THE FIVE "CONFUCIAN" CLASSICS

THE
FIVE
"CONFUCIAN" CLASSICS

MICHAEL NYLAN

YALE UNIVERSITY PRESS/NEW HAVEN & LONDON

Designed by Mary Valencia
Set in Bembo type by Best-set Typesetter Ltd., Hong Kong.
Printed in the United States of America by Sheridan Books, Chelsea, Michigan.

Library of Congress Cataloging-in-Publication Data

Nylan, Michael.
The five "confucian" classics / Michael Nylan.
p.   cm.
Includes bibliographical references and index.
ISBN 978-0-300-21200-6
1. Wu jing.   I. Title.
PL2462.Z6 N95 2001
299'.51282—dc21
00-054998

A catalogue record for this book is available from the British Library.

The paper in this book meets the guidelines for permanence and durability of the Committee on Production Guidelines for Book Longevity of the Council on Library Resources.

For friends

CONTENTS

ACKNOWLEDGMENTS

There is a Buddhist saying: *kaikou biancuo*, "Open your mouth and you've made a mistake." To write a book of this length is to make many mistakes. This book is therefore dedicated principally to four women friends, who three years ago kept me from quitting in despair over the prospect of so many error-ridden pages: Ch'iang Tz'u, Mary Erbaugh, Anna Canavan, and Sister Elza Soetens of CICM (Belgium). These four women provided me with models of personal integrity, practical wisdom, and courage under fire; more extraordinary still, they taught me lightheartedness. My debt to these four is, therefore, inexpressibly great.

Having said that, I hardly know where to begin, so many are the busy people who have taken valuable time to read my drafts and criticize them. In the early stages of the book, when the writing was particularly graceless, Hu Ying, Dick Kraus, and Keith McMahon performed this service with patience and delicacy. Jane Hedley and William Mullen steered me to readings on the modern canon controversies; Stephen Durrant and Moss Roberts, to those on early China; Raoul Birnbaum, to those on ritual and the body. Xiaobin Ji lent me his excellent paper on the *Chunqiu*. Eric Henry and Jens Petersen were kind enough to correct many errors in the *Chunqiu* chapter. Work by Eric Henry and Freda Murck prompted a rethinking of the entire *Odes* chapter. Carine Defoort arranged for me to try out some of my ideas on ritual in her class at Leuven, in a visit that afforded me the opportunity to meet one last time with Father Paul Serruys, with whom I had been reading the *Documents*.

Midway through the process, Michael Loewe, Ronald Egan, Donald Harper, Haun Saussy, Lothar von Falkenhausen, Matthew Portal, Mark Edward Lewis, Nancy Norton Tomasko, and Stuart Aque gave suggestions on at least one draft chapter. Naomi Noble Richard showed me how to unsnarl prose passages and the faulty reasoning behind them. Roger Ames and Henry Rosement were enthusiastic about the draft manuscript when it really counted. Then, in the final year of revision, William Boltz, Martin Kern, Nathan Sivin, David Schaberg, Kidder Smith, Frederick Tibbetts, and Yi Songmi labored long and hard to save me from bad style, fuzzy logic, sloppy errors, or all three. Benjamin Elman and Thomas Wilson lent me draft papers on relevant topics while arguing with me the nature of classicism. Andrew Plaks gave me consistent encouragement, even when my formulations hardly warranted it, as did David Knechtges and Anne Cheng, though all three of those scholars were wrestling at the time with their own monumental projects. In the final stages of revising, Willard Peterson quietly talked me through one mental morass. (Toby Peterson had slogged through most of the manuscript the summer before, offering a number of astute observations.) Perhaps this is the appropriate place to note that one of the chief pleasures of writing this book has been the steady collegiality that my former tutor, Michael Loewe, and my American teachers have offered. For the consistent feeling they have fostered in me—that I have written this book less on the shoulders of giants than in the arms of friends— I am profoundly grateful. I also thank Professor Chen Shun-cheng of National Taiwan University, Chinese Studies Department, who is never far from my thoughts when I read classical Chinese.

Thanks go to a number of scholars, including Ed Shaugnessy, Paul Goldin, and Michael Puett, for their incisive comments at conferences on certain points raised here. Each in his inimitable way has taught me the justice of Gu Jiegang's remark, "The problems of ancient Chinese history are extremely complicated, concerned as they are, with data of two and three thousand years' standing which has become still more confused by millennia of irresponsible criticism."

During various stages of this project, support has come from the entire staff of Gest Library and Marquand Library at Princeton University and of Canaday Library at Bryn Mawr. At Gest, I would particularly like to thank Soonwon Y. Kim, Mariko Shimomura, Gunul (Gayle) Yurdakul, Martin Heijdra, and Emily Nyguen for their unfailing helpfulness and good humor; at Marquand, Frank Chance and Xia Wei Edgren deserve particular kudos. At Bryn Mawr College, similar tributes are owed to Anne Slater, Charles A. Burke, and Ethel Merry. John Moffet of the Needham Research Institute (Cambridge) and the fellows of Clare Hall made me welcome during my sabbatical spring in England. Lorraine Kirschner over the years has made my life at Bryn Mawr more pleasant, as have many of my students (most recently, Jennifer Salen, Robin Workman, Miho Nasu, and Lisa Lee, to name just a few). Oliva Cardona kept track of every single permission slip I needed for the illustrations. Jerome Silbergeld provided speedy help on copyrights. Were I to begin to render thanks properly to friends at Princeton, the acknowledgments would never end. I should at least mention Dosier Hammond and Jane Sloan for their good advice on the book and library worlds; Dora Ching, Cary Liu, Virginia Bower, and Bob Bagley for their instruction in matters inscriptional and art-related; Jamie Fuller and Gerry Boswell for their keen interest in the sacred; and Robert Litz, for his proofreading and good cheer at every stage.

Joseph Richard saved me at short notice with his computer skills. Finally, I should like very much to thank five people connected with Yale University Press: Jim Peck, who has always thrown me an oar when I am navigating tricky waters; Otto Bohlmann, who responded clearly to each and every one of my queries during the long process from submission to publication; Lawrence Kenney, whose probing queries and comments prompted me to rethink a number of sloppy passages; and the two anonymous readers for the manuscript.

CHRONOLOGY

10,000–ca. 2100 B.C.	NEOLITHIC PERIOD
ca. 1600–ca. 1100 B.C.	SHANG DYNASTY
ca. 1100–256 B.C.	ZHOU DYNASTY

        Western Zhou ca. 1100–771 B.C.

        Eastern Zhou ca. 770–256 B.C.

            Spring and Autumn Period 770–475 B.C.

            Warring States Period 475–222 B.C.

221–209 B.C.	QIN DYNASTY
206 B.C.–A.D. 220	HAN DYNASTY

        Western (Former) Han Dynasty 206 B.C.–A.D. 9

        Xin Dynasty (Wang Mang Interregnum) 9–23

        Eastern (Later) Han Dynasty 25–220

220–265	THREE KINGDOMS
265–420	JIN DYNASTY

        Six Dynasties 220–589

386–581	NORTHERN DYNASTIES
581–618	SUI DYNASTY
618–907	TANG DYNASTY
907–960	FIVE DYNASTIES (in the north)
907–979	TEN KINGDOMS (in the south)
907–1125	LIAO DYNASTY
960–1279	SONG DYNASTY

        Northern Song 960–1127

        Southern Song 1127–1279

1115–1234	JIN DYNASTY
1271–1368	YUAN DYNASTY
1368–1644	MING DYNASTY
1644–1911	QING DYNASTY
1912–1949	REPUBLIC
1949–	PEOPLE'S REPUBLIC

Chapter One

INTRODUCTION TO THE FIVE CLASSICS

FOR MOST OF THE TIME FROM 136 BC TO 1905, the study of the Five Classics of the "Confucian" canon—the *Odes*, the *Documents*, the *Rites*, the *Changes*, and the *Spring and Autumn Annals*—formed at least part of the curriculum tested by the government examinations required of nearly all candidates for the Chinese imperial bureaucracy. Thus the more cultured members of society in premodern China, even those who had failed the examinations or had passed but never held office, enjoyed a familiarity with the Classics that afforded them a common store of knowledge. As successive governments throughout East Asia came under the cultural sway of the Chinese system, the Classics came to influence thought and politics in Korea, Japan, and

Vietnam, so that the collection as a whole once occupied in East Asia a position roughly analogous to that of the Bible in the West, its compelling arguments couched in elegant formulations, "subtle phrasing with profound implications" (*weiyan dayi* 微言大義). These texts associated with the Supreme Sage, Confucius, were thought to set the pattern of what it was to become a fully developed human being, and also the principles that allowed for the complex and interrelated processes of political, social, and cultural reproduction. Thus, generation after generation tied the maintenance of the state and of personal identity to the propagation of this textual tradition. In assuming the world to be both moral and intelligible, the views articulated there to a degree challenge the dominant modern and postmodern conceptions. But insofar as the real science of men has less to do with analyzing the world than with promoting justice, the Five Classics are well worth revisiting. To ignore, disdain, or misinterpret those same Classics is to squander their riches.

The modern rubric "Five Confucian Classics," however, has tended to skew understanding of these texts, as it implies both a direct connection with the historical Confucius (551–479 BC) and a closer relationship among them than is warranted by their early histories. Most of the texts were evolving in oral as well as written forms for centuries before they acquired the designation "classic" or "Confucian";* hence vastly differing approaches to social, political, and cosmic issues are discernible among and even within the texts. Beginning in Han (206 BC–AD 220), state-sponsored classical learning—often dubbed "Confucian" when "orthodox" or "official" would be more appropriate—drew freely on the teachings of many non-Confucian thinkers, the better to cope with the complexities (many unforeseen by Confucius) of ruling an empire. This pattern of borrowing, usually unacknowledged, continued throughout imperial history. Meanwhile the teachings, texts, and activities attributed to Confucius and his chief disciples affected many aspects of Chinese life and thought, but they most certainly did

---

*I restrict the use of "Confucian" to the self-identified followers of Confucius's ethical teachings and their cultural products. No premodern scholar ever referred to the Five Classics as the Confucian Classics. Ru, conventionally translated as "Confucian," means "classicist," though dedicated Ru were said to regard Confucius as their "ancestral teacher" because of his monumental efforts to preserve ancient traditions. While the Cheng-Zhu moralists (see Key Terms) in late imperial China sought to reserve the term "Ru" for their adherents only, popular usage continued to use Ru in more complex ways, often as a loose synonym for the broad social category *shi*, which referred to cultured men prominent in their local communities, even when they did not hold government office. Until the twentieth century, Ru always referred to people; it was never thought to refer to a set of ideas juxtaposed to that of the Buddhists or Daoists. See below for an analysis of the term *jia* 家, often (mis)translated as "schools."

not affect them all in the same way, to the same degree, or at the same time. In addition to "official learning" in China, there lay a host of conflicting interpretive lines and practices favored by various groups, not to mention the quite separate histories of orthodox learning in Korea, Japan, and Vietnam.

To tell the story of the Five Confucian Classics in its entirety would in theory require a lengthy overview of four complex civilizations over the course of some two millennia, recording the shifting issues and fashions in classical scholarship that both reflected and altered the realities of life in imperial China, mapping the changing significance of each Classic as successive commentators and readers invested it with their own diverse interpretations and emphases. And even such a monumental tale would still patently be false. False because the stable entity that later scholars have called Confucianism has never really existed. "Confucianism" is an abstraction and a generalization—apparently useful but always obfuscating— a product of ongoing intellectual engagement as much as a subject of it (fig. 1).

Significantly, the premodern Chinese, to whom this sort of learning mattered most, had no single term corresponding directly to the neat English term "Confucianism." It was, in fact, well-meaning interpreters of China, motivated by their search for an exact counterpart within the Orient to the monumental presence of Christianity in European history, who coined the terms "Confucian" and "Confucianism" to translate the Chinese *Rujia* 儒家. The original term *Rujia* (classicists) indicated not a precise moral orientation or body of doctrines, but a professional training with the general goal of state service. Not all Ru, in short, were devotees of the Confucian Way identified with the Ancients. Even today, the multiple confusions engendered by these seemingly innocuous neologisms continue to complicate discourses on morality, politics, and gender in China (see Key Terms). Modern proponents of a Confucian Revival—following the lead of some of the most famous advocates of Confucian values (for example, Mencius and Han Yu), who deliberately sought to prove the ultimate validity

→

Figure 1. Confucius as a grave, bearded Augustan, majestically taking his place in an Imperial Academy (that looks more like a European library of calf-bound books), from Philippe Couplet et al., *Confucius sinarum Philosophus* [*Confucius, philosopher of the Chinese*] (Paris, 1687, now in the Niedersâchsische Landesbibliothek Hannover), p. cxvi, illus. from David Mungello (1985), 274. A translation of three of the Four Books, this text depicted Confucius as the "Preeminent Teacher" holding, quite inexplicably, in his hands his own spirit tablet in a building that is both temple and library. The eighteen spirit tablets that appear along the bottom of the eastern and western walls commemorate Confucius's most famous disciples, including Zengzi, putative author of the "Great Learning"; Zisi, putative author of the "Doctrine of the Mean"; Yan Hui, Confucius's favorite disciple; and Mencius. Inscribed in both Chinese and romanized forms across the bookshelves flanking Confucius are the names of the Five Classics, the Four Books, and the "Great Commentary" [or "Xici"] to the *Changes*.

of Confucius's Way by tying it to the preservation of a distinctive Chinese identity—have muddied the terminology further by speaking of a Confucian classicism that constitutes a worldview, a social ethic, a political ideology, a scholarly tradition, and a way of life in a China bound by tradition to its neighbors. As early Confucian learning was inextricably intertwined first with pre-Confucian ideas about the central importance of family obligation and ancestor worship (which it reflected and through which it was interpreted) and later with other non-Confucian theories, it is no more possible to cleanly distinguish a Confucian history from the rest of history and civilization in China* or East Asia than to neatly disentangle the history of Christianity from the European enterprises sponsored by state and church.

This book therefore aims to introduce a few of the major issues in the early history of the Five Classics, in the hope that readers will be inspired to consult more specialized studies on the subject. The introduction sketches the main events leading to the adoption of the Five Classics as state-sponsored learning in 136 BC under the Western Han dynasty (206 BC–AD 8) and the refinement during Eastern Han (AD 25–220) of the basic patterns of use of the Five Classics. The book's concern with Han and pre-Han studies responds, I hope, to academic concerns as well as to personal predilections. Early classicism has received surprisingly little intellectual attention, and Han studies—the Chinese counterpart to Roman history—continue to languish in relative obscurity. Recent works on Confucian learning continue to emphasize one particular branch of ethical thought, the Daoxue, or True Way Learning movement, which by a lengthy process begun in AD 1241 came to be enshrined as the Cheng-Zhu orthodoxy. This book intends to redress the current imbalance in the standard tale, thereby providing a more nuanced portrait of the Ru traditions. At the same time, a greater familiarity with the early history of the Five Classics might keep modern scholars of late imperial China from attributing to the thinkers who constitute the chief subjects of their study a host of "new ideas" that already had a well-established history in early classical thought. Finally, many aspects of early classical learning seem more apposite to the modern age than some later state-sponsored traditions attached to the Five Classics, which tend to be more authoritarian, more solipsistic, and consequently less congenial. In light of the recent clamor for a New Confucian Revival, one should remem-

---

* Chapter 3 discusses Chinese identity as it is perceived in relation to "Zhongguo," a term that originally referred to the Central States on or near the Yellow River valley but now refers to either Chinese people or the Chinese nation. National identities were relatively late and loose inventions, fleshed out in response to successive major "barbarian incursions," including those of the Western powers in the late nineteenth and early twentieth centuries.

ber that there are manifold classical traditions to draw upon in any attempts to reconfigure and enrich the present. Still, as the final chapter of this book demonstrates, this once-rich complex of classical traditions is in danger of being reduced to mere slogans, and that will make it more difficult for future generations to reconstruct the genuine insights of early classical masters.

Because much of the earliest history of this standard collection of Five Classics remains a mystery, this introduction perforce begins at the middle of the story. Although later texts claim a remarkable antiquity for the canon, no extant work dating before the late third century BC discusses this group of texts as either canon or collection. It is not clear even now how many or how much of the texts had been written down by that date. Equally astonishing, no recorded tradition prior to 100 BC identifies Confucius as author, editor, or compiler of this collection.* But just about that time, in mid–Western Han, there occurred a virtual explosion of interest in the Five Classics, prompted in part by imperial patronage, which eventually standardized the form the canonical texts would take and privileged a few readings associated with each, while tracing every teaching ultimately back to the figure of Confucius, either directly or through the construction of scholastic lineages. All efforts to establish a single authoritative interpretation for each of the Five Classics, let alone reach a consensus on the overarching meaning of the corpus, were doomed to failure, however. Not only did the Five Classics vary greatly in origin, style, and content, so that any endeavor to harmonize them only prompted controversy, but also every literate person in the empire was to some degree a student of the Classics, able if not determined to come to a personal understanding of the corpus.[†]

---

*Unconfirmed reports from the Shanghai Museum, however, speak of (as yet unpublished) bamboo slips from ca. 300 BC that include an unknown commentary on the *Odes* attributed to Confucius. The commentary appears to be written in the special characters of the Chu state. It is not certain when Confucius came to be regarded as the author of the "Great Commentary" to the *Changes*.

[†] Since the publication of Evelyn Rawski's *Education and Popular Literacy in Ch'ing China* (Ann Arbor: University of Michigan Press, 1979), an increasing number of scholars (Cynthia Brokaw, Benjamin Elman, David Johnson, and Angela Ki Che Leung, among others) have sought to distinguish levels of literacy more precisely in order to arrive at more meaningful figures for functional and full literacy rates. Functional literacy, defined as the possession of the most basic reading and writing skills, was probably high in late imperial China (roughly 50 percent among male city dwellers), but full classical literacy (attained by 5–10 percent of the adult male population during the eighteenth century) presupposed a thorough knowledge of the Five Classics, Four Books, chief commentarial traditions, dynastic histories, and great literature that empowered members of the elite in the political and cultural arenas.

Concerted attempts to reach consensus nonetheless established the dominant patterns for official learning in imperial China, patterns that inextricably linked moral concerns with the art of governance.

The introduction reviews what little information is known about the origins of the Five Classics and their coming together as a single corpus. Theories about their compilation prior to being elevated to the canon are presented in sections 2–6. Current debates over the canon in China and in America, recounted in the second half of section 3, call attention to the cultural and political significance of forming and keeping a canon. The introduction ends in sections 7–9 with observations on the dominant pattern of classical exegesis. Section 7 reviews the political motives underlying Emperor Wu's (r. 140–87 BC) decision to canonize these five texts as a set and to omit others, a case which nicely illustrates the point that the composing, designating, and interpreting of sacred texts are always highly political acts, as is the establishment of critical editions and state-sponsored readings. Section 8, which touches upon the compromises and contradictions that marked Han classical scholarship, is meant to remind readers of the kinds of problems that commonly arise when idealized prescriptions must be adapted to state needs. The final section of the introduction, devoted to post-Han exegetical developments, does not attempt a detailed narrative for three reasons. First, the history of the post-Han schools of interpretation presents a continual reworking of this Han linkage between hermeneutics and politics. Second, significant shifts in interpretation tended to hinge on turns of phrasing within the ongoing commentarial traditions, of a subtlety and allusiveness comprehensible only to advanced students of the culture and language. Given the lengthy exegetical disputes depending on highly technical discussions or semantic extensions of key words, no amount of explication could keep readers unfamiliar with the grammar and vocabulary of premodern literary language (*wenyan* 文言) from the erroneous impression that classicists in China were obsessed with the arcane or precious. Third, to borrow a Chinese metaphor, the sheer abundance of the timbers used to construct the magnificent edifice of Confucian classicism makes the task of reassembly daunting, especially when that original building was designed in a style and with a purpose quite alien to modern academic activity. To suggest the wide range of Ru models available in the empire to ardent students of the past, the penultimate section of this introduction discusses three leading figures who were both celebrated and excoriated by fellow classicists. The final section offers only the briefest overview of the later history of the Five Classics, explicating their eventual displacement in the standard curriculum by the so-called Four Books collection, comprised of the *Analects*, the *Mencius*, the "Great Learning," and the "Doctrine of the Mean."

Having offered, in the Introduction, a broad sense of established paradigms and problems, I devote each of the following five chapters to the history, meaning, and interpretation of one of the Five Classics. I have chosen here not to assess the corpus as literature, as historical narrative, or as a literary source for early views on ritual, cosmology, music, and divination, as these topics demand far more specialized treatments. Readers interested in such topics may consult the bibliographical essays in the Suggested Readings.

I. THE FIVE CLASSICS' RELATION TO CONFUCIUS

As listed above, the Five "Confucian" Classics are the *Odes*, the *Documents*, the *Rites* (originally one text to which two others were eventually added), the *Changes*, and the *Spring and Autumn Annals*. (Tradition speaks of a *Music* classic, but if it ever existed it has been lost or incorporated into one of three *Rites* classics.) The classics can properly be called Confucian in only two senses: Confucius and his followers may have used some—but not all—of them as templates for moral instruction, much as the Greek pedagogues once used Homer. And early traditions ascribe to Confucius the tasks of compiling, editing, and in some few cases composing the separate parts in this repository of wisdom texts, although modern scholarship generally disputes those pious legends.

Because the corpus of the Five Classics contains materials that vary widely in date, style, subject matter, and point of view, its interpretation was hardly less problematic to its early readers than it is to modern scholars. The *Odes* is a collection of songs reflecting everyday life in court and countryside during the Eastern Zhou period; the same collection includes a series of hymns, composed specifically for state rituals, which relate much of the mythological lore transmitted from the early Zhou dynasty. The *Documents* purports to be a collection of archaic archival materials that preserves important edicts and memorials outlining the responsibilities of the ruling elite toward Heaven and the common people. Usually treated as a single canon, the three Rites classics, the *Ceremonials* (*Yili*), *Rites Records* (*Liji*), and *Zhou Rites* (*Zhouli*), include as many as three thousand discrete rules of conduct, in addition to fabulous descriptions of an ideal government structure and anecdotes about paragons of Confucian virtue. A divination manual eventually expanded for use as a philosophical text, the *Changes* attempts to recreate through its graphic symbols and attached texts the full range of shifting phenomena that proceed from the unitary prime mover, the Dao. Finally, the *Annals* takes the form of a court diary detailing the activities of the rulers of the small state of Lu during the years 722–481 BC. Notwithstanding this variety of materials, Confucian masters postulated a single, coherent message underlying all Five Classics.

As far as we can reconstruct, self-identified followers of Confucius prior to 136 BC emphasized a set of practices (now recognized as distinctly archaizing), including ritualized chanting, dancing, and dressing. They also upheld a number of basic notions, the most important of which was the perfectibility of human relations through *shu* 恕 (profound empathy) leading to *ren* 仁 (human kindness). According to Confucius, such developed humanity was typically realized by a two-step process: unremitting study of the Way of the Ancients, which ensured a gradual habituation to goodness through immersion in the ancient models preserved in ritual, to be crowned by a profound awareness of one's place within the community of civilized human beings. In theory, this sort of cultivation dramatically increased the charisma of the adherents, thereby inducing the transformation of less fully realized human beings who came in contact with such moral exemplars. Civilization, for Confucius, was both embodied in and enhanced through the distinctive ritual acts that inevitably govern most aspects of human interaction; if those in power would only take the trouble to express their human feelings through time-honored rituals, there would be no need for repressive penal codes and punishments to control the bestial impulses. Life in society, no longer solitary, poor, nasty, brutish, and short, would be harmonious, comfortable, peaceful, cultivated, and stable. Social realities would finally correspond to the language of prescribed social roles, for fathers would act as fathers should, rulers as rulers, and so on.

According to Confucius, a speedy restoration of the Golden Age that purportedly prevailed during the early days of the Western Zhou dynasty (tradit. 1122–770 BC; revised ca. 1050–770 BC) might be better led by men of noble character than by men of noble birth.* Good men needed only to become so adept in the ritual usages, the verbal and gestural language for dignified human interaction, that cultivation became virtually second nature, at once spontaneous and graceful. Obeying the dictates of Heaven, such men would then naturally espouse the Good. Lesser men, of course, would still require the loving support of a strong family system and the suasive model of a just ruler to arrive at a corresponding nobility of character. But given the right social conditions, all people, regardless of family status and background and despite vast differences in innate intellect and talents, might reach a true nobility of spirit. As one Confucian master put it, "All men are capable of becoming [the legendary sage-kings] Yao and Shun," insofar as they learn to weigh the relative claims of incommensurate goods in order to find the single most humane solution to problems arising from

---

*The same binome, *junzi* 君子, was used for both groups. An excellent summary of the term is to be found in the introduction to Arthur Waley's translation of *The Confucian Analects*.

social interaction. Such solutions would then confirm the perfection of the Middle Way.

Today, a student seeking to understand the basic tenets of Confucius and Confucianism would most likely turn to the *Analects*, which takes the form of notes on conversations that Confucius purportedly held with his disciples. Not so in early China. Until relatively late in the history of Confucian classicism, during the Sui-Tang period (581–907), the *Analects* was considered far less important as a source of Confucius's ideas than the Five Classics, especially the *Chunqiu*, or *Spring and Autumn Annals*, a text widely believed to have been written by Confucius. Contemporary documents state that the more important texts were written on longer strips. During the Han period, for example, the Five Classics were written on bound bamboo strips two feet four inches in length (measured in Han-time units), twice the length of those used for a minor classic entitled the *Classic of Filial Piety* and three times the length of those used for the *Analects*.

Certainly until late in the Song period (960–1279), the Five Classics were generally considered more essential to Confucian learning than the now more famous collection of Four Books, which are the subject of the vast majority of current Chinese and Western studies on early thought in China. Understanding the early prominence of the Five Classics is a prerequisite to a more precise understanding of the first millennium and a half of classical learning, from 136 BC to the fifteenth century, when all literati intending to sit the exams had to master the Cheng-Zhu orthodoxy. That reconsideration of early classical learning, in turn, should help us better appraise the dramatic turn that Chinese thought took during the Song dynasty, which represented a virtual reassessment and reinvention of the Confucian message, as sweeping in its own way as the Protestant Reformation of Catholicism. Aside from its intrinsic interest, a rediscovery of early classicism must serve to dispel lingering stereotypes about an eternal and unchanging China. I begin, then, at the conceptual beginning, since the chronological beginnings of the Five Classics corpus cannot be traced.

2. CANONICAL SIGNIFICANCE: THEN AND NOW, "EAST" AND "WEST"

What was a classic, a *jing*, in China, and where did the term come from? Apparently, early Confucians were not the first scholars to call an authoritative text a classic. Priority goes to the Mohists, vociferous critics of the Confucians in the preimperial period, who sometime in the fourth century BC christened the ten basic doctrines of their founder, Mo Di (d. 390 BC?), the Mohist Classic; by implication, these ten points represented an authoritative summary of the founder's teachings. It seems to have taken the Confucians nearly a century to borrow the term "classic" and apply it to their authoritative sources of learning. Xunzi (d. 238 BC) is the first known Confucian master to write of "classics" in connection with a corpus of four texts (the Five Classics minus the *Changes*) utilized as sourcebooks by committed Ru.* Xunzi treated these four texts—conceived as oral or written traditions—as a single system wherein each delivered a distinct but complementary body of knowledge to the student of antiquity. According to Xunzi,

> As to program, learning begins with chanting the Classics out loud [to memorize and internalize them] and ends with the reading of ritual. . . . The *Documents* is a record of government affairs; the *Odes*, a repository of appropriate sounds; the *Rites* are the great source for models and the complete outline for categorizing. Thus, learning reaches its completion with the *Rites*, for they may be said to represent the highest excellence of the Way and its charismatic power. The reverent patterns of the *Rites*, the fit harmonies of music [the *Music Classic*?], the breadth of the *Odes* and *Documents*, the subtlety of the *Spring and Autumn Annals*—these encompass all that lies between Heaven and Earth.†

Only as a group, then, could the Classics reveal the entire workings of the divine Way and its operation within human society.

Happily, Xunzi also tells us what he means by his use of the term "classic" (*jing*), and he does so by a typical Chinese rhetorical device: a pun. The character *jing* 經 was a near homophone for *jing* 徑, meaning a straight path or direct route. These texts were seen as the best route to the original teachings of the ancient sage-kings, as transmitted by Confucius. And because the word *jing* by extension also conveys the verbal sense of "passing through," it served equally well to describe whatever has stood the test of time because of its excellence. Xunzi then plays with the root meaning of *jing* 經 (literally, the lead thread or warp). Because the warp serves as fixed framework for the entire length of a weaving, "classic" is an apt metaphor for whatever imparts definition, order, and utility over the long course of history. Thus the earliest Chinese dictionary, the *Shuowen* (composed ca. AD 100), defines *jing* as "weaving," a definition which

---

*Xunzi's reasons for excluding the *Changes* will be discussed below.

†The decision to italicize *Rites* (*li*) and *Music* (*yue*) here reflects the dominant tradition that these terms indicated the titles of two classics that had been set down in writing in the classical period. However, in all probability the terms *li* and *yue* referred to performance traditions, some parts of which were written down only in Han and some parts of which were never transcribed.

recalls the Han view that the Five Classics are not only tightly woven (that is, integrally connected) texts but also texts that weave together the constant principles underlying the sociocosmic fabric.*

By a further twist on the weaving analogy, certain texts regarded as important supplements to the canon were called *wei* 緯 (woof or weft); like the weft threads that the weaver passes over and under the long, fixed warp threads to create the fabric, the *wei* were apocryphal writings that filled in the warp of the Five Classics with political predictions, cosmological speculations, and punning sound glosses. Reflecting also contemporary interest in the technical arts associated with astronomy, medicine, and geography, the apocrypha helped to bridge the gap between ancient phrasing and contemporary theory. In the minds of many pre-Song readers of the Classics, the weftlike apocrypha were so closely tied to the warplike Classics that authors sometimes made no distinction between the two when citing authorities. But the underlying political motivations of some of the apocrypha, which predicted specific dynastic changes, left all the apocrypha liable to periodic suppression by strong rulers, who feared such pronouncements would incite rebellion. In consequence, only fragments of the apocrypha exist today.

The apocrypha had failed the test that Han classical masters devised to determine whether a work qualifies as a true Classic: (1) the classic or set of classics must constitute a complete and perfect order of sufficient breadth to answer every moral question put to it; (2) the classic must be "easy to know" and "easy to follow" in the sense that it contains no "treachery or trickery," that is, no internal contradictions; (3) the classic must be eternally relevant in the ever-changing present, so that its traditions remain alive in every generation; (4) the classic must function as a kind of access route to the ethical makeup of its sage-author(s), providing models of inner strength and integrity, if not conventional power; and (5) on both the literary and ethical levels, reading of the classics must yield such reliably exquisite pleasures as to forge in the most knowledgeable adherents—the connoisseurs of morality—the strong desire to emulate the ethical exemplars of the past. Dong Zhongshu (176–104 BC), Yang Xiong

---

*If "warp" is the original etymology of the Chinese word for "classic," early Chinese usage parallels the evolution of the word "sutra" in Indian tradition, from "connecting thread." (The English word "text," of course, derives from the Latin *textus*, meaning "woven.") The characters for both *jing* (warp) and *wei* (apocrypha, woof or weft) share the silk 系 signific. That led Zhang Binglin (1869–1935) to surmise that the character *jing* originally referred to the thread that bound inscribed bamboo strips in bundles to form early texts. Also, prior to the invention of paper in Han, deluxe editions were likely to be transcribed on rolls of woven silk, rather than on bundled wood and bamboo slats.

(53 BC–AD 18), and Ouyang Xiu (AD 1007–72), three Confucian masters spanning more than a millennium, commented as follows on the Classics:

> Each and every one of the six branches of learning 六學 is great, but each has that in which it excels. The *Odes* tells of the aspirations of the heart and mind; therefore, it excels in substance. The *Rites* mandates moderation; therefore, it excels in refinement. The *Music* intones virtue; therefore, it excels in influence. The *Documents* illustrates merit; therefore, it excels in human affairs. The *Changes* bases itself in Heaven and Earth; therefore, it excels in regularities (*shu* 數). The *Spring and Autumn* rectifies notions of right and wrong; therefore, it excels in governance.
>
> —Dong Zhongshu

> Asking about divinity, an interlocutor gets the response: "What is divine is the heart/mind (*xin* 心) [the single seat of the intellect and emotions]." "May I ask more about it?" "Divinity is to immerse oneself in Heaven and become Heaven; to immerse oneself in Earth and become Earth. Heaven and Earth are divine patterns of unfathomable greatness. Yet when the heart/mind immerses itself in them, it can nearly fathom them. . . ." The interlocutor then asks, "How is one to enter [such a state of extraordinary understanding]?" Reply: "Through Confucius. Confucius is the door, the one and only door. How can any of us . . . refuse to go by that door? . . . And just as no one can ever cross a river without a boat, so no one can attain the Way without the Five Classics."
>
> —Yang Xiong

> In the *Odes* we can see the mind of the Master Confucius. From the *Documents* we can know his judgments. With the *Rites* we can shed light on his models. With the *Music* we can grasp his virtue. With the *Changes* we can examine his character. And with the *Spring and Autumn* we can preserve his purpose.
>
> —Ouyang Xiu

Over the course of imperial history in China, prominent thinkers affirmed the supreme importance of the Five Classics, but for many in the early twenty-first century, ancient Chinese testimonials carry less weight than debates since the early 1980s on the Western canon, conducted by philosophers intent upon devising a theory of value, literary critics hoping to reform the old curriculum, and anthropologists preoccupied with the mechanisms of cultural selection. Such controversies seem to have established at least five important, if contested, notions concerning canon formation, each suggesting that the survival of the Five Classics under state sponsorship is not attributable solely either to an orchestrated conspiracy by establishment institutions or to their continuous appreciation by succeeding generations over the course of two millennia: (1) a person arrives at decisions about value on the basis of information received from members of the community. Within a particular community, tastes tend to converge, except in the case of the unacculturated (the young, the untutored, and the barbarian), so that appreciation of the canon will be adjudged simply as "good taste" and "rational choice"; (2) the inclusion of a work in the canon depends as much upon the successive subjective judgments of influential tastemakers who find the work in fundamental ways to be timeless (that is, applicable to their own situation) as upon the original authorial design, labor, and skill; (3) texts are plural and ambiguous from the beginning; given that methods employed to address such indeterminacy vary over time, new meaning can in theory be generated endlessly from the same classic; (4) once a work has been in the canon for a sufficient length of time, it begins to perform key cultural functions, for example, as an unquestioned authority, as a witness to persistent community interests, as a testament to cultural superiority, as a selective compendium of ideals and traditions; it then no longer merely reflects but also shapes and creates the culture that transmits its values, as often by setting limits to the parameters of cultural discourse as by the direct promotion of a set of values; (5) certain purportedly objective truths embodied in the canon can sometimes serve as enabling alibis or cultural cover for the relentless pursuit of special economic and political interests by those who have or wish to attain power. At the very least, members of the elite tend to disregard the judgments of less privileged groups in the complex processes of canon formation and canon interpretation. But that is not all. The establishment of the canon invariably brings movement to culture because the improvisation, exchange, and revision required to maintain the canon end in a blurring of cultural boundaries. The continual borrowing from and imitation of the canon do not necessarily signify, then, "imaginative parsimony, still less . . . creative exhaustion" or pernicious social engineering. Appropriating well is the very basis of the creative act, and an ardent desire to restore or reinvigorate tradition frequently opens new avenues of expression.

In any case, official transmission of the Classics often continued in tandem with unreflective cultural selection and reproduction because a defined canon performed a variety of functions that appealed to divergent sectors within society. It allowed some degree of state control over the interpretations of texts that the culture took seriously, through official exegesis and exclusion. It also helped to locate cultural authority, historical knowledge, and ethical wisdom in the throne, thereby associating imperial patronage with infallibility, perfect comprehensiveness, and divine inspiration. Insofar as it represented a conservative product of an imagined past, the canon could reflect and promote widely shared ideals; to many, it symbolized the triumph of—or at least the persistence of—tradition, the metropolitan culture, or the universal order over and against the modern, the regional, the chaotic. For this reason, empire and the classical canon remained mutually reinforcing imaginative constructions. Those curatorial and normative functions of the canon whereby the Five Classics preserved and transmitted culture and ideology made the canon as a whole appear essentially "timeless," even when individual writings in the canon and attached commentaries clearly reflected the contemporary preoccupations of their separate authors. This very timeless quality made learning of the canon especially valuable as an appropriate class marker and index of civility. It lent a sturdy framework within which to construct aesthetic experience and cultural ideals. It could even allow the delicious escape to worlds beyond humdrum everyday existence.

In China, the political elite's desire for self-representation could not but be highly gratified by the content of the Five Classics; as the Classics are almost uniformly devoted to stories of rulers (good and bad) and their advisers (forthright and fawning), the canon depicted members of the political elite as the sole legitimate subjects of history. And although elites in China were hardly the single self-perpetuating entity portrayed by certain Marxist historians, at any one time they tried to reserve for themselves a monopoly over correct interpretations of the Five Classics, the better to enhance their status and reduce access to power by the members of other groups. For these reasons, although Confucian learning in the strict sense—the faithful reproduction of specific ethical patterns of social interaction associated with Confucius—remained only one of several options open to thinking individuals throughout the course of imperial history, classicism in its broader sense permeated much of society and culture so profoundly that it is hard to distinguish it from "things Chinese." This form of classicism was reflected in a reverence for learning and an aesthetic cultivation of the past; in an "epistemological optimism," a belief that there is sufficient moral knowledge to reform the self and others; in the consequent demand that ideal government foster rectitude; in the meticulous performance of key rituals reinforced by law; and in the very maintenance of certain institutional structures. When even armed guards stationed in the imperial palaces were assigned the Five Classics to master, it was inevitable that "within the four seas" interpretive lines explicating the Classics would "grow as numerous as trees in the forest."

The very pervasiveness of classicism in imperial China made it, of course, the scapegoat of every modern reformer intent upon rapid Westernization in late imperial China. More recently, political conservatives have muddied the waters by pushing a "suitably revised" Confucian ideology as the chief antidote to the spiritual pollution that supposedly derives from contact with the West. As a result, China, Taiwan, the Chinese diaspora, and Euro-America can expect no cessation of the highly politicized debates over the original value of the classical canon as it bears upon modern life, debates conducted among elites who have all been trained in Western-style curricula. Readers would do well to keep these debates in mind as they come to consider the general history and specific content of the original Five Classics, when compared with the Four Books favored by later Confucian masters.

3. WHO WROTE THE FIVE CLASSICS?

Over the course of Chinese history the question of the authorship of the Five Classics has received differing responses. By and large, however, scholars in imperial China tended to attribute the composition of the Classics either to the ancient sage-kings of the legendary Three Dynasties of Xia, Shang, and early Zhou or to Confucius himself. Because Confucius taught his disciples that the sage-kings of hoary antiquity had discovered and then elucidated important ethical patterns weaving through past and present, his early followers reserved the title of *jing* 經 for works on politics, ritual, and cosmology popularly ascribed to those sage-kings. The Classics, then, by definition, contained the ancients' blueprints for civilization, which were assumed to be of enduring value.[*] It was precisely because the Classics were said to be ancient texts, contemporaneous with or at least closer in time to the Golden Age projected onto an idealized past, when perfect justice reportedly prevailed among men, that texts like the *Odes*, *Documents*, and *Rites* were held to be classics. Even the *Spring and Autumn Annals* was presumably included in Xunzi's early list of Classics not because of its popular attribution to Confucius, but because the *Annals* captured the flavor of antiquity in preserving genuinely old archival material.

By the first century BC, however, during the Han dynasty, the figure of Confucius had been so elevated in the minds of the faithful that he was in effect apotheosized or deified.[†] To his most fervent adherents, at least, Confucius had

---

[*] Modern readers need not, of course, uncritically adopt this view of the Classics as the ancients' blueprints for civilization. Early Western Han and pre-Han works frequently expressed doubts about claims to great antiquity made on behalf of some of the Classics. The "antiquity-doubters" of the early twentieth century, building upon observations registered by earlier scholars in imperial China, demonstrated just how late many of the so-called antique traditions actually were (some being Han in origin), though the Classics do preserve ancient material.

[†] Confucius in history and in legend is discussed in some detail in chapter 6. The increased stress in Han on Confucius's editorial role may represent scholars' attempts to recast the august figure of Confucius in their own image.

become not merely the last in a long line of antique sages, but the Supreme Sage-Master of all, the *suwang* 素王 (uncrowned king), whose extraordinary wisdom so far surpassed that of all others before or since that he would in effect reign, without benefit of the throne, over the rest of Chinese history. Proponents of Confucius, never anticipating that future exigencies might one day render past experience wholly useless, were apt to portray him in one of three roles in which his teachings might arguably apply to all situations in all ages: as a divinely inspired prophet, a fabulous magician the repetition of whose verbal formulae (written and spoken) could dramatically alter current conditions, or an incalculably wise man who had cloaked his esoteric teachings in "subtle words with profound implications," words whose real meaning could be unlocked by specialists trained in the use of allegory. For such avid followers of Confucius, in other words, a Classic was created at the point when its text was assumed to say ineffably more than it appeared to say.

Many Han thinkers came to believe that Confucius had not only predicted the triumph of the Han ruling house, but also laid the groundwork for the new Han political order by his careful editing of the Five Classics. According to the theory, Confucius as the special patron of the Han ruling house had carefully culled from the ancient records those teachings that would lead Han dynasts to effect a grand universal and eternal peace. Ideas elaborated in the Classics must therefore legitimate the Han's social and political institutions, aligning them with both archaic institutions and cosmic patterns; if necessary, new institutions should be devised on the model of prescriptions found in the Five Classics. Inevitably, this thoroughgoing reassessment of the figure of Confucius, converting him from cultural transmitter to political activist, affected the way in which the Classics themselves were viewed. For the next three centuries, until the collapse of the Han dynasty, the Classics were said to deserve veneration not so much as ancient repositories of wisdom and culture but as the sacred works of a divine and infallible (if once-undervalued) Confucius, who had personally written or edited every book in the corpus with the express intention of benefiting the Han state. As one Han text put it, "The Classics are what Confucius put in order. They are the great canon of the Sage." Such assumptions go far to explain the hermeneutical approach adopted by many Han commentators, who tended to view the texts as entrée to the ethical commitments of the Master, Confucius. Many hoped that by studying the Classics they could immerse themselves in the revealed mind of the sage Confucius until they became so habituated to his orientation that it seemed second nature to them—at which point, they would themselves naturally become latter-day sages.

The collapse of Han institutions in the late second century AD almost inevitably spelled the demotion of the Han's special patron, Confucius, from divine to human status. Those inclined to see Confucius more as man than as god put forward a different point of view about the Classics: "The term 'classic' refers to anything of lasting relevance. If a book has lasting relevance, it becomes a classic. Moreover, the fact that a book was not written by Confucius surely does not preclude its becoming a classic!" This reappraisal of the canon returned it in one sense to nearly the same place it had occupied prior to Han, in that the chief value of the corpus now supposedly resided in its enduring relevance. In another sense, however, this seemingly innocuous statement made the category of classic far more open-ended than it had seemed before, for in theory latter-day sages could continue to create new classics eligible for inclusion in the state-sponsored canon. Indeed, the corpus of the Five Classics was unusual in the degree to which it remained open, subject to continual amplification and revision. In Han times, the list of Classics was generally limited to five, but by Tang (618–906) texts refer to the Nine Classics, and by Song (960–1279) the list had grown to thirteen. Additional candidates for inclusion in the canon were proposed throughout the course of imperial China, Wang Su's (195–256) fabrication of as many as five new minor classics being an excellent case in point. Even certain noncanonical but neoclassical texts, for example, the *Canon of Supreme Mystery* (*Taixuanjing*) by Yang Xiong (completed AD 4), were accorded quasi-canonical status by many orthodox classicists.*

To summarize, by the end of Han in the third century AD, three main theories about the character of the Classics had been advanced: that the Classics were valuable as ancient repositories of wisdom lore; that their chief value lay in their association with Confucius as author and editor; that their number was not fixed, as any book of continuing utility qualified for inclusion in the canon. Today, few intellectual historians of China assume that the Five Classics represent either the collective teachings of the ancient holy sage-kings or the edited corpus of the historical Confucius, though a great number still believe, despite evidence to the contrary, that the *Spring and Autumn Annals* represents the "praise and blame" of the Supreme Sage himself. Most probably, Confucius did not compose any texts at all. Like Socrates, he seems to have preferred dialogues

---

*To some degree, this openness was a reflection of the propensity in early China to conflate canon and commentary. It was not until the time of Ma Rong (79–166), according to tradition, that Chinese authors began to distinguish canon from commentary by making two lines of commentary equal in width to one line of canon. As late as the Tang dynasty, commentaries and main text were not always clearly demarcated. In any case, so completely did commentators and their readers conflate canon, apocryphal traditions, and commentary that when scholars argued for their preferred readings of Confucian texts, they were often making implicit assertions about the relative merits of the interpretive traditions attached to those Confucian texts, rather than about the texts themselves.

with his students to the creation of texts. Still, the traditions associated with his name by disciples and disciples of disciples point to the general orientation of his teachings.

4. THE EARLY HISTORY OF THE CLASSICS

Early accounts speak of four main subjects of classical learning in Lu, the home state of Confucius: the odes, historical documents, rites, and music. Prior to the time of Confucius, learning in these four fields, not necessarily tied to study of canonical texts, was basically reserved for aristocrats in the Zhou feudal state, for whom cultivation was both a political necessity and a desirable personal attainment. Young scions of noble houses probably acquired the rudiments of such training informally as guest-attendants in the houses of other members of the nobility, just as their European counterparts did during the medieval period. So far as we know, Confucius was the first teacher to make the training of students his vocation, though there is no indication that he ever founded an academy. Tradition also claims that Confucius was the first teacher to admit students to his circle on the basis not of their hereditary rank or social estate, but simply of their eagerness to learn. Confucius declared, "From the very poorest upward—beginning with the man who could bring no better present than a bundle of dried meat—none has ever come to me without receiving instruction." In substantiation of that claim, an *Analects* passage shows Confucius's willingness to instruct a young village boy who has adequately prepared himself for the initial interview.

From this same source we also learn that Confucius required his students to learn the contents of an odes collection related if not identical to the received text of the *Odes* in our possession. One memorable anecdote in the *Analects* depicts Confucius chiding his lazy son for his signal failure to study the odes; according to Confucius, his son will surely, in consequence, "find himself at a loss in conversation." And because Confucius insisted that the noble man model himself upon the Way of the Ancients in seeking to attain the supreme goodness called *ren* 仁 (human kindness), his disciples must have been fully conversant with the contents of historical archives, which contained the necessary examples of appropriate and inappropriate behavior. Still, Confucius seems not to have had in hand the received *Documents* text because he repeatedly laments his ignorance of the pre-Zhou period, the main subject of the early chapters in the received text of that name. In addition to guiding his students through these traditions, Confucius advised each of his disciples to practice the rites and music as a means of self-cultivation.

No reliable information is available concerning the followers of Confucius in the succeeding centuries, but the threats to the Central States culture preserved in Zhou and Lu must have escalated as interstate warfare intensified during the Warring States period (475–222 BC). In that pressured climate, accounts supposedly based on the early rites and music came to be written down. Meanwhile, several alternative collections of authoritative state documents circulated, perhaps in competition with one another. But because the ancient Chinese script had no mechanism by which to distinguish the specific titles of texts from mass nouns (for example, the *Odes* from "odes" or the *Documents* from "documents"), many readers of the late Warring States and Qin-Han periods, understandably enough, took Confucius's pedagogical references to odes, to documents, to rites, and to music to mean that the Master's chosen curriculum consisted of four specific texts: the *Odes*, the *Documents*, the *Rites*, and the *Music*. This misapprehension set the stage for later canon construction in China, which focused on texts and textual transmission rather than on praxis.

The famous Confucian philosopher Mencius (d. 289 BC) advanced this process of canon construction—taking, not coincidentally, the first step toward the deification of Confucius—when he argued that the text of the *Spring and Autumn Annals*, composed by Confucius, was equal in importance to the canons associated with the legendary sage-kings of antiquity. But judging from the texts they left behind, most thinkers in the Central States cultural sphere of the late third century BC seem less intent upon defining a set corpus of canonical texts than upon championing the traditional Six Arts (rites, music, archery, charioteering, composition, and arithmetic), the polite arts of the aristocracy. (Successive attempts to unify China and to fix an orthodox canon, as we will see, are roughly contemporary in time and similar in impulse.) Neither is there any indication that the Five Classics were exclusively identified with a Confucian camp. Indeed, there is ample counterevidence that such texts were regarded as part of the general cultural heritage or patrimony of all educated Chinese. No less significantly, neither Mencius nor his later critic Xunzi identified Confucius as either editor or compiler of a standard collection of Confucian texts, though Mencius and Xunzi were the two most ardent proponents of Confucius's message in the period prior to unification of the empire in 221 BC.

Sometime during the late fourth or third century BC, certain groups of Ru finally added the *Changes* divination text to the list of sacred Classics, a move that either prompted or responded to the inclusion in the *Changes* of some or all of the famous "Ten Wings" (or Appendices) devoted to cosmic correlations and human history. These appendices allowed all components of the many-layered text to be read as one organic treatise of considerable sophistication on man's changing place with respect to the experiential world.* With the inclusion of the *Changes* into the canon, classicists now had a set curriculum of Six Classics (*liujing*)—sometimes labeled the Six Arts as if to co-opt the older frame of reference—which were said to give the would-be gentleman the necessary educational attainments: the *Odes, Documents, Rites, Music, Changes*, and *Spring and Autumn Annals*.

It was centuries later, in mid- to late Western Han, that a scholastic impulse to group things by fives, in imitation of the Five Phases 五行 (see Key Terms), worked to suppress mention of a *Music* classic in connection with the corpus, possibly resulting in the incorporation of a *Music* text (an abridged version of the earlier classic?) into a text on rites. For a while under Han, even ardent Five Phases proponents like Jia Yi (200–168 BC) had emphasized groupings by six, symbolizing the Five Phases and their supreme overlord, the Dao. Gradually, however, talk of six yielded to talk of five, for by this final change, ostensibly devised to restore the old rubric of the Five Classics, the newest aesthetic, cosmic, and intellectual theories could be satisfied.† With that the Five Classics—the *Odes*, the *Documents*, the *Rites*, the *Changes*, and the *Annals*—came into being as a set collection in the original Modern Script order.

As we have seen, there is little question that an *Odes* anthology existed in some form, oral or written, before the time of Confucius. Most scholars now date the compilation of an *Odes* anthology from earlier materials no later than 600 BC, though the text may not have been fixed in its present form much before the third century BC. The *Documents* followed. Though the *Documents* contains some indisputably early material dating from early Western Zhou (tenth century BC), rival collections of authoritative historical documents were

---

*Although classical Chinese usually does not indicate gender, there is no doubt that in most cases early authors imagined their subjects and readers to be male, in part because more males than females could read and in part because most authors presumed a "constant norm" by which females "follow" males. As historian, I feel that the automatic substitution of "he or she" whenever the Chinese text says "person" can create a serious distortion of the distant past. Accordingly, I refer occasionally to "man" rather than "human." Elsewhere, I have argued that women in the classical period were not nearly so downtrodden as modern stereotypes suggest. But ultimately each reader will decide for herself whether the Five Classics' gender construction disqualifies them from serious consideration.

†Six may have devolved into five by a relatively simple mechanism: the six powers (= Heaven, Earth, and the four directions) became five (the four directions plus the center) by the elevation of the sixth power, Heaven or Dao (symbol of the ruler), above the five. Originally, however, the alternative groupings of six or of five reflected two quite distinct political and cosmological visions, as Michael Loewe's work shows.

circulating as late as the end of the Warring States period. Only with Xunzi (that is, only a few decades before the Qin unification in 221 BC) can we safely assume that a text similar to the *Documents* known to us was used for teaching by a Confucian master. As for the texts of the rites and music, it seems doubtful they were written down much before the Han dynasty, though the teaching of prescribed rites and music had been considered essential to the education of true gentlemen for centuries. Last to claim a place in the canon were the *Changes* and the *Spring and Autumn* texts—texts certainly known by the fourth century BC but not regarded as full-scale Classics until the late Warring States. The so-called Modern Script order* that the Warring States and early Han texts use to list the Six Classics—*Odes, Documents, Rites, Music, Changes,* and *Spring and Autumn Annals*—seems to reflect, then, the approximate stages at which the written texts were incorporated into the canon.

These Five or Six Classics fall neatly into three groups, not only in their date of entry into the canon but also in their content. The earliest sections of the *Odes* and the *Documents* claim to preserve both the literary style and rhetorical preoccupations of the early Zhou court. Although this claim is surely false as regards most chapters, it is possible that such traditions preserved on bronze, stone, silk, or bamboo were known to Confucius, who referred to them when he located his vision of ideal antiquity in the early Zhou reigns. The *Rites* and *Music* texts alike present models of the civilized practices current among the lower nobility of the Warring States, whose outward attainments were said to match the perfection of their ethical standards. Finally, the *Yijing* and the *Chunqiu* share five similarities: they are the only texts (1) whose major commentaries have been regarded as integral components of the classic;† (2) that are traditionally attributed, at least in part, directly to Confucius, for Confucius was said to have written the "Great Commentary" to the *Changes*, included in the Ten Wings or Appendices, as well as the entire *Spring and Autumn Annals*; (3) that are thought to require an extensive hermeneutic for their meanings to be revealed in all their profundity; (4) that take as central theme the effect of human

---

*This ordering of the Five Classics appears in all early texts, including the *Zhuangzi*, Dong Zhongshu's various writings, and the *Shiji*. The Archaic Script (*kuwen*) order, which, judging from extant sources, first appears in Eastern Han, lists the texts in order of the relative antiquity attributed to them; hence the *Changes, Documents, Odes, Rites,* and *Chunqiu*.

†The work of commentaries and sayings in constituting a canon can hardly be overestimated. Writing an authoritative commentary on a venerated text (a) closes the text, after which nothing, except more commentaries, may be added; (b) marks the canonical status of the text; and (c) adapts the message of the venerated text to present concerns. Han writers like Wang Chong (AD 27–97) were fully aware of this.

behavior upon fate, demonstrating their points by reference to a wide variety of examples culled from history; and (5) that devote considerable attention to omens, prognostications, and cosmological speculations. In consequence, most Han classicists, despite their avowed intention to revere antiquity as the model, came to believe the *Yijing* and *Chunqiu*, the two latecomers to the canon, were the most important of the all-important Five Classics.

5. WHY WERE THE CLASSICS WRITTEN DOWN?

Rujia 儒家, the term usually mistranslated as "Confucianism," literally means "the weak" (possibly a taunting reference to the classicists' propensity to value ritual learning over military prowess that later served as an apt jibe for bookworms) or "the pliable" (as the classicists were likened to bamboo, which bends but does not break under pressure). Two traditional tales told about the origins of the Ru classicists, and in both their weakness and pliability are born of sociopolitical events. In the first of these, the Ru were descendants of the Shang people overthrown by the Zhou about 1050 BC. As a conquered people, they had little choice initially but to preach the virtues of yielding to the strong (hence their reputation for weakness), lest they be accused of treason by the new Zhou rulers. At some point, however, the surviving Shang descendants found that they could support themselves by teaching their superior knowledge of classical learning, music, and ritual to members of the Zhou court. (In versions of this tradition, Confucius was himself a scion of the survivors of the Shang royal house located in Song [fig. 2].)

A second legend also has the Ru supporting themselves by teaching, but it identifies them as collateral members of the Zhou royal family who had been disinherited after the breakdown of the feudal order in 770 BC. Bereft of their hereditary rank and feudal emoluments, these aristocrats were supposedly compelled to make a living from their superior knowledge of the ancient texts and rituals associated with the founders of their lines, especially the Duke of Zhou, regent to the second king of Zhou and first ruler of the appanage of Lu. Interestingly, both legends confer a royal origin on this group of classical scholars, doubtless in order to elevate their status and emphasize their vital importance to the state. Both also depict the profession of classical learning as a means to cope with dispossession, a notion that strengthened the appeal of classical teachings to men frustrated at being out of office. Probably neither legend is grounded in fact, but both surely convey an emotional truth: all great literature, as the most influential historian of China observed, is born of insights gained from suffering and dislocation. This observation bears in turn upon the question, Why were the earliest Classics (for example, the *Odes* and the *Documents*) written down at all?

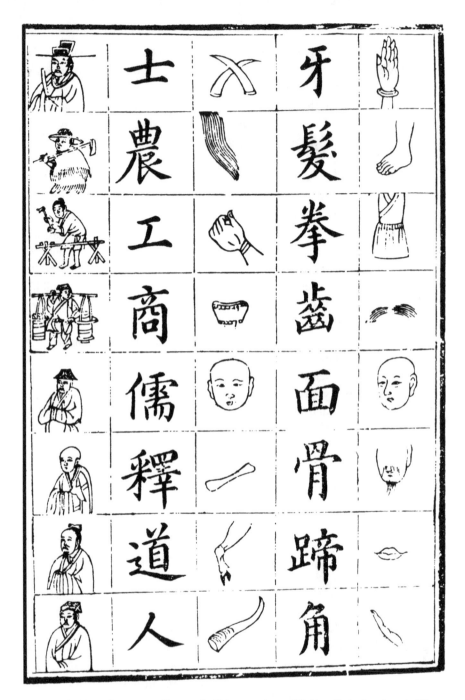

Figure 2. Fifteenth-century illustrated Chinese primer (*Xinbian Dui xiangsi yan*) (Hong Kong: Hong Kong University, 1967), n.p. The character Ru, the classical scholar, is illustrated in the leftmost column, fifth from the top, below the peddler and artisan and above the Buddhist monk and Daoist priest. At the top of the column is the *shi*, literatus of prominent social standing.

To frame a plausible answer to this question, one must consider the early history of the Ru classicists after the death of Confucius in 479 BC. Not so long ago, they were viewed mainly as sober scholars divided into two main schools, the idealist followers of Mencius and the rationalist followers of Xunzi. Between them the two schools supposedly dominated the four intervening centuries from Confucius to 136 BC, the date when the Five Classics were officially elevated to canonical status. A closer look at extant accounts suggests that both the sobriety and the simplicity have been overstated. Where one might imagine stern taskmasters or elder statesmen on the model of *Hamlet's* Polonius, the early classicists' contemporaries evidently viewed them as eccentrics who dressed in archaic robes and gathered in sectarian communities. Here are two descriptions, the first a Mohist critique of the Ru, the second an ostensibly more neutral account preserved in the dynastic histories:

> They bedeck themselves with elaborate dress. . . . They strum and sing and beat out dance rhythms to gather disciples. They proliferate rites . . . to display their decorum. They labor over the niceties of ceremonial gaits and flapping gestures to impress the multitudes.

> Now, when it came time for the High Sovereign Emperor [Liu Bang, founder of Han] to execute [his chief military rival] Xiang Ji, he led troops to surround Lu [the center of conservative classicism, where Xiang Ji was staying]. All the Ru in the state continued to discourse [upon the Way], to chant their lessons and practice the rites. The sounds of their strumming and singing never stopped [throughout the siege]. Did not Lu as a state exemplify the residual influence of the sages in its love of learning?

However united in their love of learning, even in Confucius's lifetime his disciples fell into at least four distinct groups, as the *Analects* itself reveals: (1) those like Yan Hui, who exemplified humane conduct; (2) those like Zigong, who specialized in perfecting their rhetorical skills; (3) those like Ran You, who aimed for government service; and (4) those like Zixia, who pursued cultural refinement. By Confucius's own account, his disciples were "headstrong and careless, perfecting themselves in all the showy insignia of culture without any idea of how to use them." If Confucius's assessment was accurate, their arrogance and superficiality may have spurred factionalism within the ranks of the classicists. At the same time, some evidence suggests that members of the Kong family clan—few of whom were esteemed by the Master—attempted early on to monopolize whatever benefits might accrue from their familial connection with Confucius, so they, too, may have formed factions promoting alternative accounts that would better serve their interests. In any case, by the late third century BC, one opponent of classical learning, Hanfeizi (d. 234 BC), spoke of eight types of classicists, each with its own separate political and ethical orientation. Even the writings of Hanfei's teacher, Xunzi, a strong proponent of Ru learning, reveal deep rifts among the classicists marked by theoretical differences and liturgical variations.

Such disputes were bound to arise, given the proliferation in the fourth and third centuries BC of brand-new philosophical questions demanding cogent answers. As the exponential growth in interstate relations ended in repeated culture shocks, a number of issues rocked the world of late Warring States thinkers:

What is the definition of human nature?

What lessons may be derived from history?

What is the relation of words to reality?

What form of government is most likely to ensure the well-being of its subjects?

Does any tie exist between the natural and human orders?

Confucius had said little or nothing on questions like these, possibly because he thought them unanswerable, more likely because in his lifetime such topics did not yet engross educated men. Nonetheless, later followers of Confucius's Way of the Ancients had to address such issues, if their mode of learning was not to be dismissed as mere antiquarianism. After all, Confucius himself had taught his disciples that true learning consists of "reanimating the old" through the creative adaptation of core behavioral modes to changing circumstances. And once the Five Classics were linked with Confucius, it was obvious to later followers that new material must be added to the corpus, either as interpolations into the texts or as appended commentaries, for the Classics, insofar as they drew upon genuinely old material, failed utterly to address the urgent new speculations. In other words, when the Classics simply could not be made to say what was required, "discovered" chapters and supplementary passages would supply the lack.

Not surprisingly, the continual reformulation of the classical message in response to changing theoretical concerns did not go unnoticed or unchallenged by all committed followers of Confucius. Centuries after Confucius, in mid-Han, good Ru would characterize the philosophical contentiousness of the Warring States period as a symptom of its stunning intellectual and moral decline—in stark contrast to many modern historians who see it as evidence of exciting intellectual ferment. This confusion associated with the surge of new ideas was merely heightened by the conundrums generated by the transmission or transcription of oral traditions. Especially in early China, where numerous dialects were spoken, many of which were very different from one another, oral transmission from teacher to student would have occasioned frequent misunderstandings. In the absence of inexpensive writing materials (silk, bamboo, and wood were available in the pre-Han period, but silk and bamboo were expensive in north China, then the site of Central States learning), information was held in the memory, but that is never wholly reliable.

Good reasons existed in the pre-Qin period, then, for writing down the Classics. Having so much invested in their truths, students and teachers would have naturally wished to establish a corpus of authoritative texts, the better to advance their own readings while stanching the flood of strange readings based on alternate versions. The real push to standardize crested, of course, in reaction to the cacophony of opinions that erupted in the Warring States period with its "Hundred [Theoretical] Lines"; it was hardly coincidental that the desire to transcribe and propagate the Five Classics intensified in response to the intellectual ferment resulting from increasing interstate military and cultural contacts. In China, as in so many other cultures, venerable traditions were set down in writing when masters disputed meanings.

States, no less than the adherents of Confucius, had a clear interest in establishing written texts for authoritative works: written texts are easier to control than sayings attributed to charismatic teachers.* Consequently, the first recorded attempts to impose state control over the dissemination of texts—including those associated with the Five Classics corpus—date not long after the establishment of centralized empire under the First Emperor of Qin (known to many as Qin Shihuangdi, r. 246–210 BC). The first ruler ever to succeed in unifying the whole of the territory then considered civilized (see the accompanying map), Qin Shihuangdi was not averse to co-opting certain kinds of authority through his patronage of leading teachers. Besides, the First Emperor understood that state-mandated unity would aid in consolidating his power and facilitating communication. To this end, he decreed throughout his empire uniform weights and measures, a single writing system, and a unified road system. Unity in the physical sphere naturally cried out for ideological unity, and the more highly routinized the bureaucratic state, the greater its need for stable precedents. For these reasons, the First Emperor appointed academic advisers to his palace staff.

---

*Many traditions record a fear that the writing down of texts will distort subtle concepts, ossify a cultural heritage, or open legal loopholes. In early China, as in classical Greece, written laws were also associated with tyrannical governments. Thus, some Ru insisted that the Ru had always objected to the writing down of laws, and they proved their contention by citing the *Annals* for the sixth year of Duke Zhao. Certainly such a fear seems to underlie the legend that ghosts wept at night when the sage Cang Jie invented writing.

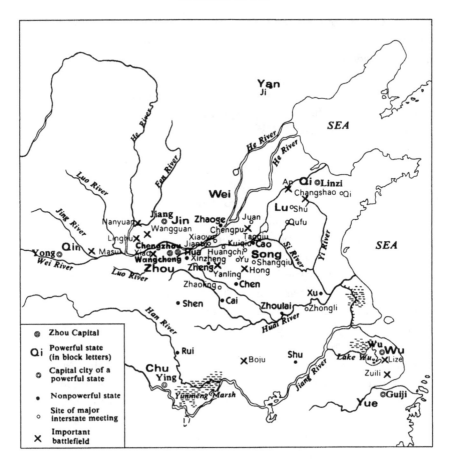

Map of the Chunqiu period, after Yu Weichao, *A Journey into China's Antiquity* 1:186.

Among such advisers were several masters appointed on the basis of their knowledge of two texts associated with the Five Classics canon: the *Odes* and the *Documents*. Presumably, then, the Qin imperial library in the palace complex at Xianyang (near modern-day Xi'an) contained some version of the *Odes* and the *Documents*, if not of the *Rites*, *Annals*, or *Changes*, along with a host of supplementary writings on ethics.

Certain classical scholars operating on the fringes of power at the Qin court tried to use their specialized knowledge to win over the ruler to their beliefs. Before long the First Emperor began to complain that the classical scholars exhibited a wicked propensity to "use the past to criticize the present" and to "harp on the past to injure the present." Stung by the classicists' political criticisms and infuriated by the duplicity of the court magicians loosely associated with them, the First Emperor in 213 BC, on the advice of his chief minister, Li Si, prohibited all "private learning" that had not received explicit government sanction, as well as all "private discussion" outside government circles. Singled out for special condemnation were the historical records of the pre-Qin feudal states, since these records undoubtedly would have contained criticisms of Qin. Still, Qin Shihuangdi's famous edict specifically exempted three important groups of texts: (1) those stored in the palace archives or used by government-appointed academic advisers; (2) those recounting the historical glories of Qin; and (3) technical manuals on medicine, herbs, and divination. All other books in private collections were to be burned. Those found guilty of disobeying the prohibitions were to be drawn and quartered. The severity of the prescribed punishment reveals just how troublesome these classical scholars and their associates had become to the ruler.

The Han, which conquered the Qin in 206 BC, circulated allegations that this Burning of the Books was responsible for major lacunae in each of the Five Classics (with the possible exception of the *Changes*, which was legally exempted from destruction as a divination text). It was said, for example, that the original pre-Qin *Book of Documents* ran to 100 or even 120 chapters, as compared with the early Western Han version of only 29 chapters. Many classicists after the Han victory joined forces with the new ruling house to decry the tyranny of the despotic Qin, for Qin statesmen like Li Si had denounced the classicists as despicable vermin whose theoretical constructs and ethical qualms impeded the machinery of state.

Despite its mythic significance, the Burning of the Books legend does not bear close scrutiny. First, researchers know that several classical scholars who specialized in the *Odes* and the *Documents* were appointed as court advisers under the First Emperor. The edict to burn the writings, the text of which has been preserved in an early historical account, explicitly exempted all writings in the possession of the Qin court academicians as well as all manuals of divination. Therefore, at least three of the Five Classics (the *Odes*, the *Documents*, and the *Changes*) should have escaped destruction entirely. Second, this same record links the draconian prohibition against private learning to a court debate over the advisability of reinstituting the feudal system under Qin. Given that none of the remaining Classics (the *Rites*, the *Annals*, and, if it existed, the *Music* texts) especially glorified the vanquished states of the late feudal system and that neither the *Rites* nor the *Music* contained "histories of a defeated kingdom" (a potentially inflammatory subject), what reason could Shihuangdi have had to consign them to destruction? Indeed, one early Han text associated with the classical master Jia Yi has the Qin burning quite another type of text: the old "wisdom lore" then in general circulation. While it is not implausible that a newly unified state would wish to foist a unified memory of the past upon its conquered subjects, in essence, the charge that the Qin specifically targeted the Ru canon for destruction probably evolved partly from the Han interest in slandering the defeated Qin, abetted by a misapprehension of the history of classical scholarship. Men of Han, moreover, writing after the Five Classics had been securely labeled Confucian, would have simply assumed that the texts of the Five Classics was anathema to the despotic Qin, whose rulers embraced the rival modernist theories of government. But as no extant text earlier than 100 BC ties the figure of the sage Confucius to any Classic except the *Chunqiu*, there was no reason for Qin's First Emperor, in his annoyance with interfering advisers, to single out the Five Classics for their support of contrary political views because in Qin times those texts simply represented the standard authorities containing old traditions handed down from the past.

Though mass destruction never befell the Five Classics in 213 BC, contrary to Han legend, surely texts of all types were lost when the Qin capital was razed in 207 BC, during the prolonged civil wars that ended the unstable Qin empire. By contemporary reports, the imperial palaces in the capital of Xianyang burned for three whole months. Three months may be hyperbole, but the conflagration was sufficiently massive to consume the entire contents of the imperial library. It was this Burning of the Books, the work not of the Qin government but of antigovernment rebels, that may have prompted classical masters to write down the many traditions hitherto dependent upon oral transmission. The devastation wrought by a single calamity of this magnitude might well have convinced scholars of the need to transcribe more texts for wider dissemination throughout the empire.

Yet even the loss of many texts would not have meant a sharp break in classical studies, for the teaching of ancient learning, prior to the invention of paper or paper substitutes in mid-Han times, perforce depended mainly upon oral transmission and memory. The Qin prohibition against private learning, in force for only two decades, was lifted by the second Han emperor in 191 BC. Many mature scholars would have retained the pre-Qin versions of the Classics in memory, especially the relatively short texts like the *Documents*. The Han histories, in fact, tell of several classical masters like Master Shen of Lu, a specialist in the *Odes*, who quickly resumed their teaching careers, presumably interrupted under Qin, once peace was restored under Han. In any case, the main effect of the Qin burnings (rumored and real) may have been to persuade the Han house to throw its considerable weight behind the task of cultural reconstruction. Not surprisingly, then, as soon as Han rescinded the Qin prohibition against private learning, many Han subjects "rediscovered" (that is, took out of hiding, wrote down, or in some cases forged) private copies of forbidden texts supposedly hidden away or held in memory during the dark days of Qin. As soon as

Figure 3. The visit in 195 BC by the Han dynastic founder, Liu Bang, to Shandong to offer sacrifices to the sage Confucius, apparently the first time a Chinese emperor paid homage to the Sage. As shown in the *Shengjitu*, late Ming edition purporting to be the 1444 original, Beijing Library (Rare Book no. 166645), scene 38. After Zheng Zhenduo, comp., *Zhongguo gudai banhua congkan*, Appendix A-6.

relative stability came to the new Han empire, specialists in the *Odes*, *Documents*, and *Annals* once again served as academic advisers at the courts of Emperor Hui (r. 194–188 BC), Emperor Wen (r. 179–157 BC), and Emperor Jing (r. 156–141 BC) (fig. 3).

6. THE CLASSICS AS STATE-SPONSORED IDEOLOGY

The single most important prerequisite for the formation of canons is the continual reproduction of the work or works. Given human frailties, the physical reproduction of knowledge in texts helps to ensure that traditions will be transmitted to successive generations of readers. It is easy to forget that the Five

Classics eventually triumphed over their rivals simply because more parts of the collection existed throughout the empire in more copies. Possibly the alternative canons (for example, the Mohist) were no longer copied in sufficient quantity to influence cultivated opinion, since classical learning by Han had already incorporated many of the most distinctive elements from the other theoretical traditions. One early source states that Mencius and Xunzi had been remarkably successful in making the Five Classics learning appear "glossy and appealing" to the men of their time, with the result that there flourished in the last century prior to unification a strong tradition of teaching and learning this corpus, a large part of which had been written down by that time. Unfortunately, little is known about how literary works were reproduced, disseminated, read, and taught in early China, though recent archaeological finds have clarified matters a bit. Some evidence exists that self-identified Confucian circles may have undergone a momentous change in identity during Western Han: whereas in the pre-Qin period the authority of such groups centered on their transmission of archaic rites, whose performance and explication were aided by a few old texts, by late Western Han (with Yang Xiong and Liu Xin) the classicists' authority began to derive mainly from their reputation as faithful keepers of ancient texts. Two anecdotes, the first dated to 208 BC and the second to AD 24, point up the contrast. In the first, the Ru, "spreading out their long robes and carrying on their backs the ritual vessels belonging to the family of Confucius," are heading for the camp of the Qin rebel Chen She, in whose service they intended to enlist. In the second, recorded some two centuries later at the time of rebellions against Wang Mang, the inheritors of the Ru tradition go seeking office only with "their charts and texts"; "from then on," the story tells, "there were none who did not carry in their arms or on their backs stacks of texts, when they gathered like clouds in the capital." This shift in emphasis from authoritative praxis to authoritative texts, already under way in the pre-Qin period, may relate to Emperor Wu's (r. 140–87 BC) decision in 136 BC to elevate the Five Classics to canonical status.

Extant historical records offer little more than intriguing glimpses into that decision. From those we surmise that three discrete acts during the reign of Emperor Wu confirmed the Five Classics as basis for state ideology: Sima Tan's (d. 110 BC) analysis of divisions between six fields of expertise in early China, which seemed to reserve the texts of the Five Classics specifically for the Ru; the statement by Sima Tan or his son that all the Five Classics were either written or edited by Confucius; and Emperor Wu's decree favoring those Five Classics as the official basis for state-sponsored academic activities.

According to the *Shiji* of Sima Tan and his son Sima Qian, it was Sima Tan who, as official archivist for the Han court, had conceived the idea of compiling a history of civilization from its earliest days down to his own time, a project so ambitious that it could be completed only by his son after Tan's death. The *Archival Records*, as the history came to be known, includes the entire text of Sima Tan's "Essentials of the Six Lines," an essay outlining six competing approaches to political rule. The influential essay not only acknowledged but strengthened the special ties between the Ru and the Classics, even as Sima Tan registered his reservations about the utility of Ru learning. As Sima Tan wrote,

> The Ru consider the Six Classics [that is, the Five Classics plus the *Music*] to be their law and model. But the canonical traditions for the Six Classics number in the thousands and tens of thousands. One could not master their learning over several generations. Nor could a man in his lifetime thoroughly comprehend all their rituals. . . . Still, when it comes to their rituals ranking ruler and subject, father and son, or their distinctions ordering husband and wife, elder and younger sibling, not one of the other Hundred Lines can improve upon them.

It was this same *Shiji*, submitted to the throne about 100 BC, that first asserted (or recorded an earlier assertion?) that Confucius was the author or editor of each of the Five Classics. Perhaps because the textual traditions had evolved so recently from disparate oral traditions, binding the corpus together required the authority of a single notable figure from antiquity.

Sima Tan's ruler, Emperor Wu, soon after his accession to the throne, is said to have conferred canonical status on the Five Classics by making them the basis for "official learning" (*guanxue* 官學) in 136 BC. Thenceforth, some proficiency in one or another of the Five Classics would be required of most candidates for most official positions in the imperial bureaucracy. If the dynastic histories are to be trusted, this momentous decision sprang from very complicated motives. On the one hand, Emperor Wu, noting the enormous prestige accorded princely bibliophiles in previous generations, would have been determined to outdo them all, for as one astute observer remarked of such patron-collectors, "Those who gained the hearts of scholars became powerful while those who lost the scholars perished." At the same time, the young emperor and empress undoubtedly hoped to use imperial patronage to undercut the influence of the powerful faction led by the Dowager Empress Dou; because she and her cronies preferred a political theory called Huang-Lao, Wu, with the backing of the Wei family, would favor the activist programs touted by their rivals, the Ru, who had considerable support in the ranks of the educated. As "authority once achieved must have a secure and usable past," the emperor would benefit from having the Supreme Sage as his patron, all the more since Confucius's teachings were recognized for their superb "rituals ranking ruler and subject." Aside from such starkly utilitarian motives, the initial decision to favor Ru classicism may have reflected the court's genuine admiration for the bold vision enunciated by one Dong Zhongshu, who imagined radically expanded powers for the Han throne and argued that the continued success of the Han sovereignty ultimately rested on its ability to undertake major political reforms. Han must be put on an entirely new basis: though the dynasty had been founded by force, it would be legitimated by a demonstration of supreme moral authority. The primary task of Emperor Wu, then, should be to show his subjects that the throne repudiated the deeply flawed model set by the tyrannical Qin. As Dong memorialized in 136 BC, "The proverb says that rotten wood cannot be carved nor a wall of dry dung be trowelled. Now in adopting Qin policy, the Han is just like rotten wood and dried dung. Even though it wishes to repair conditions, how can it possibly do so?"

Once the throne accepted the initial premise that major policy reforms were necessary—a premise bound to appeal to an energetic young ruler intent upon glory and restive under the supervision of senior advisers with a pronounced conservative bent—the activists had only to persuade the emperor that the Five Classics associated with the Confucian Way of cultivation were indispensable to any enlarged conception of Han sovereignty. This Dong proceeded to do, according to one Han account, by outlining his theory of the "Harmony and Unity between Heaven and Man" (*Tianren heyi* 天人合一). According to this theory, the human and cosmic spheres are closely linked by a network of sympathetic correspondences resonating within the triadic realms of Heaven-Earth-Human, with high Heaven taking a special interest in the works of the Son of Heaven, the emperor. Almighty Heaven would favor a radical expansion in the powers of the Han Son of Heaven, exempting the dynasty even from the natural forces of historical decay, so long as the emperor acts always in strict conformity with Heaven's ordained program of rites and music as set forth in the Classics. Should the emperor backslide, however, gracious Heaven will issue repeated warnings to its Son in the form of prodigious omens. Such omens should then be interpreted in light of the hallowed texts of the classical tradition, for these texts hold the key to understanding the latent sympathies tying the macrocosm, the world of Heaven-and-Earth, to the microcosmic world of human action. Their superior training in analyzing those Heaven-sent omens, of course, makes Ru classicists the best advisers to the throne on imperial policy matters. And when the Son of Heaven himself embraces the underlying message embedded in the Five Classics, he may hope to commune with Heaven directly. Together, the joint efforts of the emperor and his classicists to promote strict adherence to prescribed practices and doctrines will not only unify and shape society under Heaven's blessing, but also draw in the entire universe (perceived as intelligible by Dong) to the royal domain. And this was not all: Dong in his enthusiasm alleged that Confucius, as "uncrowned king" and deputy to Heaven, would deign to act as patron for the Han, interceding with Heaven so long as the Confucian Way was upheld by its emperor:

> In my humble opinion, the *Spring and Autumn Annals* seeks the ultimate ends of the Kingly Way. . . . Confucius once said, "The phoenix does not come! The Yellow River does not put forth its chart! It is certainly all over with me!" Confucius' own despair over the situation would have been enough to elicit these signs [indicating his kingly appointment], had he not been of low rank. Now your majesty, honored as Son of Heaven and commanding the wealth of all within the Four Seas, dwells in a position powerful enough to elicit these [signs of Heaven's favor]. . . . Nevertheless, Heaven and Earth do not respond to him. Good omens do not come. Why? Because his suasive moral example has not been established and the masses are not yet upright. Now Confucius wrote the *Spring and Autumn Annals* . . . to set out the text of the "uncrowned king" in it. . . . When Confucius wrote the *Annals*, he measured it above by Heaven's way; he based it below on human feelings. He checked it by antiquity; he tested it by current events.

In response to successive memorials along these lines, Emperor Wu in 136 BC is said to have reserved all the official Academicians' posts at court for specialists in one or more of the Five Classics. Presumably any other court Academicians were summarily dismissed. A decade later, in 124 BC, Emperor Wu founded the Imperial Academy (*taixue* 太學), an institution of higher learning whose course of training was based primarily on the Five Classics. Success in the classical examinations periodically administered by the Imperial Academy, where students reportedly numbered some three thousand by the end of the first century BC, became one recognized route to bureaucratic appointment and prestigious official careers. Tradition hailed these decisions by Emperor Wu as glorious precedents by which the classical texts so recently ascribed to Confucius became central to the political life of the state—all the more readily since the other belief systems that later gained mass followings in China (principally religious Daoism, Buddhism, Islam, and Nestorian Christianity) said comparatively little about the requirements or mechanics of bureaucratic rule. Almost immediately, enviable careers at court were granted those fully conversant with the Classics. Classical learning would begin to be transmitted in a more controlled fashion through the state's designation of prescribed texts, through state rewards for model behavior, through apprenticeships to state-approved Academicians, and through formal participation in a variety of state-sponsored rituals at all levels, including court academic conferences. And, as the culminating revelation in history, the Five Classics could be wielded to further the throne's interpretive monopoly.

Tradition therefore credits Emperor Wu* (and, of course, Dong Zhongshu) with establishing the orthodox pattern governing the relationship between the state and the intellectual, between power and influence, and between politics and culture, a pattern it sees as persisting throughout imperial China. Emperor Wu is said to have determined the content of learning in imperial China, for prior to his time learning presumably referred to the entire complex of Six Arts in which the aristocracy had trained or to the peculiar praxis transmitted through the classic master-disciple relation. Because the nascent civil service examinations begun in the Han period tested a candidate's familiarity with one or more of the Five Classics, the conventional story goes, a new sort of political elite evolved, one whose primary qualification was full literacy. Tied to government service, learning in imperial China would come to mean more than mere cultural refinement or antiquarian practice; it would entail at times the push for programs to integrate personal ethics with pragmatic politics.

For Emperor Wu and many of his successors, however, the primary attractions of classicism would have lain not in any cultural or moral benefits it might confer upon an emerging literate elite, but in the irresistible package of benefits it offered the state in its centralizing efforts. The Ru were famed for their eloquent phrasing, a skill that could be put to use in publicizing the advantages of state policies. Classicism afforded a wealth of precedents, including some that justified a relentless push for the consolidation of state power. Moreover, it attracted a literate group whose members knew how to preserve and transmit

---

*Historians conventionally speak of "Emperor Wu's decisions" in the same sense in which commentators refer to Nixon's policies. Most historians agree that Emperor Wu was largely under the thumb of the Dowager Empress Dou and her senior advisers until the empress's death in 136 BC. There is a strong possibility that the Wei family, the relatives of one of Emperor Wu's empresses, determined the direction of policy later on in Wudi's reign. Note also that from the beginning, mastery of the Five Classics always presupposed an acquaintance with a far larger corpus of texts, including the works of prominent thinkers and literary figures.

Borrowing Benjamin Elman's formulation in *Education and Society in Late Imperial China, 1600–1900* (Berkeley: University of California Press, 1994), I equate orthodoxy with "that which the late imperial state, represented by the overlapping but asymmetrical interests of the bureaucracy and the throne, publicly authorized and . . . the core of the civil service examination curriculum."

documents and who were also masters of symbolic action and cosmic principles, the miranda and credenda of government. In upholding, rationalizing, and yet subordinating the ancestral clan system with which most of the population identified, state classicism fostered the formation of a highly loyal literate class eager to interpret and adapt government policy. The very "emulation of models" proposed by classical masters—provided that its concomitant emphasis on moral order was downplayed—served as an excellent tool for social control, mandating strict conformity on the part of political inferiors with the announced wishes of their superiors. Still, from an emperor's point of view, favoring the classicists could prove costly, for any marked gain in the classicists' authority could come at the expense of rival thinkers and strategists who were often more ready to strengthen the royal hand. History had shown that proponents of a single authoritative interpretation might effectively challenge the throne on key issues of policy. That explains the marked ambivalence shown classicism by Emperor Wu and his successors. (At one point, Dong Zhongshu himself was sentenced to die, accused of parlaying false doctrines.) Emperors tended to favor classicists only when they perceived the interests of the royal house to coincide with those of their classically trained officials.

Although the later histories stress the monumental consequences of Emperor Wu's decision to reserve certain kinds of patronage for scholars trained in one or more of the Five Classics—so much so that Emperor Wu is principally remembered for this in later history—the Han histories focus less on the edicts of 136 and 124 BC than on his ritual reforms and expansionist campaigns in Central Asia for the purpose of controlling the profitable trade routes along the Silk Road. The Academicians, for example, receive no official notice again until 51 BC, suggesting their lack of influence at court. The early historians, unlike most of their later counterparts, knew that Emperor Wu never fully imposed the state's interpretive monopoly over a closed canon via an examination system or the Academy. It is doubtful that Emperor Wu was ever committed to doing so. For why set up so many opposing interpretive traditions (at least one and usually several for each Classic, for a grand total of up to fourteen competing state-sponsored Academicians' versions of the Way), if absolute political and philosophical unity was the principal goal? Why call for the ancient texts to be stored in secret archives? And why not mandate the continued financial support of specifically Ru institutions, including the Imperial Academy, instead of leaving those decisions to each successive emperor? For without mandated support, sooner or later the official schools would "fall into decay, with cowherds tending cattle and grass cutters gathering fodder on their grounds."

State-sponsored classical learning in Han was never intended to culminate in a complete "victory of Confucianism," despite some modern claims. Hence, the lack of any orthodox synthesis in Han, let alone a Confucian synthesis, is hardly astonishing. In any period, it would have taken a conjunction of imperial patronage, self-promotion by the literati, and perfect interpretive consensus among classical masters to make the Five Classics the single moral and literary standard throughout the empire, for if, as they say, a dialect becomes a language only when it has an army behind it, then surely an orthodox classic presupposes an entire empire behind it. No such victory could ever have been achieved unless three fundamental conditions had been met: (1) the transformation of classicists into a distinct group having a separate ideology; (2) a clear and consistent articulation of the empire's pressing need for a single ruling orthodoxy, as some later Confucian masters advocated; and (3) consistent and effective state support for specific projects and activities, leading to a notably greater uniformity in thought and in practice than had existed in the pre-Han period. The Han histories give no clear evidence that any of these conditions were met under Han. To the contrary, they portray a world in which even self-identified Confucians are determined "each and every person to have his own mind."

This is not to deny that certain Han thinkers longed to forge something like an orthodox synthesis based on Confucian principles. (Dong Zhongshu and Yang Xiong come to mind.) It is rather to observe that such attempts could not succeed, for several cogent reasons: The pool of professional classicists pushing diverse and self-interested agenda was always so much larger than the pool of committed Confucians. And once most candidates for office became nominally classicists (by virtue of their long schooling in the Classics), an enormous range of thought and activity, some of it not Confucian by any measure, was apt to be introduced into official learning, winning the dual sanction of antiquity and the state. Then there was the fact that the classical traditions contained internal tensions, puzzles, and paradoxes that resisted easy resolution. Most important, for its transformative influence (*jiaohua* 教化) to be accepted by the relatively uncivilized masses, classical theories had continually to adapt to political shifts and local conditions. As some classical masters conceded, "He who differs with the customs of the time will find himself isolated from [both] the lower officials and masses." In the process, the canonical traditions were altered—greatly for the worse, many devout adherents insisted—by their close association with the state. Furthermore, the state was determined to shift priorities among the classical virtues, so that filial piety and loyalty, two virtues not especially stressed in the teachings of Confucius, would be ranked far above humaneness. (The state's reasoning was impeccable: steadfast devotion to the state's interests found its closest analogy in loyal service to the patriarchal family.) For the remainder of the Han dynasty, the Han classicists, whether committed

Confucians or not, would try, but fail, to bring some order to the ensuing jumble of competing readings.

Had a state-sponsored orthodox synthesis been forged in Han, it could never have entirely dominated culture in China in the thousand years between Han and Song, despite the contrary claims of some present-day cultural nationalists. There were so many strands within Ru thinking—not to mention the Daoist and Buddhist teachings—each exerting strong countervailing influences to the state teachings. Even the dominant version of state-sponsored learning in late imperial China (the Cheng-Zhu interpretation) was never fully hegemonic in Antonio Gramsci's sense; its spirit, in other words, never mandated all taste, custom, and religious, political, or philosophical principles. Our perceptions of the imperial examination system, frequently mislabeled as one key component of a Confucian educational system, deserve a related clarification. The examination system became the principal avenue to official careers only in the last millennium of imperial rule, the period from Song to Qing (AD 960–1911). Before that time, upward mobility usually depended far less on the examination system than on family lines and on patronage by highly placed families with connections at court; besides, the early examinations tested literary ability (for example, the ability to compose poetry) as often as a knowledge of the Five Classics. Moreover, the examination system, contrary to common wisdom, was never intended specifically to increase social mobility, a goal the ruling classes expressed little interest in, except insofar as a degree of social mobility might foster social stability. Rather, the examinations were meant to define what kind of education qualified a person for the prestigious job of serving in government. Access to the imperial examinations was open, during most of the period from the Han to the Qing, to almost anyone who could manage to get an education. But for obvious reasons, comparatively few of the truly poor ever rose to high public office in imperial China. Their memorizing of bodies of written literature made the literate elites the virtual embodiment of culture. Thereby empowered, they found it relatively easy to bar from their ranks any unwelcome newcomers.

These caveats notwithstanding, it would never do to discount the monumental (if sometimes unintended) consequences of the imperial sponsorship of classical learning. Two anecdotes drawn from Han literature dramatize these. The first shows Emperor Zhang of Eastern Han meeting with his old tutor Zhang Pu in AD 85, some two centuries after Emperor Wu, and submitting to a lecture based on the *Documents*, while "performing the ceremonies of a disciple." Like the throne's sponsorship of the Five Classics, the emperor's purely formal submission was meant to bolster the strong connection between political and moral authority, considered crucial to legitimate authority. But to some minds this raised an ominous specter: that the empire's patronage of the Five Classics might limit state power, if committed Confucians sought to curtail initiatives and abuses by quoting the very classical traditions backed by the throne.

A second anecdote portrays another worrisome prospect, for the ranks of career-minded classicists at court included omen interpreters, some of whom were willing to manipulate portents flagrantly for personal political advantage—against the best interests of the throne. As the story goes, Minister over the Masses Zhu Zhang, holder of one of the three highest ceremonial offices at court, was the subject of a critical memorial addressed to the throne by one Yu Xu. The statement charged that Zhu, then over ninety years of age, was too decrepit to perform his job. Learning of the memorial, Zhu screamed at his assistants, "Of what use are such as you who see their master falling but do nothing to prop him up? Remember: 'When the master is in trouble, his men are disgraced!'" Zhu's subordinate, Zhou Ju, then advised him, "Every one of the sage emperors and enlightened kings of bygone days kept astronomical records of the sun, moon, stars and planets, as mirrors of Heaven's warnings. Recently, the planet Mars has exhibited unusual changes. Could you not draw up a letter on that subject to be secretly passed on to the emperor?" Zhu liked the idea, so he ordered his subordinate to draft a fine memorial to the emperor chock full of classical allusions to flatter as well as edify the royal person: "On reading Zhu Zhang's memorial, the emperor was so gratified by [the unctuous tone of] its loyal proposals that he decided that whatever the weakness in Zhu's eyesight, he still wrote a very fine hand. Assuming that Yu Xu had merely built a case against a major official to further his own personal ambitions, the emperor had Yu remanded for trial. Yu was subsequently forced to apologize to the emperor while Zhu Zhang was showered with approbation."* Factor in the self-

---

* The skillful manipulation of omens to coerce the throne continued without interruption down through Ming and Qing, as when the Ministry of Rites by such means persuaded the undereducated Ming founder to resume the civil service examinations.

Omen interpretations prompted complex questions about the nature of ultimate authority in the empire. Such questions were matters of grave concern to many early scholars, as is clear from one Han anecdote that would have readers consider whether ultimate authority lay in the canonical pronouncements or in the emperor's will. Fan Ying offended Emperor Shun (r. 126–144) by his obvious disinterest in a career at court. The emperor in his fury said to Fan, "I can keep you alive or I can kill you. I can have you honored or dishonored. I can enrich you or impoverish you. Why have you neglected our royal orders?" To this Fan Ying calmly replied, citing the *Analects*, "I received life from Heaven. And it will be Heaven that grants me life to live out my days or sentences me to death. . . . How could it be your majesty that keeps me alive or kills me? I view a tyrannical ruler as my enemy" (HHS 82A:2723).

righteous tone adopted by many Ru moralists and one sees why the more inde-
pendent-minded Chinese emperors—Emperor Wu among them—were often
inclined to discredit or ignore whichever classical sayings were apt to prove
inconvenient or disruptive of state power, despite their loud professions of
boundless admiration for the Supreme Sage, now safely dead. But that is,
perhaps, to get ahead of the story.

7. AUTHORITATIVE VERSIONS OF THE FIVE CLASSICS

Historical complexities aside, the decision to reserve certain kinds of imperial
patronage for the Five Classics presented their adherents with an immediate
problem: how best to choose an authoritative edition for each of the Classics?
After all, well into the mid-Han period (first century BC), relatively few editions of the individual texts now called the Five Classics had circulated among
the early masters, many of whom, adopting the model of Confucius, relied on
informal tutorials supplemented by occasional lectures to pass along their own
distinctive traditions to students. After the Han state announced its decision to
select candidates to office on the basis of their classical learning, students flocked
to recognized Ru masters, demanding instruction. Ironically, the new market
value of learning, calculated in proportion to the fame of the teacher, probably
increased the potential for serious errors in transmission. One famous anecdote
recorded about Dong Zhongshu, for instance, says that "he used to lower the
curtains of his room and lecture from within them, his older disciples passing
on what they had learned to the newer ones, so that some of his students had
never seen his face." In another tale, recorded centuries later, Zheng Xuan
(127–200)—the most famous of the Han exegetes—never once encounters his
renowned teacher Ma Rong (79–166) during his first three years of study ostensibly under Ma's direction. Such anecdotes suggest that a lack of personal contact
between beginning students and their masters was not unusual. (They incidentally highlight the enormous difference between Han scholasticism's propensity
to exalt and mystify the figure of the great master and the down-to-earth conversations, relaxed jokes, and individualized question-and-answer sessions used
by Confucius himself.)

So long as the Five Classics had been nothing more than receptacles of ancient
learning, their uniform transmission, either orally or in writing, was not necessarily a top priority among scholars. But as soon as the Five Classics were seen
as essential legitimating documents for the dynasty, representing at once sacred
scriptures and political programs, practical concerns demanded the establishment
of a single authoritative written recension for each Classic, in part to provide

an objective standard by which to gauge each student's knowledge, in part to fix the teachings and thereby render them more controllable than loose oral traditions. It was equally necessary to disseminate the authoritative written texts as widely as possible in order to promote the values and behavioral modes favored by the state. The very concept of a sacred canon or scripture had sprung from the imperial desire to impose tighter connections between the central state and local traditions of scholarship. Over time, the continual proliferation of public offices increased the demand for coordinated efforts referring to a stabilized, normative set of texts (fig. 4).

Given the nature of language in early China, establishing authoritative texts of the Classics was no easy task. The earliest written texts that we know of had originated in response to the perceived need of the Shang ruling clan from 1300 BC to record their applications to the illustrious ancestors-become-gods residing in heaven. While the script remained in the hands of a small circle of people drawn from the highest ranks of the political-religious elite, who understood the meanings of the written graphs by virtue of their rigorous training in ritual, it could function as a kind of aide-mémoire for that group, who did not always feel the need to differentiate phonetically similar words by the use of graphic radicals. But in the centuries after the collapse of Shang about 1045 BC, the Chinese script came to be ever more widely used for secular purposes by an ever larger and less homogeneous literate population, with the result that significs (also called radicals or determinatives) were often added later by those anxious to distinguish homonyms, near homonyms, and extended meanings of the same character. That early Chinese was unpunctuated only compounded the possibilities for misinterpretation.*

Though the ferocity of the Han scholastic debates over the correct readings of pre-Qin texts was vastly overstated by polemicists in late imperial China, the Han controversy between Modern Script texts, those transcribed in Han-time script, and Archaic Script texts, those transcribed prior to unification in 221 BC, would become so crucial to later self-mythologizing among the Ru that it is worth a short digression to review the facts. A surprising number of modern scholars seem to hold the mistaken impression that enormous caches of genuinely old texts resurfaced early in the Han dynasty, after the Qin prohibition against private books was rescinded in 191 BC. Actually, relatively few texts or parts of texts, genuine or spurious, reappeared in Han

---

*Much later, Zhu Xi (1130–1200), perhaps the most famous classical scholar of all times, remarked that he would sometimes have to read a classical passage some forty or fifty times to understand some 60–70 percent of the text. See *Zhuzi yulei* chap. 81.

Figure 4. In the premodern period, families that could produce five healthy sons were thought to be blessed by the Lord of Heaven, as this woodblock print suggests. Such families had reason to hope, then, that the family fortunes would be secured by at least one son doing well in the civil service examinations. From *The Graphic Art of Folklore* (Taipei: National Museum of History, 1977).

times.* The most notable rediscoveries reportedly included some material attributed to the *Documents* classic (at least one complete chapter, plus scattered passages and chapter titles), along with the entire texts of the *Zhouli* (*Zhou Rites*) and the *Zuo Traditions* attached to the *Spring and Autumn Annals*.

Despite the small number of texts concerned, the sudden reappearance of multiple texts transcribed in Archaic Script could not but unsettle the academic establishment in Han because it was claimed that the recently "rediscovered" texts in pre-Qin script were genuinely older editions containing "many archaic characters and ancient phrases." Were these texts really old? If so, did their relative closeness in time to Confucius make them more authoritative? (Some, though not all, of the Han scholars rightly discerned that older editions were not necessarily better editions.) Serious scholars, not just career academics concerned for their government stipends, were understandably loath to urge state approval of texts of such uncertain provenance, when the texts transcribed in Modern (Han-era) Script were so much better known. After all, the Five Classics had originally been valued less as a group of ancient texts than as a storehouse of ancient traditions. (For example, Han scholars certainly knew that at least two of the three *Rites* canons had been written down only during Qin or Han.)

Just beneath the surface of such qualms and quandaries over authenticity lay larger political issues, as one might expect of any court-sponsored ideologies. So apt were the Han literati—and their successors into the Song—to conflate

---

* Other so-called Archaic Script texts were basically the same as the Modern Script texts, except for a few variant characters. Generally there were no more variants between the Archaic and Modern Script versions than among the Modern Script interpretive traditions. Sometimes the Modern and Archaic Script texts differed by the inclusion of a single additional short passage, as in the *Xiaojing*, whose Archaic Script version contained a single passage of 120 characters not found in the Modern Script.

Much of the growth in commentarial traditions, then, was driven less by conflicting interpretations of the Five Classics themselves than by conflicting interpretations of the commentarial traditions attached to the Five Classics. Commentaries sought to reflect the different rhetorical uses to which the same Classic might be put. They also tended to supply three main sorts of information: (a) detailed philological analyses of words and clauses; (b) allegorical explications of passages; and (c) cross-references to other canonical texts. The strong Anglo-American bias in favor of original works as against "derivative" commentaries (inherited from Thomas Hobbes and John Locke) would have baffled many literati in imperial China, as well as the modern Continental philosophers, who have been happy to see themselves working in the school of an intellectual master. But each age in China has registered its protests against unthinking scholarship. In an amusing story recorded by Ji Yun (1724–1805), a ghost reveals that scholars preoccupied solely "with a mound of exegesis" emit an aura of nasty black smoke, dense clouds, and fog.

canon and commentary that when scholars argued for their preferred interpretations of Archaic or Modern Script texts at court, they were really making implicit assertions about the relative merits of entire interpretive outlooks connected with those canonical texts. The most important of the Modern Script traditions attached to the Five Classics had been completed by the first century BC, in contrast to the Archaic Script textual traditions, which began to be elaborated some two centuries later, in Eastern Han. In the intervening centuries, enormous social and intellectual changes had taken place. As government gradually became less centralized, ethical ideas favoring meritocracy and contingency yielded to those emphasizing hereditary prerogatives and fixed rules. The throne itself exemplified—and so furthered—such impulses; while Western Han thinkers could hardly forget that the wily Han founder, an upstart commoner, had wrested supreme authority from aristocratic Qin, the Liu ruling clan by Eastern Han had held the throne for centuries, so it had grander pretensions to divine right. Meanwhile, with the power of the Han weakening under a series of underage, indifferent, and incompetent emperors, it became ever more difficult to subscribe to Modern Script claims that a deified Confucius had himself conferred his eternal blessing upon the Han mandate.

Han scholars were fully aware of the major inconsistencies between the Modern Script and Archaic Script commentarial traditions. Those who had written the Modern Script commentaries stressed the commonalities between emperor and commoner, in the belief that the same ritual rules bound "everyone from the Son of Heaven on down to the lowest commoner." For example, one commentary to the *Gongyang* began its discussion of the first entry in the *Spring and Autumn* classic with the daring pronouncement, "No one under Heaven [including the emperor] is [necessarily] born to high rank." By contrast, for most Archaic Script proponents it was axiomatic that the emperor enjoyed a unique position by virtue of his patrilineal line. At one point during Eastern Han, for instance, the Archaic Script counterpart to the *Gongyang*, the *Zuo Traditions*, won the court's backing precisely because its adherents persuaded the reigning emperor that their tradition "exalted the sovereign and the father, while belittling the minister and son, reinforcing the trunk while weakening the branches." On the other hand, in denying that a semidivine or divine Confucius had bestowed his specific imprimatur upon the Han experiment, some Archaic Script commentators may well have been considering their self-interest. By the mid–to late second century AD, with the decline of Han, the Archaic Script scholars would have had at least two reasons to dissociate the figure of Confucius from the Han imperium: to ensure the continued validity of the Classics in the future and to command increased respect as protectors of a surviving civilization rather than as lackeys in service to a moribund Han court. To understand the position of a group of scholars risking much to promote a single group of agreed-upon texts as authoritative guides for private morality and public administration, we need think only of the current impassioned debates over the content of textbooks used in the public school curricula. Reputations and revenue from lucrative official posts, from publishing, and from teaching, no less than the fate of one's culture and the state, were conceivably at stake in early China. (Chapter 3, devoted to the *Documents*, returns to this problem.)

When such debates proved too divisive for the court, the throne would summon scholars to resolve inconsistencies and contradictions within the Five Classics. Indeed, successive courts under successive dynasties convened multiple court conferences whose sole aim was to resolve problems in textual interpretation. Sadly, such court conferences seldom functioned as cooperative exercises by literati well schooled in patterns of deference. One Eastern Han history, for example, shows a classical master, Dai Feng, engaging in the very sort of aggressive competition that violated Confucius's dictum "Gentlemen never compete." At a court audience, Dai Feng refused to take his assigned place. When the emperor asked him why, Dai replied, "None of the Academicians is my equal in explicating the Classics, yet they are ranked above me." The emperor responded by testing those present on problematic passages in the Classics. Finding that Dai did, in fact, know more than the official Academicians, the emperor raised him to a higher office. As it was the custom in court academic conferences that those who could not offer a satisfactory explanation of problematic passages had to cede the mats they sat upon to those with plausible answers, one court conference ended with Dai Feng sitting atop a pile of more than fifty mats taken from eminent scholars whom he had bested.

The dynastic histories relate how all too often the conferences degenerated, as the appointed "Imperial Academicians and their disciples all argued from personal opinion, without adhering to the Ways associated with their scholastic lines." Scholars pushing new ideas usually found it politic to utilize the authority of the Classics, and so they forged new works attributed to the Master or appended explanatory apocrypha to the Classics to uncover the "hidden meaning" in what were then commonly regarded as the "Secret Classics" of Confucius. As one Han skeptic noted, "The average person today holds the ancient in high esteem but looks askance at the new. . . . Today, if writings by new sages were to be taken and labelled as those of Masters Confucius and Mo, then certainly many adherents would express admiration for the works and accept them." Because imperial patronage was always more readily forthcoming for an interpretive line that fit into the framework of accredited theories and thereby wore the aura of hallowed tradition, scholars sought, consciously or not, to couch their ideas safely in the language of the approved commentarial traditions. That is how commentaries and commentarial modes of think-ing came to dominate later intellectual history.

The increasing reliance on written commentaries rather than on oral trans-mission initially seemed to represent at least a stopgap solution to nagging ques-tions about authenticity. Nonetheless, the practice soon created problems of its own. Scholars intent upon making a name for themselves felt a powerful impetus to overinterpret each line in a Classic. And proponents of new ideas found that the voluminous subcommentary format afforded a conveniently safe cover; under the pretense of explaining old texts and their commentaries, new ideas could easily be inserted into older textual traditions. As a result, within a century after Emperor Wu, commentaries and subcommentaries of incredible length came to be composed for the Five Classics. One Han text cites an extreme case in which a single three-character phrase had appended to it some 300,000 phrases (*yan* 言) of explication. But apparently, it was not unusual for Han com-mentaries and subcommentaries to go on for hundreds of thousands of charac-ters. By comparison, the entire text of the *Laozi Daodejing* [*Lao tzu's Tao te ching*] is some 5,250 characters long. (As early literary Chinese language is far more compressed than modern English, the numbers of characters must be quintu-pled to approximate the word length of the Han commentaries when converted to the highly inflected English.)

Such verbosity earned vigorous condemnation. The Western Han master Liu Xin (53 BC–AD 23), for example, asserted that in the good old days of antiquity scholar-farmers had mastered one entire Classic every three years, and they knew them all by heart by age thirty. Nowadays, he continued, even the most dedi-cated of students needed a lifetime to read the commentaries and subcommen-taries on a single chapter of a single classic, so in the end he forfeited any overall understanding of their content. Such protests went largely ignored, however. State-sponsored classicism could never reconcile the bureaucratic desire to treat a particular topic exhaustively with the contrary need, especially of beginners and those outside the academic profession, to distill the heart of the ethical message.

Moreover, the state's need to disseminate texts as widely as possible so as to forge a uniform social morality itself undermined real uniformity. For the greater the number of copies of the Five Classics that came into general circulation, the more the Classics became a kind of common intellectual property, open to wider literate audiences for acceptance, revision, or rejection. Whatever tenuous unity the original Confucian vision may have had in the pre-Qin period, thanks to careful transmission by masters to small circles of adherents, that unity easily dis-sipated. By the first century AD, texts of all types were to be found in the mar-ketplaces at reasonable prices. The penniless scholar Wang Chong (27–97) is said, for instance, to have "roamed the Luoyang market, examining the texts for sale" at the bookstalls—texts that he sometimes interpreted in a most iconoclastic fashion. With texts becoming more accessible, the temptation grew for the general public to try to make sense of the Five Classics and their commentaries without the benefit of a long apprenticeship under an acknowledged master. Paradoxically, then, the very attempt to establish a single authoritative edition of each of the Five Classics tended to spawn multiple versions of them, each claiming to be authoritative. Clearly, if the imperial house was to retain, let alone increase, its control over the dissemination of learning in the empire, it would have to take decisive measures to determine which of the variant editions of the Five Classics and attached interpretive traditions to authorize for teaching in the Imperial Academy.

Attempting to curb an increase in variant editions, many Han emperors extravagantly rewarded scholars who carefully "preserved the [approved] interpretive lines." Such measures failed to stem the interpretive flood, for the most vociferous of the polemicists, it was widely rumored, were daring enough to bribe the imperial librarians to tamper with the Five Classics texts themselves. Accordingly, the Han emperor in AD 172 ordered a definitive edition of the Five Classics to be carved on stone tablets at the Han capital, outside the Imperial Academy, so that students and teachers would have a standard to consult for ready reference. Cai Yong, heading the team of scholars, may have labored eight full years (175–83) on that first set of Stone Classics. His efforts hardly brought an end to doctrinal disputes, however, as is obvious from the following lengthy yet partial list of later Stone Classics carved for precisely the same purpose (fig. 5):

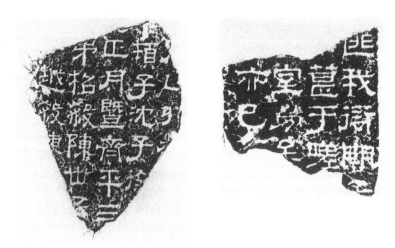

Figure 5. Stone Classics of Han, after Jessica Rawson, *Mysteries of Ancient China* (New York: Braziller, 1996), 215, fig. 117.1–2.

1. an incomplete set on which Hantan Chun worked for eight years (240–48)
2. a set associated with Xi Kang about AD 260
3. a Western Jin (265–316) set of unknown date
4. a Northern Wei (386–534) set of unknown date
5. a Northern Zhou set (completed 581)
6. the Tang Stone Classics (833–37), with repairs and supplemental stones made during the periods 874–80, 907–22, and in the Ming (1368–1643)
7. a Five Dynasties set carved in Chengdu (begun in 938)
8. a Northern Song set carved in 1040–61
9. a Southern Song set carved in 1135–43
10. a Qing set carved in Peking during 1791–94.

Even carved into massive stone steles erected in the capital within sight of the imperial palaces, the texts of the Five Classics could not be fixed or the scholarly debates halted. It was hardly more likely that the publication and empirewide distribution of the *Correct Meanings of the Five Classics* (*Wujing zhengyi* 五經正義) in AD 653, despite all the attendant fanfare, would settle such questions once and for all. Essentially, as long as the Five Classics were in any way authoritative, they would remain important subjects of controversy. Even within the professional academic community, the impulse to invent or manipulate the past—whether deliberate or subconscious—animated those hailed as the greatest of Ru scholars. History records, for instance, that Kong Rong (153–208), a direct descendant of Confucius and a most erudite commentator, extemporaneously invented a legend in utter contradiction to traditions attached to the *Documents*, merely to save the two most powerful men of his time, Cao Cao and Cao Pi, from embarrassment over their sexual peccadilloes; by such means the most renowned classical masters were brought to see that "their freedom [need] not be constrained by classical principles." And notwithstanding the popular image of the Chinese as docile, submissive, and conformist, records culled from early and medieval China attest not only to lengthy disputations among scholarly rivals but also to healthy skepticism toward the state-sponsored canon on the part of those outside the official sector. One anecdote from the Six Dynasties period (317–581) illustrates this point beautifully:

Lady Liu, wife of Senior Tutor Xie An (320–385), would not allow him to house any favorite concubines in separate quarters, though his lordship, who was very fond of music and female beauty, wanted to set up female entertainers and concubines in separate establishments. Xie's nephews on both sides of the family intuited his feelings, so they banded together to admonish Lady Liu to make some accommodation, citing the first and fifth odes in the Classic, said to illustrate the virtues of a lack of jealousy. Lady Liu, realizing what her nephews were about in their criticisms of her, asked them, "And who wrote those songs?" They replied, "The Duke of Zhou." Lady Liu retorted, "The Duke of Zhou, being a man, wrote them for his own benefit, that's all. Now if it had been the Duchess of Zhou, the tradition would never have contained any such words!

The crux of the matter was this: any decree reserving special patronage for certain texts associated with Confucius occasioned dilemmas that the state could never resolve by fiat. For instance, how could the state on the one hand regulate official teachings about the Five Classics and on the other instill deep reverence for the Classics in its subjects? And how to distinguish the relatively few who studied the Classics for their moral-didactic value from the legions of opportunists who did so only to worm their way into government office? Presumably only the first group were trustworthy; those in the second bore watching. That the state failed to devise such a gauge is suggested by the fact that in many periods candidates for public office shunned the most difficult of the Five Classics, which tended to have the longest commentarial traditions, and took the state examinations in a shorter Classic with more concise commentaries, confident that this would not prejudice their chances for appointment. Under Emperor Wu's grandson, Emperor Xuan (r. 73–49 BC), a certain Wei Xuancheng had been appointed chancellor, the highest office in the land, purely on the strength of his classical learning. From that time on, conventional wisdom held that "to leave your child a trunk of gold is less good than leaving him a text of one Classic." Conversely, the lowborn who lacked talent for classical study had to be resigned to living out their days down on the farm. But as soon as classicism was widely seen as a marketable commodity, complaints mounted about poseurs polluting the ranks of government, crowding out better men. One typical early complaint, registered by the Han thinker Wang Chong, alleged that "the vulgar students in the end are unwilling to thoroughly master the Classics, making a comprehensive study of ancient and new. They are preoccupied with mastering the 'chapter and verse commentaries' of one interpretive school, so as to get its general idea."*

---

*The *Documents* and *Changes* were always considered the most difficult of the Classics, given their archaic language. As the two shortest classics, however, with about twenty-five thousand graphs in each, the *Documents* and *Changes* proved to be perennial favorites among civil service examination candidates; in Ming and Qing, for example, roughly 50 percent of all candidates specialized in one or the other of these two canons.

In addition, there was always a certain ambiguity, if not downright contradiction, in the roles that the Five Classics were required to play for the benefit of the state. The divergence first glimpsed in Dong Zhongshu's early memorials to Emperor Wu became ever more obvious over time: the Classics served both as mundane administrative tools for the running of government and as magical "weaving strands" joining society and the cosmos into a seamless whole. Which function or functions of the Classics should the state value most? In one popular story circulating in late Han, the grand patriarch of Confucian scholars, Dong Zhongshu, courageously repulsed a dreadful shamaness's curse by donning court robes, facing south (the direction of light and enlightenment in China), and chanting the Classics. That these talismanic properties of the Classics were equally available to quite ordinary individuals is shown by another popular tale dating to the end of Han, wherein a certain Zhi Boyi defeats a bloodthirsty demon out to destroy him by reverently chanting the *Changes*. But the magical, even talismanic attributes that the texts of the Five Classics quickly acquired were less likely to be taken up by the sober souls who preferred to locate the center of classicism in a this-worldly ethic, downplaying its profoundly religious character.* All could agree that the Classics taught men how to be both "inner sage" and "outer king," that is, how to govern oneself as well as others. But how were these roles to be defined and which should take precedence, if only one could be achieved? Inasmuch as no clear conceptual boundary separated the Classics from history, literature, or political philosophy, did the Classics simply comprise the highest achievements in those intellectual genres?

8. THE CLASSICS IN THE POST-HAN PERIOD

Despite the occasional imperial patronage awarded the Five Classics and their consequent propagation outside the court, the Han dynasty made notably little progress toward the anticipated Great Peace. Modern historians have suggested even that the tremendous attention devoted to state-sponsored classicism may have itself contributed to the eventual breakdown of the centralized state, insofar as it helped to create a welter of conflicting obligations, all in theory absolute, to ruler and bureaucratic patron, teacher and patriarchal family. Certainly the steady proliferation of competing readings of the Classics (many verging on the bizarre)

---

*In 1923, nearly two decades after the abolition of the traditional civil service examinations, peasants in Phoenix Village, Guangdong, reportedly still invested the Five Classics with magical potency. Even today, Chinese medical prescriptions may include ashes from the texts of the Classics. Down through the ages, some humanistic scholars have scoffed at the supramundane properties associated with the Five Classics, preferring to associate such wild "superstitions" with the religious Daoists and the Buddhists. But many self-identified Confucian literati have credited the Five Classics with special magical powers.

did little to enhance the general prestige of either the Classics or classicists. Hence the repeated critiques at the end of Han in response to the perceived dual collapse of Han power and Han classicism. Many law-and-order proponents blasted the Han court for failing to impose a greater standardization of thought. Others argued that Ru institutions needed supplementing, if not correcting, by infusions from rival traditions, especially those associated with the Legalists, later Mohists, Laozi, and Zhuangzi. And some thinkers came to the belated realization that the historical process, including the rise and fall of dynasties, could not help but diverge from moral prescriptions. Why not, then, make practical ability, instead of moral conduct or classical training, the main criterion for government posts?

Xun Xu, living just after the disintegration of the Han (during the Wei dynasty, 220–64), acknowledged this restored sense of the conceptual separation of morality from power in his bibliographical categories, which sharply distinguish the classics from both history and political philosophy. Long before the late Song, when the Cheng-Zhu school asserted the primacy of inner self-cultivation over external political rule, the connection between inner sage and outer king had broken down. Thus many came to see official learning as the diligent study of statutes, precedents, and bureaucratic management techniques, utterly without reference to ethical principles. Some literati, in arguments that recall present-day disparagements of academe in the world of Realpolitik, went so far as to assert the total inapplicability of the Five Classics to political life. Perhaps the Classics as history were of little use as guides to the future; perhaps the Classics, after all, represented at best "only the dregs of the sages."

During the so-called Period of Disunion (220–581) following the Han, when no single state managed to control all of Chinese territory, official classicism declined, in part because the monies that the Han state had regularly devoted to civil enterprises, including classical scholarship, were more often diverted to war budgets and also because rulers and scholars alike turned to two religions newly institutionalized in China, Buddhism and religious Daoism. (In this period, the Buddhists produced their own literary canon, whose contents challenged many Han and pre-Han conceptions of society and cosmos, and they introduced forms of social organization hitherto unknown in China, including the celibate monastic system). Some interpretive traditions associated with Han classical learning, lacking the financial support of an imperial court, failed to survive in the cultural marketplace. But historians have tended to vastly overstate the diminution of interest in the Five Classics during this period, many accepting at face value the rhetoric of Han Yu (768–824), who proclaimed that the one Confucian Way had been unrealized in China since the fall of the Han. In AD 241, when Dao teachings were in vogue, for example, the Wei court still conducted a seminar on the Confucian *Analects*, at which an exposition of the text was accompanied by solemn sacrifices to Confucius's spirit. By such deliberate acts, the Wei emperors reaffirmed the principle that "honoring classicists and valuing learning is the basis of kingly teachings." And it was in AD 489, under the Northern Wei (386–534), that possibly the first temple to Confucius was built in the capital.

By no means, then, did Six Dynasties statesmen and thinkers entirely reject the teachings of the Five Classics. Most sought insight into a unitary Way that embraced Daoism and Buddhism as well, valuing pluralism over ideological purity, just as most of their predecessors had done. Even during the Tang period, the high point of Buddhist influence in China, scholars showed substantial "commitment to the preservation and study of the . . . canons and to official service on Confucian terms." One modern classical scholar, Pi Xirui (1850–1908), whose history of Chinese classicism remains the standard work on the subject, considered it altogether beneficial that Confucian ethical teaching was largely left to privately funded academies led by private scholars. Absent court patronage, the intense study of the Five Classics was left once again to those who prized the texts themselves rather than the expected material rewards.

But the fate of Ru classicism during this Period of Disunion is also subject to a less sanguine interpretation. It may be that the Han exegete Zheng Xuan, one of the few scholars who could plausibly claim to have mastered the entire spectrum of commentarial traditions in Han, had synthesized the divergent interpretations of each of the Five Classics so satisfactorily that no further need was felt for the many separate textual traditions. Zheng had stated his ultimate scholarly objective thus: "By raising one principle, to open up ten thousand items; by explaining one chapter, to clarify many sections, so as to reduce effort and minimize [the need for prolonged] consideration." Never doubting the universal appeal of reduced effort and thought, Zheng was apparently oblivious to the possible negative consequences of his syntheses. But once "the learning of Zheng had unified All-under-Heaven," the classical traditions were impoverished, deficient in the play necessary to fire scholars' imaginations and prevent scholastic ossification. The timing of Zheng Xuan's neatly collated texts and a conservative syncretism could hardly have been worse; they appeared just at the dawn of a period of incessant warfare, forced migrations, and repeated sackings of the old capitals of Luoyang and Chang'an, with their impressive libraries, in AD 189 and 311. In the face of the neglect of so many early scholarly traditions compounded by the physical destruction of so many texts, many classicists, acknowledging the multiple losses, concluded sadly that further developments based in authentic Confucian traditions were unlikely.

By the time the empire was unified under Sui (581–617) and Tang (618–907), the main thrust of classical scholarship was therefore directed at elucidating not the Five Classics themselves but rather the ethical norms that presumably informed the commentaries—so impossible did it appear to be to bridge the long conceptual and chronological gap separating the later exegetes from the distant figure of Confucius as author and editor. Living in an age when scholastic approaches to the various branches of thought tended in any case to be highly compartmentalized, Kong Yingda (574–648) and his coeditors in the massive *Correct Meanings of the Five Classics* project, aimed only to adjudicate among the extant Han and post-Han commentaries. For each classic they selected what they deemed the most reliable commentary and to it appended their subcommentary, which mainly amplified, "for the most part mechanically," the arguments of the commentary. But between Han and Tang there lay a major difference: for generations of dedicated Han classicists, the compelling motive was personal immersion into the presumably unified moral perspectives of the Classics' sage-authors, whereas for the Tang scholastics seeking to recover and revive Ru learning, it was the classical texts and their prescriptions of duty (*yi* 義) that constituted the primary hermeneutical concern.

Few students of classical learning may have noticed the shift at the time because the Han attempt to find the sages behind the Classics was less an attempt at psychobiography than a search for examples of the ethical orientation of the fully realized person. In general, the ranks of the Tang elite may have contained fewer serious students of the Five Classics than in the heyday of classical learning under Han. Under Tang, as during the earlier Period of Disunion, only one of the groups competing for power within the imperial court, the *shi* 士, measured qualifications for office by its literary training. Moreover, the men of Tang tended to gauge literary ability by skill in composing verse, not by any specialized knowledge of the Five Classics. This would not change till early Song times, when the demise of aristocratic lineages cultivating the polite arts left greater power in the hands of the self-consciously classicizing *shi*; in Song, for the first time, such literati had no significant rivals for political power at court except the emperor himself (and not coincidentally, imperial patronage of the cult of Confucius as model classicist escalated then).

With so many important players gathered into the fold, it is hardly surprising that Song thinkers quickly threw off many of the constraints that the Tang *Zhengyi* approach had exemplified. One interpretive school in Song, which developed out of the teachings of two brothers, Cheng Hao (1032–85) and Cheng Yi (1033–1107), as transmitted by Zhu Xi, claimed to have rediscovered an inner-oriented hermeneutics devoted more to questions of human nature than the old Han learning, which had sought to define shared patterns of sympathetic interaction operating in the political, social, and cosmic realms. From 1241, when it received state sponsorship, through the last three dynasties (Yuan,

Ming, and Qing), the Cheng-Zhu school dominated state ideology. Adherents of the Cheng-Zhu, or True Way Learning, branch of Confucian learning were apt to downplay the two sources of extracanonical authority that were most central during Han, the received classical legacy as it had evolved through history and the physical world of Heaven-and-Earth as precise model for social action. The first, they argued, had long been tainted by heterodox ideas, and the second was somewhat peripheral to the central Confucian task, the attainment of perfect self-cultivation through a contemplative interaction with set texts. Such preoccupations with relatively interiorist metaphysics probably originated in political opposition to Wang Anshi's (1021–86) New Policies and in political despair over the Song's disastrous military situation. Although the new mental style of the Cheng-Zhu masters predicated a startling degree of autonomy from current sociopolitical events, the masters themselves nonetheless intended to exert a considerable influence over those events.

Building upon certain Tang developments in exegesis, the Song masters elaborated something of a new approach to understanding the Classics: (1) a general preference to explicate a Classic by juxtaposing passages within it rather than by reference to additional works within the canon; (2) an inclination to draw freely from many separate commentarial traditions in explaining the text of a given Classic; (3) a propensity to locate in each Classic one or more touchstone passages that presumably functioned as condensations or keys to the whole; and (4) a tendency to attribute contradictions within any one text to either (a) a sequence of authors living in different periods or (b) a single author's decision to adjust his replies to address the varying concerns of different audiences. In Han times, all parts of the Five Classics were accorded immeasurable value, even if certain passages proved eminently more quotable than others, but now the Classics were to be viewed on the model of anthologies, whose selections might vary in worth.

Armed with these general interpretive principles, the leaders of the True Way Learning posited the ability of each literate male to interpret the Classics with intellectual independence, following, of course, long years spent in intensive moral self-cultivation under the guidance of a True Way Learning master. In some ways, then, this dominant strain in the movement represented a revolution comparable in kind,* magnitude, and scope to the Protestant Reformation.

*I say "in kind" because the desire to return to the pristine core of the canonical texts, unencumbered by exegetical traditions, reflects the same impulse to effect untrammeled communication with the Ancients. Thus Zhu Xi urged his followers to discard the Han commentaries on the Classics, but five centuries later, when Zhu Xi's own commentaries had themselves become encumbrances to the desired direct insight, Zhang Dai (1597–1679) in his *Encounters with the Four Books* urged readers to put aside Zhu Xi's commentaries.

Whereas Han Confucians had considered a thorough grounding in the exemplary sage-kings' traditions the best possible preparation for practical political action in an ever-changing world, Zhu Xi (1130–1200) and his followers sought to elicit directly from their texts a set of eternal ethical precepts that would lift them entirely out of the realm of change. And whereas Han Confucians had sought to bring together in a comprehensive whole all of the startling insights proposed by various thinkers in the pre-Han period, thinking that "all roads led to the Dao," Zhu Xi and his followers, following Han Yu, desired to locate in history the single, straight line of the correct Confucian Way conveyed directly from the heart of one Confucian sage to that of another; by this process, they hoped to strip away faulty accretions stubbornly adhering to what they saw as the greatest of all teachings. (It is hardly coincidental, then, that with respect to the contents of the Five Classics, "no one before him [Zhu], and none after him, has uprooted the authenticity and authority of so many works." Zhu Xi considered some of the *Odes* less than properly elevating; he doubted half the standard text of the *Documents*, the so-called Archaic Script chapters; and he dated the *Rites Records* to a time many centuries after Confucius.)

Just as the Protestant Reformation focused on select portions of the Bible, Zhu Xi's three-part educational program (see below) elevated the Four Books over the Five Classics. Believing that a thorough knowledge of this small group of ancient materials would serve students better than a nodding acquaintance with the lengthy Five Classics, Zhu advised his students to engage in deep rather than broad reading, lest they draw unorthodox conclusions when faced with an overwhelming amount of material. Zhu further warned his disciples not to mistake mastering details with mastering the text: "Not the places where you have questions, but rather the places where you have none: that is where you should focus your energies." In essence, Zhu Xi was determined to fix a program of study to help students avoid the two most common scholastic errors: the tendency to subscribe uncritically to long-held interpretations and the countertendency to cling to one's presuppositions, however idiosyncratic. Zhu Xi therefore asked committed students to (1) read less and recite what they read until it became absolutely familiar to them; (2) turn the text continually over in their minds; and (3) apply it in their lives. (In this program, Zhu Xi borrowed freely from the Buddhists, who continually recited sutras in order to internalize their meanings.)

Zhu Xi preferred the Four Books to the Five Classics for at least three other cogent reasons besides their relative brevity. First, the Five Classics emphasized good rule, whereas the Four Books were more concerned with personal self-cultivation. Zhu held self-cultivation to be unquestionably the first step along the ancient "Way of Yao and Shun." Though he affirmed the transformative influence of moral virtue and the deep affinities between the person and society, Zhu considered that only a strong priority on self-cultivation would eventually ensure a better-governed world. Second, the Four Books, far more often than the rest of the Five Classics, dealt with psychology, human nature, and meta-physics. It was essential that these topics be developed if the new ethical teach-ings were to satisfy members of the elite long accustomed to the Chinese Buddhists' sophisticated discourse on the connections between original mind and the universe, which had already been adopted by leading proponents of institutional Daoism. Third, dedicated scholars over the ages had often been unable to discern in the Five Classics corpus a coherent vision of the world and a single, unified message. Zheng Xuan had gone so far as to trace the same scholarly frustration to the Sage-Master Confucius himself: "Since the subjects and meanings of the Six Arts [here referring to the Six Classics] differ so much from one another, Confucius worried that the Way might fall apart, with future generations unable to grasp its basic essence." As centuries of debates focused on inconsistencies in the Five Classics had resolved little, why not seek a new path out of an age-old problem?

A curriculum based on Zhu's beloved Four Books undoubtedly eased the students' lot. Being more recent and less terse than the Five Classics, the Four Books were easier to read. Also, they had all been composed within a shorter span of time (late fifth–second centuries BC), making them more coherent and more intelligible to most beginning readers. One famous classical scholar in Japan, noting this, recorded his suspicions about Zhu Xi's motivations in pro-moting the Four Books in notebooks dating to 1717:

> By the time Han Yu made his appearance in the Tang, . . . writing had undergone a great change. Then came the two Chengs and Zhu Xi, admittedly scholars of great stature, yet nonetheless unacquainted with the archaic language. Unable to read and understand the Six Classics properly, they showed a preference for the "Doctrine of the Mean" and *Mencius* because these texts were easy to read. This is how such . . . writings came to be mistaken for the true expression of the Way of the Sages in its original form.

Although the famous classicist Gu Yanwu (1613–82) cast no such slur upon the founders of the Cheng-Zhu school, he likewise alluded to the considerable effort required just to read the Five Classics corpus and its resulting unpopular-ity among students: "With competitive fellows who want to establish a reputa-tion quickly, speak to them of the Five Classics and you'll find that they are unwilling to study them." Most Ming scholars, for example, when faced with the many interpretive problems presented by the Five Classics, simply resorted to the Four Books for their explications.

Inevitably, such an emphasis on the Four Books provoked a reaction, so that by late imperial times many of the finest scholars were once again working to understand the "subtle phrasing" of the Five Classics texts via their Han and pre-Han interpretations. One of the first notable signs of the concomitant retreat from the Four Books in favor of the Five Classics came in late Ming, when some scholars urged that the Great Learning and Doctrine of the Mean chapters be returned to their original status as chapters within the *Rites Records* text. Such proposals implicitly challenged the legitimacy of the Four Books as an independent corpus representing the supreme distillation of the fundamental message faithfully transmitted by Confucius from his paragon, the Duke of Zhou. Proponents of Han Learning accused Song Learning of an overpreoccupation with personal morality grounded in metaphysics and a corresponding failure to address pressing issues of statecraft and scholarship. Their complaints, which continued during the Qing period (1644–1911), were acknowledged by the state in changes made to the examination system in 1756, changes that put the Five Classics on a more equal footing with the Four Books. The revived interest in the Five Classics was not always apparent outside elite academic circles, however. Arthur Smith, an early missionary fluent in Chinese, reported in his *Village Life in China* (1898), "It is a strange fact that one occasionally meets schoolmasters who have never studied anything beyond the Four Books, and who therefore know nothing of the Five Classics,—an outfit comparable to that of a Western teacher who should only have perused his arithmetic as far as simple division!"

Over time the corpus called the Five Classics had risen from its original non-canonical status to the status of official scripture in 136 BC, only to be reduced, some thousand years later, to secondary canonical status. And although the Han Learning scholars' advocacy of these texts in late imperial China excited interest in the Five Classics in some quarters, it could not save the corpus from serious decline. By the turn of the twentieth century, the Five Classics had become an attractive target for a new set of reformers protesting the perceived conservatism and elitism of the old society, in large part because such a high level of erudition was required just to read them. In 1912, the very first year of the Republic (1912–49), formal study of the Five Classics was promptly dropped from the prescribed national studies curriculum. And by 1930, most colleges and universities in Peking had canceled such courses as "The History of the Confucian Classics" and "General Survey of the Confucian Classics." As the course of classical learning in twentieth-century China is the subject of the final chapter in this book, I note here only that modern scholars of Chinese classicism seem to have absorbed many of the prejudices common to the

Cheng-Zhu followers of late imperial China and the May Fourth reformers. For example, the eminent sinologue William Theodore de Bary, in a book devoted to the Oriental Classics, makes no mention at all of the Five Classics (only of the Four Books), to all intents and purposes ignoring the first fifteen hundred years of Confucian classicism.

9. EXEMPLARY FIGURES

As we have observed, the classical Way was by no means synonymous with the Confucian Way. In order to appreciate the special commitments undertaken by those dedicated to the Way associated with Confucius, three short biographies of famous classicists will show the main concerns holding that imagined community together through history: a dedication to improving state policies so as to "aid the king" and "educate the people"; a preoccupation with certain rites associated with transmission of the ancient Way; and a belief that the study of past events could illuminate present predicaments. Fundamental to each of these was the equation of moral excellence with the cultivation of self and others; ideally, through the joint exercise of *jingyi* 經義 (canonical principles) and *zhishi* 治事 (managing [practical] affairs) humans might come to realize "the perfect out of the finite existence of humankind." Such concerns with governance, ritual, and history did not necessarily predispose a committed classicist to political or social conservatism. In their attempts to realize the standard of moral excellence demanded by Confucius, ethical classicists were just as likely to propose reformist, even radical programs designed to "reanimate the past." Neither did such concerns predetermine the personal choice between the partly competing priorities of internal self-cultivation versus the improvement of society through benevolent government. They only ensured that the polite arts, including book learning, would always be thought the means to, rather than the end of, the good life.

Any selection of exemplars is bound to strike some as arbitrary, but three men are treated here because of their lasting influence over history: Han Yu, the Tang prose master who urged that minds clouded by the foreign religion of Buddhism return to the classical teachings of ancient China; Wang Yangming (1472–1529), whose theory of "unity of knowledge and action" challenged the very premises of state-sponsored Cheng-Zhu orthodoxy; and Kang Youwei (1858–1927), the religious reformer and political iconoclast whose peculiar vision of Confucius as religious savior demanded the rejection of nearly half of the "Confucian" Classics. (Readers particularly interested in the subject of classically trained women might start with, *Pan Chao: Foremost Woman Scholar of China*, Tseng Chi-fen's *Autobiography of a Confucian Woman*, and *The Sage and the Second Sex*, listed in Suggested Readings.)

Han Yu

Han Yu is best known today in two capacities: as an advocate and practitioner of a literary prose style modeled on the "patterns of antiquity" (*guwen* 古文) and as a tireless promoter of a specifically Chinese Way, which he regarded as inherently superior to that of the "foreign" religion of Buddhism. Determined to transmit aspects of the antique culture, Han Yu is usually perceived as the central conservative figure bridging pre-Tang intellectual trends and those of later imperial China. But Han Yu, at least in his early, idealistic years, before disillusionment and disappointed ambitions set in, never claimed the conservative mantle. He preferred rather to present himself as no particular respecter of persons or conventions: "My [only] teacher is tradition. . . . It matters neither whether one is rich nor poor, old nor young. Where the tradition lies, there my teacher is."

Though Han had been a precocious child, reciting the classics by the age of six, he was thirty-six or thirty-seven years old before he began to make his name by his political and ethical positions. A stickler for regular bureaucratic procedures and a staunch opponent of bureaucratic corruption, Han Yu was progressing slowly but steadily up the ladder of success at court, when by a single audacious act that he later came to regret he nearly ruined it all. Early in AD 819, the emperor ordered members of the court to venerate a relic of the Buddha for three days at the palace; the relic was thereafter to be displayed for the public at various temples in the capital. Han Yu promptly sent a memorial to the emperor, asking him to rescind the order. The memorial was less than tactful. Portraying the preservation of the empire as a monumental contest between civilization and barbarism, it argued that the relic should be destroyed, lest the Chinese emperor show himself to be a mere servant of a barbarian, the Buddha. Moreover a bone, as it partakes of death, might kill off the emperor in the absence of proper exorcisms, and Buddhism has no precedent in China, nor does it support filial piety.

Anticlericalism was common enough among late Tang literati, even among those who were adherents of the Buddha in their private devotions, but Han Yu certainly went further than most when he publicly denounced not merely the evident abuses perpetrated by wealthy and powerful Buddhist institutions but also the fundamental character of Buddhist teachings. For Han, the true excellence of classical teachings lay in their presumption that self-cultivation could occur only in the real world of political and social action, not in the seclusion of the monastery. But the emperor was so infuriated by Han Yu's memorial that he considered condemning him to death. Thanks to the intercession of patrons and friends, the sentence was commuted to exile. One year later, a general amnesty allowed Han to come home and resume his bureaucratic career.

Perhaps because of that near catastrophe, in later life Han Yu distanced himself from his earlier anti-Buddhist, anti-Daoist positions; he even ceased advancing some of the educational ideals for which he had been celebrated. His final years saw Han appointed director at the Imperial Academy, a job somewhat isolated from the main political arena. There his official attitude toward the capital's educational institutions proved so thoroughly conventional as to be in conflict with his unofficial opinions on teaching. He declared blandly that the examination system should encourage the broad humanistic training that was likely to supply a firm moral foundation. He also wanted candidates for office to demonstrate their consistent concern for the welfare of the populace. Still, there were remnants of the old firebrand left. In court debates, he tended to side with those factions determined to root out separatist movements, for Han believed that Confucius had written the *Spring and Autumn Annals* classic to clearly demarcate the cultural boundaries between the Chinese and the "uncivilized."

All too often portrayed simply as forerunner of the orthodox masters of late imperial China, Han Yu was distinctly a man of his times. He placed greater value on sublime literary expression and high office than on scholarly activities or introspective metaphysics. He enjoyed his drinking bouts. Indeed, his sly sense of humor and his playful quips sat better with his contemporaries than his pretensions to sagehood. (It surprised none of them that he composed a poem entitled "Ridiculing the Snorer.") But even the serious advocates of True Way Learning had to acknowledge Han Yu's contribution to their rethinking of Confucian tradition. For Han was one of the first after Yang Xiong to insist upon Mencius as the foremost disciple of Confucius in place of Xunzi, whose writings had been far more influential up to his time; also, despite his celebrated opposition to certain Buddhist practices, one of the first to popularize a new style of exegesis modeled on the traditions of reading the Buddhist classics, the style that would later be adopted by Zhu Xi (see above). Add to this Han Yu's advocacy of the *guwen* "archaic" literary style, which embodied the hope that a return to antique models might restore the moral perfection and political puissance attributed to the empires of antiquity, and it is easy to see why many late Confucian masters considered Han's writings a turning point in the history of Chinese thought. Thus in AD 1084, Han Yu was officially recognized as a master of the Way, and his spirit tablet placed for worship at the Confucian temple in the capital.

Wang Yangming

For most of his adult life, Wang Yangming pondered with rare single-mindedness one of the central puzzles of the moral life: the nature of reality as it relates to knowledge and action. Confucius and his early followers—in contrast to the Buddha—had averred that the human faculties, including the senses, are reliable tools in the service of human development; that the phenomenal world is real and apprehensible enough to true insight; and that humans can attain the Good not by detachment but by an ever-greater attachment to human society and cosmic norms. The Cheng-Zhu synthesis, enshrined as state orthodoxy from 1313, suggested that a person's best path to moral understanding lay in the thorough investigation of material things and events (*gewu* 格物), which afforded a basic knowledge of the unseen cosmic principles (*li* 理) that could "extend" (*zhi* 至), by further speculation, to the moral (fig. 6).

Wang Yangming, as scion of a reputable scholarly family, was trained in the Cheng-Zhu tradition, but early on he put to the test Zhu Xi's assertion that cosmic principles were to be discovered in every tree or blade of grass. With a friend, Wang spent seven days in intensive contemplation in a bamboo grove, after which he fell dangerously ill. At first, Wang was unsure whether his inability to apprehend cosmic principles resulted from insufficient virtue or from a defect in Zhu Xi's axiom. Over time, however, he came to reject outright Zhu Xi's recommended course of "investigating things," in which "the principles of things and the mind remained dual," and to resist its implicit abstract intellectualism that required perfecting knowledge and words before taking ethical action.

Despite his disdain for conventional learning, Wang took the examinations and passed them at the highest level, the *jinshi*, in 1499, after which he was appointed a minor court functionary. In 1506, he submitted a strongly worded memorial protesting governmental abuses, a particularly unexpected act in view of Wang's relatively low status as junior secretary. As a result, Wang was imprisoned, publicly flogged, and exiled to the malarial mountains of distant Guizhou. In despair, he had a stone coffin made, before which, filled with a sense of the urgency, fragility, and ephemerality of human existence, he practiced the quiet sitting associated with devotees of Chan (Japanese: Zen) Buddhism. Eight years in exile proved an inadvertent gift, for one night while meditating Wang came to the realization that values and commitments are not external to the self but part of the very structure of our beings. Recalling Mencius's formulation that "the ten thousand things are all complete within me," Wang reasoned that "knowledge and action are one," meaning that moral understanding and right social practice are indivisible. One does not know (that is, correctly value) a

Figure 6. "Wang Yangming contemplating the bamboo," from *K'ung tzu: On the 2540th Anniversary*, 207.

specific moral act unless one feels compelled to act on it. Real goodness may be achieved only by unrelenting efforts to care selflessly for others, efforts that required an unflinching moral courage.

Recalled from exile after eight years of intensive practice, Wang had a chance both to test his newfound convictions and to teach by personal example when he was appointed governor in 1516 over a large area in southern Jiangxi overrun with bandits and rebels. To restore social order, Wang used every means at his disposal: the newest military strategies and the most advanced weaponry in the field, together with strict controls over the civilian population to prevent enemy infiltration. As governor, he also instituted local schools and village compacts in order to engage the local people. Within three years, the area was pacified. Wang was transferred to a new post, where he quashed a local rebellion under the Prince of Ning. His brilliant success in that undertaking nearly proved to be his undoing, for certain court factions, anxious to claim credit for the victory, questioned his pacification methods, his failure to make the pro forma declaration giving credit for victory to the capital powers-that-be, and hence his basic character. To these experiences, which helped Wang realize the inherent difficulties of knowing when and where and how to act, he responded by redoubling his efforts to discover within them the path to sagehood.

During the period 1521–27, Wang committed himself to teaching groups of disciples his most important insight: that the basic substance of the mind was formed slowly by unremitting moral effort consisting of caring for others; that the highly educated mind did not, in other words, contain more innate awareness of the ultimate good than that of an ignorant commoner. The Confucian Way once more—as articulated by Confucius himself—was not to be a privilege or polite art reserved for the literati, but a way of acting open to all humans with the requisite courage and vision. Determined to have all men strive simultaneously for both inner sageliness and outer kingliness, Wang and his disciples promoted a kind of muscular Confucian teaching that envisioned the full integration of all intellectual, spiritual, and physical activities as the first step toward the perfection of self and society; in this they pushed in effect for a virtual return to pre-Qin ideals, though their sayings were often couched in Buddhist vocabulary.

Wang spent the last two years of his life working to pacify a tribal rebellion in Guangxi and Guizhou. Exhausted by public service, Wang died in January 1529 while on his way home from a successful military campaign. After his death, many honored him as a witness to the Confucian Dao, though others excoriated him for "false learning" that allegedly broke with the Ancient Way of the Sages. Wang's condemnation of pedantry and scholasticism offended the classicists prone to such literalism; his reduction of the basic Confucian teachings to the single phrase "apply one's [acquired] knowledge of the good" (liangzhi 良知) implicitly denigrated the elaborate theorizing of many thinkers. As a result, Wang's loyal supporters were unable to defuse the animosity of his fiercest detractors, some of whom went so far as to hold him responsible for the downfall of the Ming in 1643 on the grounds that Wang's influential teachings were empty, heterodox (that is, beholden to Chan Buddhism), "hot-blooded," even "mad," and conducive to the worst kind of self-indulgence. It is hard to square this accusation with Wang's twenty-eight years of practical service as an effective local administrator, tactician, general, and teacher. In 1584 Wang's merits were recognized, and a memorial tablet was erected to his spirit in the capital Confucian temple.

Kang Youwei

By his own self-promoting accounts, the charismatic Kang at long last was thrust into the position of national prominence he so richly deserved when he gained unprecedented influence over the young Guangxu emperor (r. 1987–1908) during the period of the Hundred Days Reform (16 June–21 September). Faced with an unceasing barrage of imperialist assaults on China's territorial integrity, Kang allegedly persuaded the emperor as a "self-strengthening" measure to issue a series of edicts committing Manchu rule to a vast array of policy initiatives inspired by Kang's thorough acquaintance with foreign models, initiatives that would have required a complete revamping of the dynasty's chief educational institutions, a reorganization of its military, rationalized administrative procedures, and rapid capital expansion in agriculture, commerce, and industry. Though Kang in 1898 was by no means as influential, as knowledgeable, or as radical in his politics as he later claimed, there is no doubt that the ambitious "scholar-celebrity" Kang ran afoul of the relatively conservative coalition of powers behind the Manchu throne that included the age Dowager Empress Cixi Taihou, the chief ministers, and the Manchu princes. As the Reform alerted the coalition to the speed with which the most ambitious reformers had evolved in their thinking from "barbarian affairs" to "foreign affairs" to "current affairs," the coalition panicked, fearful lest Manchu sinecures be lost and the dynasty's authority weakened. Accordingly, the emperor was placed promptly under virtual house arrest, and orders went out to execute Kang Youwei and other activists accused of multiple acts of treason: beguiling the innocent with talk of "protecting national China but not the great Qing"; playing into the hands of rival foreign powers during a time of grave national crisis; and conspiring to murder the emperor or members of his court. More fortunate than five associates and his younger brother, Kang narrowly escaped with his life, then wandered with a price on his head in exile until 1913, seeking to convert to his way of thinking Chinese residing in Europe, America, Japan, Hong Kong, and Penang. Kang then was able to return home to spend most of his final years in

China, where he was still at the center of controversy—decried as an archreactionary rather than as radical reformer. Swiftly moving political events had in 1912 toppled the Qing dynasty and brought the Republic of China into being, but Kang remained outspokenly loyal to his ideas of a constitutional monarchy. Unknown to the political revolutionaries, however, Kang was sketching plans for an incalculably more revolutionary world than they could ever imagine: a utopian Great Commonwealth that would unite all the world in a single democratic state of perfect gender, class, and age equality guided by Confucius's chief virtue, developed human kindness.

Trained in the practically oriented Qing (1644–1911) Modern Script school, the youthful Kang Youwei had reacted to the imperialist presence in China, with its gunboats and missionaries, by concluding that only a complete reconceptualization of relations among the monarchy, the classical tradition, and "Western learning" would enable China to remain "at the center of world evolution." Reinventing tradition, Kang came to portray Confucianism as the dominant religion in China, occupying a position comparable to that of Christianity in Europe and America. Confucius was to be transformed into a Savior, first for the Chinese people and ultimately for the entire human race. According to Kang, Confucius, having received from Heaven a direct revelation concerning the future, had set himself the task of writing—not editing—each of the Five Classics, in order to ensure that each Classic contained the "hidden message" (*weiyan* 微言)* that the whole of humankind would inevitably (if gradually) progress through successive stages of institutional reform until it attained an era of complete harmony and equality in which all things and relations would be held in common. In this final ideal state, contemporary institutions, including the secular state, would fully be imbued with the spirit of *ren* 仁, which Kang understood as the Heaven-sent capacity to recognize one's kinship with all the "ten thousand things" of the cosmos through empathetic social interaction. The world could confidently expect to approach this futuristic Great Commonwealth of unparalleled moral autonomy, egalitarianism, and material abundance in three discrete stages Kang located in the *Spring and Autumn Annals*: the present era of Chaos, the succeeding era of Increasing Peace, and the final era of Great Peace. By the time of the Great Peace, the world community would have transcended all those particularistic distinctions and boundaries that give rise to human suffering, including gender and racial biases, to form a federally organized and democratic universal state. To demonstrate that countries in the West were tending toward the exact same Way, Kang loosely equated *ren* with

---

*That was Kang's idiosyncratic rendering of the binome usually understood as "subtle phrasing."

universal love, utility, and enlightened self-interest, arguing that *ren* inclined human beings to make the most socially productive choices over the long term, thereby achieving ever-greater human happiness. The Chinese government must therefore do its part to hasten this healthy transformation of world institutions by establishing Confucianism as the official state religion. For once official evangelizing missions had been sent abroad to propagate the Confucian message and worship of the immortal Sage, a reinvigorated China, "restored" to religiocultural parity with the foreign powers crusading under the banner of their "heretic faiths," would then be braced to resist the imperialists' aggression and to undertake a cultural renaissance better adapted to Chinese ways.

To account for what he perceived as China's current backwardness along the universal path to perfection, Kang offered an explanation. By adopting the Modern Script versions of the Classics during the Warring States and Han periods, China had embraced the most advanced and civilized spiritual heritage in the world at that time. But in late Western Han (206 BC–AD 8), Liu Xin, corrupt ally of the dastardly usurper Wang Mang, passed off a number of forgeries he had written as canonical scriptures in order to further Wang's bid to seize the throne. Those forgeries gained credence as the Archaic Script texts and, being included in the Five Classics, naturally obscured the original revelations transmitted from the Sage. Once China's spiritual preeminence was lost, its competitive edge over other nations followed. Derailed from the True Way, China became increasingly backward relative to other nations, so that many Chinese had mistakenly come to assume the inherent superiority of Western cultural models over the Chinese.

Reactions to Kang Youwei's ideas and to his undeniable charisma varied dramatically. At the height of Kang's influence, Liang Qichao (1873–1929), his foremost disciple, praised Kang, portraying him as a "volcanic eruption and a hurricane," a virtual Martin Luther of Confucianism. Liang Shuming (b. 1893), often called the "last Confucian" in treatments of the Republican era (1911–49), said that the idea of a Confucian church made him "nauseous," even if Liang essentially concurred with Kang's belief that the special genius of Chinese culture lay in its early grasp of the absolute value of "personal disinterestedness."

These three famous classicists, so dissimilar in their beliefs and actions, suggest the variety that has marked classical traditions from the beginning. Confucius himself had most admired two disciples who could not have been more different in their virtues: the bookish Yan Hui, "who had but to hear one part in ten in order to understand the whole" and who despite his wretched poverty "was capable of occupying his whole mind for three months on end with no thought but that of goodness"; and Zeng Dian, who expressed the desire "at the end of spring, to go with thirty newly capped youths and forty-two uncapped boys to perform the ritual lustrations at the River Yi, take the air at the Rain Dance altars, and then go home singing." (From the example of Zeng Dian no less a figure than Wang Yangming had concluded that the Master's "teachings are not so restrictive or difficult to endure. Nor do they mean that people should assume the appearance of a rigid, strict schoolman.") Certainly the Master, when asked his fondest wish, had replied with utter simplicity, "In dealing with the aged, to be of comfort to them; in dealing with friends, to be of good faith with them; in dealing with the young, to cherish them." Dedicated adherents of the Way of the Ancients knew that exact imitation of the past was neither practical nor desirable, for noble virtue, as one authoritative text stated, does not "necessarily rest in one principle alone." Each person's efforts to achieve the Way necessarily represented a distinctive response to the unpredictable turns that life takes. Though this central teaching of the Classics was lost to vulgar classicists preoccupied with the trappings of culture, like-minded friends and teachers engaged in mutual criticism and encouragement could help the would-be sage keep firmly to the path of moral virtue.

* * *

In spite of steady advances in the study of the archaeology and history of ancient China, we still know little about how the Five Classics came into existence. Clearly they were the heterogeneous products of various oral and written traditions that flourished over time notwithstanding social upheavals. In the long process of canon formation, those responsible for the actual compilation and editing of particular texts may have done their best to obscure their identities, as they believed the texts to have a transhistorical value in themselves. Relatively late in the process, in response to conflicting scriptural traditions and repeated acts of physical destruction, the decision was made to collate a single authoritative version of the entire corpus, though agreement on such a version was never destined to last. And even after the state elevated the Five Classics to canonical status in 136 BC, it took centuries for the collection to become truly canonical in the sense that its teachings were reflected in law and considered binding by most of the literate population. By that point, in the Tang and Song periods, there were fewer debates over questions of authenticity, for many found it unthinkable to challenge the basic authority of texts hallowed by such a long tradition. Still, disagreements about the proper moral applications of canonical passages to daily life continued, for each new generation and each reader had to try to establish the relevance of a given Classic to a variant context. If they were now most often read in light of standard readings of the Four Books, the Five Classics were far from static entities. The interpretations attached to them at any one time mirrored larger changes in Chinese society and state, no less than personal concerns. Chapters 2–6 in this book will therefore address the central question, What did readers see in these Five Classics, that the texts remained so powerful throughout imperial history in China?

Some modern scholars assert that the Five Classics really have little or nothing in common—a position that needlessly exaggerates problems in interpretation, for the Five Classics as a group brilliantly articulated a number of core cultural assumptions in early China. Standing outside the tradition, one can see that inconsistencies and contradictions within the Five Classics, no less than the variety of topics and approaches, insights and analogies, allowed the canon as a whole to continue to perform many disparate functions for many minds over many centuries. It was also fortunate that such cryptic texts as the *Changes* and the *Spring and Autumn Annals* came to be included in the canon when more systematic treatises were excluded. Only texts sufficiently laconic in style and mysterious in message could inspire endless constructions appealing to successive generations of later exegetes, each of whom came to the texts with specific personal preconceptions about sociocosmic order.

Why study the Five Classics at all? Some readers will want to examine the early culture of the Pacific Rim, given its increasing economic and political impact on their lives today. And some, no doubt, will be led to this corpus by reawakened fears of the Yellow Peril, occasioned by an ever-present awareness that "from the Western point of view, China is simply the other pole of the human experience." American history buffs may be drawn to consider the Five Classics because of the Founding Fathers' abiding interest in things Chinese and in Confucius.* Even today the justices of the United States Supreme Court hear oral arguments in a chamber whose frieze depicts Solon, Hammurabi, Lycurgus, Augustus, and Confucius as the most eminent lawgivers in ancient history.

But a reconsideration of the Five Classics is called for less by global politics or American history than by contemporary debates in ethics. There have always

---

*West European and American Enlightenment figures were full of praise for China, seeing it as a state wonderfully free of regional wars, religious persecution, and undue influence by an established Church—as proof positive, in other words, of the moral power of natural human reason. Under the influence of late-eighteenth- to early-nineteenth-century philosophy, beginning with Montesquieu (especially in German Idealism under Hegel), China came to be viewed as a backward Oriental Despotism populated by unthinking slaves. Max Weber popularized that view, seeing in the "relentless canonization of tradition" the chief barrier to rationalism, when he might well have viewed it instead as a carefully framed attempt to locate the normatively valid. After all, the classically trained Carsun Chang, as China's first ambassador to the United Nations, was significantly involved in the wording and content of the Universal Declaration of Human Rights in 1948.

been two standard ways to consult a classic: ask what it meant to the author and his immediate circle of readers, a question whose answer largely depends upon philology and history, or ask what it can mean to readers now, if they make the effort to meet the Classic halfway, allowing some measure of accommodation and adaptation. The first approach tends to treat the Classic as a closed book that learning can partly open; the second, as a universal text from which new meaning can spring ad infinitum. A synthesis of the two approaches—careful research into classical learning on the assumption that it has much to teach us—has the blessing of tradition in China, where the Classics by definition were capable of speaking to all types of subjects in all kinds of situations. Certainly, over the course of imperial history in China, the Classics were brought to bear upon a host of conditions quite unimagined by their authors. In this determination to bridge the gap between philosophy and history, such adaptations of the older readings may prove truest to the spirit of Confucius, for it was the Sage himself who instructed his followers to think how best to "make the ancient new" [that is, relevant], using ancient models to inspire necessary innovations.

In keeping with this maxim, chapters 2–6, each of which is devoted to one of the Five Classics, attempt to balance two tasks: to situate the Classic within the context of its early history and to treat one or more major themes in the Classic in such a way that may engage readers today. Each of those five chapters follows the same format: opening remarks on the Classic are followed by a section devoted to questions of dating and authenticity, which in turn precedes a broad discussion of one or more ethical themes associated with the Classic. Readers with no particular interest in the technical issues of textual history should feel free to skim or skip the sections on dating and authenticity, which are clearly marked. (The notes, which are posted on the Internet at www.yale.edu/yup/nylan, are likewise meant primarily for the advanced reader in that they often refer to texts written in foreign languages.) But the discussions of ethical themes that follow are essential to arrive at some sense of early classicism. Ways of knowing and acting effectively are the subject of the *Odes* chapter. The relation of past to present identity comes up in connection with the *Documents* chapter. The transformative effect of the rites is discussed in the *Rites* chapter. With the *Changes*, the main topic is the sages' duty to act selflessly in behalf of others. Traditions associated with the *Spring and Autumn Annals* inevitably raise questions about the power of language and of exemplary models.

Of course, to assign one basic topic to each of the Classics is somewhat arbitrary, given that these same themes and related ones thread through the whole corpus of the Five Classics with their commentaries. (The *Odes* and the *Changes* are equally preoccupied with types of knowing, for example, though they define the parameters of knowing somewhat differently.) My main concern has been to resist the twentieth-century call to reduce the Classics to mere history likely to be of interest only to antiquarians. For that reason, the seventh and final chapter, on the use and abuse of Confucian classicism in modern China and beyond, assesses the general impact that political events in modern China have had upon the current appreciation of early tradition.

Chapter Two

THE *ODES* (*SHI* 詩)

The Master addressed Boyu [his son] saying, "Have you done the first two
sections of the odes yet? He who has not done even those is, in effect,
standing with his face pressed against a wall."
—*Analects*

One must write of merit on bamboo and silk,
and leave traces in sound in pipes and strings.
—Fan Ye, *Hou Hanshu*

T H E   *O D E S*   (*S H I*   詩) , *   A   C O L L E C T I O N   O F
what appear to be polished folk songs, sophisticated occasional pieces, and

---

* *Shi* 詩, the title of the Classic, has generally been translated in one of three ways:
"poems," "odes," or "songs." In that the *shi* were unquestionably set to music, "songs" or
"odes" is more accurate than "poems." I have chosen "odes" to emphasize the performance
aspect of these songs. Unfortunately, scholars have no idea who composed the individual
songs or who compiled the anthology. As performance texts, in most cases, they would
have had no individual authors, even though a small number of odes bear internal references, such as "I, Jifu, have made this song." Note that in this chapter the term "*Odes*"
refers to the received anthology, whereas the term "odes" refers to particular songs, not
necessarily in their current written form.

solemn dynastic hymns, is the most uniformly old compilation of texts included in the Five Classics—and the first to be recognized as canon. Some of the odes now included in this collection of 305 verse pieces may have been in existence as oral performance texts by the fifth century BC—in time for Confucius himself to have used them in his teaching—though a fixed anthology of these particular lyrics may not have existed in written form before unification in 221 BC. No evidence, of course, supports the pious legend that Confucius himself compiled the received version, culling "the three hundred odes" from more than three thousand; and yet the received anthology in all likelihood crystallized out of a much broader repertoire of performance songs, just as in the myth.

The *Odes* collection is arranged in three main sections, each with a distinctive metrical and linguistic pattern, though over 95 percent of them employ the tetrasyllable:

- 160 State Airs (*Guo feng* 國風), which tend to be single-theme songs, mostly quite short, on subjects of daily life, including courtship, unrequited love, and the hardships of war. The majority of the Airs, supposedly drawn from fifteen different states in northern China, including the former royal domain of Zhou (called *Bin* 豳 after the area), have three stanzas each, in which regular rhymes, refrains, repeated tropes, and symmetry are very common. Odes of two and four short rhymed stanzas, each composed of three to eight lines each, make up most of the rest of the total, so that a surprising number of the Airs rhyme on almost every line.
- 105 Court Songs (*Ya* 雅) divided into two categories, Minor (74 in number) and Major (31 in all), which were presumably composed by music masters for state dinners, entertainments, and audiences; they include as well a few important sacrificial hymns (for example, Odes 209–12). The customary Minor/Major distinction suggests the greater preoccupation of the Major Court Songs with royal activities, though it is often explained in terms of the different average length of odes in the two subsections, the median length of a Minor ode being 18 or 30 and that of the Major, 54 lines. The comparative brevity of the Minor Songs, their reliance on metaphors drawn from everyday life, and the frequency of rhymes reminds readers of the Airs.
- 40 Hymns (*Song* 頌) in honor of the Shang,[*] Zhou, and Lu ruling houses, performed often in conjunction with the dances, short plays,

---

[*] In the case of the Shang Hymns, performed by the small state conferred by Zhou on scions of the Shang royal clan after its conquest.

and pantomimes that formed a routine part of state sacrifices, archery contests, or "merry" feasts. Scholarship has long differentiated the Zhou Hymns from the Lu and Shang Hymns, as the latter two seem not only later in date but also different in nature. In the entire *Odes*, only the Shang and Zhou Hymn subsections lack clearly identifiable rhymes (and thus the stanzaic divisions based on rhyme); in those two subsections, pieces without rhyme constitute slightly more than half the total number (21 out of 40), and the Zhou Hymn section contains songs of particularly irregular form.

Because knowledge of some odes was common to members of the ruling elite by mid- to late Zhou times, the received text opens the widest window we have on the material culture, habits, attitudes, and characteristic forms of association of this group. Occasionally the *Odes* canon offers glimpses into a past so archaic that it must have seemed obscure to many long before unification. All the odes, as highly rhetoricized accounts of memorable situations, must be used with some caution by present-day specialists, but in imperial China they were regarded as a guide to a distant past by an elite culture that deeply venerated antique traditions. The *Odes* was also thought to represent a cultural legacy to which each major region tied to the Central States had made a signal contribution. Given the requisite sophistication, any member of the cultural elite near the Yellow River—and apparently even any "barbarian" neighbor—could conceivably use and respond to citations from the *Odes*. From its very inception, then, the *Odes* was regarded both as the common coin of official discourse and the supreme distillation of the very highest expressions of culture, although the collection in translation has struck those readers bound by late-eighteenth-century European poetic conventions and ignorant of complex and subtle Chinese literary conventions as too naive to qualify as literary art.

The multiplicity of functions assigned the *Odes* is one good measure of its early importance. The *Odes* was consulted for its exhaustive lists of the names of "birds, beasts, plants, and trees." A virtual encyclopedia of early times, it was moreover valued for its wealth of information bearing upon legendary history, as in the following ode, which neatly encapsulates the entire predynastic genealogy of the Zhou ruling house:

> Distinguished was Qiang Yuan [ultimate female ancestor of the house],
> Her virtue without flaw.
> The High Lord settled on her,
> So that without injury or harm,
> Her time fulfilled,

> *She gave birth to Houji,*
> *On whom all blessings were conferred.*
> *He taught the people to sow and reap . . .*
> *Continuing the work of Yu [the primeval flood-queller].*
> *Descended from Houji*
> *Was the Great King, Danfu,*
> *Who made his home south of Qi.*
> *[So great and compassionate a ruler was he that]*
> *There the ruin of Shang began,*
> *So that with Kings Wen and Wu*
> *Continuing the Great King's work,*
> *Heaven's purpose was accomplished*
> *In the plain at Mu [with their conquest of Shang]. . . .*
>
> (Ode 300)

The earliest traceable exegesis perceived the *Odes*, in fact, as "history told in verse." With the institutionalized cultural memory preserved, celebrated, and reinforced through successive performances of the *Odes*, it was to this sort of lyric "recording" that early thinkers in China looked to find the information needed by knowledgeable men in the political and social arenas. Happily, the *Odes* as didactic instrument, a source of lessons drawn from political precedents and exemplars, was entirely consonant with the *Odes'* teaching of another sort of knowledge much more difficult to attain than recorded facts and even more valuable to have: "knowing men" (that is, understanding human capacities and aspirations and how to motivate them). Through that kind of knowing, students of the *Odes* could gain a sense of the subtle sympathies linking themselves with others, the strengthening of which radically enhanced their faculties for intuitive intellection and genuine feeling and so produced deeper and more satisfying sorts of engagement. Ode after ode celebrates the joys of this type of knowing or laments its lack, tying the arts to "wisdom in the person's heart."

To answer why this book of songs has proven to be of such great interest to the Chinese since Zhou times, and what kind of influence it has exerted over classical formulations of the Confucian Way, the main functions of the odes must be considered, along with the difficult topic of social knowledge and pleasure in relation to the canon. Difficult, because most recent sinological approaches to the *Odes'* traditions presume that the Chinese more or less overlooked the pleasures associated with the collection in their eagerness to read nearly all the songs as pointed allegories criticizing specific political situations in the Zhou. James Legge, Bernhard Karlgren, and Marcel Granet, for instance, all scoffed

at the "far-fetched" "absurdities" occasioned by the old-style exegetical interpretations. A beautiful woman bemoaning a lover's rejection makes a poor figure,
the sinologists insisted, for the righteous minister spurned by his neglectful
ruler.* But if we set aside the sinological scorn, seeing it as a reflection of recent
scholastic trends that value knowing facts more than knowing specific persons,
three simple observations spring immediately to mind. First, courtship songs
were probably used to deliver political messages from the moment they were
composed because courtship is about as political an activity as one can imagine.
Second, the Chinese commentators spoke so often of political allegories in
connection with the *Odes* because they had watched men of every class and
condition—emperors and kings, slaves and grave diggers—for generation after
generation employ the *Odes* to convey social and political criticism neatly
through literary conventions. Third, schooling in the didactic readings of the
Odes seldom blinded Chinese to the extrapolitical opportunities presented by
the *Odes* for fostering bonds between humans in the know.

No love of moral didacticism alone can account for the intensity of feeling
that sophisticated Chinese brought to the *Odes*. Once we alert ourselves to the
possibility, even the court Academicians' glosses on the *Odes* sometimes convey
as strong a sense of the magic of literary creation and the delights of social
engagement as they do of sober moralizing or literary criticism. It was sublime
literary creation, after all, that ensured that the captivating woman serving as
metaphor for an upright official comes alive in her dual capacities—that, and a
fine appreciation of the multiple possibilities of seduction. Working on such
assumptions, this chapter begins with a brief summary of what little is known
about the history, dating, and content of the *Odes*, reviewing certain traditional
theories as a way of situating the *Odes* in relation to the themes of historical
recording and good rule. It then addresses the place of the *Odes* in classical education and in moral learning, tying the text both to music and to pleasure in
order to introduce the complex associations that many brought to study of the
Odes. Then the remainder of the chapter is devoted to the three related themes
of knowing, pleasure, and human integration—types of social knowing that
would eventually all be seen as benefits accruing from training in the *Odes*.
Though we can never be sure about the original intentions behind the composition and compilation of the *Odes*, given that the anthology was largely the
product of anonymous authors working over centuries, we can say with

---

*This is not to deny the production of far-fetched analogies, once the formal *Odes*
interpretive conventions had been well established. Adopting the official model of the *Odes*,
poem 265 in the Tang 300 poems, for example, has a nubile woman applying her makeup
serve as metaphor for a bureaucrat in the division of water management.

assurance that the strong associations forged between knowledgeable use of the *Odes* and convivial pleasure helped to ensure the survival of the collection over the centuries. Given that performing appropriate verses (in Zhou) or writing them (in the post-Han period) was not usually a distinct profession in China, but rather a prerequisite for recognition and communication as a person of insight and cultivation, the *Odes* played a monumental role in the production of social knowledge and classical learning.

The folk etymologies once supplied to explain the origins of the anthology are provocative, if ultimately inconclusive. One tells us that the odes "record" events and feelings (*shi = zhi* 誌). Another relates the odes to "commitments" and "aspirations" (*shi = zhi* 志), on the grounds that the singer's choice of lyric and melody inevitably reveals to a knowing partner what is on the singer's mind. A third glosses the word "ode" as "to hold" (*shi = chi*, 詩 = 持), arguing that an ode holds things and people together so that "the two halves fit" in a harmonious whole. And a fourth (favored by the first century AD "Great Preface" to the *Odes*) breaks the graphic form for "ode" into its three component parts, "speaking," "foot," and "hand," as if to indicate that men exulted in singing the odes to waving hands and tapping feet. Early thinkers considered all these powerful associations when assessing the history, lyric beauty, and social utility of the *Odes*.

HISTORY, DATING, AND CONTENT OF THE *ODES*

Over the centuries, many have formulated theories to explain the composition and collection of the *Odes*. Wen Yiduo (1899–1946), one of the most original scholars to grace the field of Chinese studies, argued in a pathbreaking essay that in preliterate China speech whatever the archaic community intended to remember was rhymed and set to a melody. (That song is the best medium by which to possess and preserve knowledge is an idea repeated in the *Odes* itself.) According to Wen, in those early days valued speech took two distinct rhymed forms, each having its own function: There was the sung lyric (*ge* 歌), whose chief function was to express the emotions, and the sung ode (*shi* 詩), designed to transmit information about historical events. After the emergence of a developed writing system ca. 1300 BC, state archivists increasingly began to record events in prose, for the very fact of writing enabled events to be chronicled in more exhaustive detail without mnemonic devices. Somehow, the expressive songs and the narrative odes came to merge, probably during late Western Zhou, with the result that many individual songs in the *Odes* anthology combined both characteristics and fulfilled both functions.

Wen Yiduo's explanatory paradigm is noteworthy, less because it resolves the debates over commemorative speech than because it directs attention to a number of important issues, among them the question whether state archivists existed in the archaic period and the probability (contra Wen) that writing functioned as servant, rather than substitute, for the word spoken in stylized performance texts. Thus we are still left with few answers to the most fundamental questions about the *Odes*' early textual history. Certainly, the limited number of rhyme schemes that appear in the received text and the fairly consistent voice of the anthology suggest that the extant group of odes was reworked at least once into final, more consistent form at a single specific time and place. In China, as elsewhere, oral traditions tended to be fixed in writing relatively late, either to enhance and perpetuate the spoken text or to gain an advantage in doctrinal disputes among competing oral traditions. Most scholars would agree that in the centuries preceding unification the anthology existed in some form (oral or written) similar to that found in the earliest extant redaction of the received text—[called the Mao *Odes* after two early masters, Mao Heng 毛亨 and Mao Chang 毛萇]—being already divided in the same three main sections that appear in the received Mao version.* That conclusion derives from a single *Zuozhuan* entry (dated to 534 BC but certainly compiled later) that tells of a court performance of the entire sequence of the State Airs, Court Songs, and Hymns, with only four sections of the Airs played in a slightly different order from the Mao Odes. (Note, however, that the *Zuo* passage describes a sequence in performance, not an arrangement in a text.) Musicological analyses have often posited a distinct character for each of the *Odes*' three sections, theorizing that they were initially sung to different types of musical accompaniment: the State Airs, to small jingling bells; the Court Songs, to lacquered pipes and strings; and the Hymns, to ceremonial bells, chimestones, and drums. Current, admittedly fragmentary, evidence suggests that the early classicists regarded the odes more as musical compositions than as set lyrics, let alone as texts; and they did so until the early melodies were inexplicably lost.

The State Airs

Classical exegetes typically chose one of two complementary approaches to interpretation, sometimes combining both within the same commentary: either they celebrated the broad applicability of an ode's moral infrastructure, so that the ode could comment on widely disparate situations, or they sought to ascer-

---

*Through early Western Han at least four variant editions of the *Odes* circulated, each associated with masters from different geographical areas. Eventually the Mao recension and Mao readings became dominant, so much so that only fragments of two traditions and roughly a half of the third have been preserved. And although Zhu Xi issued his own version of the *Odes*, he did not alter the basic arrangement by Mao.

tain the precise historical time and place of composition, seeking the ode's meaning in the precise circumstances of its authorship.*The anonymous makers, generic tropes, and timeless feel of the State Airs generally confounded the most determined attempts by traditional commentators to assign each ode in that section to a particular time, place, or social origin. (By contrast, a few odes in the Court Songs section reveal their aristocratic authors' specific dilemmas and names.) In consequence, early traditions on the origin of the State Airs, the section that came increasingly to be considered the paradigm for the whole *Odes* anthology, emphasized governmental responsibility and collective compilation. Poetry set to music was widely regarded as the spontaneous expression of public sentiment, so the story went out that Zhou officers gathered verses from the various states in their cultural horizon because their rulers intended to use the odes essentially as diagnostic tools revealing the material and psychological welfare of the common people. The *Han shu*, a history compiled circa AD 100, says of the State Airs that (fig. 7),

> In the first month of spring each year, just before the many inhabitants were to scatter [for farmers went out to live in their fields during the growing season], the envoys would come shaking their wooden clackers all along the roads, in this way intending to gather up the local odes, which were then presented to the Grand Master [at court]. It was he who arranged their musical scores, at which point they were performed for the Son of Heaven. Hence, the saying, "The king knows All-under-Heaven, without ever peering out from his windows and doors."

Another Han text made it the job of the head musician who accompanied the Son of Heaven on his periodic tours of inspection to gather local folk songs "that the ruler might witness the manners of the common people." Every five years that information was tallied, in concert with other data, including market prices, so that the Son of Heaven might acquire a good idea of the general success or failure of his administration in each locale. In seeming corroboration of such traditions, an anecdote from the *Lüshi chunqiu* (circa 239 BC) has the wise minister Yi Yin correctly predicting the downfall of the despot Jie, the last

---

*The image of Confucius-as-*Odes*-editor corresponds to the general moralizing impulses, whereas the traditions that derive the odes from local folk songs reflect the historicizing impulse to tie each ode to a particular time and place. To Zhu Xi, however, the *Odes* were neither generalized didactic messages nor specific historical expressions, but the spontaneous outpourings of the common people's emotions (some of which would have been better suppressed).

Figure 7. A scene from the movie *Yellow Earth*, in which the Communist party, like so many imperial governments before it, sends officials out to gather folk songs from the people, which will be of use to the new government in gauging the temper of the times. Slide courtesy of Jerome Silbergeld.

ruler of Xia, as soon as he heard the rhymed ditties that Jie's subjects were composing and circulating.

The political subtext of some State Airs was absolutely transparent, as in verses taken from Ode 113:

> *Big rat, big rat,*
> *Do not gobble our millet!*
> *Three years we have slaved for you,*
> *Yet you take no notice of us.*
> *At last we are going to leave you*
> *And go to that happy land;*
> *Happy land, happy land,*
> *Where we shall find our place.*
>
> *Big rat, big rat,*
> *Do not gobble our corn!*
> *Three years we have slaved for you,*
> *Yet you gave us no credit.*
> *At last we are about to leave you*

> *To go to that happy state;*
> *Happy state, happy state,*
> *Where we shall get our due!*

But what political meaning lay hidden in State Airs like Ode 8, whose subject and style seem charmingly detached from court concerns?

> *Thick grows the plantain.*
> *Here we go a-plucking it.*
> *Thick grows the plantain.*
> *Here we go a-gathering it.*
>
> *Thick grows the plantain.*
> *Here we have our aprons.*
> *Thick grows the plantain.*
> *Apronsful tucked in at our belts.*

If the confident assertions alleging political motivations behind every folk song were little more than folklore themselves, they reflected the common wisdom that the wise ruler "never uses water to see his own image; instead, he uses the people as a mirror." Similarly, when classicists argued that "the ways of selecting odes and writing histories are the same," they meant that the principles and precedents conveyed in the *Odes* could be used to assess the great societal patterns that had propelled historical evolution in each region, with a view to improving custom. One could tell a great deal from the melodies and timbres of the accompanying instruments alone, they said, insofar as harmony in government created harmony in music: "The tones from a time of good rule are peaceful and happy, as the government is balanced. The tones from a time of chaos are resentful and angry, as the government is unbalanced. And the tones of a state that is failing are woe-stricken and brooding, as the people are in trouble."*

In line with such theories on composition, many recent studies (for example, by Granet, Wen, Yiduo, Shirakawa Shizuka, and C. H. Wang) have tended to stress the oral-formulaic character of the State Airs and some of the Court Songs as well to explain why stock formulae are regularly grouped together or substituted for one another. For example, that "the fish go deep" while "falcons fly high" signifies inexpressible yearnings, but climbing a hill and gathering wild

---

*The questionable assumption that the common people are more likely to express what they really feel and think informs many early elite discussions of authenticity in music and, by extension, poetry.

plants conveys, more precisely, longing for a lover. And when those same fish appear in conjunction with a heron (a fish catcher), they refer to lovemaking, for fish are symbols of fecundity as well. The motif of aster gathering always signifies a return or a desire for the return of a loved one, and so on. Audiences could more easily penetrate the emotional subtext of an ode whose composition largely consisted in piecing together such stock formulae, each indicative of a particular mood or theme. With minor variations on those formulae, an ode could transmit a potent message that was both personally expressive and culturally coherent.

The newest studies pointing to the oral-formulaic character of many parts of the Five Classics (including the *Changes*, *Documents*, and *Zuozhuan*) owe a debt of gratitude to the early folklorists' studies, but the folk character of the State Airs in particular and of the *Odes* in general has often been overemphasized. Hence the continuing struggle by many late twentieth-century redactors to determine which of the State Airs were genuine folk songs, which were folk songs artfully revised by scholar-editors, and which were original compositions cast in the form of folk songs by members of the elite, even when no evidence attests to any folk involvement. The fundamentalists see the original folk texts of the Ur-odes being corrupted by courtly revision of the folk lyrics or courtly readings imposed on them, presumably at the very moment the songs passed from the mouths of the multitudes to the repertoire of court musicians and the literary bureaucracy. But oral composition, performance, and transmission of the odes by court elites should never be confused with folk activities, and set formulae are just as likely to mark elite ceremonial speech as folk compositions. The record shows that many of these most beloved odes were performed in a wide variety of ritual, social, and diplomatic settings (see below); and the State Airs are as apt to be the work of court musicians and literati-bureaucrats as politicized peasants. In essence, the stanzas in the *Odes* anthology are unquestionably too polished, their rhymes too regular, and their choice of language too elegant and too uniform to represent unedited folk poetry gathered from different dialect regions. (These qualities led both Karlgren and Gu Jiegang to conclude that all the odes in their extant versions must be the products of "well-trained, educated members of the gentry.")

Doubting that all of the State Airs were unmediated products of uneducated serfs functioning as moral-political barometers, some scholars in imperial times devised a supplemental theory to account for this. The more complex State Airs, they reasoned, along with the Court Songs, must represent loyal submissions to kings enlightened enough to canvass worthy ministers and nobles for their opinions on policy. Presumably, such opinions could have been expressed either in verses of the elites' own making or in suitably edited versions of the rude, crude, or sexually transgressive folk songs, since either type of expression functioned at once to "display [inner] intent" and to register conditions in the political realm. Building upon such arguments alluded to in the Minor Prefaces associated with the Mao exegetical tradition, the "Great Preface" generally ascribed to Wei Hong (first century AD) credits high-ranking members of the ruling elite with creation of most of the State Airs section—and indeed the entire *Odes* anthology—though the preface implicitly posits a range of creative potential at all levels of society. Claiming that the ode is the site "to which there go the aspirations" (*zhi* 志, a term that connotes ambitions and intentions as well), Wei's preface to the canon situates ode-making within *ganying* (reaction-response) theory, seeing the ode as the product of sensory and intellectual reactions to external conditions that provoke the *zhi*. The initial responses, when deep enough to imprint the body and soul, subsequently take the form of patterned speech and ritualized gestures.

Given the marvelous basic capacities that all humans share, it is conceivable that some unschooled genius responding to unfolding events can make wonderful songs. But insofar as those at the highest levels of cultivation have mastered the entire range of admirable social and cosmic patterns, they can more reliably produce the clearest, most powerful messages of the very kind that can, in turn, affect the development of things, situations, and people beyond the poet. A songmaker's efforts, when spurred by undisciplined passions, may not assume a shape coherent enough to move others in predictable ways. But heartfelt lyrics informed by careful training in the arts, when carried on the ordained pitches and timbres of recitation, chanting, and music, can be expected to rouse all hearers, thereby "rectifying excesses and deficits [in the person and the state], moving heaven and earth, and stirring the ghosts and spirits." Thus Wei Hong's conclusion—that the affective power of the odes, those entirely natural reflections encapsulated in movements of song and dance, nonetheless increases to the degree that high cultivation for the maker has become second nature—leads inevitably to the notion that the elite's *zuo* 作 of the odes (their initiating, making, and raising of them) serves the community well as the vehicle par excellence of ritual communication and social change.

Even today, Wei Hong's preface remains a touchstone for students of the *Odes*. Still, the notion of an original text being attached in a one-to-one relation to a certain situation, place, or single author, whether folk or elite, seems entirely misleading in the ritual setting of antiquity, where conscious repetition and variation clearly endowed oral performance texts with greater normative and aesthetic power. Thus it may be more fruitful to pose the larger hypothetical question here: Why would cultured members of the elite ever adopt the voice of the State Airs, if that section of the *Odes* was associated with their social inferiors?

At least four answers come to mind. First, as mentioned above, the *Odes* may have been one of few available sources upon which elites could build a shared lingua franca accepted across the entire Central States cultural horizon. From this perspective, the *Odes* do not collect aspects of discrete local cultures but instead spread Central States culture to the peripheries. Second, many of the themes treated in the State Airs and Court Songs (for example, harvests, love-making, and festivals) were of interest to lord and subject alike. For a long time, thinkers in China had seen the wisdom of proclaiming their material and emotional ties with the masses rather than advertising their differences. Third, political elites quickly realized the unique efficacy of rhymes set to music in persuading commoners of the inherent wisdom of the elite's version of the social order; the *Odes* as repository of ceremonial language wielded particular authority. Fourth, many of the most familiar images were eminently adaptable to political uses by the ruling elite. The abandoned lover was easily transmuted into the discarded official, to take one overworked example. As good poetry evokes shared realities even while it remains open to individual interpretation, teachers and rhetoricians with a modicum of imagination played with the odes to adapt them to particular situations.

The Court Songs and Hymns

Tradition held that many of the Court Songs and the Hymns were composed in joyful response to the establishment of Zhou dynastic power or as sharp criticism of later Zhou rulers. But aside from some few Zhou Hymns whose formula may date to the ninth century BC, most Hymns do not offer even roughly contemporary descriptions of archaic institutions, and it is even less likely that the Court Songs—Odes 242, for example, hailing the legitimate state power of the true kings of early Western Zhou—provide reliable accounts. The vast majority of odes in these two sections instead supply "a pattern and a model" for high-ranking contemporaries impatient with allusions to a more distant period; rejoice in the activities that foster cohesion among members of the ruling elite; address the most powerful dead to solicit their blessings; and where protest is registered—for instance, in connection with a king's deceitful dealings with his men and his exploitation of his subjects—employ stock phrases to present quite standardized messages. Odes that bemoan the "near extinction of the Zhou ruling house" presumably function as last-ditch cultural salvage efforts made in what Jan Assmann, in another context, called the "experience of deficiency": the sense that the good times are irrevocably gone. Perhaps the more optimistic composers dared also to hope that aristocrats who "do not stand in awe of Heaven" might be persuaded to rededicate themselves to the task of restoring the past, now idealized and under the aegis of mythic figures. The unstinting praise for unimpeachable exemplars of long ago becomes more explicit only in certain Major Court Songs and Hymns that seem quite specific on the subject of the early Shang, Zhou, and Lu rulers. Their extended descriptions, in seeking to capture the anterior halcyon days in song, accomplish at one stroke three not unrelated aims: giving praise where praise is due, attracting boons from distant ancestors, and reproaching, however indirectly, their unjust and unmannerly descendants for failure to live up to their good names. Hence the following ode, which commemorates the glories of an imagined predynastic Zhou:

> *Great dignity had Tairen,*
> *Mother to King Wen.*
> *Well loved by Lady Jiang of Zhou,*
> *Bride of the noble house.*
> *Taisi carried on the fine name.*
> *Hence, the multitude of sons.*
>
> *King Wu was graced by the ancestors,*
> *The spirits having no cause for complaint;*
> *And no occasion for dissatisfaction.*
> *He was a model to his chief bride,*
> *And to his brothers, young and old,*
> *A model in his rule over house and fief.*
>
> *Affable was he in the palace,*
> *Reverent in the ancestral hall.*
> *Before his fame, watched over by Heaven.*
> *Ever and always in Heaven's protection.*
> *Neither war nor sickness did destroy*
> *His bright eminence without a stain.*
>
> *He was a model before he was taught.*
> *Ready to admit his guilt before a rebuke.*
> *(Ode 240/1–4 [Major Court Songs])*

Many of the Minor and Major Court Songs may have been composed by court officials for set occasions since nine of them (nos. 162, 191, 199, 200, 204, 252, 257, 259, and 260) name their authors. Tradition assumes that all their authors were high officials advising the king, some professional music masters, a class of men who held a high place in pre-Han courts.

The Hymns of Zhou, of Shang, and of Lu record the texts of prayers chanted as part of song-and-dance suites performed by ritual specialists at these three courts prior to Qin unification in 221 BC. Designed to edify the court audiences, the living and the dead, the hymn cycles celebrate the history of their states' heroes, laud the impulse to perpetuate state sacrifices to such exemplars, and enjoin the living to emulate them. Nonetheless, the Zhou Hymns are best separated from the other two. Even though the Lu and Shang Hymns may have taken the earlier Zhou Hymns as one of several inspirations (which would account for certain thematic similarities in all three groups), the Lu and Shang hymns are dynastic eulogies of greater length and more regular rhyme (with rhymes determining stanzas). The Hymns of Lu and Shang, being much closer in form and meter to the Major Court Songs, differ, then, from the Zhou Hymns, which seldom display either consistent line lengths or consistent rhyme schemes.

Much of the scholarship on the Hymns is devoted to explaining these stylistic disparities. Modern scholarship often ascribes some of these to chronology because the Zhou hymns may date to several centuries earlier than the Lu and Shang Hymns, which were probably composed during the mid-Chunqiu period within a fairly short period of time and in loose imitation of one another. Traditional scholars, however, following the lead of the main Han exegetes, had no such easy answer available to them, for legend supported a much earlier set of dates for all three Hymns sections. It was said that "when King Wu conquered Shang, the Hymns were composed," so the Zhou Hymns had to have been composed during the regency of the Duke of Zhou for King Cheng (successor to King Wu). The inconvenient fact that the Zhou Hymns include explicit references to Kings Cheng and Kang—where Cheng and Kang are posthumous titles that could never have been employed during those kings' lifetimes—was explained away by successive commentators, who saw in the martial vigor and stately beauty of the Zhou Hymns a suitable reflection of the "great peace and virtue" ascribed to the first reigns of Western Zhou.

Similar historicizing premises were also applied to the Shang and Lu Hymns by the dominant *Odes* interpretations. It was a tenet of Han classicism that "knowing the man, one could evaluate his era." Therefore, commentators sought to link the societal perfection described in the Hymns to the sage-rulers of antiquity. The Shang Hymns were said to preserve traditions of the Shang people prior to the Zhou conquest, and the Lu Hymns to reflect societal conditions prevailing under the renowned Duke of Zhou, who was not only regent for the second Zhou king but also first ruler of the vassal state of Lu. And since the Shang Hymns were tied to the Shang dynasty, which preceded Zhou, it was logical to date the Shang Hymns many centuries before the Zhou and Lu Hymns, joint products of the regent-duke. Naturally, Tang the Victorious (tradit. r. 1766–1753 BC), the legendary founder of Shang state, was the candidate most often mentioned as composer or commissioner of the Shang Hymns. Elabora-tions upon that theory suggested that, following Shang's conquest by Zhou, the Shang Hymns had come into the eventual possession of Zheng Kaofu, alleged ancestor of Confucius and minister to Duke Xiang of Song (r. 650–637 BC), as Song was the small successor state assigned the defeated Shang after the Zhou conquest. Very few scholars before the Qing, except for Ouyang Xiu (1007–72), troubled over the chronological impossibilities inherent in such traditional attributions, let alone over another curiosity: the fact that the Zhou Hymns are unexpectedly strong and simple, in contrast to the elaborate Lu and Shang Hymns—which would be distinctly odd, if the Shang Hymns were much the oldest or the Zhou and the Lu Hymns contemporaneous attempts based on Shang models.

But eventually Wei Yuan (1794–1857) and Wang Guowei (1877–1927), among others, urged a return to an earlier account, much neglected, that had first appeared in Sima Qian's *Shiji* (comp. ca. 100 BC). By that account, the Shang Hymns had been written down during the Chunqiu period by men of Song—with Zheng Kaofu possibly among them—who claimed descent from the Shang ruling clan. To that Wang Guowei, followed by Liang Qichao (1873–1929), added the further conjecture that the Lu Hymns, composed in direct imitation of the Shang Hymns, were commissioned either late in the reign of Duke Xi of Lu (r. 659–627) or shortly afterward for the consecration of a new ancestral temple built to honor the Lu ruling house. Of course, some Hymns may have been compiled even later, from well-established liturgical formulae, but the precise dating of a stable text for the Hymns is perhaps of less importance than what these scholars pointed to in their research: the ritual character of odes' performance and the aus-picious quality of commemorative odes singing, designed to lend dignity and grace to the singers, subjects, and audiences alike.

THE THREE SECTIONS' DATING AND DIVISIONS

On questions of dating, most specialists today see the Zhou Hymns as the oldest section; they would put the Court Songs next, followed by the State Airs. The Shang and Lu Hymns seem to preserve some lines, phrases, and themes from truly ancient praise-songs, though they may have been put in final form much later. Traditional scholars got it nearly right in putting the Hymns first, the Court Songs next, and the State Airs last. But one can sometimes arrive at the right answer by faulty logic: they believed that compositions could safely be dated by the degree to which each relied on rhyme; by their lights, a steady evolu-tion from simple to complex made rhyme more complex and less natural than unrhymed lines. By that criterion, the State Airs, in which rhymed lines are the norm, must be somewhat later than the Court Songs, in which fewer lines are rhymed, and vastly later than the Zhou Hymns, in which the fewest rhymed lines occur.* But a close study of datable inscriptions from the pre-Qin period shows that rhyming's presence or absence cannot date examples of ceremonial speech, since such speech, typically quoted or sung, in relying heavily on commonplace compounds and consonance, may lack or use rhyme. Underlying traditional scholarship was a sublime faith in two questionable assumptions: first, that the odes represented genuinely spontaneous works, unmediated expressions of emotion or reports of events allowing for little, if any, slippage between the songmakers' experiences and the forms of the songs themselves; and second, that the individual odes, once written down and included in the collection, had not been significantly reworked. As the adage had it, "The odes expressed what was on the mind," and few traditional scholars could ignore powerful legends about the submissions of odes to the court's collection by ordinary villagers and noble ministers.

In simple fact, however, the formal characterizations later used to distinguish State Airs, Court Songs, and Hymns probably did not exist at the time the music of all three sections was first devised for formal occasions, including sacrifices and banquets. Audiences and composers may have been much the same for each section, just as their later anthologizers and exegetes were. Thus, though one can assign to each section a "typical" structure, with specific lengths of lines, lengths of stanzas, and numbers of stanzas (as above), exceptions abound within each section. Moreover stylistic devices and themes spill over from one section to the next. For rhetorical purposes a folk song mode may be used in the Court Songs. And while the State Airs are musically more inventive than the Major Court Songs, whose metrical regularity led several early rulers to pronounce them stupefyingly dull, a great many themes are shared by the State Airs and the Minor Court Songs, on the one hand (for example, young love, early abandonment, the sorrows of war), and by the Major Court Songs and the Hymns on the other (for example, the steady expansion of Zhou power). Still, tests that measure the reappearance of specific syntactic structures and stock vocabulary from one ode to the next reveal the intertextual cohesiveness of the State Airs section, and also the high degree of intertextuality exhibited across the Court Songs and Hymns sections, as the early binome "Ya-Song" would indicate.

Certainly, all this blurs the traditional tripartite division of the *Odes* based on function or origin. Nonetheless, commentators over the centuries usually saw fit to attribute a wide range of significances to this very division. One or more

---

*By this logic, modern free verse must precede poems of the Victorian era. Traditional analysis relied upon fairly simple notions of rhyme. The work of William Baxter corrects their views.

of the following five explications attracted most traditional commentators, with some commentators applying several of them simultaneously in their interpretations of individual odes:

- *Small or great import*   On this theory, the State Airs depict the mundane affairs, both public and personal, of a single state; the Court Songs, the government affairs of the Zhou kings; and the Hymns, the deeds of the gods and sage-heroes, each of whom served as perfect exemplar of virtue for All-under-Heaven. In this order, the spiritual potency of each section exceeds that of its predecessor, a ranking that reflected the traditional commentators' views of the historical devolution in morality away from the Way of the Golden Age of antiquity (since commentators judged the Hymns to be the oldest section of the *Odes* and the State Airs the most recent).

- *Blame or praise*   On this theory, a majority of the State Airs satirize the lax mores prevalent in the fiefs; the Court Songs describe in fairly equal measure the dramatic successes and failures of the Zhou kings; and the Hymns praise the former sage-kings, who followed the perfect examples of the gods and Ancients.

- *[Sexually] impure or pure*   On this theory, the State Airs section is decidedly tainted in its moral outlook, given its high concentration of sexual escapades and innuendoes, and the Court Songs, only somewhat less mixed. The Hymns, by contrast, register the pure, unmediated voice of goodness.

- *Social class of the authors*   On this theory, the State Airs were composed by commoners, male and female; the Court Songs, by worthy ministers, councillors, and courtiers; and the Hymns, by blind musicians in court employ who were mere vehicles for divine inspirations.

- *Performance type*   On this theory, the State Airs were chanted without musical accompaniment. The Court Songs were performed with some musical accompaniment (the Major Songs at the Zhou royal court, which presumably commanded a larger orchestra, and the Minor Songs at the courts of local rulers). And the Hymns were accompanied by music, dance, and pantomime in the ancestral temple.

Commentators in the early imperial period (Han through Tang) were primarily interested in the implications of the first two classificatory schemes, in contrast to the classical exegetes of later imperial China, who concerned themselves mainly with the supposed moral purity of expression in relation to authorial status. Modern commentators have been increasingly preoccupied with the musical and folk foundations of the *Odes*, so that even today some scholars seem reluctant to abandon the search for an underlying principle capable of elucidating the tripartite division of the *Odes*.

Over the centuries a no less influential division has been that between the so-called upright odes versus the turned (*bian* 變, "changed from the norm"). This dichotomy ultimately derived from Confucius's statement deploring the popularity of the "new music" of Zheng, whose voluptuous tones supposedly encouraged dissipation.* Classical scholars of late Han through Tang, including the author of the "Great Preface", then proceeded to distinguish the lyrics of what they called the upright odes from those of the turned. The turned lyrics, like the music of Zheng, were characterized by great metrical irregularity and many were found—not coincidentally, the scholars opined—in the Zheng State Airs. Despite the correspondences, the early classicists did not generally characterize the turned odes as inherently depraved; they merely assumed that their metrical irregularity reflected the (appropriately) agitated responses of worthy folk to the turmoil accompanying the decline of Zhou.

By contrast, in later imperial China, when gender segregation and chastity were far more strictly enjoined, straitlaced exegetes went considerably further in their condemnation, characterizing both the turned odes and their makers as utterly depraved, the proof being the odes' explicitly romantic, even salacious content, no less than their irregular meter. Accordingly, a few prominent defenders of contemporary mores, Wang Bo among them, insisted that the turned odes be excised from the anthology since utterly immoral men must have inserted them into the canon. Such serious charges were often countered by the argument that the turned odes must have been included in the hope they would serve as cautionary tales of ruin through debauchery. Good men surely would not have composed, compiled, or studied the turned odes had they not served as warning signs presaging the downfall of men and states.

No pre-Han evidence supports the theory in late imperial China that classicizing moralists condemned the turned odes. Indeed, every scrap of available literary evidence works against such an idea. After all, the Confucius of tradition insisted that a "single phrase"—"thoughts with no trace of deviance"—summarizes the underlying meaning of the entire collection. Evidently, the Supreme Sage discerned no moral turpitude in any part of the collection. Neither did other moral exemplars, if evidence culled from the state-sponsored canons can be trusted. The statesmen of the *Zuozhuan* chose to employ the State

---

* All Warring States and Western Han discussions about the lascivious character of the new music concerns tones, melodies, and rhythms, not the wording of its songs. The increasing preoccupation with the wording of certain odes over the course of time corresponded to the very gradual transformation of culture in early and medieval China from rites centered to text centered.

Airs and Minor Court Songs frequently in diplomatic exchanges, not to issue grave remonstrances or dire warnings, but to convey greetings, compliments, and felicitations during diplomatic missions (see below). Prime Minister Zichan of Zheng, one of the great heroes of the *Zuozhuan*, was especially fond of citing the Zheng odes because with "all music, one takes delight in one's place of birth." Ji Zha of Wu, a worthy gentleman, pronounced the Zheng Airs—considered doubly corrupt by the later moralists owing to their illicit themes and relative metrical irregularity—excellent, while noting that their "excessive fineness" bespoke a certain measure of effeteness. Pre-Qin discussions of the supposedly depraved melodies associated with new music were elaborated and exploited over the centuries for political reasons. But this sharp distinction between turned and upright odes, however influential in later imperial China, can easily divert attention from the significance of the *Odes* in elementary and advanced training.

THE ODES AS TOOLS FOR LEARNING

In Elementary Education

If surprisingly little is known about the composition and compilation of the odes, all traditions portray the *Odes'* vital importance as a cultural repository of eminent utility and as a teaching tool for the social graces. Therefore, even in the pre-Qin period, for those intent upon acquiring "all the insignia of culture," study of the *Odes* began early. By the imperial period, it commenced about the age of nine and continued into young adulthood. Skilled social practice required sensitive yet stylish and improvised yet informed responses to the subtle interplay of human relations. Ideally, speech was to seem "designedly done but without overstepping, subtle yet in everyone's sight." As a textbook of style and the language of diplomacy (in both senses of the word), the *Odes* could hardly be outdone. A storehouse of elegant language and refined formulae, preferably intoned with special pronunciations in set keys,* it served as a kind of early thesaurus and book of etiquette rolled into one, whose limited format was of limitless applicability.

The social graces in turn were what made for an impressive character: the "sound of virtue" 德音 capable of influencing others for the good. Good students of the *Odes*, according to tradition, could "incite [others'] emotions, observe their feelings carefully, keep company with others, or express grievances, either in the service of their fathers at home or their princes abroad." Simply

---

*An unofficial report from the Shanghai Museum speaks of an excavated text that explains the scales to which the odes should be sung, but as the text is written in Chu characters, it has so far resisted decipherment.

Intoning the Cocklebur (Ode 3),
  made loyal ministers rejoice.
Singing the Thick Tarragon (Ode 202),
  made filial sons grieve.
Declaiming Big Rat (Ode 113),
  made greedy officials depart.
Trilling the White Colt (Ode 186),
  made noble men return.

This potential for suasive power, the most typical motive cited both for study of the *Odes* and for the inclusion of the canon in the curriculum of polite arts, rested on an admirable virtuosity. The ability to select on the spot an apt citation from the anthology so as "to round out meaning" displayed erudition and perceptiveness. To go on to compose minor variations on an ode or to match or "cap" a verse, returning it with one as good or better, took greater improvisational insight. The ultimate test of a person's discernment—the capacity to make perceptive connections—occurred in the social arena in contests of oratorical skill in which the recitation of short selections from the odes or extemporaneous variations on them could sway the course of events. The inherent ambiguity and the multivalence of the odes allowed songmakers and audience alike to thrill to witty displays of learning imparting a single meaning to lines quoted within a specific context. In effect, then, an ingenious, flexible, yet guided response, reaching ever higher levels of insight, became both the prerequisite for and the end product of *Odes'* learning.

To the degree that the social skills and intuitions that made for profound charismatic influence could be taught at all, they were best taught by the *Odes* anthology, which itself showed incredible musical and literary invention throughout, the latter most evident in its dazzling composite images, each relating to one another and to the ode's main theme while having wider implications for the social world outside the text.* Given the variety of persons, situations, and milieux described in the *Odes*, a work that seems to embrace every aspect of the world—past and present, living and dead, male and female,

---

*The inherent difficulty of learning the *Odes'* complex and semiarchaic language of civilized discourse was greatly augmented by the multiplicity of nuances that each poetic image could be made to convey. That the same lines could impart many messages should not be surprising, considering the speed with which the best-known lines from present-day pop lyrics acquire new meanings, some of which reverse the original intent of the lines. Naturally, as professionals the classical masters in the empire, especially those on state stipend, felt it their duty to educate their students, each a potential candidate for office, in the main tropes used.

aristocratic and commoner, human and nonhuman—the anthology provided a series of manageable test cases by which the beginning student could gradually become well versed in constructing feasible connections and distinguishing similarities and differences. Many of the odes included paired utterances like "Who says I am X? / I am in fact Y" or "It is not that X / It is rather that Y," admirably designed to teach the fine art of discrimination. Mastery of these techniques might lead the aspirant toward the more advanced stages of knowing required in less controlled circumstances, in which the proper modes of social interaction were harder to establish, though the stakes were as high or higher. Armed with such valuable knowledge, the gentleman could expect to "exercise his own initiative" wisely, extrapolating from principles learned through the odes to any situation he might encounter.

As a result, those who could chant odes and respond appropriately to them were considered "qualified to become great officers" who would "turn their merits to account." Conversely, the lack of such abilities was deemed sure proof of the person's loutishness, ignorance, insensitivity, and lack of suasive influence, in that "words lacking pattern and refinement do not go far [in persuading others]." Based on his knowledge of odes, one could get a fair grasp of a man's training, self-discipline, and resourcefulness. And this ability to know men via their knowledge of the *Odes* was considered the most valuable type of knowledge available to the ruling elite. To know others and be known favorably by them was the one skill essential to those wishing to acquire or retain high rank. At the same time, those already in power needed to exercise their powers of discernment in knowing others, lest they fail to measure merit accurately, employ it suitably, and reward it proportionately, for only thus can a superior attract good men to his service and secure their loyalty.

The preferred method of employing the odes in public discourse was to skillfully "break off a stanza or line" from the ode, usually the first or the last, and then offer its message for consideration by those present. The reciting of one part of an ode could convey a highly specific meaning unambiguously and succinctly, if indirectly; alternatively, it could recall the main themes or dominant mood of the entire song, the better to criticize, satirize, or extol. Depending on the location and relative formality of the event, the verses would be sung or chanted, and to underscore the message instrumental accompaniment might be added, for the more compelling the rhythms of an ode, the greater the likelihood that its audience would absorb its meaning deeply.

Two anecdotes (among the many recorded in the *Zuozhuan*) demonstrate the public function of odes as coded language in diplomatic meetings, at the same time revealing them as "tools for knowing" the moral, emotional, and intellectual states of others. The first focuses on Zhao Meng, a great officer of Jin:

Zhao Meng was on his way home from a diplomatic mission to Song, when he stopped in Zheng, where seven officers were all in attendance on the earl. Zhao Meng asked each of the seven gentlemen to do him the honor of chanting his favorite ode, for from that he intended to discern their characters. Bo You chanted an ode describing a bickering quail and a fierce magpie that occupy the same nest. By this, he inadvertently revealed his desire to edge his ruler out from the seat of power. Zhao Meng, feigning ignorance of Bo You's intent, managed to forestall further discussion of the matter when he reminded the court that details of domestic politics are never to be divulged to envoys from other states. Soon, it was the turn of Zichan, the famous prime minister of Zheng, who proceeded to chant a refrain from the "Lowland Mulberry" (Ode 228),

> *When I see noble men,*
> *How great the pleasure is! . . .*
> *How can I not be glad? . . .*
> *Their good name binds me to them! . . .*
> *Never will I forget them!*

Understanding this as a compliment to himself, Zhao Meng replied, "Permit me to accept only the last stanza of the same ode":

> *My heart is full of love.*
> *Why should I not say so?*
> *The core of my heart will treasure him.*
> *What day could I forget him?*

With this, Zhao Meng promised never to forget Zichan's generous treatment. And so it went. After all seven had chanted their favorite odes, Wenzi, an officer of Jin, remarked to his fellow officer, Shu Xiang, "We use odes to express what is on our minds." Following that logic, Wenzi confidently predicted that Bo You was bound to come to a bad end, given his ambitions to usurp the ruler. But he considered the other six, whose choices had all been appropriate to the occasion, to be men of virtue who would help their families retain noble rank for generations. "The family of Zichan will be the last to perish. For though he occupies a high rank, he does not forget to humble himself."

example 2:

One year later, the marquis of Jin sent his minister Han Xuanzi on a diplomatic mission to Lu. When Han Xuanzi was shown on his visit the state archives of Lu, a signal honor, he returned the compliment by remarking upon the exemplary virtue and wisdom of Lu's founder, the Duke of Zhou. Responding to this expression of courtesy, Duke Zhao invited Minister Han to a feast, where Ji Wuzi of Lu welcomed Han Xuanzi by reciting the last stanza of the "Long Tendrils" (Ode 237), which reads:

> *Yu and Rui made their peace,*
> *Having been moved by King Wen's virtues.*
> *I say, some at a distance allied with him.*
> *And those who came first led those who came later.*
> *I say, some ran to do his bidding.*
> *And some to defend against insults.*

By implication, Lu would always "run to do the bidding" of the marquis of Jin, Han Xuanzi's lord and master, whose virtues matched those of old King Wen of Zhou. Such an alliance between Lu and Jin would strengthen their mutual "defense against insults" from other states. To this welcome announcement, Han Xuanzi responded with lines from the "Horn Bow" (Ode 223):

> *Well fashioned is the horn bow,*
> *And swift its return.*
> *Brothers and relatives by marriage*
> *Must not be treated distantly.*

In intoning this ode, Han Xuanzi promised that Jin would maintain and improve its relations with Lu, symbolized by the family ties that bound the rulers of the two states. Ji Wuzi, who had hoped for exactly this kind of response, bowed to Minister Han, saying, "I venture to thank you for your kindness to our poor city. Our ruler may certainly expect a strong alliance!" To reiterate his appreciation, Ji Wuzi offered Han the last stanza of "High-crested Southern Mountains" (Ode 191), which says:

> *I, Jiafu, composed this song,*
> *To lay bare the king's quarreling.*
> *In hopes that you, in your change of heart,*
> *Would nourish the myriad states!*

Ji Wuzi with these lines not only thanked Jin for strengthening its alliance with Lu, but also predicted that their alliance "would nourish all the myriad states," insofar as it lessened the likelihood of war.

When the formal feasting was over, the group moved to the family home of Chief Minister Qi, to continue the entertainment. Within the

Qi family compound, there grew a beautiful tree, which Han Xuanzi singled out for particular praise. Inspired by the beauty of the tree, Ji Wuzi drew upon the odes' traditions to extemporize two elegant compliments that implicitly compared Han Xuanzi with Duke Shao of Zhou, a man known for his forceful yet judicious character. Han Xuanzi modestly declined the comparisons, saying, "I am unworthy of such compliments." Secretly, of course, Han Xuanzi could not have been more delighted. He later proved faithful to Lu's interests.

Time passed and Han Xuanzi was sent as envoy to Qi to present a marriage gift to its marquis. There he visited the two ministers Ziya and Ziwei, who had him meet their heirs. When Han Xuanzi expressed his disapproval of both younger men, the great officers tended to laugh at him. Chancellor Yanzi was the exception. He reasoned, "That man is a gentleman. A gentleman has those whom he trusts. And he has a means by which to recognize them, surely!" Han Xuanzi then left Qi and went to Wei, where he was entertained by the marquis at a similar feast with literary exchanges.

In these two anecdotes drawn from the *Zuozhuan* (abbreviated somewhat here), the odes' public function is unmistakable: they are elegantly allusive vehicles for conveying sentiments and intentions in diplomatic contexts. In a society ordered by patron-client relations, knowing men was particularly crucial and, as the proverb said, "The *Odes* expressed what was on the mind." Yet in any social gathering, true virtuosi of the *Odes*, whether male or female, could safely express their innermost feelings without fear of offending others. (Early traditions attributed a number of odes to women.) It was not only that the odes were intoned during court feasts, when the participants, under the influence of wine and good food, were generally more receptive to the concerns of other parties. With odes, a person could broach delicate matters indirectly, allusively, and in accepted strophes and thereby reprimand or voice the unexpected without embarrassing anyone. For "when a person governed by patterns [patterned language and ritualized behavior] offers an indirect admonition, it creates no offense." Regarded as the product of suitable emotions aroused in the singer, the odes served as a versatile rhetorical tool by which to arouse sympathetic emotions in audiences public or privileged, lettered or unlettered. Set to music, the exchanges "flooding the ear" "would penetrate deeply into others, so their transforming influence was swift." And what better model existed for the convivial give-and-take of diplomatic alliances than singing a stanza from the odes and receiving in reply a perfectly apt quotation from or variation on the same anthology? Such an exchange forged or reinforced a bond between participants, based in part on their shared identity as members of a tight community of those in the know, even—or perhaps especially—when little information was communicated and no substantive argument made.

In the political domain, then, acts of knowing and persuading rested upon wise use of the *Odes*. Where the *Documents* canon enjoins rulers to know men, the phrase is always in the context of selecting the very best men for bureaucratic office. But if the odes, or at least the State Airs, were in any part the powerful expressions of unlettered commoners, then the task of knowing men ultimately required at the same time the development of a fine sensitivity to the less overtly political, an attention to the essential, irreducible nature and feelings common to all people at all eras, regardless of rank, so as to arrive at the broadest, most long-range, and most compelling views possible. Admittedly, some literati found imaginative identification with a peasant-composer of the archaic past far easier than brushing up against his unwashed counterpart in real life. Nevertheless, the very existence of the *Odes* anthology and its reputed origins implied the necessity for members of the ruling elite to attend closely to the stories, ditties, and songs circulating among the very lowliest subjects in the state, even the fuel and fodder gatherers, for only in that way could one know enough men well enough to persuade and be persuaded by them, as appropriate.

Ethical Training by the Odes

Adherents and opponents of Confucius alike had the followers of the Sage continually "reciting the three hundred odes, playing them on strings, singing them, and dancing to them." Early texts give some idea of the important role that the *Odes* played in ethical training. Two of the most famous anecdotes from the *Analects* record spirited interchanges between Confucius and his disciple relating the value of ethical training to specific odes. In the first, the disciple Zixia asked the meaning of a particular lyric, "Oh, the sweet smile dimpling, / The lovely eyes, so black, so white! (Ode 86) / [Like] plain silk to take for colored stuff."

> The Master replied, "It means that the painting comes after the plain groundwork." To this Zixia responded, "Then that means that ceremonies must come after [the basic groundwork has been done to establish humanity, integrity, and respect for others]?" The Master said, "Zixia, it is you who bears me up [in my troubles]! At long last, I really have someone with whom I can discuss the *Odes*!"

In this one encounter Confucius taught three important lessons: that mastery of the polite arts is valuable only to the extent that it is predicated on an acute moral sense, whose ultimate worth is greater than conventional beauties of form; that the *Odes'* literary figures nonetheless supply apt metaphors for the process of moral cultivation; and that cultivation of one's humanity would have undeniable attractions for those who witnessed it.

In a second anecdote, the brash disciple Zigong tries out a fine phrase, "Poor without cadging, rich without swagger."

"How is that for a line?" The Master said, "Not bad. But better still would be 'Poor, yet delighting in the Way; rich, yet a student of ritual.'" Zigong said, "I suppose that the *Odes* saying, 'Like [a jade] cut and filed, / like one chiselled and polished' conveys much the same meaning as the lines you have just spoken?" The Master replied, "Now, I can really begin to talk to you about the *Odes*, for when I mention what came before you know what comes next!"

Playing off select lines from the *Odes*, Confucius and his disciple tackle the all-important subject of moral self-cultivation through a series of images implicitly positing the simultaneous and complementary development of knowledge of the *Odes* and of ethics. The disciple Zigong opens by suggesting that self-cultivation is a matter of attitude toward one's position in life: Whether rich or poor, the cultivated person will neither boast nor beg. True, replies Confucius, but insufficient, for people with fine manners may yet have an underdeveloped moral sense. Moral self-cultivation is itself a kind of an exquisite taste: the truly cultivated have learned to delight in the moral Way and to appreciate the beauty and utility of ritual. Such sophisticated powers of discrimination keep them on the path of full humanity (*ren*), painstakingly refining their initial impulses toward sympathetic understanding, like the jade cutter who cuts and files, chisels and polishes the precious material. People who know enough to take pleasure in the Way find that the end products of their efforts, their lives or their jades, have become exquisite works of art.

This talk of knowing delight makes much more sense when we remember that in early China and well into medieval times the odes were performed to music. Today, the odes are usually read in silence, but silent reading was considered markedly eccentric in early and medieval China. (In classical and medieval Europe, too, reading also meant reading aloud.) At the very least, the odes were chanted, sometimes in special pronunciations. Regarded primarily as musical pieces, they were more often sung to well-known melodies. Indeed, one early standard definition for the odes is "poetry set to music." Cultivated amateurs among the elite, no less than professional musicians, were expected to sing and play the odes, for music was one of six polite arts. Imagine for a moment the scene at one of the Zhou courts where the musicians have

> *Set up the cross-boards and music stands,*
> *The upright hooks, the planted plumes.*
> *The small drums and the big drum for beating,*
> *The tambourines and stone-chimes, signal bells and scrapers.*
> *With these all ready, they begin to play,*
> *Full sets of pipes and flutes raised high.*
> *Their sounds sweetly haunting,*
> *Then, in unison, the answering calls.*
> *Our forebears lend an ear.*
> *As do our guests who came.*
>
> *(Ode 280)*

With the text of the odes indissolubly wedded to musical lines, so that lyric and melody each carried meanings in complex interplay, early musical performance and study of the odes went hand in hand. It was the impulse to harmony and rhythm that initially prompted poetic composition, after all, and the Confucians attributed special transformative powers to music, including those "to broaden one's guiding ideas, . . . to make the eyes and ears more perceptive, to calm the bodily humours, and to improve local mores." Learning to keep time to music fostered self-restraint and self-discipline, along with a keen appreciation of the vital importance of good timing to all activities. As one ode put it, the perfect gentleman "in dancing counts [the steps] / then in shooting pierces the target / . . . preventing violation of the rules." Moreover, with music inhabiting the body as passing scenes could not, songmakers, like the shamans of old, could introduce receptive audiences into unseen realms, imparting a visionary intensity.* Sensing through this intensity the spectrum of human possibilities for integration and for immortality, friends joined in choruses: "Set the tune and I will sing with you! / Set the tune and I will follow you!" "Performed in communal settings, where the old and young joined in listening to it, then each and every one felt this spirit of accord." Moreover, as music embodies an "unchanging harmony," the singers could trust to meter and rhyme to preserve their songs in memory long after the makers were gone. For music, one of the most ephemeral of the performing arts (at least until the invention of the

---

*Especially before the introduction of Buddhism, emotion, intuition, and moral judgment were thought to work in tandem, rather than in opposition to one another.

gramophone) and the least amenable to adequate written description, has often proved the most enduring.

Such strong connections between music and the odes were bolstered by the apparent identity of *yue* (music) and *le* (pleasure, joy, delight), two words written with the same graphic sign 樂 from early on. As similarities in graphic form or in sound were thought to indicate a common semantic origin, music, particularly the melodic component of odes, was by definition equivalent to joy. (Compare the English word "glee.") A joyful ease came with knowing the musical odes. Performing them, not to mention composing them, made moral learning at once the most natural and so most delightful of all human activities—far more than a polite accomplishment, a significant source of gratification. It was hardly surprising, then, that moralists were apt to employ musical performances of the *Odes*, often conceived of as multimedia theatrical events, to foster in the immature an ardent taste for self-cultivation, thinking that such performances forged strong links between physical enjoyment, the willingness to harmonize with another's sensibilities, and cultured attainments. A story told about Confucius illustrates the power of music to transform the hearts of even those of dubious morals. One day, some people in the state of Kuang threatened Confucius, mistaking him for an evil man, Yang Hu of Lu. Confucius's disciple Zilu, always one to swagger, drew his dagger in preparation for a counterattack. Confucius stopped him, saying, "Let us join together in a song!" At this Zilu plucked the zither and sang, Confucius accompanying him. Before the two had finished the third stanza, the hostility of their would-be attackers had dissipated.

Later in history, in self-conscious imitation of Confucius, some of the empire's best bureaucrats tried to apply this very lesson, reasoning that a return to the kind of genuine emotion expressed in song was a prerequisite for moral cultivation; also that rhymed songs were the best means to inculcate moral ideas in those less socialized to virtue. Thus Feng Menglong (1574–1646), who served as educator and magistrate in Fujian, devoted himself to preserving and employing the style of the local popular songs of that region. And Zhang Boxing, governor of Fujian during 1707–1710, issued three versions of the *Sacred Edicts*: a plain text of the imperial pronouncements for the literati; an illustrated version with popular sayings for those "of medium intelligence and scholarly ability"; and one with catchy jingles for simple country folk.

Study of the musical odes, therefore, was credited with the power to raise humans to loftier aspirations. The *Odes* anthology itself repeatedly draws our attention to the human desire for social engagement and the sense of mutual well-being engendered when that engagement is adept and loving:

If along the highway
I catch hold of your sleeve,
Do not hate me.
Old ways take time to overcome.
(Ode 81/1)

The pond at the east gate
Is good for steeping hemp.
That lady, lovely and fine,
Is good at capping odes.
The pond at the east gate
Is good for steeping nettles.
That lady, so lovely and fine,
Is good at capping lines.
The pond at the east gate
Is good for steeping rushes.
That lady, so lovely and fine,
Is good at capping talk.
(Ode 139)

Once I have seen my lord,
Side by side, we will sit and strum the lute.
Not to make music now or to feel our joy
Is to let time pass till we are too old.
(Ode 126/3)

Just as the odes taught that skillful and rewarding relations depend on a proper appreciation of the objects deserving admiration, so the deeper pleasures available to humans—self-knowledge, friendship, sexual pleasure, and connoisseurship—relied on an extraordinary capacity to cultivate in oneself and others the desire for more refined social interplay.

In the end, the ethical followers of Confucius claimed this province of ordinary human interaction, with its marvelous potential for imbuing men with greater vision, as their own special area of expertise, in contrast to those thinkers now labeled Legalists, Mohists, or Daoists. To see the justice of the claim that a breadth of moral vision could develop from the close observation of the most mundane human activities, we need examine only one famous ode, the "Cypress Boat" (Ode 26), which early commentators took to be the lament of a young woman of good family, whose parents intended to marry her off to one man, though she fancied another:

Tossed, that cypress boat,
Wave-tossed it floats.
Disturbed, unsleeping,
Such is the secret grief.
It is not that I lack wine
Or the means to sport and play.

My heart is not a mirror, for
There's more than meets the eye. . . .
My heart is not a stone, for
It cannot be turned.
My heart is not a mat, for
It cannot be rolled and put away.
My conduct has ever been correct.
It cannot be singled out for blame.

My sorrowing heart wastes away,
Harassed by hordes of petty men.
The vexations I have met are many,
And the insults borne, not few.
In silence I think of it, and
Startled from sleep, I rend my breast.

Oh, sun; oh, moon!
How have you cycled and dimmed?
Sorrow clings to my heart
Like an unwashed robe.
In silence, I think of it: that
I cannot spread wings to fly away.

The song opens with an "evocative image" (*xing* 興),* precisely drawn to convey the complex feelings the singer—like the early commentators, one may assume a woman—cannot bring herself to divulge fully. Comparing her emotional volatility to the wave-tossed boat and her innate value to the precious cypress

---

*The 305 individual lyrics included in the *Odes* are structured on two basic models or a combination thereof: the first, parallel or contrasting images; the second, sequential or reverse sequential narration. Note that the odes employ three types of description: (1) the *fu*, straight exposition; (2) the *bi*, simile or obvious metaphor; and (3) the *xing*, or evocative image. *Xing* was defined as a concrete thing, often a plant, bird, or beast, that by some subtle sensory association arouses (also *xing*) in the receptive reader, adept in interpreting such signs, an important insight into an aspect or quality pertaining to the subject of the lyric.

wood, the singer avows her integrity through a series of contrasts suggesting that she would fain not be an object acted upon, like the mirror that merely reflects whatever is before it, the stone that can be turned this way and that, or the mat that can be lain upon and then set aside for the next user. The next two stanzas spill out a tangle of emotions—despair, anger, resentment, confusion, and not a little self-loathing—at her inability to escape her troubles. But all the while, the evident perturbation is offset—and so intensified—by the standard metrical regularity of the ode, whose clipped tetrasyllabic form, though symptomatic of nearly all the State Airs, nonetheless contributes to an impression of the woman's rigorous self-containment and irreproachable behavior.

Committed followers of Confucius sought to know the singer of an ode by every means at their disposal. As students of the past, their first search for knowledge might be somewhat detached and abstract, with the singer treated mainly as author of multiple signs in significant juxtaposition: the condensed impressions imparted by the opening evocative image; the composite images of the main content building from one another; the formal metrical structure of the ode; the melody itself. But as the careful correlation of these signs strengthened in the listener a sense of the singer's identity and situation, they would come not only to feel her pathos, but also to recognize the sadder fact that her plight is duplicated whenever anyone, male or female, is betrayed by close friends or trusted colleagues. Real distress at the outrageous betrayal would stiffen their resolve not to become like those unfeeling "petty men." So catching the basic human note could ready them to engage in more ethical conduct themselves, and understanding one particular singer could increase their empathy for all.

Citation of the "Cypress Boat" shows that the intuitions gained from long training in the odes—the ability to see beyond one's own ego and the social externalities—could often end in a heightened awareness of human frailty. Only frailty or, worse, downright perversion could account for the utter subversion of the Odes' enormous moral potential, apparent when, for instance, select odes were used to mock the Sage himself or to justify immoral conduct. Ode 34, one of the odes chanted by Zhao Meng on another diplomatic mission, opens with images portending a grave reluctance to embark upon a risky business ("The gourds have bitter leaves [that is, they are useless] / The ford is deep to cross [that is, trouble lies ahead if one continues one's present course]." A respondent in the ode then replies, "Where deep, step on stones / And where shallow, wade," in effect, telling the first speaker to proceed with his business. As the story goes, once, during his exile in Wei, Confucius bemoaned his troubles with an allusion to the opening lines of Ode 34: "How is it that I have become a bitter gourd? Why am I merely hung as ornament on the wall and not devoured?

[Why am I disdained and my services rejected?]" Came the sarcastic retort: "How stupid he is! And how stubborn! When no one recognizes him, he just quits! [As the ode says,] 'Where deep, step on stones. And where shallow, wade!'" When Confucius despairs over the repeated rejection of his advice, his critic, equally adept in the language of the odes, lambastes the Master's basic unwillingness to adjust his message to contemporary audiences in order to achieve his goals. Bewailing the world's ingratitude is self-indulgent and point-less, so one does better to make opportunities, adapting quickly to time and cir-cumstance, as the speaker must in every instance of breaking off a stanza.

Moralists might express outrage at employing the very sacred odes sup-posedly collected by Confucius to ridicule the Master. But because the odes were so widely known across society, one could never be sure who might use them or how, as an anecdote from the late second century AD suggests:

> In the household of [the famous commentator] Zheng Xuan, even the male and female slaves were literate. Once while Zheng was being waited on by a female slave, she failed to satisfy his wishes. He was on the point of flogging her when she began making elaborate excuses for herself. In a rage, Zheng had her dragged through the mire. A moment later another female slave came by to ask, in the words of an ode, "What are you doing in the mire?" The female slave replied in the words of another ode: "I went to him and pled my cause / But there I met only with his wrath."

Knowledge and use of at least the oral texts of the odes were so ubiquitous, in fact, that a cruel parody in the *Zhuangzi* had classically trained grave robbers swapping lofty citations from the odes as they stripped corpses of their gold and pearls. Pointing to the gap between moral cultivation and polite attainments and the ever-present potential for the perversion of factual knowledge, such passages obviously disputed the notion that one could come to true knowledge of oneself and others simply through knowing the sacred odes. Nonetheless, for a small group of men determined to seek self-cultivation for its own sake, the odes afforded not just a storehouse of memorable phrases to play with and master, but a host of antique moral exemplars and an avenue to appropriate pleasures.

KNOWING AS A PATH TO FRIENDSHIP AND PLEASURE

Earlier I focused on, first, the practical uses of knowing men through the odes in a political context of state affairs and state service, and, second, the moralis-tic readings employed in the ethical arena. In both cases, the hortatory value of an ode and its value as the legitimate expression of feeling converged neatly, heightening the impact of any citation. But literary traditions attached to the *Odes* show that the early Chinese were equally concerned with other reasons for knowing men. Thus we will consider the less official uses of the odes, setting aside the fairly extensive literature coupling the musical and the predictive arts, which is discussed briefly in chapter 6 on the *Changes* divination manual.

Given their strong belief in humans as social beings, the Chinese held that the good life required at least one soul mate, male or female, living or dead, heart to heart. In early court etiquette, as we have seen, singing the odes was the standard method by which to initiate closer relations. By definition, accomplished singing at court worked to enhance mutual understanding and trust between partners, to effect accurate yet moving self-representation, and to invite others' confidences. Outside court, the exchange of odes was a tested method to discover friends and deepen friendships in private life: "The gentleperson uses patterned [behavior and writing] to meet friends, and friends to support his virtue," seeing the identification of patterns as a continual delight to instructed minds. There, too, knowing and being known constituted the greatest of all delights, for shared enjoyments are always the best.

Successful odes singing in some sense partook of the model for good friendship, in that it required far more than a willingness to express one's own ideas completely yet inoffensively. Attention to the delicate interplay between another's unconscious rhythms and expressed intentions was crucial in fostering a successful exchange of ideas. Even the minor incremental repetitions found in some odes mimicked the successive stages of "getting to know" a good friend over the years, allowing one to savor the familiar that was ever new. Hence the lines of Ode 165:

> *Takk! takk! thwack the axes.*
> *Ying! ying! sing the birds.*
> *Out from the valley dark,*
> *Up to the treetops high,*
> *Ying! goes the cry,*
> *Searching out the sounds of friends.*
> *Look at those birds.*
> *Birds, though they be,*
> *They still search out the sounds of friends.*
> *How much more, then, shall men*
> *Go to seek their friends?*
> *Spirits attend to it, hearken to it,*
> *For its end is peace and harmony.*
> *(Ode 165/1)*

Not surprisingly, given the strong association between singing the odes and friendship, major traditions attached to the *Odes*, for example, the *Hanshi waizhuan* (*Master Han's Outer Traditions for the Odes*), draw upon well-known descriptions of superb friendships, including some never mentioned in the *Odes'* anthology. Among these, the friendship of Guan Zhong and Bao Shuya is a testament to the marked advantages of collegial knowing within the court bureaucracy, whereas that between Bo Ya and Zhong Ziqi portrays an ideal friendship operating outside the official sphere. According to legend, Minister Bao Shuya took a considerable risk when he pressed the Lord of Qi to employ Guan Zhong (d. 645 BC) in his place. Bao swore that Guan surpassed himself in no fewer than five aspects: the scrupulous honesty of his dealings, the farsightedness of his plans, his skillful management of bureaucracy, his manly courage, and his absolute loyalty. And this even though Bao had watched Guan Zhong misappropriate funds, bungle businesses, and fail in government office, all the while acting the coward and ingrate. True recognition, in this instance at least, required Bao to look well beyond surface events to Guan Zhong's essential character. Like a good doctor, who never confuses the symptoms of an illness with its root cause, Bao Shuya rightly sensed that Guan Zhong's peccadilloes were owing to his talents being squandered in inappropriate jobs. Guan Zhong would surely rise to a challenge of sufficient magnitude.

And so it came about that Guan Zhong, in faithful service to Duke Huan of Qi, eventually "organized the feudal princes, uniting and reducing to good order All-under-Heaven, so that even today people benefit by what he did for them." But for Guan Zhong, as Confucius once remarked, the empire would surely have succumbed to barbarian invasions with disastrous losses to the Central States culture. Late in life, pondering Bao Shuya's perceptiveness in reading his character, Guan told others, "It was my mother and father who bore me, but it was Bao Shuya who really knew me." Many might call Guan Zhong, Prime Minister of Qi, the true success story. The Supreme Sage, on the other hand, gave nearly all the credit for the pair's achievements to Bao Shuya, the man who gladly yielded his ministerial post to a friend he knew had greater potential. Confucius commented, "To recognize a sage is wisdom; to advance a sage is humanity; to introduce a sage is righteousness. Who could ever excel someone who possessed these three virtues?"

Unfortunately, the Guan Zhong cycle of legends associated with the *Odes* never explains how Bao Shuya came to develop his superb talent for discerning merit. But an equally famous story, also discussed in the early *Odes* commentaries, offers a second glimpse of knowing men, one germane to the *Odes'* functions in private friendship. In this legend those in the know are the skilled musician Bo Ya and the skilled listener Zhong Ziqi, figures who parallel the songster and his audience. As one famous Han commentary to the *Odes* tells it,

> Bo Ya played the zither while Zhong Ziqi listened. As he played, Bo Ya happened to think of Mount Tai, so Zhong commented, "How well you play! The music is lofty as Mount Tai!" After a while, Bo Ya thought of flowing water, at which point Zhong commented, "How well you play! The music is as expansive as the Yangzi or Yellow River." Sometime later, when Zhong Ziqi died, Bo Ya split his zither and broke the strings. To the end of his days, Bo Ya never played the zither again, insisting that no one left in the world was worth playing for.

In the story about Guan Zhong and Bao Shuya, the bureaucratic milieu over-shadows the sense of exchanges between the two men; between Bo Ya and Zhong Ziqi, the knowing seems both more reciprocal and more intimate. The quality of their friendship, in fact, is symbolized by the musical instrument of choice, for lutes were generally played in less public settings, often at home. As the story opens, Zhong Ziqi recognizes the innermost thoughts of Bo Ya. By the end, Bo Ya is acutely aware that no other listener will ever be as sensitive as Zhong Ziqi. Both men, then, have come to know the hearts of others, with Zhong Ziqi seeing into one and Bo Ya seeing into all. Bo Ya, moreover, has been brought to self-knowledge: recognition of his superlative talent is coupled with a realization of the enormity of the loss he has sustained in his friend's death.

The ancient sages themselves were credited with exemplifying and pro-moting the ideal of perfect friendship, intentionally composing the *Odes* in such a way that they "can be used to foster groups," for "the sages who created music did not think it right to do so for their own enjoyment." To the Chinese way of thinking, the very desire for friendship was predicated on the desire to know oneself and others; hence, the pressing need to communicate one's aspirations. Ideally, the achievement of true friendship is a process of many steps, each of which directly relates to the musical odes. First, because personal "moods are not open to easy analysis, but neither are they vague," a person can read his own mind and those of others through intensive study of the many striking figures in the *Odes* anthology. One schooled in the *Odes* became in effect a blind musi-cian, a person who had so honed his intuitive capacities and his sensory facul-ties that he could discern and replicate more profoundly the complex of patterns that underlie the surface social reality.

Once he has achieved that level of perception, a person knew how to ascer-tain the type of person best suited for friendship, for the same training and taste that allowed one to "recognize the [prevailing] tone" (*zhiyin* 知音) in another's musical performance helped one read the essential substance of that person's expressive speech and deeds. Then came the period of acquaintanceship, during which the exchanges of citations and paraphrases among potential friends showed, sometimes through conscious design and sometimes through unconscious revelation, what potential friends had on their minds, especially in situations evoking great emotion. As one Han text put it, "A person's ability to follow in song or to sing in response issues forth in the quality of his voice, takes shape in the way he looks and listens, reveals itself in his face, and animates his body." The would-be friends, eager for clear yet subtle communication, turned naturally to patterned language, of which the most intricately patterned was poetry set to music in the manner of the *Odes*. Poetry set to music was not merely the truest test of another's mettle, the surest mirror of one's own character. It was also the safest vehicle for necessary, periodic release of the volatile human emotions, which must be properly regulated lest they damage oneself or another. As the Preface to the *Odes* put it,

> What goes into the *Odes'* verses is what is on the mind. Within the mind, it is an aspiration or commitment (*zhi* 志). Issued forth in words, it becomes an ode. When feelings are stirred at the core of one's being, they take form in words. And when words are not enough, feelings are expressed with exclamatory sighs. And when exclamations are not enough, we then extend them in song. And when extending them in song is not enough, feelings are expressed unconsciously with a waving of hands and a tapping of feet.

Developed appetites for both commitment and empathy and the satisfaction of those appetites: all this was appropriate. And with friends, the selection of verses need not be guided by special genius, but by an intuitive reaching out to the heart of another—facilitated perhaps by long years of training, but fundamentally based in a readiness to form steady attachments, so as to experience the pleasures of stable friendships. The mutual esteem of close friends generates the true bliss that comes from correctly valuing and being valued; in the words of Zhao Meng of Jin, "Never again will I know such joy!"

True friendship inevitably begets this elation, or so the Chinese say, because shared aspirations and shared pleasures so greatly exceed solitary goals and pleasures, given that the very definition of human nature connotes a capacity for empathy far greater than that of any other creature, surpassing even the strong appetites for food and sex. The spontaneously responsive phenomena in Heaven-and-Earth themselves were proof that even the subtlest of connections invariably held strong for appropriate partners, as when "the *gong* or *shang* note struck on a lute is [invariably] answered by *gong* or *shang* notes from other stringed instruments, which sound without being plucked." With music furnishing the example par excellence of the mutual sympathy binding the cosmos, its own sound merging with Heaven and Earth, the musical odes were surely the most effective instrument by which to solicit and sustain friendship, to school oneself in the twinned pleasures of the process by which in going beyond oneself one remains truest to oneself. "Music . . . originates in the heart-and-mind's response as they are influenced by external things. . . . for when the heart and mind are acted upon by external things, they stir." And "the odes exist for the sake of uniting hearts and minds, just as melodies exist for the sake of singing odes." In consequence, to neglect the study of the *Odes* set to music was, as the *Analects* put it, to willfully decrease one's chances of discovering persons of like mind, even to reject the possibility for congenial society—in effect, "to stand with one's face pressed against a wall."

Only this sort of deep friendship, best attained via the odes, could bring the psychic security that accrues from recognizing one's fundamental kinship with other people and with the past. And not coincidentally, virtue's path was more easily walked when one knew the security and the consummate pleasures of mutual esteem and shared tastes. This was a theme constantly reiterated in Han art, especially murals from Shandong and Sichuan, the most important centers of classical learning: the companionable pleasures to be had from such shared enjoyments as learning, attending musical performances, and feasting. In Shandong, for example, at Wu Liang and Yi'nan, murals that depict banquets accompanied by song and dance are placed near respectful portraits of the most famous classical masters, from Confucius to Fu Sheng. In Sichuan, too, portraits of the classical masters teaching their students appear among scenes of convivial feasting and music that delineate the shared pleasures of married life (fig. 8).

Commentators could not help but notice that the *Odes* anthology opens with an epithalamium, or marriage song:

> *Guan-guan, cry the ospreys*
> *On the Yellow River isle.*
> *The fetching yet chaste girl:*
> *The noble man's good match.*
>
> *Long and short, the duckweed.*
> *Left and right we cull it.*
> *The fetching yet chaste girl:*
> *Dreaming and waking, he seeks her,*
> *Seeking her, only to fail.*

Figure 8. Two pictorial bricks from Sichuan province: (*top*) a convivial banquet scene with men and women in attendance; (*bottom*) a scholar (Wen Weng?) instructing his students in the Classics.

Dreaming and waking with longing.
Pining and pining!
Tossing and turning in bed.

Long and short, the duckweed.
Left and right we gather them.
The fetching yet chaste girl:
The lute and se befriend her.
Uneven grow the water-reeds,
Left and right we pick them.
The fetching yet chaste girl:
Drums and bells to please her.

Ode 1 most directly speaks to the signal importance of finding and knowing one's true mate, though its metaphors by extension apply to similar searches, for example, the search for a soul mate of either sex or a congenial colleague. The opening lines draw a parallel between the osprey and the young woman soon to become the nobleman's mate, presumably because of a pertinent tension associated with the osprey: Unlike other waterbirds, which were thought to form monogamous pairs (like humans), ospreys were usually said to be solitary. Still, ospreys used "songs to seek one another out," their songs revealing their "pure and undefiled" nature. The image of the osprey therefore admirably conjures up the societal demands for female chastity before marriage and legitimate sexuality after, giving just a hint of the aloofness that marks the truly noble soul whose tastes preclude coarser ambitions for mere satiation or conventional success. The symmetries in spirit are nicely confirmed by fortuitous symmetries in sound, the regular alternation between strong and weak syllables in the opening lines; also the fact that the osprey's favored resting place, the "isle" (*zhou*), rhymed with and so punned on *qiu* (the word for "seeking" the duckweed and seeking the girl). And just as the lyric builds to an ever-greater intensity of feeling, beginning with the first yearnings for the "right girl" and ending with a promise of conjugal joy, the sounds themselves crescendo, as scattered birdcalls give way to the solemn orchestral music of the wedding ritual drums and bells.

Knowing whom to seek and how in courtship and marriage was a matter of the greatest importance to oneself and one's family, and ultimately even to the world: "As human nature's greatest sort of love, no pleasure is more complete than that of husband and wife. . . . The matter is profound and subtle, dark and mysterious. This is the start of [all] right and proper relations." Or, as one early commentary to the *Odes* said, "Mysterious and dark, . . . its transformations like those of the divine dragon [symbol of fecundity]. It is that which connects all things, that on which the life of human beings depends." Hence Confucius's rather more prosaic reminder to his followers: "If Heaven and Earth had not mated, the myriad things would not be born. It is by means of the great rite of marriage that mankind subsists through the myriad generations." It was entirely in character, since certain of the odes may have been composed to accompany rites of sexual or psychic union (for example, marriage feasts and lustration festivals), that each rendition of particular odes reiterated the desire for a more perfect union. Themes of courtship and marriage thread through the *Odes*, voicing sweet tension, loving pledges, and the yearning to be satisfied:

> *She tossed me a quince*
> *I returned a girdle-gem.*
> *Not just to requite her,*
> *But to pledge eternal love.*
>
> *She tossed me a peach,*
> *I returned a greenstone.*
> *Not just to requite her,*
> *But to pledge eternal love.*
>
> *She tossed me a plum,*
> *I returned a jetstone.*
> *Not just to requite her,*
> *But to pledge eternal love.*
> (Ode 147)

> *That a mere glimpse of the plain coat*
> *Could stab my heart with grief!*
> *Enough! Take me to your home!*
>
> *That a mere glimpse of plain leggings*
> *Could tie my heart in knots!*
> *Enough! Let us two be one!*
> (Ode 147)

> *My lord is all a-glow.*
> *In his left hand, he holds the reed-organ,*
> *With his right, he beckons me to make free with him,*
> *Oh! the joy!*
> *My lord is carefree.*
> *In his left hand, he holds the dancing plumes,*

With his right, he beckons me to sport with him.
Oh! the joy!

(Ode 67)

The Chen and Wei
right now swelling waters.
The men and women
everywhere, valerian in hand.
Woman: Have you been to see?
Man: Yes, once already.
But let us go again to look.
Beyond the Wei
Great was our pleasure and then some more.
Thus do these very men and women
sport with one another,
gifting lovers with small peonies.

(Ode 95)

The eroticism of the Airs Xunzi took for granted because the satisfaction of desire is right and proper so long as "humans do not err in where they take their rest," that is, in choosing life's companions and models. Centuries later, Yan Zhitui (531–591) in his *Family Instructions*, a guidebook for domestic management found in many gentry households, concurred with Xunzi's assessment. "Men of virtue do not personally teach their sons" about sex, Yan remarks; they do not need to, for the children can figure it out easily enough from certain classical texts, especially the *Odes*. Ode 1 itself, as the commentator Zheng Xuan observed, had begun with "music / pleasure in the inner chambers." And even the sacred Hymns, in recounting the establishment of the great dynastic lines, sang of the founders' mothers lying with the Lord of Heaven out in the fields. This association between sexual knowing and the *Odes* was abundantly clear to literati in imperial China, judging from the sheer number of popular poems and plays that spun off from the canon. To take but three famous examples: The "Rhapsody on a Grisette" by Cai Yong (133–192) describes the sexual dalliance between a dashing young gent and a maidservant almost entirely through images drawn from the *Odes*, successfully merging the sexual frisson with the pleasures to be had from knowing the canon. Centuries later, in the Tang, the short romances detailing the lives of *caizi jiaren* 才子佳人 (talents and beauties) relied heavily for their romantic conventions on similar poetic exchanges. And later still, in the *Peony Pavilion*, completed in 1598, a single tutoring session introducing the young lady of the house to Ode 1 leaves Bridal Du swooning from a "spring sickness" (that is, lovesickness) of uncommon severity. That the chanting of an ode brings literary form to the young maid's "spring-struck" condition is made doubly clear by two incidents in the play: when Bridal Du's predestined lover first appears in her dreams, he asks her to exchange a poem with him, so that he may better know her and thereby arouse her passion.* Then, some time later, Bridal Du's tutor, who fancies himself a learned doctor, tries to effect a homeopathic cure by reciting lines from the *Odes*. In the case of human sexuality, then, just as in that of good friendship, the *Odes* implied that the wise use of the great passions, which invariably prove self-consuming and socially destructive when put to ill use, increases one's potential for the sublime sociable delight that fosters and sustains, rather than dulls, the most rarefied of sensibilities.

Still, upon occasion the very best humans with the highest capacity for sociable delight might find themselves with no suitable outlet for their emotions, either because they had failed to find a soul mate or because unhappy fate had separated them from the one they knew. According to the early classicists, connoisseurs of knowing men then have three recourses open to them. They can vent their sorrow and frustration in writing great literature, trusting that cultivated persons of future generations will come to know and delight in them through their compositions, since the very existence of the *Odes* anthology attests to the eternal powers of expressive song. They can seek kindred souls among those who have made artful lives, placing themselves in aesthetic lines through connoisseurship. Or they can devote themselves to "making friends with the Ancients," immersing themselves in texts like the *Odes* in order to know their authors. Underlying this last course is the assumption that only the unmediated voices of true sages can guide humans in extremis to the therapeutic process that will in the end assuage their troubles. The three paths were in fact one because adherence to the Way of antiquity was thought both to quicken one's sensitivity to cultivated patterns of the past and to inspire one's artistic expression. It was in this context that Mencius, the self-styled defender of the Confucian faith, had said to Wanzhang, "But if befriending the good men of the world is not enough for a man [for any reason], then one can still discuss the men of antiquity. In chanting their odes, in reading their documents, can one possibly not come to know these men? This is why evaluating their era is another name for 'upholding friends.'" One reads the ancient texts to know what kinds of persons these extraordinary exemplars were, to immerse oneself in their inner selves so as to widen one's acquaintance beyond one's immediate

---

*There being no cult of the nude in premodern China, sexual charms were apt to be shown through less obvious forms of self-display.

circle of like-minded persons and to attain the finest model, the truest match, across space, time, and social standing.

By the implicit promise of the *Odes*, at some point in the course of considering every possible source of literary allusion and impulse to elegant phrasing, the person chanting or singing the odes "will use his ideas to trace back the intention [of the poet] and he will be able to get it." The Classics in general, but the *Odes* most particularly, guaranteed the reliable and repeatable transmission of insights achieved by memorable predecessors, for had not the blind musicians of old managed to contact the dead sage-kings through recitations of the songs? And did not many of the odes envision a time of being "together again, he and I," in their "longing for noble men." From this great men could apparently derive immense comfort: "When Yang Xiong wrote [his masterwork, the neoclassical] *Supreme Mystery*], people ridiculed him. But he said, 'That my age does not know me does not pain me. In later ages there will come another Yang Xiong who will surely commend my work.' . . . From this it is clear that writers do not beg others to recognize them. They wait, never doubting, that a sage a hundred generations hence [will appreciate their merits]." Countless examples of "making friends in history" through such imaginative excursions into antiquity can be culled from the annals of Chinese connoisseurship. Important historical figures resorted to song and poetry to register their respect for those they saw as their friends in history, as when the gifted but unappreciated Jia Yi composed his *fu* rhapsody extolling the purity of the discarded Minister Qu Yuan, who had lived centuries before, or when Wang Yangming left a poem commemorating his visit on the wall of the temple dedicated to his sixth-generation ancestor, the upright official Wang Gang:

> *In a hundred or even a thousand ages*
> *How many attuned ears would a lifetime find?*
> *True communion leaves notable traces*
> *May they not betray the original mind.*

Full immersion into the personality of past heroes frequently entailed replication of not only the spirit but the very patterned structures employed in antiquity. Therefore poets wishing to suggest a strong moral or aesthetic affinity with the archaic exemplars tended to adopt for their new poems the *Odes*' four-character lines. Sometimes the formal similarities went further, as when Su Shi (1036–1101) and his friend Wang Shen (ca. 1046–after 1100), inspired by Du Fu's (712–770) staunchly moralistic poetry, borrowed Du's rhyme schemes to communicate their distress at a recent turn of political events, in the process affirming literature's age-old part in revealing and shaping the course of politics

Figure 9. "Scholars gathered in the garden for literary activities," ink and colors on a silk scroll, 33.9 × 195 cm. dated to ca. 1499. Property of the Palace Museum, Beijing. From *Ming Qing huihua*, ed. Yang Xin (Peking: Palace Museum, n.d.), 20–21.

(fig. 9). And in the same way that "matched images" linked generations of literati poets, painters, and connoisseurs, "reversed rhymes" highlighted jarring emotional and physical changes over the ages. This rapport developed between friends across the ages—this true meeting of minds based initially on savoring lines from a text—could, as the proverb said, form a bond stronger than mere metal and stone. No less an authority than Zhu Xi wrote, "I was born a thousand years too late! My best friends lived a thousand years ago." By approaching the texts of antiquity in the proper spirit, part openness and part reverence, modern aspirations and ancient writings could finally "fit together like two halves of a tally, with no gap in between." Well into this century, numerous witnesses remarked on this unparalleled power of the sung word. One turn-of-the-century writer remembered his childhood entry into self-conscious identity in just this light: "Someone would start off with a story. . . . And whenever the action became exciting, he would burst into lines of poetry that said so much in so few words, often chanting the words in a sing-song fashion that appealed to us. And that night, before we could fall asleep, we had to repeat those lines of verse until they too became a part of our being. We had become heirs to our great literary tradition."

Study of the *Odes* was valued as one path out of human alienation,[*] the immersion into the past leading to an awareness of the perfect "unity of Heaven and Man." By intense study and practice of the *Odes*, one learned both to refine one's temperament and to fathom other people, things, and events, so as to take the first steps toward harmonizing and finally integrating the self with the larger

---

[*] By contrast, the only other pre-Han poetic tradition, that of the *Chuci*, seems to relate high refinement with an antisocial, disaffected, even self-indulgent disposition, leaving the *Odes* as the sole compendium of verse conducive to integration as well as cultivation.

social and phenomenal worlds. The measured rhythms and equal line-lengths found in most odes facilitated singing in unison or in harmony, which stimulated feelings of good fellowship: "Sing and I'll sing in harmony with you!" The frequent juxtaposition of images (human and nonhuman) further emphasized the mutual sympathy and wholeness of all aspects of All-under-Heaven, the subtle interplay of the associations contributing to the sense of community. For as listeners searched their own experience to supply definition, correlation, and completeness to the images, they, in their roles as interpreters, participated in the construction of meaning along with the song's original composer. With the song's effect depending as much on the listeners' response as on the singer's song, singer and listener were inextricably joined; thus "where the written word ended, the meaning went on," the text "at its end, joining the vast," "merging with Heaven and Earth." Perhaps this explains why so many of the odes' lyrics seem to avoid closure, leaving audiences with a curious sense of weighty matters left unsaid. Connoisseurs of poetry considered this sense of open-endedness to be one criterion of excellence.

Thanks to such long-standing traditions celebrating literary imitation, variation, and capping, great pleasure could be had in what must seem to many now a most unlikely quarter: the vast commentarial traditions attached to the *Odes*. As with all the Five Classics, there are as many different *Odes* to be reconstructed as there are commentaries and allusions to that Classic.* The odes "rarely seem to have carried their original context with them when pressed into rhetorical usage," and with commentators piling up so many different visions, tradition obviously acted less as an iron cage on the imagination than as a sacred space within which one could find and form beauty, engaging in those creative formulations of meaning that some have termed yet another kind of poetry. That almost every reading in the old commentaries presupposed an ability to cross-reference other odes and other Classics made the process of building coherence into the sacred classics akin to playing music, for music "commences with playing in unison" but soon breaks into "improvisation that is mellifluous, clear, and unbroken." That pleasures are still to be wrested from the rich traditions of exegesis is the working premise of a growing number of young and sophisticated *Odes* scholars, who see each ode as a vessel for institutionalized cultural memories preserved through multiple performances, ongoing explications, and complex forms of intertextuality.

---

*Ode 1, for example, eventually prompted no fewer than three divergent readings in Han times: one interpreting the ode as describing and censuring an immoderate and therefore destructive union; another as describing and applauding a moderate and therefore constructive union; and a third describing a moderate and constructive union, as a way of rebuking an immoderate and licentious king.

In pre-Han literature from the *Analects* to the *Zuozhuan*, the *Odes* appear as songs to be employed in courtly rhetoric. Exegetical traditions of the late Warring States and Han periods often made concerted efforts to historicize each song and supply it with didactic meaning, thereby building and completing the groundwork by which the anthology became a Classic. But rhetoric and morality, especially in the post-Han era, sometimes yielded to an ever more elaborated notion of the *Odes* as fountainhead of lyrical poetic expression. What unites these various readings of the *Odes* is their heartfelt commitment to people and values; what informs them is a single-minded preoccupation with *wen* 文, the laudable patterns that include cultivated social interactions no less than literary pursuits; also a firm belief that the arts, starting with song and music, are "messengers of the heart," the means to "display one's wisdom, ornament one's ability, order affairs, guide the masses . . . and so perfect one's virtue," that others may learn of it.

Early in the twentieth century, Hu Shi (1891–1962) complained that two thousand years of research into the *Odes* had yielded almost no results, in part because scholars in imperial China had focused on separate problems in interpretation, rather than on building a synthetic view. Hu's criticism was manifestly unfair, for classicists, however much their personal interests and approaches varied, were united in their understanding of the cardinal benefit—to composers and singers, hearers and readers alike—implicit in all the *Odes* traditions: that the *Odes* provides the appropriate patterned language, no less than the range of social patterns, by which kindred spirits might recognize one another. Fellowship within the *Odes* could transcend time, space, and ignoble obscurity, assuaging the anxiety of those who felt that to be known, that is, to be valued at one's true worth, was life's chief goal and to remain unknown, that is, misunderstood, slandered, unappreciated, an unbearable calamity. Once in speaking of his Way of commensality, Confucius remarked that "to know it is less good than to love it, which is less good than delighting in it." The path of discovery from first knowing to delight likewise informs the opening statement attributed to Confucius in the *Analects*, which in its listing of the heady joys and calm satisfactions to be gained from successive phases of acculturation seems in turn to epitomize the *Odes*' traditions: "To learn and then at the proper time to practice what has been learnt, is that not a pleasure? To have friends come from distant parts, is that not a delight? And to remain even-tempered and optimistic, even when others fail to recognize one's merits, is that not true nobility?"

Traditional readings of the *Odes*, whether Confucian or not, tend to assume a transparent, integral, and ultimately integrating relationship between the moral character of an author and the quality of his literary work. Good poems binding author, performer, and audience in a cycle of self-representation and self-recognition could not, in theory, be the work of reprobates and scoundrels. To the Chinese literati, each ode "was not the object of its writer; it was the writer, the outside of an inside, . . . for when the heart of sorrow and happiness is moved, the sound of chanting [invariably] comes forth." Certainly, the marvelous power of the *Odes* derived, at least in part, from this prevailing belief in its capacity to reveal the hearts and minds of great men, unimpeded by the passage of time or the slanderous remarks of "petty men"—a capacity by no means credited to every piece of polished writing. To the crabbed souls who cynically insisted that "the best men never achieve their aims" (*xianren bude zhi* 賢人不得志), the *Odes* traditions offered a substantive rebuttal. All who write an ode or who cite, chant, and savor the odes or who seek to engage the spirit of the odemakers of old by living a noble life—all these "achieve their aims" to know and be known. For persons of sufficiently elevated nature, the *Odes* itself is an excellent meeting place, one where, as a songmaker phrased it, "we happened to meet, / And to be with you is good." Thus in ages when daring deeds, even dramatic suicides, comprised the principal proofs of extraordinary devotion and integrity, study of the *Odes* yielded a more constructive way to reveal the heart and, in so doing, secure the heart's desire for all eternity.

Chapter Three

THE *DOCUMENTS* (*SHU* 書)

Please tell me who the Chinese are,
Show me the way to firmly cherish the memory,
Please speak to me of the greatness of this people.
—Wen Yiduo (1928)

APART FROM THE *ODES*, THE THREE MAIN
literary sources for ancient China are oracle bone inscriptions, bronze inscriptions, and a compilation entitled the *Documents*. Although the veneration
accorded all three sources reflects a prevailing impulse to reach back to an ancestral past for guidance, the sources differ markedly in the kinds of information
they provide. The bone inscriptions, known mainly through twentieth-century
archaeology, record pious injunctions, forecasts, and statements of intent, often
posed as sets of alternative charges, that were put to the divine ancestors in
Heaven by the late Shang (ca. 1300–ca. 1050 BC) kings or their representatives:
"There will be rain today. There will not be rain today." "Lady Hao will bear

a son. Lady Hao will not bear a son." They also record the divinities' replies, interpreted from the pattern of heat-induced cracks in the bone or shell, and often the actual outcome. The relatively brief Zhou bronze inscriptions, prized by antiquarians throughout history for their connection with the glorious dynasty (1050–256 BC) praised by Confucius, employ fairly standard formulae to commemorate, for the edification of their descendants, the meritorious deeds of members of the ruling elite who received or commissioned the bronze vessels. At first reading, the *Documents*, a single source claiming to cover a huge span of history, from 2500 to 500 BC, appears to offer a much richer and more nuanced portrait of life in ancient China. Less circumscribed in form and in content than either the bone or bronze inscriptions, the fifty discrete chapters in fifty-eight *pian* (bamboo bundles)* of the *Documents*, which are mainly accounts of ritualized speeches, are not assigned, either by traditional attribution or by modern scholarship, to a single region of China. Moreover, the contents of the *Documents* promise to reflect more than the preoccupations of the royal house, insofar as part of the *Documents* ostensibly addresses audiences beyond the immediate members of the royal house and its ancestors.

But study of the *Documents*, no less than that of the bone and bronze inscriptions, is beset by a host of interpretive puzzles. Beyond the problems with the basic decipherment of the text (for every chapter contains variant characters, loan characters denoting homophones,† and scribal errors) there lurks a host of additional problems, as the *Documents* fails to provide accurate dating, provenance, and internal context for the persons and events referred to in its fifty chapters. Though scientifically excavated materials, including many bones and bronzes, help to suggest some of the physical and cultural contexts for the composition of individual chapters and the events and persons described therein, no reliable and substantive information, either internal or external to the text, exists to suggest whether and how these *Documents* chapters fit together in a narrative whole. The amplification, reinvention, and reinterpretation of the *Documents* text over thousands of years, through successive commentaries, apocryphal texts, and works of popular literature, only further complicates problems of understanding.

---

*Excavated *pian* typically occur in units of thirty to sixty strips. Some Han *pian*, however, are known to have contained only one or two slips, so the unit does not neatly correspond with the English terms "essay" or "chapter." Given the weight of bamboo bundles, figured in terms of kilos or cartloads, texts did not circulate widely in the pre-Han period, and those in circulation usually represented no more than a few bundles, not lengthy works of many chapters.

†For an explanation of the term "loan characters," see the Introduction, pp. 41–42.

Nonetheless, these *Documents* texts, subject to continual emendation and elaboration, altered to fit different times and shifting needs, were somehow made to yield satisfactory answers to perennial questions about what it means to be Chinese under Chinese rule. The chief value of the *Documents* for literate Chinese has always resided, so far as we can tell, in its presumed ability to shed light on certain central questions of their political existence: how does the distinctive Way of Central States civilization differ from that of the barbarians? what form of rule is most just and therefore most enduring? how to define the role of the scholar-official in relation to the commoners and rulers? Insofar as the "compilers of the *Book of Documents* created . . . the nation they celebrated," those intending either to bear witness to past mores in China or to change them have found it rewarding to explore the worlds revealed by the canon.

Though the *Documents* text, often dubbed in English the *Book of History*, is invariably treated today as the first history of China, it bears little resemblance to any modern history. The *Documents* material that purports to deal with China's earliest times sketches the distant past in terms of discrete sage-kings and worthy officials, often hundreds of years apart, each of whom purportedly contributed to the formation of a distinctive Chinese culture. Yet the text makes no attempt to weave these separate tales into a continuous whole. In fact, all the *Documents* stories are profoundly ahistorical, in the sense that they have not been preserved in order to construct a connected sequence of events but rather to illustrate, with considerable variation in manner and content, instances of normative conduct by exemplary kings and officials. The sociologist Marion Levy has observed that premodern societies experienced historical change as "jerky, discontinuous, and slow," in contrast to modern societies, which tend to see change as "continuous and fast." This seemingly simple assertion goes a long way to explain the content of the early *Documents* corpus.* But in the centuries immediately preceding and following the unification of China in 221 BC, when the push for unification in many ways prefigured modern nationalism, a succession of intellectual upheavals occurred. As a result, learned men made strenuous efforts to attach to the *Documents* additional traditions and texts that would transform this jerky and discontinuous picture—a picture that to some degree reflected the realities of China prior to unification—into a persuasive model of quite different character: the glorious sweep of a single, continuous history issuing from the mists of antiquity to culminate in the glories of the

---

*By the phrase "early Documents," I refer to the *jinwen* chapters of the Documents, as opposed to the *guwen* chapters.

Han dynasty, the time when Confucius would become uncrowned king and sponsor of a vast, unified, and just empire legitimized by the Mandate of Heaven (see below).

Partly by conscious design and partly by unwitting desire, then, the *Documents* came to be far more than a collection of edifying portraits of moral action. The scholars who over the centuries compiled, interpreted, and emended the *Documents* so altered the venerable Mandate of Heaven theory, for example, that it became a dispensation whereby Heaven heeds even the least of its subjects in the area under its special protection. By this they elevated the status of the *Documents* from a set of disparate source of memorable precedents to a sacred history. Over the centuries, the essential allure of the *Documents'* traditions has lain in their romanticized image of China, which appears not only as the oldest continuous civilization on earth, but also as one whose manifest superiority is confirmed by fine traditions of governance and the legitimating sanction of benign Heaven's Mandate. Turning and returning to the *Documents* as a guide to principled action, using its evocation of the past as ample justification for present deeds—these activities have lent political culture in China its distinctive dynamic down to the present day. Arguably, it is this dialogue with the illustrious dead that has made the *Documents* a keystone of the Five Classics.

BACKGROUND AND DATING

On the Origins, Formats, and Titles

The *Documents* consists of separate pronouncements on the theme of governance, each attributed to a famous ruler and minister of the distant past. The Zhou royal court almost certainly initiated the circulation of these official pronouncements to glorify the ruling house and so legitimate its rule. After all, the Zhou founders had achieved such glorious feats that their descendants felt it was true piety to emulate them and carry on their work. At local courts within the Central States, the ruling families would have been careful to store away in the family archives documents relating the Zhou rulers' charges or instructions to their ancestors, for such documents, in specifying the origins and deeds of their lineages, also confirmed the basis of their political authority. For this reason, even quite minor states kept collections of source materials relating to their histories. Later in the Warring States period (fourth–third centuries BC), policy makers and clients competing for patronage bolstered their arguments with plausible stories about and speeches from the past. Thus the thin line between myth and history, between fact and propaganda, hard enough to discern at any time and any place, seems especially blurred in the case of the *Documents*, whose chapters mostly purport to record, though they inevitably to some degree reconstruct,* the major speeches of ancient sage-rulers and famous officials.

Many of these originally separate traditions, whether based in truth or in invention, eventually made their way into competing collections of political documents that constituted the stock-in-trade of diplomats, ministers, and professional persuaders. The many sets of proto-*Documents* that resulted, each with its own major policy statements, preserved for posterity samples of renowned rhetorical skill. They introduced an impressive body of precedents by which to assess and justify major political decisions. In line with the most advanced theories of their day, they also fostered an idealized picture of strong central rule, designed to undercut countertendencies toward political fragmentation. And always they bolstered the authority of any ruler who could conceivably claim descent from the ancient sage-kings and sage-officials, as well as the prestige of the classicists who transmitted the precedents, accounts, and genealogies.

But for modern readers who may bring to the *Documents* the expectation that heroic deeds are the stuff of ancient history, it is striking how very few *Documents* chapters recount any deeds at all, and those few are now known to be quite late. Battles receive short shrift. Omens and royal progresses are accorded brief notices, as are state funerals and transfers of the capital. Only a handful of chapters, including the famous Pan Geng chapter, intersperse rhetorical speeches with short accounts of specific deeds. Moreover, the speech and deeds chapters in the *Documents* are strikingly unalike in many aspects. The speech chapters tend to be surprisingly brief, whereas the more theoretical chapters devoted to deeds or to speeches and deeds are noticeably longer. For example, the entire texts of two speech chapters entitled the Sacrificial Day of the Noble Ancestor and the Western Protector Attacks Li average a mere 100 characters, while the Tribute of Yu and Pan Geng chapters, the first a deed chapter and the second a mixed chapter, are ten times longer, with 1,196 and 1,285 characters, respectively. As to content, while the speech chapters occasionally lapse into laudatory references to idealized rulers of the hoary past, they are apt to be remarkably

---

*In ancient times history was generally regarded as a repository of lessons from the past. No ancient historian felt constrained to offer an objective recording of facts, in the manner of the modern social scientist. Thucydides, for example, remarks of his *Peloponnesian War*, "My method has been, while keeping as closely as possible to the general sense of the words that were actually used, to make the speakers say what, in my opinion, was called for in each situation." Herodotus repeatedly says of his narratives that he "merely records the current story, without guaranteeing the truth of it" and, with even more brutal clarity, "My business is to record what people say, but I am by no means bound to believe it—and that may be taken to apply to this book as a whole." See Thucydides, sect. 22; Herodotus IV.195; VII.152.

frank about the reigning dynasty's continuing struggle to impose its will on the loose confederations of allied states and families nominally under its control. In contrast, every chapter devoted to deeds portrays a highly centralized empire under the compelling leadership of an extraordinary Son of Heaven endowed with nearly unlimited sway over the known world—a portrait utterly anachronistic for early times but reflecting in its outline the rapid expansion of the Central States cultural sphere from the Warring States period.

Curiously, traditional commentators on the *Documents* classic tended to ignore this obvious division between speech and deed chapters, perhaps because effective speech was itself considered an act. They did, however, classify the *Documents* chapters into six basic types of account: canons (*dian* 典), counsels (*mo* 謨), oaths (*shi* 誓), injunctions (*xun* 訓), proclamations (*gao* 告), and decrees (*ming* 命). And from Han at least, the received text has been arranged chronologically in four major sections, corresponding to the four periods that were held to constitute China's history prior to unification under Qin: Yu [or pre-Xia], Xia, Shang, and Zhou. Because modern historians find no evidence of a developed Chinese writing system that predates the late Shang period (ca. 1300 BC), the Yu and Xia sections of the text, which claim to present the very earliest source materials, cannot possibly represent edited transcripts of actual court documents originally recorded on bronze, bone, or silk. Indeed, judging from grammar and content, the earlier the chapters in the Xia and pre-Xia sections purport to be, the later their probable dates of composition. Upon reflection, it is easy to see why this is so: The notion of a coherent, continuous history of Central States civilization gained strength over time, generating a demand for a plausible history projected onto distant eras long before the invention of writing. Rhetoricians, advisers, and thinkers, all of whom would have wished to lend weight to their ideas, did so by attributing them to the earliest sage-rulers. Simply put, the longer the heritage that one could claim for one's ideas, the greater the chances of acceptance of those ideas, for most Chinese have tended to locate the Golden Age in the very distant past. One Han text admits all this with refreshing candor: "The average person of today holds the ancient in high esteem, while looking askance at the new, so those who work out methods of rule must attribute them to [the legendary emperors of antiquity], the Divine Farmer and the Yellow Emperor, and only then will [their innovations] be admitted into the debate."

In trying to devise groupings of the *Documents* chapters, the vast majority of literate Chinese, then and now, have been content to assume that the texts collected in the *Documents* canon are faithful and approximately contemporaneous records of key speeches and events. Indeed, so authoritative did the *Documents* material appear that the early Chinese simply called the *Documents* the *shu* 書, meaning *The Text*. Because the Chinese term *shu* can apply to any written document, to name this specific set of documents *The Text* is like calling the Bible The Book.

It seems that in the fourth century BC, however, those trying to distinguish one particular collection of materials from similar collections in circulation at the time, devised a special appellation for that part of the *Documents* collection believed to be of greatest antiquity (that is, pre-Xia and Xia): they called it the *Shang shu* 尚書 (Venerable [section in the] documents). At first, the qualifier "venerable" (literally "upward" in Chinese, which means backward with respect to time) was applied only to those sections of the *Documents* that purported to reach the furthest into antiquity, but as the passage of time made later periods seem venerable also, the rubric was naturally extended to cover their documents as well. Some time in the second century BC, *Shang shu* (Venerable text) was used for the entire *Documents*, the better to claim an antique provenance for the whole collection. By a linguistic extension parallel to that in modern English, the epithet "venerable" was read as an obvious, if implicit injunction to venerate the text as a repository of models of correct behavior promoted by the moral-political elite of antiquity. (Later apocrypha, spinning out the pun, said the title *Shang shu* signified the text's reception by sages from Heaven on high, since *shang* also means "high.")

The most popular name employed for the *Documents* today, the *Shujing*, or *Documents Classic*, came into general use only in the tenth century AD, when some classicists felt impelled to defend the text's canonical authority in the face of critical salvos launched against parts of it. But Song scholars, if anything, pushed the *Documents* canon to the very center stage of politics and classicism in late imperial China. Wang Anshi justified his New Policies (1075–1086) by his own "New Classics" *Documents* commentary, so that successive generations of Wang's partisans and their opponents had continually to refer to the *Documents* text in framing their debating positions. And both the Cheng brothers and Zhu Xi cited a single *Documents* passage consisting of four linked sentences of four characters each as the essence of the entire Way embodied in their Dao Learning. Only in the seventeenth century, when revisionist historians launched devastating attacks upon no fewer than twenty-one *Documents* chapters in twenty-five *pian* (see below), did Chinese classicists reluctantly begin the monumental task of sorting out the complex history of their chosen *Text*. Many modern historians, the notable exceptions being Gu Jiegang and his circle of iconoclastic "antiquity-doubters," have been equally reluctant to recognize the clues suggesting that individual *Documents* chapters were written down in their final form centuries, and in some cases, millennia, later than tradition supposed. The vast majority of readers has embraced the *Documents'* narrative history, and even the best scholars have often found themselves in unwilling thrall to it.

Recently, the political gerontocracy in Beijing seems intent upon confirming accounts in the *Documents* by various manipulations of archaeological evidence, the better to shore up nationalistic slogans touting China's historical uniqueness and unquestioned superiority. So much confusion has been generated by claims and counterclaims about both the authenticity and the authority of the *Documents* that a sober reexamination of the history of its compilation must precede further discussion.

History of the Compilation

The *Analects* shows Confucius's disciples studying the odes and familiarizing themselves with official documents. Men training for careers in government service needed to master both the language of polite discourse and diplomacy (hence the odes) and also historical precedents (hence the documents). In addition, since at least the time of the earliest bronze inscriptions, repeated injunctions to emulate the sage-rulers of the distant past had established the principle by which past occasions became models for present behavior. As a result, collections of government documents would have been required reading for any gentleman with pretensions to culture, let alone for good classical scholars, of whom broad learning was expected.

In part because of the linguistic confusion between the *Documents* and "the text(s)," very little is known about the early history of the *Documents*. However, in the fourth to second centuries BC, rival thinkers knew and expounded upon several key *Documents* chapters, according to one or more traditions. No single version of the *Documents* appears to have been accepted as especially authoritative among the self-identified followers of Confucius. The standard collections of documentary materials included passages similar to parts of the received *Documents* text, but they clearly were not identical with it; some passages may have been precursors to parts of the present text. It is well-nigh impossible, then, to settle upon a single date of compilation for the block of reputedly authentic, or pre-Han, chapters, simply because so many competing versions of *The Text*, some in oral and others in written traditions, were circulating as late as the second century BC, centuries after a fairly definitive *Odes* collection had been compiled.

Given the number of competing versions of Chinese history supported by these variant *Documents* traditions, with some implying competing moral visions, it is hardly a surprise that the early Confucian masters expressed greater skepticism toward parts of the *Documents* collections then circulating than did many classicists of the late empire, who knew only a single, state-sponsored edition. For example, in the third century BC, the master Mencius (d. 289 BC) wrote, "If one were to accept every portion of the *Documents*, it would be better not to have the *Documents*. I myself accept at most only two or three passages from the 'Completion of the War' ('Wu Cheng') chapter." Writing in a similar vein some fifty years later, the Confucian master Xunzi (d. 238 BC) scoffed at the scholastic traditions concerning the early sage-emperors Yao and Shun and then more generally questioned the utility of the *Documents* materials "dealing with ancient matters." Classical masters would have registered no such skepticism had they believed that any of these pre-Qin versions of the *Documents* could plausibly claim Confucius as author or editor. Put another way, there is no indication that the *Documents* was seen prior to unification as anything more than a collection of reference materials of varying authenticity and applicability.

Notwithstanding various attempts around the time of Xunzi to determine a definitive edition of the *Documents* for use in the curriculum, the first known standard edition in twenty-nine *pian* was achieved sometime between 179 and 156 BC, during the reign of the Han emperor Wen. This standard edition is now called either "Fu Sheng's text" (after an Academician at the Qin court whose explications were transmitted to younger scholars in early Han) or the Modern Script (*jinwen*) text (since the text was transcribed in the clerical script in current use during Western Han). Though individual chapters in the Modern Script version must have had widely disparate origins, the polite formulae and grammatical particles employed are fairly uniform throughout, suggesting a single editor or group of editors who regularized the language of the *Documents*, presumably at the time of its final compilation. Perhaps Fu Sheng himself selected what he considered to be the most authentic material from several collections circulating in the pre-Han period, appending his explications to the main text. In any case, it was this Fu Sheng or Modern Script *Documents* in twenty-nine *pian* that won recognition as the official canon during the reign of Emperor Wu of Han in the first century BC (fig. 10).

As so many courts and lineages had existed since antiquity, many Western Han thinkers came to feel that Fu Sheng's text must represent only a small portion of a much longer *Documents* collection said to be in either 100 or 120 *pian* and originally compiled by the Sage-Master Confucius.* (Perhaps the early classicists arrived at the nice round figure of 100 *pian* by combining the twenty-nine bundles in Fu Sheng's version with the seventy-one bundles in the *Remnant Zhou Writings*, or *Yi Zhoushu*, parts of which apparently contained materials dating to Western Zhou.) It is true that certain pre-Han and early Han texts

---

*Later apocryphal traditions had Confucius, after gaining access to the archives of the Zhou vassal court in Lu, the vassal state founded by the illustrious Duke of Zhou, compiling a 100 or 120 *pian* Documents from a total of 3,240 chapters, so as to provide an exhaustive record of source materials for the entire early history of civilization.

Figure 10. "Fu Sheng transmitting the *Documents*," anonymous, ninth century AD? (attributed to Wang Wei, 699–759), ink and colors on silk (H 10 1/4"). Osaka Municipal Museum (former Abe Collection). Illus. from *Bunjinga suihen*, vol. 1, *Wang Wei*, ed. Ishikawa Jun (Tokyo: Chûô Kôronsha, 1975), plate 1.

mention titles of lost chapters or cite brief passages attributed to some version of the *Documents* no longer extant, although the ambiguous citations may come from some other, unspecified "text." Still, such legends alleging an original *Documents* of stupendous length most likely developed in response to the growing expectations of literate persons in the Qin-Han period. As an ever-increasing number of once-distinct local traditions presenting culture-heroes of distant antiquity had to be accommodated within the discourse of Central States civilization with their legends projected onto antiquity, readers in Qin and Han came to learn of a glorious and unified past that stretched way beyond the third millennium BC to the time of the Yellow Emperor, the legendary ruler whose reign supposedly predated by millennia that of Emperor Yao, the first emperor to appear in Fu Sheng's twenty-nine bundles of explicated *Documents*.

For the unaccountable loss of so much invaluable material, popular wisdom blamed the legendary Qin Burning of the Books in 213 BC (see the Introduction). The Qin court Academician Fu Sheng, it was said, had secreted an original *Documents* text of either 100 or 120 *pian* in the adobe wall of his house, hoping to keep his precious but illegal copy from the repressive Qin police. Unfortunately, by 191 BC, when the Han rescinded the Qin prohibition against private scholarship, great portions of that copy, inscribed on fragile silk or bamboo strips, were said to have rotted away, leaving only twenty-nine *pian* sufficiently legible to be transcribed into the script mode then in use (the Modern Script). Two main historical fallacies cast doubt on this account: (1) by the terms of the Qin proscription, court Academicians were exempted from turning in their own copies of texts, so the Academician Fu Sheng would have had no reason to hide his copy of the *Documents*, and (2) the Academicians of Fu Sheng's time, before the great availability of paper, were far more likely to memorize an endangered text than to consign it to expensive, fragile silk or bamboo. These improbabilities notwithstanding, the Han emperors and their court scholastics signaled their mutual readiness to have additional ancient texts "discovered" and accepted by the dynasty.

Accordingly, in the years following the submission of Fu Sheng's twenty-nine *pian* to the throne, there surfaced no fewer than seven distinct sets of chapters or fragments allegedly recorded in pre-Han script, the so-called Archaic Script, or *guwen* 古文. As each of these sets purportedly came from an original (that is, pre-Qin) *Documents* edition, each upon submission to the throne was promptly incorporated into the Han traditions, winning its sponsors rich rewards. Two of the finds were particularly celebrated, the first being an Archaic Script submission to the throne of a Great Oath (*Taishi* 泰誓) chapter by a "woman of Henan" that served as replacement for an earlier, lost Taishi chapter. But the largest such Archaic Script "rediscovery," a single cache containing some ten-odd additional *pian* written in pre-Qin script, came to light a half century or so after Fu Sheng as structural repairs were being made to the walls of Confucius's old home. Surely these chapters, too, had been walled up to save them from destruction during the Qin proscriptions. The scholar Kong An'guo, a direct lineal descendant of Confucius living on the site, set about deciphering the pre-Qin texts. Seizing the chance to strengthen the Kong family monopoly on the purveyance of classical culture, Kong An'guo rendered the Archaic Script materials into contemporary (that is, Han clerical) script, readable by the ordinary literate public of his time—or so the legend goes.

Except possibly for the forged *Taishi*, those first seven separate sets of Archaic Script chapters or parts of chapters (all eventually transcribed in clerical script) unaccountably disappeared during the Han period.* In the early fourth century AD, a new set of *guwen* discoveries (now recognized as pastiches of materials, some genuinely old)—or maybe two—was submitted to the throne during the reign of Emperor Yuan (r. 317–322) of the Eastern Jin. Reputable classicists in medieval times mistook these later forgeries for Kong An'guo's early transcriptions, perhaps because they confused the Han scholar Kong An'guo with a namesake-descendant (d. AD 208) who may have had a hand in producing the later set. In any case, the twenty-one pseudo-Kong chapters, as they are now known, in twenty-five *pian* gained wide acceptance among Chinese literati, especially in the south of China, by the fifth century AD. Soon proponents of the pseudo-Kong chapters touted them as even more authentic and so more authoritative than Fu Sheng's Modern Script chapters on the grounds that they came directly from pre-Qin editions written in Archaic Script and so antedated Fu Sheng's redaction.

Despite the misgivings registered by a few scholars, before three centuries had elapsed the allegedly rediscovered pseudo-Kong chapters, called the Archaic Script chapters, were included with the twenty-nine *pian* of Fu Sheng in the authorized *Documents* recension produced by the imperially sponsored *Correct Meanings of the Five Classics* (*Wujing zhengyi*) project in AD 653, which is the version known today. From that date until the mid-Qing (AD 1644–1911), most scholars would assume that all the *pian* in the *Correct Meanings* recension had been transmitted from Han, partly from Fu Sheng and partly from Kong An'guo, in three separate transmissions:

- Fu Sheng's Modern Script (*jinwen*) version in twenty-nine chapters (later rearranged to make twenty-eight and arranged in thirty *pian*);

---

*Aside from the forged *Taishi*, it is not clear that any major texts other than Fu Sheng's twenty-nine *pian* of explicated text were ever available to scholars during the formative four centuries of Han rule (206 BC–AD 220). The prestige accorded any old manuscript associated with Confucius and his family would surely have gained it imperial patronage, and no record exists of such patronage. Quite possibly, the original Kong An'guo find consisted of little more than additional chapter titles plus passages that differed from Fu Sheng's version mainly in the use of variant characters. Based on present evidence, it appears also that the Kong An'guo *guwen Documents*, some possibly genuine, were no longer extant by ca. AD 100, when Xu Shen's *Shuowen jiezi* was compiled. For when Xu refers to *guwen* script styles and texts, he cites only passages drawn from Fu Sheng's version, which drew upon pre-Qin period traditions originally transcribed in Archaic Script that centuries before Xu's time had been transcribed into Modern Script.

- an additional "Great Oath" (*Taishi*) chapter in three *pian* supposedly restored to the original *jinwen* version of Fu Sheng to fill in a lacuna;
- some additional twenty-one Archaic Script chapters in twenty-five *pian*, originally written on silk, bamboo, or lacquer.

These made for a total of fifty chapters in fifty-eight *pian*. Scholars in the late seventeenth and early eighteenth centuries, the most famous being Yan Ruoju (1636–1704) and Hui Dong (1697–1758), were the first to offer detailed proof that the twenty-one pseudo-Kong chapters must be inauthentic. Though a few scholars, including Mao Qiling (1623–1707), remained unconvinced, over time most have come to accept the idea that, despite the confusion engendered by the nomenclature, the extant Modern Script texts must predate by centuries the so-called Archaic Script texts.

How did the late pseudo-Kong chapters come to be so readily accepted by generation after generation of classical scholars in China? The answer is that they were almost certainly not pure inventions intended to dupe a gullible court in the early fourth century AD. These Archaic Script chapters are in some sense deutero-canonical in that they contain genuinely old material, possibly copied from the bronze inscriptions known to early antiquarians. This older material, identifiable by its grammar and vocabulary, was spliced with newer bridging passages of later date to form coherent narratives. As a result, even careful scholars could plausibly find the Archaic Script chapters authentic in two important repects: they contained genuinely old material, and they exhorted faithful adherence to the classical Way.

Given the possibility of multiple interpolations, even the genuine Modern Script texts confront the historian with extremely complicated questions of dating and context. It is probably wrong to think in terms of a composition of the *Documents* text, as some passages at least must represent a loose synthesis of shared truths about the past continually reformulated over centuries. Individual passages of even a single chapter may well have originated in different times and places. It may take decades of textual analysis, therefore, before scholars are able to fully utilize any new evidence in their study of the *Documents* to estimate the dates of the troublesome passages. Further, when and if firm dates are determined, there will remain a methodological question no less taxing: What kind of date is most meaningful in the study of a given chapter: the dates when individual passages were composed? the date when most or all of the chapter was compiled, barring later interpolations? the date when the entire chapter was written down as a unit? or the date when the chapter, in part or in whole, was inserted into the *Documents* collection? The Canon of Yao chapter represents a fairly typical case of such complexities. Though its final compilation must postdate Confucius (551–479 BC) by three to four hundred years, since it refers obliquely to Qin or possibly even Han institutions, some of the Canon's information appears to tally with Shang oracle bone inscriptions and Shang astronomical observations. That one chapter may comprise information from periods as widely separated in time as Shang, Warring States, and Han.

Because present knowledge of early China is still rudimentary and because the *Documents* offers a trove of problematic information about early China, modern scholars may find it helpful to scrap the traditional division of the book into purported pre-Xia, Xia, Shang, and Zhou "dynastic" periods, substituting for it a new four-part classification of the chapters based on vocabulary, grammar, syntax, and stock formulae:

- *Group A* Five chapters collectively termed the Five Proclamations (the Great Proclamation, the Proclamation to Kang, the Proclamation on Drink, the Proclamation at Luo, and the Proclamation at Shao). Almost certainly these state proclamations, traditionally assigned to the latest section in the received text of the *Documents*, represent its earliest stratum, for many of the formulae they employ, though not all, echo the ceremonial utterances of the rulers recorded in the early Zhou bronze inscriptions. Each of the Five Proclamations relates to the founding of the new capital under Zhou. Each has the Duke of Zhou professing his commitment to continue the virtuous model laid down by King Wen, the predynastic founder. Centuries of readers have found these five chapters extremely difficult. In retrospect, the reason is plain: In both grammar and vocabulary the Five Proclamations correspond to that unusually compressed archaic language inscribed on Shang oracle bones and on early Zhou dedicatory vessels. But the language, institutions, and ways of thinking of early Zhou would have seemed as foreign to Chinese of the early empires as to those of modern times.

   Chapters bridging groups A and B probably include the following: Catalpa Wood (*Zi cai*), Take No Ease (*Wu yi*), Many Knights (*Duo shi*), and Many Regions (*Duo fang*).
- *Group B* Those Modern Script chapters that purport to date either from the last reign of Shang or from early Zhou, but that may be attributed to the late Western or Eastern Zhou periods. As a group, these eighteen chapters are generally somewhat easier to read than the Five Proclamations because they are significantly closer in grammar and vocabulary to the better-known works of the Warring States period philosophers, which are familiar to every student of classical Chinese.

The Pan Geng chapter in three *pian* appears to bridge groups B and C in three respects: (a) it contains some genuinely older formulae and arguments; (b) it does not attribute to a reign in the distant past an impossibly perfect ruler; (c) it uses *min* 民 (people) to refer to the king's men, not to commoners.

- *Group C* Six Modern Script chapters, including the highly influential Canon of Yao, Tribute of Yu, and Counsels of Gao Yao chapters, two of which purport to date from early to mid-Shang and four of which purport to date more than a millennium earlier than the Five Proclamations. None, however, can possibly date much earlier than Qin unification in 221 BC, and some may postdate unification. Ever since the Han, these group C chapters have been the ones most often cited, ostensibly because they contain the most antique (and so the most venerable) of models, but more likely because the grammar, vocabulary, and ideas in this group, being far less archaic than tradition claimed, felt more familiar to readers in imperial China.

- *Group D* The twenty-one chapters (in twenty-five *pian*) once identified as the Archaic Script chapters and now more often called the pseudo-Kong chapters, known to be late compilations, dating possibly as late as the early fourth century AD, though they contain much earlier material that presumably circulated in the Warring States, Han, and Wei periods in the form of oral traditions. As the famous Confucian philosopher Zhu Xi (1130–1200) pointed out, these chapters tend to be the easiest to read. Now we see why: having been transcribed at a comparatively late date, their grammar and vocabulary were closest to current usage.

The accompanying table summarizes the correlation between the traditional and proposed classifications. Obviously this proposed reclassification essentially reverses the conventional chronology of the *Documents* chapters. The marked differences in grammar, style, and vocabulary between the various *Documents* chapters have been there for all who cared to see. But relatively few traditional Chinese scholars undertook to reexamine issues of dating.[*]

In the eyes of scholar-officials long used to citing the *Documents* when advising their rulers on policy, it made little sense to dispute the antiquity of

---

[*]Even within the present reclassification, unexplained anomalies remain. For example, since Qing times nearly all scholars have assumed that the present Canon of Shun chapter was once the second half of the Canon of Yao chapter. But the fact that a standard grammatical feature of the Canon of Shun (the particle 也) cannot be found even once in the Canon of Yao calls that assumption into question.

Documents (Modern and Archaic Script)
Modern Script chapters attributed to Fu Sheng

Chapter title	Supposed date	Probable group
1. Yaodian 堯典, Canon of Yao	pre-Xia	C
1b. Shundian 舜典, Canon of Shun	pre-Xia	C
2. Gao Yao mo 皋陶謨, Counsels of Gao Yao	pre-Xia	C
3. Yugong 禹貢, Tribute of Yu	Xia	C
4. Ganshi 甘誓, Oath at Gan	Xia	C
5. Tang gao 湯告, Proclamation by Tang	Shang	C
6. Pan Geng 盤庚 (in 2–3 parts)	Shang	B–C
7. Gaozong rongri 高宗肜日, the *Rong* Sacrifice to Gaozong	Shang	A?*
8. Xibo kanli 西伯戡黎, the Western Baron's Conquest of Li	Shang-Zhou transition	B
9. Weizi 微子	Shang-Zhou	B
10. Taishi 泰誓, Great Oath	Shang-Zhou	original not extant
11. Mu shi, Oath at Mu	Shang-Zhou	B
12. Hongfan 洪範, Great Plan	Zhou	B
13. Jinteng 金縢, Metal Coffer	Zhou	B
14. Dagao 大告, Great Proclamation	Zhou	A
15. Kanggao 康告, Proclamation to Kang	Zhou	A
16. Jiugao 酒告, Proclamation on Wine	Zhou	A
17. Zicai 梓材, Catalpa Timbers	Zhou	A–B
18. Shaogao 召告, Proclamation of Shao	Zhou	A
19. Luogao 洛告, Proclamation at Luo	Zhou	A
20. Duoshi 多士, Many Officers	Zhou	A–B
21. Wuyi 無逸, Take no Ease	Zhou	A–B
22. Junshi 君奭, Lord Shi	Zhou	B
23. Duofang 多方, Many Regions	Zhou	A–B
24. Lizheng 立政, On Setting up Rule	Zhou	B
25. Guming 顧命, Testamentary Charge	Zhou	B
25b. Kangwang zhi gao 康王之告, Proclamation of King Kang	Zhou	B
26. Lüxing 呂刑, Punishments of Lü	Zhou	B
27. Wenhou zhi ming 文侯之命, Charge to Wen hou	Zhou	
28. Bi shi 費誓, Oath to Bi	Zhou	B
29. Qin shi 秦誓, Oath by Qin	Zhou	B

* Taishi 泰誓, Great Oath (3 parts) and Wu cheng 武成, Completion of War, both dated to the Shang-Zhou transition; the originals = pre-Qin, the received = forged. Group D = Archaic Script chapters, the most important being the "Da Yu Mo" 大禹謨, Counsels of Great Yu, said to encapsulate Cheng-Zhu neo-Confucian learning.

one's chosen citation, as this would only undermine the authority of one's present counsel.* Prior to unification and in the early empires, the *Documents* had derived its aura of textual authority from the firm (if sometimes mistaken) conviction that it had incorporated the most important early writings on turtleshell, bronze, bamboo, and silk, providing a reliable record of ideal government in the past on which to base present policy and plans for the future. The later classical scholars' marked disinclination to question the *Documents'* dating and authority is surely attributable in part also to the real confusion engendered by designating the chapters as Modern Script and Archaic Script, terminology which inevitably suggested that the latter must be older than the former. In any case, the frequent recurrence throughout the entire corpus of five major themes (see below) only increased the scholars' inclination to read the collection of disparate chapters as a fully coherent whole. Even now, long after the Five Classics are said to have lost their hold on Chinese ways of thinking, newer motivations sometimes spur modern scholars to insist upon the authenticity of one or more *Documents* chapters: Many Chinese invoke the *Documents* (1) to strengthen national identity in the face of threats (actual or perceived) from the aggressive and "polluting" cultures of industrialized Euro-America and Japan; and (2) to support the claim that China's native traditions boast such universal values as democracy and equality. To understand the *Documents* as it relates to questions of Chinese identity and universal definitions of just rule, we must now examine the content of the Modern Script *Documents* in some detail.

"DISCONTINUOUS" TALES OF SAGE-RULERS AND SAGE-OFFICIALS

Five major topics hold the *Documents* together: (1) the operation of the Mandate of Heaven; (2) definitions of true kingship; (3) portraits of worthy officials; (4) discussions of the relative merits of rule by punishment versus rule by virtue; and (5) explications of the role of "those below" vis-à-vis the ruler. These topics are treated again and again within the context of the exemplary conduct of famous sage-kings and sage-officials. Yet the *Documents* chapters do not offer a single ideal model for just and enduring rule. As changing circumstances required changing visions of the good, a range of models was needed to convey the full scope of human potential. Of that range, five models have proved particularly influential in the course of political debates in imperial China:

---

*Usually, the most cited lines were the quotable lines, those which were epigrammatic in their pith and brevity but nonetheless easy to understand. After all, the quotations' purpose was to (a) parade the scholar's erudition and so (b) bolster his authority but also (c) get his point across. Thus, passages from Group A are seldom cited, though the stories recounted there had passed into popular lore at a very early stage in history.

1. Yao in the Canon of Yao chapter, model of cosmic control;
2. King Wu, in the Great Plan chapter, model of bureaucratic control;
3. King Wu and the Duke of Zhou in the Five Proclamations chapters, royal models of filial duty, sibling concord, and collegial rule;
4. Pan Geng in the Pan Geng chapter, model of the ruler as rhetorician, who thereby controls the people (first construed as the inner circle of aristocrats and later as the commoners);
5. The Duke of Zhou in the Metal Coffer chapter, model of the self-abnegation and "secret virtue" of worthy officials.

What are the implications of so wide a range of ideal patterns for behavior, as opposed to a single type of political heroism? Since the canonical status of the *Documents* as a whole ensured that each ideal type would be praised and imitated, alternative or even competing definitions of good government, the good ruler, and the good official coexisted and contended throughout history, giving the lie to the timeworn cliché of a monolithic and unchanging China. All five models, however, incorporate three common presumptions: (1) that strong, wise central leadership is necessary to society; (2) that communities are inherently beneficial to members; and (3) that communities should function at every level of state and society, being as diffuse in nature as the cosmos itself, as disparate as the commoners, or as tightly organized as the bureaucracy and royal house. Thus, the direct discourse "recorded" in the *Documents*, far from dramatizing a gulf between authorities, the speaker, and the audience, attests the mutual benefits binding together members of a great union, benefits that extend in some measure to those readers prepared to enlarge their own understanding by imaginative immersion into the scenes depicted.

Three variant models exist for ideal rule, as presented in three sets of texts: the Five Proclamations, the Great Plan, and the Canon of Yao. Current scholarship (reversing the traditional chronological order) would date the compilation of these chapters respectively to roughly the tenth, fourth, and second centuries BC. Next, we shall take up the Pan Geng chapter, which implicitly advocates the ruler's nuanced employment of rhetorical skills, and then the Metal Coffer, which considers as well the benefits of secret virtue. The lengthy Pan Geng and Metal Coffer chapters each combine protracted speeches with short passages on deeds. While their dates of composition are still matters of debate, their dates of transcription are in all probability quite late.

These particular texts are presented in this order to suggest the following possibility: that the *Documents* represents a repository of sequentially developed approaches to good rule, though to classicists of Han and post-Han times these same approaches would have appeared as simultaneously available.

THE FIVE PROCLAMATIONS (TENTH CENTURY BC?)

Tradition says that the Five Proclamations were issued in rapid succession in response to a tense political situation. The martial founder of the Zhou dynasty, King Wu, died only a few years after the conquest of Shang, leaving the Zhou's new domain incompletely pacified. Because King Wu's successor, King Cheng,* then in his teens or early twenties, was insufficiently mature and experienced to assume full responsibility, King Wu's brothers, the Dukes of Zhou and of Shao, acted as Regent and Senior Protector, respectively, for King Cheng. Almost immediately, the regency had to contend with a revolt led by the scion of the conquered Shang ruling house, allied with two brothers of the good Dukes of Zhou and Shao. Fearing lest "the fire [of rebellion], flickering small, blaze up," loyal members of King Cheng's family circle vigorously defended their Zhou rule on the battlefield. No less crucially, the Duke of Zhou and the Duke of Shao, on behalf of King Cheng, waged two separate propaganda campaigns against the Shang camp in the civil arena. In the first, they argued that the Shang deserved to lose the throne because of the decadence and cruelty of its last king. In the second, they insisted that they, the Zhou rulers, had rebelled against their Shang overlords out of filial piety, which required them to avenge the maltreatment of their father, King Wen, by the evil last king of Shang. By his consistently virtuous conduct, King Wen—whose posthumous name denotes his exemplary behavior—had built so strong a foundation for the Zhou ascendancy that he would be remembered always as the dynasty's virtual founder, though he died before the overthrow of Shang. For King Wen's descendants to allow the wicked Shang ruler to continue in power would be tantamount to ignoring the example of good King Wen, even to agreeing that Shang's imprisonment of King Wen was just. In one Proclamation, speaking on behalf of King Cheng and mindful of the oversight of the ancestral spirits, the Duke of Zhou made the following powerful analogy:

> As in building a house, if, once the father has chosen the model, the son is reluctant to proceed to laying out the foundation platform, how much more reluctant will he be to raise the roof. As in cultivating a new field, if, once the father has tilled the soil, the son is reluctant to sow it, how much more reluctant will he be to take the trouble to harvest it.
>
> Plainly put, how could I dare refuse to discharge the great mandate inherited from King Wen? . . . I intend to follow the accomplished men [that is, my Zhou ancestors].

*Wu, Cheng, and Wen (see below) are posthumous, or "temple," names. Although the names were never used during the kings' lifetimes, historical convention uses them as if they were personal names.

Soon afterward, during an elaborate ceremony granting his brother rule over lands to the east, the Duke of Zhou in his role as regent reiterated the obligation that the newly victorious Zhou owed to its ancestors. The Duke of Zhou charged the newly enfeoffed lord, "Think on it! Now you are on the point of making a commitment reverently to submit to the plan of your accomplished ancestor. You shall carry on what you have heard from the ancestors and heed their virtuous words." The ancestors' good example must be perpetuated and the ancestors' will obeyed, for the ideal king, in point of fact, rules by virtue of his ancestors' charisma. It is the ancestors (especially Kings Wen and Wu) whose admirable actions fundamentally defined the "great task" of governing for their hardworking descendants. It is they who laid the moral foundation for the new empire, which can be realized only through their descendants' efforts. The enthroned ruler must at all times please his dead ancestors because they sit in Heaven with the Lord on High and can persuade the Lord to bless or curse those on earth. Besides, the people are wisely disposed to follow King Wen's enterprise and may rebel against anyone who appears to deviate from it.

For these reasons, it is essential that the conscientious ruler ascertain and adhere to the ancestors' mandate. This may be done by reverently recalling their deeds and words; by cooperating with one's brothers and uncles to continue the ancestors' work, so that the ancestors live on in their descendants' deeds; and by determining the ancestors' wishes through acts of divination. If in doubt about whether or how to implement a proposed policy, the ruler must first consult with the men of requisite experience, the "old perfected men" who served as advisers to his predecessors. In those rare cases in which the right course of action still remains in doubt, the ancestors' will may be discerned through two reliable mechanisms: the portents that appear in Heaven-and-Earth and the aggregate counsel of the ruler's "people" (meaning the king's men, his circle of advisers, most of whom are members of the royal clan, living and dead): "Thus, his people's feelings [about a particular government policy] can be made absolutely plain." Careful determination of and reverent conformity with the will of the ancestors is both possible and necessary for those who would further the interests of the Zhou ruling house through the ages.

THE GREAT PLAN (FOURTH CENTURY BC?)

The Great Plan chapter presents quite a different model of ideal kingship from the Five Proclamations, demonstrating how much ideas of legitimate rule had evolved in the Central States region over the intervening centuries. Tradition held that a divine Great Plan of governance, originally conferred by Heaven upon Yu, the primeval flood-queller, was passed on to King Wu, the Zhou founder, by Jizi, a wise uncle of the last Shang king, who had been forced to play the court fool after his incessant remonstrations had aroused that evil king's wrath. The story of the wise Jizi, who forsook his own ancestral clan to go over to the camp of King Wu the conqueror, immediately raises a host of moral quandaries: When is loyalty to family less important than loyalty to community? How may a corrupt reign be restored to goodness? At exactly what point are conventional obligations superseded by a higher duty to the Right? And when and in what manner may one expect the Lord on High to intervene in the troublesome course of human affairs?

The Great Plan answers such questions, for it defines legitimate kingship less as reverent devotion to or conformity with the ancestors' mandate than as the efficient marshaling of all the resources available to the state, especially those human resources to be found in the pool of bureaucratic candidates for office. (Note the abrupt shift away from the old presumptions, whereby birth generally determines who will hold office.) So long as the ruler faithfully attends to the provisions of the Plan, the Lord on High will not intervene in human events, except to bless them. In nine successive sections, then, the Great Plan lists the sorts of resources available to the state; section 1 cites the natural resources of the empire: water, fire, wood, metal, and earth; section 2 constructs a parallel between those physical and personal resources (cognitive and sensory) of the ruling elite; section 3 turns to the kinds of institutional resources—from markets to diplomacy to armies—that together provide material security for one's subjects; section 4 rests the prosperity of the state upon astronomical data, as basis for the agricultural calendar; section 6 considers the appropriate function of punishments in state rule, after which sections 7, 8, and 9 list three methods (divination, portent reading, and material verification or portent-outcome) by which the ruler may ascertain the best policy in a given situation, on the assumption that what is morally right will also be of greatest utility.

Section 5, by far the longest section of the Plan, is devoted to a theory of true kingship known as *huangji* (supremacy maximized). According to this theory, the ruler plays the pivotal role in maximizing the power of his state when he induces his subjects to contribute their individual talents to his service. To this end, the ruler consults widely with his subjects, then dispenses material rewards (the Five Riches) or punishments to secure absolute compliance with his royal will. This is the central paradox of the Plan: by giving away substantial portions of his wealth and power, the ruler increases his personal sway over others, thereby accruing still more wealth and power: "Section 5: The great kings [of the past] established a perfect standard of power and authority. They brought together those Five Riches, in order to disperse them to their many people. Precisely when you [the ruler] have granted many of the people maximum expressions of favor will you retain maximum power and authority."

The ruler, however, not only binds his subjects to him by gifts, salary, and emoluments. Far more compelling is his suasive example. To his subjects, he announces, "What I love is virtue," knowing his charisma to be supported by the punctilious performance of social duty. To demonstrate his own virtue, the ruler clarifies the impartial standards that are to be uniformly upheld by all in his domain. Once the ruler has demonstrated his own absolute fairness with respect to all his subjects, in this imitating and so honoring high Heaven above, his subjects by a natural symmetry will be more easily persuaded to contribute their finest talents to the state for the betterment of all. In the words of the Plan,

> There should be no oppression of the helpless and lonely, nor should there be any fear of the highly placed and well known. As to those among your men with ability who act properly in their roles, let them advance in their respective endeavors so that their fiefs prosper. In general, once these upright men have a competency [a measure of material security], they will go on to be good. The people will gravitate toward the ruler to the degree that he embodies this standard of public-spiritedness.

Then, quite abruptly, the theoretical section of section 5 in the Great Plan gives way to rhyming couplets extolling the ruler's necessary impartiality:

> *Without predilections, follow the King's Way.*
> *Without aversions, follow the King's road.*
>
> *Being neither partial nor partisan,*
> *The King's Way is smooth and even.*

It is the ruler's fair-mindedness, in other words, that forges that ideal sense of community between ruler and ruled. Insofar as the good ruler acts in compliance with the high lord above, he naturally becomes the focus of the people's adoration on earth below. Acting always as "father and mother" to all his subjects, the good ruler induces his subjects so to identify with him that they come to imitate him. At that point, his subjects both share in and contribute to his glory.

The Great Plan consistently defines true kingship in terms of what is *gong* 公 (meaning what is "just," "public-spirited," and in the best interest of all), in stark contrast to the Five Proclamations, in which the king is said to rule by virtue of his ancestors' charisma and his own filial piety. In the Plan, after all, the king becomes father and mother to each of his subjects. To pattern oneself as *gong* is to set aside short-term personal gain and gratification for the sake of long-range dynastic stability. The motive need not be altruism, but rather the ruler's profound apprehension that only fairness and generosity are likely to evoke loyalty in the subjects on whom his throne depends. Only by acting according to a publicly recognized standard of the common good can the ruler hope to maximize his power and authority, thereby securing his personal goals. To reinforce this claim (not welcome to all rulers), a dramatic parallel is drawn between the unselfishness of the supremely successful ruler and that of high Heaven itself, a parallel well calculated to increase the allure of public-spirited behavior for the average ruler: the ideal ruler and Heaven each graciously allows those below to develop their talents fully so that all may eventually contribute to and partake of the harmonious whole. Only because he has become a byword for equity in his wielding of the instruments of state, including rewards and punishments, is the king able simultaneously to prevent factionalism, promote the public good, and foster the long-range interests of his royal house.

CANON OF YAO (SECOND CENTURY BC?)

The opening lines of the Canon of Yao suggest yet another vision of successful kingship, though the text retains echoes of earlier claims for legitimacy derived from ancestry and the public weal. The chapter begins with a hasty assurance that Emperor Yao qualifies for the post of Son of Heaven by his possession of the more traditional virtues sketched in the Five Proclamations and the Great Plan. Yao has consistently "conformed with antiquity"; and he has appropriately honored distinguished members of the hereditary elite. Consequently he has brought peace to the myriad states in All-under-Heaven. But then the main body of the Canon of Yao ascribes new, extraordinary qualifications to the sage-ruler Yao and his worthy successor, Shun, with the unmistakable implication that these qualities are essential to the success of all future Sons of Heaven. (The chapter's emphasis on these qualifications is unique in the *Documents*.) By its account, Yao and Shun have been able, despite the evil propensities of some of their closest relations, to bring perfect harmony to their inner family circles. The sage-kings Yao and Shun also understand how to order the entire range of cosmic operations, from the astronomical to the musical. And in selecting their successors, Yao and Shun, as upright men of unerring discernment, have each rejected the conventional claims of heredity in favor of the absolute claims of merit. Their readiness to abdicate in favor of meritorious officials, rather than firstborn sons—surely the ultimate expression of the ideal sage-kings' total impartiality, as first enunciated in the Great Plan—brings them rewards never envisioned in the Plan: they attain remarkable longevity (Yao supposedly reigning close to a century) and the sincere devotion of their lowliest subjects, including the birds and beasts, so that the memory of their deeds powerfully affects not only the course of human history but also the cosmic workings. The picture of ideal rule supplied by the Canon of

Yao is, then, at once less paradoxical than that found in the Great Plan (for when the sage-emperors of the Canon of Yao abdicate, they experience real loss), less realistic (for how likely is it that a ruler will reject all family claims in favor of a virtual stranger's greater merit?), and more fantastic (for even the birds and beasts dance with joy in response to their virtuous rule). Meanwhile, the Canon largely ignores the subject of filial piety toward the ancestors, though the whole empire plunges into mourning upon the death of emperors.

The Canon of Yao opens by outlining in clear progression the workings of those qualities considered essential to legitimate rule: inducing order first within one's own extended clan naturally generates perfect order throughout the realm: "Once the Nine Kin [from great-great-grandfather to great-great-grandson] had been brought into harmony, Yao selectively gave marks of distinction to [members of] the Hundred Clans (a term for the most prominent families of the empire), so that they became suitably illustrious. He then brought peace to the myriad vassal states." All of this is related in a single short paragraph, though the link between ordering the family and ordering the state is reiterated several times in the chapter. For example, when sycophantic ministers unctuously assure Emperor Yao that his eldest son is fit to be appointed heir, Emperor Yao bluntly replies, "He is prone to quarrel, so how could he possibly do as heir to the throne?"

As the chapter proceeds, Yao's advisers, in a lengthy speech ostensibly devoted to his family circumstances, introduce the subject of Shun's extraordinary worth:

"There is a bachelor living in a low position whose name is Shun of Yu." The emperor Yao said, "Ah, I have heard of him. What is he like?" The Court Guardian replied, "He is the son of a blind man. His father is stupid; the mother, deceitful. His [half-brother] Xiang is arrogant. Despite all this, Yao has been able to live in harmony with them. By his remarkable filial devotion, he has led his family members to self-government, so that they are no longer obstructive and treacherous." The emperor said, "Let us try him. I will marry my two daughters to him and observe the pattern of his behavior with regard to them."

Clearly the sage-king Yao and his advisers agree that an ability to order one's immediate family circle constitutes the chief qualification for the heroic task of ordering the state. That much is obvious, since Shun, at this point a virtual stranger, has come to the court's attention solely for his ability to bring about good relations with his family of antisocial miscreants. That attainment suggests his superbly honed powers of intuition, of flexible response, and of con-sensus building. Not surprisingly, Shun's first official act as Yao's official heir is to "carefully exemplify the Five Canonical Relations" governing the most significant social interactions, those between ruler and minister, parent and child, husband and wife, elder sibling and younger, friend and friend. This emphasis on the wider significance of ordering the family is corroborated in another *Documents* chapter, which purports to explain Emperor Yao's confidence in Shun's capacity to govern well. Emperor Yao there remarks, "If three virtues are displayed daily, early and late, the man of virtue can regulate and enlighten his family members. If six virtues are practiced daily with a serious, cautious, and respectful attitude, the man can brilliantly conduct the affairs of state."

Much of the remainder of the Canon depicts the decision-making process by which Emperors Yao and Shun assign their most capable officials the tasks of regulating the natural cycles in heaven and on earth. First, the quadrants of the sky are marked off, with each assigned responsibility over specific astronomical movements. Next, a reliable calendar is produced. As most of Yao's subjects are farmers, an accurate calendar facilitating agricultural production is a requirement for dynastic stability. Kingship has been expanded to encompass not just the social world but also the heavens and the earth. For the first time in the *Documents*, good rule must seek to comprehend, influence, and harmonize with the prevailing patterns of the triadic realms of Heaven-Earth-Man. In a magnificent gesture toward this nearly boundless empire, Yao commissions one of his ministers "courteously to receive the rising sun as guest, and to adjust and arrange the labors of spring," in nearly the same language employed to charge the lords of the land to oversee mundane affairs.

Yao's successor, Shun, in his first official act as king rather than designated heir, verifies the movements of the sun, moon, and five visible planets, in order to improve the accuracy of the calendar. Next, Shun has the musical pitch pipes standardized, so that the "spirits and men may be brought into harmony . . . and the Hundred Beasts follow in dance." Emperor Shun then orders his officials to "carefully attend to his grasses and trees, birds and beasts, in the highlands and the lowlands." And through a series of royal progresses to every corner of his empire, he enfolds the outlying areas of All-under Heaven into his domain.

Still more remarkable than the Canon of Yao's expanded vision of empire is its unambiguous assertion of meritocratic over hereditary rule. Meritocracy, the implicit argument suggests, is the highest form of watchful care on behalf of the family and state, in that it makes the state "less the empire of one man than the possession of all." Twice, the chapter shows the reigning Son of Heaven—first Yao and then Shun—selecting his successor from candidates recommended by his senior advisers. In the brief probationary period following their nominations to the throne, the designated successors demonstrate their talents for fostering social harmony. Then, as the newly enthroned Sons of Heaven, they proclaim their determination to consult widely with high officials, so that they may "see with the eyes and hear with the ears of all"; to institute regular bureaucratic procedures that test their subordinates' professional achievements; and to reward (chariots and court regalia are named) and punish officials according to their desserts. Appointments are given to no fewer than twenty-two ministers valued especially for their kindness to colleagues, their eagerness to instruct the people, and their peaceable spirit attuned to the gods and humans. Through regular consultations with such high officers, the model emperor can ensure that reverent and gentle men in office will induce even greater harmony in the empire through their collective suasive example. In this way, the emperor, on the model of Heaven itself, may rule well without much active intervention on his part. As the chapter puts it, "Without the emperor ever once moving from the throne, the empire is well ruled."*

The Canon of Yao chapter ends with a simple statement that Yao and Shun each reigned for more than eighty years. Its closing message is obvious: the wise person who succeeds in living in concert with his fellow humans, near and far, will induce order within not only his immediate circle, but also the microcosm of his physical person and the macrocosm of Heaven-and-Earth. In the making of a sage-king, family background is irrelevant and the ability to create concord is all. As the Confucian *Analects* states, "There is no greatness like that of Heaven, yet Yao could model himself after it. So boundless was it [his extraordinary greatness] that the people could not describe it."

Even so brief a comparison of these portraits of legitimate rule, as defined in the Five Proclamations, Great Plan, and Canon of Yao chapters, suggests the wide range of opinion that evolved on this important topic.† In defining the nature of ideal kingship, five major quandaries emerge, all of which would remain unanswered throughout the course of imperial history: (1) should birth

---

*Two chapters in the *Documents* challenge this model of a noninterventionist ruler. An authentically early *Documents* chapter, Take No Ease (*Wu yi* 無逸), argues that the good king must work as hard in his own sphere as his subjects do in theirs. The late Tribute of Yu (*Yugong* 禹貢) chapter portrays the sage Yu, then only an official, not yet an emperor, according to traditions, working hard to shape the configuration and boundaries of the empire. The "Great Commentary" to the *Changes*, I will argue in chapter 5, also emphasizes the interventionist aspects of sagehood.

†Popular legends, some recorded in the apocrypha, associate all the protagonists of the foregoing *Documents* chapters—Yao and Shun in the Canon of Yao, Yu and Jizi in the Great Plan, and the Duke of Zhou in the Five Proclamations—with shamanic rule. In shamanic rule, the king's main function is to contact the gods directly on behalf of his subjects, through ritual invocations and dances and through animal intermediaries, rather than through more routine methods like formal divination and regular consultation with senior advisers.

or merit determine succession? (2) how and to what degree should the ruler be unselfish, even self-abnegating, so as to enhance the common good and the royal power? (3) to what extent must the king master the extrasocietal resources of Heaven-and-Earth? (4) to what extent must he look to omens to guide his behavior? and (5) what is the correct use of punishments in a just state?

On the issue of hereditary rule versus meritocracy, there is no question that the main speaker of the Five Proclamations, the Duke of Zhou, assumes that the former subsumes the latter. The Zhou ruling house has acquired the throne in Heaven's acknowledgment of his ancestors' efforts. Not to build upon and extend the ancestors' foundation would be that most heinous of crimes, unfiliality. The Great Plan is entirely silent on the question, either because hereditary rule was still the norm at the time of its composition or (to the contrary) because hereditary rule as an institution was contested. Still, the Plan's repeated injunctions to the ruler to exemplify fairness send a veiled warning to the hereditary ruler to take special care, lest his rule appear doubly arbitrary, in practice as well as in origin. The Canon of Yao, however, openly rejects hereditary rule, advancing meritorious conduct as the only criterion for succession. Political theorists, then, could justify quite a range of notions on the subject of succession by reference to one or another *Documents* chapter.

All three chapters stress that the ruler's compliant conduct strengthens community cohesion, though they differ in the motives they adduce for such magnanimity, according to the community they address. The Proclamations would have rulers conform to the splendid model established by the clan ancestors, so that the king's men conform also; the Plan reasons that equity and liberality enhance the common people's devotion to the throne, which ultimately increases the ruler's power and authority; the Canon talks of just rule mandated by the cosmic powers and harmony among the myriad things consonant with Heaven's will. (The *Documents* chapter Take No Ease (*Wuyi*) may urge the ruler to work so sedulously that he allows himself no time for excursions or hunts, but nowhere in the *Documents* is asceticism ever valued for its own sake. The noble man "intends to have no pleasurable ease" lest he forget the manifold sufferings of his ordinary subjects. Unless the ruler has some experience of toil, he risks undervaluing and so alienating his subjects, who may then drive him from the throne.)

In its preoccupation with the ruler's moral orientation, the Five Proclamations gives only limited consideration to the more material resources of empire. Presumably, so long as an emperor heeds the will of the dead ancestors and of Heaven, as revealed in divination and in the good counsel of senior family members, good rule and therefore good harvests will ensue. Active husbanding of the empire's physical resources is unnecessary, in part because the gods in heaven control the harvests and the weather. Anthropomorphic Heaven hearkens to the other ancestors; it issues orders. Given Heaven's personal interest in the ruling circle and its policies, central government is essentially a matter of engaging the loyalties of the "right men"—those qualified by noble birth to be Heaven's kin—and placing them in office. A single reference speaks of "economizing the products of the soil," a second of trade, though managers are to be appointed in the outlying districts to oversee defense, animal husbandry, and the like. In contrast, in the much later Great Plan, consideration of the material resources of the empire starts to supersede in importance the securing of spiritual resources in the form of the ancestors' blessings. At the same time, the emphasis has shifted from keeping the loyalty of the right men within the extended family circle to the task of finding capable advisers outside the family circle. By the time of the Canon of Yao a few centuries later, the proper ordering of material resources has become a still more important aspect of good governance, not merely (as in the Great Plan) because such resources are necessary to maintain an expanded empire but, more crucially, because their proper management accords with the sublime cosmic order exemplified by the perfect symmetries of the astronomical, musical, and mathematical realms.

On the subject of portents, the fourth century BC Great Plan, not surprisingly in light of its dating, represents an intermediate stage between the earlier Five Proclamations and later Canon of Yao chapters. The Plan explicitly instructs the ruler to watch for ominous reactions registered in Heaven-and-Earth (especially the starry signs in the sky) as possible checks on royal policy. In the decision-making process, however, omens seem far less important in the Great Plan than either direct communication with the unseen world through divination or consultation with the ministers and knights. The Great Plan king, in devising his policies, has not yet learned to consult first and foremost the models presented by the patterned operations of the cosmos. Only with the second century BC Canon of Yao will the smooth running of the cosmic operations to a large degree replace Heaven and the ancestors as the immutable basis for a just order balancing hierarchy with reciprocity.

Inevitably, as the scope of his imagined empire expands, the ideal king's responsibilities swell in number and in magnitude, always reaching beyond current exigencies to visions of greater powers, verging on the godlike. Thus, the locus of concern in the *Documents* abruptly moves from a preoccupation with a small circle of clansmen in genuinely early Western Zhou texts to a vast empire imagined in mid-Eastern Zhou to fully articulated dreams of a well-ordered universe around the time of unification under Qin. In keeping with the comparatively circumscribed sway of good rule in early Western Zhou, the Five Proclamations show the early Zhou rulers struggling with the most basic political problems: bureaucratic double-dealing and incompetence, the court's regrettable tendency to overindulge in wine at state ceremonies, the treacherous defection of putative friends and allies. Centuries later, the Great Plan has ideal rulers managing to elicit from virtual strangers their very best efforts, while the still later Canon of Yao shows the sage-kings magically adjusting the calendar, calibrating the musical system, and divining the very deepest mysteries of the cosmos, including the unseen hearts and domestic arrangements of men—all without the aid of oracles. So while the Five Proclamations depict the early Zhou rulers confronting ordinary difficulties, the latest *Documents* chapters tell of omniscient demigods whose absolutely correct moral orientation impels the very workings of the universe, offering a past that is more abstracted and thus more difficult to apply as model.

This transition from human to superhuman can also be traced in the *Documents'* discussion of the place of punishments in the ideal state. Though the earliest block of chapters in the *Documents*, the Five Proclamations, devotes relatively little discussion to the topic, its arguments inform all subsequent treatments of the role of law in a just society (limited to penal law) in this important sense: the Proclamations identify the wrongdoer's intention as the single most important criterion to be used in judging the relative weightiness of any crime. Even minor crimes, if committed intentionally, may merit the death penalty, while major crimes, if committed inadvertently, are to be pardoned. (The radical nature of the *Documents'* implicit calls for revision to the standard penal codes becomes evident when comparisons are made with the detailed criminal procedures attested for late Warring States, Qin, and Han by such new finds as Shuihudi and Zhangjiashan.) Given the severity of certain punishments, which range from heavy fines to mutilation and death, the Five Proclamations naturally instruct the true king to determine guilt or innocence with care. In assessing the merits of a case, the true king must ignore his personal feelings. He must also examine his conscience to see that the blame is not his for having failed to provide his people with the requisite moral example. Only after lengthy deliberations does the king dare to announce his verdict and, acting in Heaven's name, mete out justice.

The Five Proclamations presume that even the best of kings will need to resort to penal law in the course of ruling his domain. But many of the most serious crimes listed in the Five Proclamations chapters—including sibling rivalry and disrespect to family heads or to dead ancestors—are not crimes at all under the modern legal system. Obviously, the Zhou elite believed it to be in their state's best interests to encourage family harmony, since the Zhou king ruled in coalition with his close kin. The Great Plan chapter then modifies the legitimate role of punishments in the just state in one crucial respect, seeing punishments, like rewards, as important tools in social engineering, even if they are admittedly less effective in altering human behavior than the king's suasive example reinforced by grants-in-aid. All the same, the Great Plan is bold enough to suggest that the need for punishments will be all but obviated under a good king's influence, except for the most recalcitrant malefactors. By the later Canon of Yao, the Plan's bold invention is taken for granted; punishments no longer appear as an ordinary, if secondary tool of good government. Decisive action on the part of the Canon's sage-kings, resulting in the exile or execution of a few powerful evildoers, leads to a state of Great Peace in which "all the world"—even the birds and beasts—joyously submits to imperial rule. As a result, mutilating punishments fall into disuse because mere "images" (symbols? characters? pictures?) put on the clothing of criminals are enough to induce the requisite shame and repentance, given the heightened moral awareness throughout the state.

Their divergent views on the role of punishment in government notwithstanding, the *Documents* chapters generally agree that punitive measures should play a lesser role in government. The famous Punishments of Lü chapter (composed ca. 550 BC) ostensibly makes punishment its main subject, but punishments actually play a subordinate role in the text, as compared with three other themes weaving all the disparate *Documents* accounts together: the theme of virtue as a balance between incommensurate goods, that of the good ruler's reliance upon rhetorical skills, and that of the "secret [that is, self-effacing] virtue" of top officials—themes that also take center stage in the oft-quoted Counsels of Gao Yao, Pan Geng, and Metal Coffer chapters of the *Documents*, respectively. Ironically, the most complete statement on punishments preserved in the *Documents*, the Punishments of Lü, is dedicated to the proposition that the best ruler governs primarily through suasive virtue, rather than punishment. The reigning king of Lü, one learns from the chapter, did not even devise a penal code for his state "to control the people of the four quarters," fearing that an overreliance on punishment would cause the common people to "set their hearts no more on good faith, and violate oaths and covenants," the old-fashioned, personally contracted obligations between members of society. The text concedes that even the good ruler, who principally relies upon ritual and suasive example, may occasionally need to punish. Still, the vast majority of people can be counted upon to behave well, so long as the ruling elite sets the tone in the state, acting ever with "compassion and reverence."

In this phrase, "with compassion and reverence," are two complementary virtues. Compassion requires empathy with equals and inferiors, and reverence, respect and honor toward superiors. Implicit is the notion that the finest virtue represents a delicate balance between such conventional virtues. Quite familiar to readers of Aristotle's *Nicomachean Ethics*, this notion appears in many

Documents chapters but most memorably in the Counsels of Gao Yao. The chapter opens with Gao Yao, an official of Yu the sage-king, describing the criteria for exemplary rulers and officials. The ideal is to be "broad-minded yet cautious; gentle yet steadfast; frank in speech yet dignified in manner; authoritative yet reverent; bold yet compliant; straightforward yet mild; simple yet precise; firm yet trustworthy; strong yet dutiful." "Whoever shows that he has these virtues constantly within him may be considered fortunate indeed!" Such happy persons are sure to extend their good fortune to others, for when government employs them in its service, "The Hundred Officials act as teachers for one another [so exemplary are they], and the Hundred Tasks are accomplished in a timely fashion, conforming with the planetary movements, so that the many achievements are all consolidated." Thus, if a few key members of the ruling elite can be persuaded by the ruler's example to undertake the rigorous course of self-cultivation required to achieve this superb balance in speech and action (for formal speech is understood throughout the *Documents* as a performative act), the entire bureaucracy and gradually the empire at large will begin to perfect itself as well.

This continual stress on suasive example, if it is not to verge on the mystical, imputes excellent rhetorical techniques to those who govern, though the ideal sage-rulers and officials who appear in the *Documents* chapters display no special pride in their forensic skills. In the three-part Pan Geng chapter, the good Shang king of the title appears as accomplished speaker; by turns reasoning with, cajoling, and threatening his men, Pan Geng displays each and every possible form of conventional rhetoric (chain syllogisms and arguments by analogy, appeals to antique precedents, and to the authority of the gods) before he finally persuades his people to move the capital to a more suitable location (fig. 11). As the *Documents* tells us,

> Pan Geng would have had them move [the new capital] to Yin, but the people refused to go there to make their dwellings. Like a true leader, Pan Geng summoned the leaders of the multitudes, and then, as if he were one of the family, he issued a straightforward proclamation:
>> Our former kings came here, and had their homes built on this spot. As they attached great importance to our people, there were no executions under them. Now we find ourselves unable to sustain ourselves in this location. I have divined by the turtle, examined the result, and find the spirits to be in accord [with my plan to move].

When this appeal to divine sanction fails, Pan Geng cites the suitable historical precedent for his plan:

Figure 11. Pan Geng leading his people out to the new capital site. From Sun Jian'ai, *Shujing tushuo*, 747.

The former kings in their tenure reverently attended to the commands of Heaven. Still, they did not always experience peace during their reigns. Nor did they always retain their capital cities. Up to now, there have been five capitals already [in Shang]. If we do not now continue on in the old way [moving the capital when necessary], we would be ignoring the possibility that Heaven may cut off our mandate to rule. . . . Just as a fallen tree has its new shoots, so Heaven will prolong our mandate in a new capital city.

When he finds his people still unmoved by these appeals to divine will and to historical precedent, Pan Geng extends his arguments by analogy, hoping to convince his people that they ought to rely on his good judgment: "Consider the net, which remains orderly and untangled only if it rests on the lead-rope. Consider the farmer, who gets his crop only if he works tirelessly in the fields." When all the initial arguments prove fruitless, Pan Geng in his exasperation tries to rally support for his proposed move by conducting a series of informal seminars with various groups, starting with the high officers and ending with the "small people," a term that presumably refers to those in the lowest government positions. More than once the king asserts that his sole motive is the strong desire to help his officials secure a better life: "[When I see you resist this move,] I seem to be watching a great conflagration that will consume you. Yet I had only planned to the best of my abilities to make it comfortable for you." Reiterating that his interests are identical to theirs, he points to the pattern of cooperation that has prevailed for generations between the ruling house and its lateral branches: "For our former kings shared ease and toil with your grandfathers and fathers. . . . Anciently our former rulers toiled for your grandfathers and fathers. You are all my people, whom I intend to sustain."

Pan Geng then announces that he has forgiven his men for their recalcitrance; he himself is to blame for his failure to provide sufficient leadership. Even the opposition leaders he solemnly pardons, saying, "I will not put the guilt on all of you." In return for this free "disclosure of his mind," however, he expects his closest advisers and kinsmen to report fully on "anything that the small people say in remonstrance," on the grounds that he may profit from their frank counsels. Pan Geng intends to persuade his subordinates to express their anxieties about the proposed move freely to him, that he may better dispel them. At the same time, he commands them not to whisper among themselves, lest ill-founded rumors cloud their perceptions of the true situation. With consummate skill, Pan Geng anticipates his listeners' every objection, the better to orchestrate their every response, until in the end his men find themselves accepting the move of the capital with "one heart and mind."

If the Pan Geng chapter shows the value of rhetorical skill to good government, the Metal Coffer chapter shows that wise officials exemplifying "secret virtue" nonetheless constitute the single greatest asset available to rulers. Like the Pan Geng chapter, the Metal Coffer chapter immediately engages readers' attention because it thrusts them into the middle of yet another political crisis. This time it is not the stubborn elite who refuse to change their ways and move the capital; this time the problem is the severe illness of good King Wu shortly after the Zhou conquest, and the youth and immaturity of his heir. Will the great enterprise embarked on by the new government in conformity with the ancestors survive if King Wu dies? or will the enemies of the new regime seize the opportunity to usurp the throne? To find out, the exemplary Duke of Zhou, King Wu's brother, constructs an altar to the ancestors. There, facing north in the position of a supplicant, he beseeches the most illustrious of his ancestors—a group that includes his father, King Wen—to allow him to die instead of King Wu. The Duke of Zhou's prayer, a masterpiece of rhetorical skill, then details the many reasons the ancestors would do better to accept him as ritual scapegoat. The Duke of Zhou claims, for instance, that he would make a finer personal attendant for the gods and ghosts because he commands considerably greater "talents and arts" than his elder brother King Wu. In addition, the ancestors are more likely to receive their sacrifices without interruption if they leave King Wu securely on his throne, for the people, who sincerely love and revere King Wu, would surely be distraught at his death. As he, the Duke of Zhou, is less highly regarded on earth, his demise is unlikely to occasion the extravagant outpourings of grief that might disturb the regular schedule of offerings made to the ancestors. The Duke of Zhou ends by promising that rich gifts will be given to the ancestors if only they accede to his prayers. But he does not hesitate to threaten that a denial of his heartfelt prayers will lead to the suspension of the sacrificial offerings that sustain them so comfortably in the afterlife.

When King Wu was restored to health by this marvelously ingenious prayer, the written transcript of the duke's prayers was supposedly stored away for safekeeping in a metal strongbox. Years later, when the duke, acting as regent for King Wu's successor, reluctantly took up arms to quell a rebellion led by his ambitious brothers, his campaign was widely misinterpreted as the first step toward usurpation. When the inexperienced king failed to recognize the rumors as slander, the good duke with admirable fortitude never tried to defend himself; instead he suffered the royal disfavor in silence, for to apprise the young king of his grievous error would be to show him up for a fool. Moreover, the duke enjoined all witnesses never to reveal his magnanimous act. It was only when the metal strongbox containing the transcript was opened for an unrelated reason that the duke's noble intentions were discovered and his name finally

In these chapters, the king's men and his people are synonymous with Heaven's men and people, for they are the ruling elite, related by birth to the ancestors in heaven. In relation to his clansmen, the early Western Zhou king stood as *primus inter pares*, not as absolute autocrat, for his inner circle (*qimin* 其民) represented the aggregate power of the ruling lineage bolstered through blood ties with the sacred ancestors residing in Heaven. In attending to the advice proffered by his relatives, living and dead, the king merely acknowledged a fundamental truth: his legitimacy depended upon the consent of his close family members and the sanction of the ancestors, which rested in large part upon his treatment of them.

Over succeeding centuries, however, the two terms *ren* 人 and *min* 民 gradually broadened in meaning, until they came to refer to all humans and all commoners, respectively. This linguistic extension was operative by the fifth century BC, for in discussions attributed to the Master and rival thinkers, the good ruler was expected to consider the needs and feelings of those well outside his inner circle. Later, in the Warring States period, the classicists and the Mohists, applauded or condemned for their slogan "Employ the Worthy!", took the terms *ren* and *min* to refer to even the lowliest of the king's subjects, the poor fuel and fodder gatherers, to whose advice the king, on the model of impartial Heaven, hearkened. Moreover, they quite anachronistically projected their reinterpretation onto earliest antiquity. As a result, the statement "Heaven hears and sees as the people see and hear"—the most widely quoted line in the Counsels of Gao Yao chapter, which was itself the most widely quoted of all *Documents* chapters in the pre-Qin period—was taken to mean that great power had always been invested in the collective will of the common people (reflecting Heaven's will), which could determine the fate of the ruler and his ruling house, if only through the potential for mass uprisings.

This late Warring States version of Tianming had incalculably great implications for the course of later Chinese history, perhaps the most far-reaching being the notion that Heaven had sanctioned the history of the entire Chinese people for the entire Chinese past. Equally significant was the kind of history the accumulated *Documents* traditions had constructed for the chosen people of this superior civilization. Many twentieth-century readers, predisposed to think in Enlightenment and post-Enlightenment modes about the merits of representative democracy, are apt to overlook the deep concern evinced in the *Documents* and *Odes* traditions for the full elicitation and representation of the people's will. The relevant *Documents* texts are clear. The ruler has an obligation to seek out the opinions of his people and to consider these in his evaluations of court officials or political policies; he even has precedents enjoining him to raise commoners of proven worth to the very highest ranks. Patently, the popular will is to be drawn into policy making, even if the precise techniques for doing this seem alien, vague, and inadequate, as they are rarely described in the *Documents* in sufficient legalistic detail to satisfy the modern bias in favor of constitutional protections.* No less an authority than Confucius had pointedly rejected any administration that ruled primarily by law, fearing the propensity of "mean men," among whom he numbered many of high rank, to reduce written law to the letter and thereby oppress the people. Moreover, as the Chinese traditions attached to the *Documents* evolved, they continually stressed the links between the common people's economic welfare, their political understanding, and the ruler's ultimate strength, unlike Enlightenment tradition, which assumes a sharp underlying opposition between the interests of the people and those of the state.

It would be unwise, then, for modern readers to scoff at the *Documents* traditions that envision empathetic patrimonial rulers committed to providing for their subjects a measure of material security in the form of food, housing, clothing, and community as well as moral instruction. Repeatedly, the *Documents* insists that the ordinary person whose basic material needs remain unsatisfied can never be "led to virtue." That insistence may help to explain why so many literate Chinese in the mid–twentieth century made a connection between the traditional learning espoused in classicism and the talk of social democracy to be found in the early writings of Mao Zedong; also, why so many scholars continue to characterize the dominant cultures of imperial China as humanistic or human-centered, despite the inordinate importance that Chinese of all classes have tended to ascribe to the gods and to fate. Certainly the later chapters in the Modern Script *Documents*—those more often quoted, being easier to understand—implied that good rulers need not, except in extreme crisis, trouble the inhabitants of the other world with their questions, for the ruler can easily gather all the information required to formulate and implement effective policy simply by consulting his subjects and observing their behavior—what the Confucian master Xunzi liked to call "human portents."

---

*The so-called British constitution is the name given to an unwritten set of customary arrangements and precedents; also, there are a number of variant models implicit in the vaguely federal-democratic institutions thought of as Western. The presuppositions behind the U.S. Constitution do not, for example, accord particularly well with Jean-Jacques Rousseau's idea of "la volonté générale." The complex relation between American constitutional interpretations and Protestant faith in the Bible, as outlined by Sanford Levinson in his *Constitutional Faith* (Princeton: Princeton University Press, 1988), suggests that the parallel relation between the Five Classics' interpretive traditions and modern Chinese law is not amenable to easy definition either.

FROM DISCONTINUOUS HISTORY TO
CONTINUOUS CIVILIZATION

Those *Documents* chapters that describe early Western Zhou, following the conquest of Shang, uniformly insist upon the ruler's duty to care for his men and
his people (that is, his close supporters and allies). According to these chapters,
it had been the last Shang king's twisted pleasure in torturing his high officials,
many of them blood relatives, that brought on his dynasty's demise. Hence the
delight expressed in the genuinely early *Documents* chapters, as in the early
bronze inscriptions, at the Zhou king's success in "punishing the evil men" who
had destroyed their own. But as we have seen, by late Eastern Zhou, centuries
after the Zhou conquest, the powerful notion of Heaven's commands or mandates (Tianming)—which by late Western Han would become the very center-
piece of Ru theories on political legitimacy—had been evolving in directions
that prompted reinterpretations.* To later classicists considering the *Documents*
in light of the *Mencius*, the canon offered a gratifying sense of a strong, cohesive Central States community, "all the way down from the Son of Heaven to
the commoner," stretching back into a distant past, and sustained by exemplary
rulers and officials displaying notable courage, temperance, and fortitude in their
lives.† Classicists advocating the Confucian ethical traditions could further
rejoice in the inherent justice of the imperial system, in which the right of the
very least of China's subjects to rebel against cruel or unjust rulers was guaranteed by Heaven itself.

Still, additional textual support was necessary to convince skeptics in the first
and second centuries BC that the inhabitants of the Central States area had long
enjoyed such marks of Heaven's signal favor, not only as the oldest continuous
civilization on earth, but also as the most materially advanced and culturally
progressive. Teachers of the time accordingly added at least five components to

---

*Recent work-in-progress by Michael Loewe shows that it is only in late Western Han
(not in early Zhou, as hitherto thought) that there exists the full-blown Mandate of Heaven
(Tianming) theory whereby Heaven oversees the course of dynastic cycles, insuring that
the ruling houses' rises and falls reflect precisely the degree to which the throne conforms
with standards of virtue.

†Some modern scholars believe that members of the ruling elite in imperial China never
much noticed, let alone emphasized, the idea that the Mandate of Heaven permits rebellion in extreme circumstances. They believe it was principally the nineteenth- and twentieth-century Euro-American challenges to China that inspired the determined search for
indigenous sources of suitably modern political thought. But this is to ignore multiple references to the "right of rebellion" in the Classics and their associated traditions (e.g., in the
Mencius and *Xunzi*) as well as the famous instances in which emperors sought to expurgate
those references.

the *Documents* traditions in order to convert its accounts of "discontinuous" and "slow" events within the geographic boundaries of empire into a single history of prodigious length and incomparable worth:

1. They saw to it that the Tribute of Yu chapter was included in the Fu Sheng version of the *Documents*, thereby projecting several millennia into the past an ideal, centralized Chinese rule over suitably vast territories.

2. They devised a single Preface to the *Documents* (which in some editions was interleaved by chapters) designed to join the chapters in a single, continuous history, in part by asserting the direct transmission of political and moral knowledge from dynasty to dynasty.

3. Beginning with the famous "Great Commentary" attributed to master Fu Sheng of early Western Han, they composed commentaries to the *Documents* to interrelate discrete stories within the classic. This contributed to the illusion of one smooth narrative in the political-moral history of the Central States empires, while diverting attention from the many contradictions among chapters.

4. They invented elaborate connections between historical cycles and genealogical affinities, so as to account for apparent disjunctions between different models of just political rule, thereby weaving all of the past—dating not merely from the legendary Xia, but from the Yellow Emperor at the dawn of time—into one whole whose seamless integrity was ensured both by anthropomorphic Heaven and by the cosmic processes.

5. In apocrypha and supplementary traditions attached to the *Documents* canon (conflated with the canon proper until Song), they remythologized the historical vignettes preserved in the *Documents* (some of which had once represented meticulously demythologized versions of local legends), so as to reassert the guiding presence of Heaven, fate, or biology throughout the entire course of history.[*]

---

[*] Readers will recall that the opening four-character phrase of the *Documents*, which was expected to give a historical context for the early reign of Yao, provoked an outpouring of exegesis amounting to some three hundred thousand phrases. Chinese literati, it need hardly be said, found the commentarial narratives gratifying to read and to write, since they were the single group that could reasonably claim credit for acting as responsible custodians of the grand tradition, in courageous resistance to the modernists, who questioned the wisdom of using past models to guide the present. The sanctity of history in China, in other words, provided the single best proof of the sanctity of those who devoted their lives and careers to transmitting, propagating, and appreciating that sacred history. As teachers, statesmen, historians, and exemplary leaders of communities, the literati perceived themselves and were perceived as latter-day Dukes of Zhou.

A brief review of each of these five related phenomena will suggest that the aggregate effect of historical interpolations, reworkings, and impositions has been to create a deep pride in an age-old, enduring Chinese culture. This pride has been based on the eminently simple calculation that history encompasses the collective wisdom of all the living and dead, so that the longest continuous history must by definition be the best, affording its inheritors the greatest access to civilization. If empire is a habit of mind, a presumption of vast resources, then the habit of empire in the Central States has been above all this presumption of uniquely rich chronological and human resources empowering the Chinese people throughout their history.

The current Preface to the *Documents* (a late work, despite its pious attribution to Confucius), in specifying a historical context for each chapter, aims to weave successive chapters into a single, continuous narrative. A typical example, the preface for the Proclamation at Luo, states, "When the Duke of Shao had first examined the site, the Duke of Zhou went to construct Chengzhou [the capital]. Having sent someone to report on the divinations [used prior to siting the capital], he then composed the 'Proclamation at Luo.'" Here the preface connects the Proclamation at Luo chapter (*Luo gao*) with the chapter that immediately precedes it, the Proclamation at Shao (*Shao gao*). In a few instances, however, the preface relates inherently unconnected events spanning much longer periods. For instance, the part of the Preface assigned to the Great Plan says, "When King Wu conquered Yin [= Shang], he slew the last, bad ruler of Shang. He appointed Wugeng to office. Then he got the Viscount of Ji [Jizi] to swear fealty and make the 'Great Plan.'" Such prefatory remarks almost imperceptibly but effectively tie Shang and Zhou rule to the sage-rulers of the legendary pre-Xia period mentioned in the opening passage of the Great Plan proper; taken together, the preface and chapter replace the presumption of a sharp break occasioned by military conquest with the implicit claim that moral-political knowledge has passed smoothly from one dynasty to another under Heaven's perpetual protection.

At far greater length than the Preface, early commentarial traditions attached to the *Documents*, beginning with the so-called Great Commentary 大傳 attributed to Fu Sheng, succeeded in weaving all known Chinese events into a single, progressive, yet ultrastable narrative. Like the Preface, Fu Sheng's work (dated ca. 150 BC, except for later interpolations) forges links between chapters that do not appear to be contiguous in the current arrangement of the *Documents*, the better to verify the existence of major continuities throughout the entire course of Central States civilization in China. Even the extant fragments of the Great Commentary show it going further than the Preface to link chapters whose contents have little ostensible connection. For instance, the Great Commentary relates the Canon of Shun chapter (attributed to the pre-Xia era) to the Great Plan chapter (attributed to early Western Zhou), though their only tenuous connection is the flood-queller Yu, who makes a brief appearance in both chapters. In essence, the Great Commentary seeks radically to expand the scope of the *Documents* both in time and in space, so as to convince readers that an advanced civilization has existed under Heaven's blessing from time immemorial in China. To flesh out this assertion, the Great Commentary draws into its discussion many rulers said to have reigned some two millennia before Yao (the legendary ruler whose reign begins the *Documents*), figures of myth like the Yellow Emperor (Huangdi), progenitor of the entire Chinese race; the Fire Maker (Suiren), inventor of fire; the Animal Tamer (Fu Xi), inventor of the *Changes'* Eight Trigrams; and the Divine Farmer (Shennong, inventor of sedentary agriculture). These figures, despite their roles as antique culture-heroes, are in no way differentiated from less "primitive" or bureaucratic-minded rulers of more recent times.

In fact, every passage in Fu Sheng's Great Commentary consistently attests to the fundamentally unchanging character of Central States civilization. Despite temporary reverses under bad rulers, the main features of the Central States cultures have been and must be preserved at all costs. Hence the Great Commentary's insistence on harsh punishments for those who in any way alter the ancient systems of rites and music or the ancient political institutions (thus confirming the utility of classicists in service to the state), notwithstanding the dominant pre-Han assumption among leading Confucian masters that some change was both inevitable and proper. By following Fu Sheng's commentary, one could reduce immense shifts in history to the status of temporary or illusory phenomena, for the Commentary attributed such shifts to the intersection of events with the troughs or crests produced by at least three concurrent cycles governing all history, cycles whose complex interactions might mask or heighten existing tendencies and trends. To the Five Phases theory of cycles first promoted in the late Warring States period, the Great Commentary added two additional concurrent cycles: a dyadic cycle, in which a refinement mode (*wen*) alternates with a substantial (*zhi*), and a triadic cycle ruled in turn by phases labeled as red, black, or white.

Later Han thinkers delighted in elaborating these constructed cycles, seeing in them a framework that would make history more cohesive and more intelligible. Successive elaborations allowed the conservative Han juridical expert Ying Shao (d. AD 203), for example, to suggest that every Chinese person was of royal blood, as all were direct descendants of the Five Lords engendered by the Five Phases, who had set the patterns for the sublime Central States civilization in the archaic period. By this view, chronology and genealogy, no less than geography, had joined to produce the singular greatness of the empire. In extrapolating from the core *Documents* stories backward and forward in time, this framework tended to view particular human events in terms of a larger divine history. And once the *Documents* had become part of the state-sponsored canon of the Five Classics, it was nearly inevitable that more and longer commentaries would be composed—and not merely because such commentaries had to supply the rhetorical justification for all policy changes, addressing a wide range of problems, particularly in the related fields of astronomy, geography, and politics. The *Documents* commentaries had moreover to supply highly complicated, even tortuous, explanations in order to weave separate chapters into a single sacred history. If successive generations of Chinese readers were to be completely satisfied in their yearnings for a larger identity outside themselves, the *Documents* had to be seen to correlate all the relevant sources perfectly. Only a massive exegetical outpouring could dispel all conceivable doubts about the general reliability of this most romantic notion of a continuous history stretching well back into the archaic past. (This illustrates Clifford Geertz's contention that a commentary is merely a story that a certain people relates to itself about what it means to be that people.)

Ironically, then, the same exemplary sage-kings and officials who had once been stripped of their overtly mythological qualities, so that they might appear as more relevant models for rulers and bureaucrats in the *Documents* canon, were subjected time and again to remythologizing. Given the *Documents'* monumental authority, this kind of remythologizing was bound to occur often, sometimes quite consciously. In AD 1, for example, during the reign of the "usurper" Wang Mang, a group of people claiming to be descendants of the ancient Yueshang traveled to court to present in tribute a white pheasant, in a solemn recreation of an event recorded in the *Documents*. As they could reasonably expect rewards and recognition from Wang Mang, who was known for his love of archaic models, both Wang and the tribute presenters in curious collusion invested a straightforward political act with mythological significance. This one example suggests that variations on ancient myths would be implicated in every search for metaphorical equivalence between past and present, sacred and mundane—in teaching (the presumably sober transmission of exemplary models worthy of emulation) and in entertainment (the telling of heroic tales). Remythologizing, conscious or not, was the best way to make the charismatic power of those exemplary figures come alive, especially to those not fully socialized into traditions about the past because of their youth, ignorance, or emotional immaturity.

Hence the didactic tale of young King Cheng, in which the king, then a young boy under the supervision of the exemplary regent the Duke of Zhou, plays in the courtyard with the Duke of Shao. Partly to boast but partly in jest, the king recited the formula bestowing the rank of baron upon his playmate. Next, to give a suitable flourish, he confirmed the appointment with a token in the form of a fallen sycamore leaf. A palace attendant who had witnessed this charming scene happened to report it to the Duke of Zhou. The good duke was not amused, however; he chided the young king for not realizing that his word must ever be his bond. Before the day was out, the Duke of Shao was duly raised to the rank of baron and endowed with a large fief commensurate with that high rank. Like many an excellent story, this one contains not a shred of historical truth: King Cheng was probably in his teens when he assumed the throne, too old for such childish pranks. And the Duke of Shao was the king's elderly uncle and guardian, not his boyhood playmate. Even so, there can be no finer illustration of the gentleman's solemn duty to keep his word than this sycamore leaf tale; enclosing a core of emotional truth in an unforgettable vignette, the tale was included in many an anthology read by teachers and students alike. (The requirement that history stick to relating what happened rather than what historical figures would have said and done if only they had had sufficient presence of mind is a relatively recent invention, one whose feasibility has rightly been challenged by the postmodernists.)

In many cases, of course, the remythologizing impulse has seemed calculated more to entertain than to edify. Popular accounts ("popular" meaning widely appealing to the literate and illiterate alike) could hardly resist the temptation to embroider the moral messages contained in the *Documents*. In one anecdote drawn from the apocrypha, Yu, the hero-protagonist of the Tribute of Yu chapter, appears as scion of the White God of the skies. Nine feet tall, with a tiger's snout and a bird's beak, the marvelous Yu receives from a stranger with a fish's body (who finally reveals himself as the Lord of the Yellow River) a divine commission to traverse all "Under Heaven," pacing and marking and shaping its sacred geography.

Somewhere between the parables like that of the sycamore leaf and the utterly fantastic tales like that of the zoomorphic Yu lie the only slightly less incredible stories about the superhuman heroes of the distant past. Traditions associated with the *Documents* so successfully reimagined the sober accounts of political legitimacy presented in the original *Documents* that spin-offs of the *Documents'* stories continue to inform popular literature and film even to the present. One of the best instances of this perennial impulse to remythologize the *Documents* is the Ming novel *Romance of Enfeoffing the Gods* (*Fengshen yanyi* 封神演義, now available in an English translation entitled *Creation of the Gods*). For its plot, the *Romance* takes the greatest story ever told in China, the dissolution of the Shang dynasty and the founding of its successor state, whose institutions and ethics supposedly set the pattern for all subsequent civilization in China. Not only do these events form the subject of the single largest block of chapters in the *Documents*, but they raise the great political question about man's role in relation

Figure 12. Woodblock print depicting the defeat of the wicked last Shang emperor by the forces of good, who use an evil-averting Eight Trigrams. From *Creation of the Gods*, trans. Gu Zhizhong (Beijing: New World Press, 1992), 1:242.

to the Heaven's mandates: in altering the course of history, what part is played by the gods and what by humans? The *Documents*, in answering this question, forgoes scenes of court audiences and battlefields for less dramatic scenes of filial piety, fortitude, fairness, and perseverance, with the result that the *Documents* upsets expectations raised by the great epic tales of Greece or India (fig. 12).

Readers will recall what the *Documents* traditions say: the last ruler of the Shang so abused his authority that one of his most faithful vassals, a certain King Wu (the Martial King) finally rebelled, despite the exemplary loyalty displayed by Wu's father, King Wen (the Civil King), who had served as Western Protector. The Shang tyrant had reportedly committed a host of crimes, motivated by sadism, drunkenness, and a slavish desire to please his perverse wife, Daji. But all these notorious crimes, according to the *Documents*, paled in comparison with his signal failure to appoint and keep good advisers. King Wu, in contrast, took pains to attract good men to his cause, having learned the ways of his father, the charismatic King Wen. Thus it was not King Wu's military superiority that finally carried the day but his surpassing authority. True victory for Heaven above and the people below resided in the solemn promise made after the conquest to always "employ those worthy of employment and to respect those worthy of respect."

That spare, sober account in the *Documents* evidently failed to satisfy all demands for a glorious antiquity. For the *Romance*, though it skillfully inserts materials drawn from the *Documents* into its narrative, portrays this same Shang–Zhou transition in startlingly different colors, viewing it as a single dramatic episode in the eternal struggle of rival factions among the gods and superhuman heroes for ultimate control over the supremely hallowed ground of the realm. The pretext for this particular renewal of hostilities, as readers soon discover, is a single ritual fault committed by the last Shang king, who quite inadvertently insults the goddess Nü Wa on her birthday. Nü Wa takes revenge by introducing a fox sprite into the royal palace in the guise of a seductive beauty, Daji. Daji quickly bewitches the Shang ruler, hitherto conscientious, luring him into unparalleled acts of debauchery, cruelty, and extravagance that naturally distract him from state business. Wound tight in her pernicious web, the king is deaf to the protests of his loyal senior advisers. Before long, conditions in the empire have so deteriorated that the "poor people, bearing their children on their backs and leading their wives in flight, call piteously upon Heaven" for help. At that juncture, the forces of All-under-Heaven begin to assemble under the banners of Shang or of Zhou. Up to this point in the tale, readers have witnessed mainly verbal jousting between the gods, but now the *Romance* hurls gods and men, along with assorted genii and giants, sprites and immortals, into frenzied battles that at once affirm the age-old link between the martial and magical arts and prefigure present-day Hong Kong *gongfu* movies.

Early scenes between the Shang and Zhou forces set the tone and pace. A Green Sword Cloud, concealing thousands of swords and spears within its vapors, envelops the battlefield, only to be succeeded by a Universe Muddling Canopy, which plunges heaven and earth into total darkness. There follows a dizzying succession of jade unicorns, red beams of light, and Wind-Fire Wheels, also a miraculous Yin/yang reflecting mirror and a foolproof charm that summons freezing cold in mid-August. On either side of the conflict, great heaps of warriors are slain, only to be revived by potent elixirs of immortality. In the end, of course, the skirmishes and melees lead to a Zhou victory, but not without a final twist. With the opposing forces virtually stalemated, it is the ordinary residents of the Shang capital, not the gods or their designated champions, who seal the fate of their wicked ruler by throwing open the gates of their city to the Zhou invaders. Obviously, ordinary humans, who may perceive themselves as hapless victims, act upon the course of human history no less crucially than do the gods and their heroes.

The *Romance* begins by confusing the very issues of moral responsibility that the *Documents* takes as its main theme. It then nearly buries the *Documents* version of the Zhou conquest under heaps of fantasy and gore. But the *Romance* ends by reiterating one of the main moral lessons of the *Documents*: decisive moral action can improve both the material and ethical conditions of the empire, pleasing Heaven above and humans below. The *Romance* even betters the *Documents* in its vivid portrayal of continual and continuous interaction between the gods and humans, and this fixes the sacred character of narrative history in the Chinese people, who still walk the land on which gods and heroes once fought. Hence, the strong moral sense that many Chinese have held that an "insistent present," to borrow Whitehead's phrase, is located in these, their most ancient texts. As one thirteen-year-old at the turn of the century in Sichuan put it, "All legend was history as history became legend about her. Along her rivers and about her plains—and far beyond, her fortresses and tumuli, temples and shrines, her trees over a thousand years old—were witnesses to battles fought, phrases said, stratagems of war and politics. All was in place, known, written, and recorded."

Of all the Five Classics, the *Documents* and its associated traditions have most served to facilitate this sort of cultural positioning. Faith in the authenticity of the *Documents*' message has tended to bring with it an implicit belief in a monolithic, superstable China—in utter defiance of the current historical and archaeological evidence—and, at a still deeper level, a belief in not only the possibility but also the inevitability and desirability of a salutary embrace by the present of this familial past: "Ideas and events that had occurred years before in a historical sense belong to the social present as long as they remained relevant to the sociocultural concerns. Such events are, in effect, still "happening." History is not, then, something we must study, lest we be condemned to repeat the past. History is alive, not merely 'paper' learning, but 'present' learning."

This continual blurring of the line between past and present, propelling unceasing waves of demythologizing and remythologizing of history, continues in China today, perhaps with even greater force and speed in this era of mass media. So memorable, monumental, and marvelous has this distant past come to seem to many students of the *Documents* Classic—some of whom know it only through reworkings in school set pieces, in storyteller's tales, in literati novels, in comic books, or in modern *gongfu* plots—that present experience can sometimes feel like a pale repetition of the set themes, a mere shadow of the dense, all-pervading web of words, events, and concepts that is history. This explains the marked ambivalence that certain modernizers feel toward their powerful heritage, despite the real utility of certain *Documents*' traditions to modern times, particularly the strong message that legitimate government is moral government whose chief business is to protect the weak. The undeniable force of these aggregate reconstructions, reiterated incessantly over time and reinforced through that stupendous creation of the Han officials, the dynastic cycle, has been to make China seem too grand and too absolute an entity to coexist with modernity's messy impulses toward disunity, discontinuity, interplay, and change. Moreover, in imaging a superior Chinese past and assuming a perfect identity between civilization and empire, the *Documents* traditions, which once justified the spread of Chinese empire into other parts of Asia, can exacerbate the pain and self-doubt felt by Chinese who find themselves lorded over by the relatively uncivilized states of Europe, America, and Japan. In response, popular culture, presuming the notion of China's ultrastable past, asks in productions like the documentary serial *River Elegy* whether China can ever escape the crushing weight of its long history?

But however keenly many Chinese may long to be free of their extended past, some fear its loss the more. It is like the story in the *Zhuangzi*: a would-be disciple turns up at the door of the master, begging to be admitted. The master disingenuously inquires of the newcomer, "But who are all those people you have brought with you?" Of course, when the prospective disciple looks behind him, there is no one to be seen. Clinging to one's cultural baggage seems to hold out the chance to become larger than life. As one contributor of Chinese ethnic origin wrote in a Hong Kong magazine, "China is a cultural entity which flows incessantly, like the Yellow River, from its source all the way to the present time, and from there to the boundless future. This is the basic and unshakable belief in the mind of every Chinese. It is also the strongest basis for Chinese nationalism. No matter what government is in power, the people will not reject China." Numerous academics in the People's Republic, Taiwan, Singapore, and the Chinese diaspora are busily engaged in efforts to prove the absolute historicity of the preliterate Xia and pre-Xia "dynasties" in this cultural flow, pushing Chinese history ever further into the dim reaches of the past; the genuine longing that their efforts reveal—for a superior identity secured in a teleological narrative—necessarily entails a concurrent denial of the multiple realities of a far less tidy past. Academics outside that group face a formidable task in seeking to free themselves and their students from the fabulous ensnarements of a mythic past. The inherent difficulty of that task should be obvious, for history turned into myth "does not become unreal, but . . . only a continual normative and formative force."

In retrospect, it seems almost laughable that many of the finest minds in late Ming and Qing China (Huang Zongxi, Gu Yanwu, Mao Qiling, and Chu Yizun among them) should have feared that attacks on the Archaic Script *Documents* would bring about the utter collapse of the whole classical vision, along with the academic and political institutions that had supported it. In one sense, of course, their anxiety was entirely justified because the old distinctive form of empire, along with its educational and examination systems, succumbed to modern institutions only a few centuries later. But in another, more profound sense, the most essential lesson to be derived from the study of the *Documents* traditions remains alive and well in modern times: the Chinese are uniquely superior and uniquely blessed, by virtue of their "longest continuous civilization." Transient spasms of despotism can never nullify the fundamental justice guaranteed them for all eternity by Heaven's Mandate.

Confucius may have guessed as much. Once, in answer to a personal crisis that prompted more generalized doubts about the viability of the Way of Central States civilization, Confucius remarked to a disciple, "If Heaven really intended such a culture to disappear, a latter-day mortal would never have been able to link himself to it as I have done. And if Heaven does not intend to destroy such culture, what have I to fear from the people of Kuang [who threaten to kill me]?" Of all the texts encountered in a classical education, it was primarily the *Documents* and its traditions that afforded such faith, by presenting an enduring culture formed and peopled by sages, ancestors, gods, and spirits who, whatever their historicity, inhabited the imagination as living presences. Though they may have left their *Documents* textbooks behind, many Chinese today, highly self-conscious of the past and in ongoing dialogue with their dead, maintain this same quiet confidence in their ability to preserve and possibly even extend the remarkable achievements of the sage-kings of yore.

Chapter Four

THE THREE *RITES* CANONS

The Six Classics are records of the Way, and rituals are the main structures.
—Huang Zongxi

Confucianism should be called the study of ritual (*lixue* 禮學),
rather than the study of principle (*lixue* 理學).
—Jiang Xiangnan, student of Ruan Yuan

Your gentleness shall force
More than your force move us to gentleness
—*As You Like It*

Courtesy is contagious.
—American bumper sticker

IN THE PERIOD PRIOR TO UNIFICATION
in 221 BC, the classical masters inspired by Confucius were identified above all
as masters of the rites. Words attributed to Confucius justified this identification:
in the *Analects* the Master equated supreme virtue with "overcoming self-
centeredness, so as to return to ritual." Ritual was of inestimable importance to
premodern society in China, for the single term "rites" or "ritual" (*li* 禮) denoted
the full panoply of appropriate and thus mutually satisfying behaviors built upon
emotional insights. These behaviors, expressed in dress, countenance, bodily
posture, and verbal phrasing, were designed to strengthen communal bonds
among the living, between the living and the dead, and with the gods. In addi-

tion to decorous ceremonies performed in specific settings, there was everyday *li*, encompassing circumspect behavior, considerate acts, and exquisite courtesy. Ranging from the simplest verbal formula to the most elaborate of institutions, the rubric of rites and ritual included the observance of taboos, the offering of solemn sacrifices to the dead, the institution of sumptuary regulations, and the exchange of pleasantries. One Ru master spoke of *li* as an all-embracing system whereby "to join heaven and earth in harmony, . . . to moderate [human] likes and dislikes and to adjust joy and anger, as is proper." Modern categories that differentiate the religious or sacred from the secular and the numinous from the mundane do not apply to Chinese notions of ritual. Ritual masters (even those who insisted that the dead are not conscious) ascribed mysterious, even "godlike" (*shen* 神) powers to ordinary ritual action. Ritual did for the early Chinese what tragedy did for the ancient Greeks: it schooled humans in the definition of proper social roles while justifying their necessity; at the same time, ritual performances propelled the human imagination beyond the here and now, implying both the operation of larger cycles of fate and a boundless, hence godlike, human capacity for perfection. The rites, as distinctive cultural products, also performed the useful function of sharply demarcating "the people of the Central States from the barbarian tribes." Moreover, the rites served to explain or ameliorate contradictions inherent in the human condition, to offer guidance in troubled times, even to help humans break away from their dull routines.

Ritual continues to play an equally important role in Chinese communities today. Though anthropologists the world over study the power of ritual in complex societies, students of China, in homage to the early classicists, have tended to assume that ritual played an especially dominant role in civil and military culture there. Leaders of what used to be called Free China (that is, Taiwan) have loudly credited the solidarity of the Chinese people "for four thousand years" to the traditional norms embodied in the old ritual rules, extolling these as "the only reason Chinese [continue to] exist as a people and as a country." And in the People's Republic of China, that ritual code, reworked in modern death rituals, in artful *guanxi* 關係 (calculated social exchanges), and in small-group political rituals, still promotes the vertical and horizontal integration of the society.

The *Rites* canons themselves spoke of no fewer than "three hundred major and three thousand minor rules of ritual." Hence the commonplace that "all schools of Confucianism agree that the traditional value system is revealed through elaborate definitions, regulations, and moral and ethical principles regarding individuals' roles and relationships." Such commonplaces assume that the primary goal of ritual is social cohesion with a view to preserving the status quo in this life. Quite understandably, modern cynics have viewed successive versions of the ritual codes as instruments enabling elites to capitalize upon the instinctive urge felt by a superstitious populace to sanction social relationships through custom, thereby elevating the scholar-official class while keeping ordinary people in check. In this view, the rites appear to be the Chinese equivalent of the opiate of the people. Even far less cynical students of Chinese culture presuppose (only to decry) the normative functions of ritual, seeing ritual as the routine, the rote, the inegalitarian, and the conventional, the mere "insignia of culture" in Confucius's phrase. For them, ritual is perforce the enemy of the inspired, the creative, the reciprocal, and the nonconformist. A few modern scholars pursue this line of thought so far as to condemn the rites as the source of Oriental decadence. Such critics focus on metaphors within the rites canons that stress the restraining function of the rites, metaphors that liken them to curbs, dikes, barriers, or cinches. Americans are particularly prone to denounce Chinese ritual as inherently elitist, citing in evidence a single *Rites* passage that says, "The rites do not go down to the common people." That passage, however, simply acknowledges that commoners cannot be expected to engage in the most expensive and time-consuming ceremonies. The critics not only misinterpret the passage they cite; they also overlook Confucius's injunctions to use the rites to "treat everyone as an important guest and employ the people as if performing a great sacrifice." Many Americans seem oblivious to the fact that cultivation and culture, even in successful democracies, are built upon customary practice designed to internalize a complex code of behavior. As ritual is essential to any sophisticated society, perhaps classicists in China have been right to devote so much effort to describing the origins, functions, and ideal types of rites.

To see only the normative function of ritual is to miss a great deal of the picture. More than any other of the Five Classics, the three *Rites* canons, the *Yili*, the *Liji*, and the *Zhouli*, attempt to illustrate the process by which the distinctive character of each person develops. One chapter of the *Liji*, for example, states, "The noble man must take care of what is singular to him,* . . . that is to say, his selfness." The *Rites* canons, especially the *Liji*, repeatedly warn against reducing the rites to the merely perfunctory performance of set rules; to work effectively, considerable latitude must exist for personal adjustments. And the course of Chinese history shows that the three *Rites* canons, again more than

---

*The Cheng-Zhu adherents, however, wanting to emphasize the ultimate seriousness with which all activities should be approached and the necessity of rigorous self-scrutiny, interpreted this same phrase (*shendu* 慎獨) to mean something quite different: that the noble man is gravely "attentive [to moral concerns even] when he is alone." The French sinologist Henri Maspero first pointed out their alternate construction of the phrase, which can be traced to early sources.

any other of the Five Classics, inspired dramatic attempts to rethink and reorder Chinese social and political relations. The reforms of Dong Zhongshu (176–104 BC) under the Han, of Wang Mang (r. AD 9–23), Wang Anshi (1021–86), and Kang Youwei (1858–1927) are but four of the most famous attempts to revolutionize everyday Chinese life by a radical "return to the rites." The two Wangs referred to the *Zhouli*; Dong Zhongshu and Kang Youwei based their visions of a new and better society upon one chapter in the *Liji*, the Cycle of the Rites (*Liyun* 禮運). But even the *Yili*, shortest and least theoretical of the three *Rites* canons, projected an ideal world in which model *shi* 士 (originally "knights," but by Han times "the educated in actual or potential service to the state") set the pattern for all decorous relations "from the Son of Heaven on down to the common people." The rites, then, like Janus, are two-faced. They can stifle change or facilitate it. They are just as likely to subvert the status quo as to support it.

It was this transformative aspect of ritual performance that received paramount emphasis in the early study of the *Rites* canons, mainly because early Chinese saw humans less as innately fixed natures than as loci for boundless change.* The rites made it possible to transform oneself, to transform others, and to order the cosmos. They operated principally in two ways: by training the body through the practice of choreographed physical movements, so that the physical person became "moralized" to the core, and by training the mind through a thorough knowledge of edifying texts. In early China, the two ways of ritual were regarded as equally valid and mutually dependent, with a few famous ritual masters specializing in either practice or theory (fig. 13).

But even the earliest extant discussions of ritual (dating from the pre-Han period) reflect their authors' awareness that this transformative potential of the rites, as opposed to their normative function, was in perennial danger of attenuation. Certain tendencies toward desanctification were endemic to the very nature of ritual itself. Because the rites function as a social language, addressing the gods, the dead, and other members of the local community, they must be conventionalized to some degree in order to be understood and appreciated. Though conventionalization by no means necessarily precludes variation or

---

* The Five Classics, and particularly the *Changes*, suggest that the slightest shift in gesture or verbal formula can set off monumental changes affecting multitudes of people over many generations. Mastery of the rites imparts two benefits, therefore. In teaching proper behavior, it (a) gives insight into the correct interpretation of events and their probable outcome, and (b) prevents humans from making inadvertent errors, thereby improving the ritual master's chances for good fortune. Believing ritual to be "the physical expression of life and death, preservation and ruin" (*Zuozhuan*, for Duke Ding 15), the Chinese celebrated the rites' inexplicable and incontrovertible power.

Figure 13. Woodblock print depicting Confucius as a child delighting in practicing the rites. From *Kongzi shengji tu*, comp. Kong Decheng (Taibei: Zhongguo wenjiao, 1957), 41.

modification, any routinization can undermine the experience of authenticity in the rite on the personal, social, and canonical levels. On the personal level, for example, ritual activity constitutes an aesthetic order, so that the rites are most efficacious when they have become fully internalized and seem like second nature. As second nature, however, they can easily become mere habit, stifling any impulse to change or transform. Conventionalization slips all the more easily into ossification when objects, beliefs, and practices are written down, especially in liturgical texts, which pitifully reduce vivid practices attuned to living concerns to sketchy sets of instructions. Lengthy commentaries, particularly those that extol the authority of the ritual canon, are as apt to hasten this process of ossification as to prompt new insights into multivocal traditions.

At least four specific circumstances peculiar to imperial history in China increased the potential for the rites to function as barriers, rather than gateways, to transformation: (1) the ever-increasing veneration of canonical texts, beginning with Han, tended to work against modifications of ritual practices associated with Confucius and his immediate followers; (2) from Han and notably from Tang, the autocratic state's growing reliance on "Confucianized" law (whereby parts of the ritual code were incorporated into the legal code) decreased the likelihood that certain ritual practices would be subject to ongoing experiments; (3) from late Eastern Han, the conservatives' rejection of more egalitarian readings of selected *Rites* passages reflected a complaisant acceptance of the widening sociopolitical gaps between estates occasioned by the rapid rein-feudation then in process; and (4) in Song, a further retreat from the grand orders envisioned in the three *Rites* canons and their apocrypha, accompanied by an increasing focus on texts more amenable to rational, psychological, and intellectualist interpretations, impoverished ritual practice and theory, lessening the importance of intuition, mystery, and the choreography of mind and body. Though history demonstrates a continual reworking of the classical rites, some-times viewed as a way of mediating between popular custom and the prescrip-tive demands of the canonical texts, traditions supplied no well-defined and conventionally accepted mechanism by which latter-day adherents of Confu-cius, by definition morally inferior to the sage-kings of yore, could alter the rites. Committed moralists knew only that rites, to remain effective, must always be harmonious variations on a theme; they must always exemplify the social bonds in ways that made sense for the time, the situation, and the group. In the name of preserving time-honored rites, failures to institute timely changes quashed the transformative powers of those very rites. Hence the continual irruption of rites controversies at court, some of which produced rites identi-fied as unimaginably old that were, in fact, essentially new inventions.

Systems of rites, if originally designed to "reanimate the old," became in the early twentieth century the chief target of the May Fourth reformers, who mocked them as the keystone of a hopelessly outdated "Old Confucian Curios-ity Shop." To these reformers, the rites seemed no more than a heap of state-sponsored abuses and gross superstitions maximizing the elite's tyranny and the populace's misery. Attributing to ritual a social role similar to that of the Church in medieval Europe, the reformers discounted any possible defenses, for example, that governing by ritual represented a viable alternative to governing by force and thus served to strengthen civil institutions in relation to the mili-tary; or that the promotion of a rich ritual life by secular authorities at every level tended to dilute the authority of clerical experts and their hierarchies. Only now, in the early-twenty-first century, has the influence of the May Fourth gen-eration receded enough to allow a calmer reexamination of ritual in the impe-rial era, an exercise that may make us not only better historians but also more imaginative members of our present societies.

DATING AND CONTENT OF THE THREE *RITES* CANONS

Three texts were eventually canonized as a group attesting the absolute superiority of the ritual Way over other methods of organizing society: the

Ceremonials (*Yili* 儀禮); the *Zhou Rites* (*Zhouli* 周禮); and the *Rites Records* (*Liji* 禮記). Two additional classical canons have been loosely associated with these *Rites* canons: a lost *Music Classic*, which possibly has been preserved in the Music Records (Yueji 樂記) chapter of the *Liji*, and *The Elder Dai's Rites Records*, or *Da Dai Liji* 大戴禮記, ascribed to the Western Han ritual master Dai De, which appears in Zhu Xi's preferred list of the so-called "Fourteen Classics."

The three *Rites* canons are not linked by a single author, style, or approach. To the modern eye this is obvious, even without the glaring contradictions to be found among the texts. It was probably no less obvious to many early Chinese, but pious legends ascribing the whole or part of all three *Rites* canons to the Duke of Zhou (eleventh century BC), the model founder of the Lu state in which Confucius was born, led the Eastern Han commentator Zheng Xuan (127–200) to discount the disparities in style and content. Building upon a *Liji* statement that all ritual activities "lead to one and the same end," Zheng argued that the three *Rites* canons together describe a complete ritual system, which encompasses a broad spectrum of activities from the courtesies of daily life to the most solemn affairs of state. This solved the problem that each of the individual *Rites* classics is arguably incomplete: the *Yili* because it provides liturgies only for the lowest-ranking knights or officials (the *shi*) and not for rulers, nobles, or the common people; the *Zhouli* because it mainly enumerates the official posts required in an ideal bureaucracy, without explicating the relation between the ritual and sociopolitical systems; and the *Liji* because it deals with ritual theory to the near exclusion of liturgical practice. Supporting Zheng's proposed grouping are the explicit ties between the *Yili* and the final seven chapters of the *Liji*, whose anecdotal and explanatory passages function as explanatory notes or appended essays (*wai pian* 外篇) on the *Yili*'s ceremonials.

Zheng Xuan's respectful solution, in some sense, may have softened the impact of his implied harsh condemnation of the Monthly Ordinances (Yueling) chapter in the *Liji*. (Over the objections of some classicist contemporaries, Zheng noted that the Monthly Ordinances chapter duplicated material found in the *Lüshi chunqiu*, an eclectic work reputedly sponsored by the conniving chief minister at the evil Qin court.) In general, Han scholiasts preferred to link the composition of the *Rites* canons with Lu, the state that served as supposed repository of hallowed traditions dating back to the Duke of Zhou, to Confucius's inner circle of disciples, and to his descendants. Their preference was supported by the content and attribution of a great many *Liji* chapters that seemed to preserve little-known facts about Confucius and his exemplary descendants. For instance, early Ru traditions attributed to Zisi, grandson of Confucius, a block of four of the most famous *Liji* treatises, including the Doctrine of the Mean (Zhongyong); to Gongsun Nizi, a direct disciple of Confucius, the single chapter Music Records; and to Zengzi, another direct disciple of Confucius, a block of several chapters, including the influential Great Learning (Daxue). It seems more likely that much of the *Liji* was compiled and edited in early Western Han by Han court specialists, though parts of it closely reflect ideas of the pre-Han classicists, especially Xunzi; certainly the grammar and content of the other two *Rites* canons, the *Zhouli* and the *Yili*, cannot date to a time much before Han. Han texts, in fact, admit as much, even while duly repeating the pious legends about the ancient origins of the *Rites* canons. The *Shiji* and the *Hanshu* (compiled ca. 100 BC and AD 100, respectively), for instance, agree that the rites had not been completely written down in the pre-Han period and that they were, in fact, in total disarray at the start of early Western Han. In China, as in other classical civilizations, the two ideas could be held simultaneously, for authorship often meant little more than an imputation of a pedigree for certain ideas embodied in the text.

Han scholars often presumed that texts about the rites had suffered more than any other canonical works from the Qin proscriptions against private learning in 213 BC. In reality, this disarray had at least five other sources: First, as noted earlier, Ru classicism began to focus more on written texts after the institution of the Imperial Academy in 124 BC. Second, almost a thousand years separated early Western Zhou from Han, dooming any attempt to reconstruct the outlines of the ritual system prevailing in the early Zhou courts. Third, the collapse of Zhou rule and the proliferation of local courts had spawned a host of competing official ritual practices and theories, often as a means to legitimate or innovate governance. Fourth, various attempts to adapt elite rites for use by commoners, in early China no less than in early Greece, had opened the spirit and court worlds, once strictly reserved for an aristocracy of priests and warriors, to an expanding circle of devotees, with some proposing to amend the rites and others simply rejecting them. And fifth, the razing before Han of the old Qin capital, with its imperial libraries and cult centers, must have destroyed many ritual accounts. It is hardly surprising, then, that ritual masters consulted by the Han court repeatedly confessed complete ignorance of the proper imperial rites as they debated the fundamental meaning of key ritual terms.

Given these vast lacunae in ritual practices and texts, it is surprising how quickly classicists in Western Han granted authoritative status to all three *Rites* classics, although only the *Yili* and possibly the *Liji* received official state sponsorship via a designated Academician's post during most of Han. Copies of chapters now included in both the *Yili* and the *Liji*, written on bamboo and wooden slips, have been found in Han tombs in regions as far-flung as Gansu and Shandong, attesting to the relative importance of the *Rites* classics in Han times.

Why this sustained emphasis on the rites? From the beginning, the Han dynasty's sporadic attempts to promote an orthodoxy on the classical model had much to do with the court's desire to bolster its legitimacy through cultural activities. For political reasons, successive Han emperors were determined to outshine potential rivals as patrons of the entire range of academic rites associated with antique literary authority and current literary accomplishments: book collecting, collating, and compiling; library building; the convening of academic conferences, and such. Equally important, since Liu Bang, founder of the Han dynasty, had no ancestral claim to the throne, the single most popular justification for the new dynasty lay in its promise to replace the despotism of the Qin with benevolent rule, which to many meant rule by ritual. The Han therefore thought it best to broadcast their position that violence might win an empire but could not secure it and that "classical scholars of little use when taking the offensive in war could help to retain what had already been won." Furthermore, the early rulers of Han fully realized the degree to which they could, as if by a miracle, accrue great authority from efficacious ritual, as a story drawn from Sima Qian's *Archival Records* illustrates beautifully:

Liu Bang's followers were given to drinking and brawling over their respective achievements. When in their cups, some would shout wildly and others would draw their swords and hack at the pillars [of the palace], causing the High Ancestor [that is, Liu Bang] distress over their behavior. Shusun Tong, realizing that the emperor was becoming increasingly disgusted with the situation, persuaded the emperor [to take action]: . . . "I beg to summon scholars from Lu, who can join with my disciples in drawing up court rituals."

"Can you make them not too difficult?"

"The Five Emperors of antiquity all had different types of court music and dance; the Three Kings [of Xia, Shang, and Zhou] did not follow the same ritual. . . . They did not merely copy their predecessors. I intend to pick a number of ancient rituals and some Qin ceremonies, to make a combination of these."

"See what you can do," replied the emperor. "But make it easy to learn! Keep in mind that it must be the sort of thing that I can perform."

Shusun Tong then summoned some thirty-odd scholars from Lu [the home state of Confucius]. . . . With the more learned imperial advisers and his own disciples, numbering over a hundred men, he worked out the rituals. When they had practiced for more than a month, Shusun Tong felt that it was time for the emperor to come take a look. . . . "I can do that all right!" exclaimed the emperor when he had watched them carry out the rituals, so he ordered all his officials to practice them so that they could be used in the New Year festivities.

In the seventh year of Han, at the completion of the Eternal Joy Palace, all the nobles and officials attended the New Year's formal audience. . . . During the ceremony, every single person, from the assembled nobles on down, trembled with awe and reverence. During the drinking which followed the formal audience, . . . no one dared to quarrel or misbehave in the least. At this, the High Ancestor announced, "Today, for the first time, I know how exalted a thing it is to be an emperor."

As early advisers to Liu Bang had foreseen, a return to ritual (via newly invented rituals) could exalt the authority of the early Han throne while introducing an element of salutary refinement to its court. At the same time, Liu Bang and his successors were quick to recognize that self-identified students of the Five Classics were often a cut above the usual job seekers, learned in the historical precedents and literary flourishes needed to "adorn the rigor of state law," trained in the polite arts, and reputedly reliable and incorruptible. Thus, soon after reunification, in the early second century BC, the Han court commissioned scholars to retrieve ritual materials from scattered fragments and to reconstitute long-lost imperial rites, for example, the sacred *feng* and *shan* ceremonies at Mount Tai. Early in Han, rulers perhaps failed to foresee that some strong-minded classical scholars might wish to stretch their authority, grounded in ritual mastery, check absolutism, and to hold rulers to the very strictest standards of moral accountability. Relative to the number specializing in the other classics, the number of ritual masters reported in the dynastic history for Eastern Han is so small that one imagines a ruling house increasingly exasperated by the dangerous speculations and incessant factional squabbles about the most sacred—and touchy—matters involving the legitimacy of the throne.

Nonetheless, in retrospect it is clear that the classical formulations of ritual theory inherited from Xunzi (d. 238 BC), which laid equal stress on the personal and the sociopolitical advantages to be gained from a reliance on ritual, put their stamp on Han institutions and thereby on all later Chinese dynasties. The existence of no fewer than three separate *Rites* canons both reflected and sustained the preference for civil modes of government, for all three downplay (and the *Yili* omits) any mention of military rituals and state-sanctioned violence, despite their obvious significance in the affairs of Zhou and Han. Accordingly, the pinnacle of human achievement, the ideal sage-king, is described in early Ru texts not as philosopher or conqueror, but as supreme ritual master. Officials, too, were urged to become "accommodating officials" who could without coercion improve the local customs by introducing more civilized rituals, especially the all-important rites for ancestor worship and for marriage. As we shall see, those two topics loom largest in the oldest of the *Rites* canons, the *Yili*.

THE *YILI*

The seventeen chapters of the *Yili* contain detailed, idealized prescriptions of the liturgies for the major rites celebrated by the *shi*, including marriage, mourning, and district banquets. These prescriptions are invariably presented as straightforward descriptions of actual practice in an orderly state that is, curiously, at once feudal and bureaucratic. There is no literary embellishment, no dialogue, no anecdotal material. Instead, the liturgies are accompanied (in thirteen of the seventeen chapters) by notes (*ji* 記), brief explanatory and supplementary materials containing the precise verbal formulae and injunctions that the novice student of ritual is expected to need. A single chapter, On Mourning (Sang fu 喪服), appends a series of additional "traditions" (*chuan* 傳) attributed to Zixia (d. 420 BC?), the direct disciple of Confucius. (These three separate strata, each with its own slightly different grammar, suggest that the process of compilation took place over an extended period.)

The chapters of the *Yili* divide topically into eight sections, each devoted to a separate rite. The first section describes the ceremonial capping of a boy at puberty, a public rite signifying a male's entrance into adulthood. Part 1 of this section begins with elaborate instructions for divination to determine an auspicious day for the ceremony, then turns to proper procedures for inviting guests to witness the capping, followed by a description of the three-part capping ceremony. Part 2 specifies procedures for the formal visits paid by the newly capped son to relatives and friends, as well as for assigning his courtesy name (that is, his official name to be used in public). Part 3 gives instructions for all conceivable variations on the standard ceremony, that is, for the capping of an orphan, of a concubine's son, of a son whose mother is unavailable (because she is divorced, remarried, sick, or dead), and so on. The section ends with notes that explain the underlying significance of caps and capping. The notes insist that the heir apparent to the emperor be capped in exactly the same fashion as the son of an ordinary officer because "no one in the empire is born [inherently] noble." The notes go on to argue that the bestowal of hereditary office marks a decline from the practice of the earliest sages, who chose their successors entirely on the basis of merit.

In its second section, the *Yili* recounts the steps in the betrothal and marriage of an ordinary officer. Part 1 includes the exchange of betrothal presents, the announcements of the betrothal and the wedding, the divinations required to ascertain appropriate dates for the festivities, the feasting of ushers and visitors, the preparations for the wedding feast early on the morning of the ceremony, the groom's reception of the bride in front of the ancestors at his ancestral shrine, the joint entry of the bride and groom into the main house, the ritual feasting accompanying the marriage, followed by the preparations for the conjugal act and the final watch on the wedding night by the bridesmaids. Part 2 of this section rehearses the activities of the day following the wedding ceremony, when the bride first visits her father- and mother-in-law, offering them gifts of food. After the parents-in-law taste the food she has prepared, the bride moves to eat their leftovers (to signify her acceptance of their authority), an act the father-in-law refuses to allow. Instead, because the other sauce had been soiled by his fingers, he sets down fresh sauce for the bride. The bride then proceeds to taste the food left by her new mother-in-law, after which most of the feast is removed to another chamber to be eaten by members of her wedding party. Next, in return for the bride's courtesy, the new parents-in-law personally serve first the bride and then those in her wedding party. The supplementary notes at the end of the section on marriage discuss the proper age for marriage; the provision for unblemished offerings; the pinning of girls with a hairpin to publicize their betrothals; the reasons for a three-month interim before the bride may begin to offer sacrifices in her new home as a full-fledged member of the household; and the proper forms of address for various participants during the marriage preliminaries and ceremony. The marriage ceremony, as the *Yili* itself comments, is punctuated by dramatic inversions in which the older generation cedes precedence to the young, and men (the groom, the groom's father, and their driver) give way to women (the bride and her bridesmaid). This marriage ceremony also illustrates that commingling of sorrow and joy that accompanies major rituals marking life transitions, for the son's marriage, however joyful, cannot help but call to mind his parents' impending old age and death.

The third section outlines the standard procedure for friendly visits between ordinary officers, stipulating the appropriate modes of speaking, making eye contact, giving presents or polite signals to retire, and so on. Variations on the standard visit (such as interviews with one's ruler or with visitors from abroad) follow. The fourth section relates procedures for the district symposium held by the great officer in charge of the district, who assembles all the local dignitaries for a feast followed by a musical performance and a ceremonial pledging of guests with wine. Notes at the end of this section discuss the proper vessels, clothes, and offerings for the ceremony; the proper seating arrangements for guests; and provisions of wine for musicians and assistants.

The fifth section is devoted to the proper etiquette for the district archery contests, held as an incentive to ordinary officers to master this art of war. Part 1 of this section elaborates the rituals preliminary to the archery contest, including those for apprising onlookers and participants of the time and place for the meeting, for positioning and stretching taut the target, for receiving ordinary guests and notables, for pledging in wine, for musical entertainment, and for arranging ritual archery implements. Part 2 describes the three main stages of the archery contest, in which participants wearing special clothing take turns competing in teams. A master of ceremonies keeps score, announcing the victorious team after each round. A junior member of the winning team prepares wine that the officer in charge will offer first to the losers; after that, all competitors and helpers are invited to partake of this fine wine. Part 3 enumerates regulations for the session of feasting that follows the archery contest. Appended to the main text are lengthy notes (some forty-eight in number). These permit the omission of certain ceremonies in the contest itself when "all invited are well versed in ceremonial"; they also clarify and expand the regulations, listing measurements for the target and the number of arrows in each contestant's bundle; and they limit the ruler's participation in the archery contest.

The sixth section concerns the formal banquets given by the duke for his officers, with variations for the ducal reception of visitors from other states. Thirteen notes follow, specifying the type of dress to be worn at a banquet, the location of the banquet, the choice of the principal guest, the performance of music, and the serving of wine and dainty appetizers. A seventh section covers the Great (that is, capital) Archery Meeting, a more elaborate version of the District Archery Meeting.

The eighth and final section is devoted to the preparation and conduct of state missions. Suitable gifts for the foreign host must be readied, the diplomat's instructions given, provisions made for passing through foreign territories, a dress rehearsal conducted, the send-off accomplished, and—upon the successful completion of the mission—gifts offered to the diplomat in recognition of his services. Part 2 of this section describes the formal audience and exchange of diplomatic courtesies, followed by a private interview, that constitute the mission proper. Part 3 concerns the provisioning of members of a mission, regulations governing a second interview, the ceremonial gifts to be forwarded to other dignitaries in the foreign state, parting courtesies to be exchanged in the form of gifts and farewell banquets, and the formal report made by the head of mission to his prince upon his return. Part 4 then explains variations on the standard mission, for example, what to do if upon arrival the mission finds its host court preoccupied with the solemn mourning rituals that preclude the regular conduct of public business. Forty explanatory notes follow, mandating minor points of etiquette, such as the type of presents, the kind of speeches, and the ceremonial garb to be worn by members of the mission. Following the notes, two final chapters, both extremely brief, describe a formal dinner given by the prince to honor his emissary upon his return.

Each of the eight sections of the *Yili* seems devised to emphasize one particular aspect of the ritual it describes. For instance (as mentioned above), the chapters on marriage lay stress on those junctures in the marriage ceremony at which the normal order is inverted. The chapters on archery teach the social value of "deference" (*rang* 讓) to others, even to one's social inferiors. Significantly, the competitors "bow and make way for each other." Then, after each round, the winners hasten to prepare the wine to serve to the losers, as if to exemplify Confucius's dictum that "gentlemen never compete," except in their drive to acquire learning. In the many passages in the *Yili* devoted to "family rites" (for example, sacrifices to the ancestors, mourning rites, and the "auspicious rites" of feasting, marriage, and capping), the *Yili* also clearly reaffirms the function of the household's eldest male to act as priest or ritual celebrant, for it is the eldest male who generally presents offerings and conducts ceremonies on behalf of his family members, who presides even when he appoints a professional liturgist to perform or read part of the ceremony. The conduct of the state seems largely to be family affairs writ large, for the head of state's relation to his subjects, at least to those belonging to the *shi* 士 estate, appears to be closely modeled on the patriarch's to his family members.

To some modern readers, the degree of formality prescribed by the *Yili* for social exchanges may seem stultifying, but avid readers of Jane Austen or Emily Post will find themselves on entirely familiar ground, with surprisingly little "translation" required to move from one gentlefolk's culture to another. The modern verdict that the *Yili* is dull—and so unworthy of scholarly attention—suggests, ironically enough, the stupendous achievement of the *Yili*'s compilers, who successfully projected upon a glorified antiquity an idealized code of aristocratic behavior (somewhat like the European chivalric code, minus its romantic overtones), in hopes of hastening its adoption by all who aspired to true nobility of character. This new code, embodied in an elaborate etiquette, imagines lords and retainers (often depicted as hosts and guests), no less than family members, united by their mutual determination to exemplify the charismatic virtue that alone confers true honor. But because it stipulates the exact wording, precise gestures, and clothing for each stage of major rituals, the *Yili* text, like modern etiquette books, represents an important, even revolutionary tool by which to increase social mobility, for it enabled nonelite aspirants to high culture to learn elite behavior by studying its text. The *Yili*, in other words, no less than the other two *Rites* canons, aims to advance an ethical order through patterns of ritual life among *shi*, patterns presented as accurate portrayals of hallowed customs.

THE *ZHOULI*

Quite a different picture of the state emerges in the *Zhouli*, which purportedly reconstructs the entire bureaucratic structure of the administration led by the Duke of Zhou, the powerful regent whom legend credits with establishing peace and prosperity in the first years of Western Zhou. The text supplies a roster of offices: some 360 major posts, one for each day of the lunar year, who supervise about 330,000 petty officers and menial functionaries altogether. Appended to each bureaucratic title is a complete list of pertinent duties. Given its exhaustive nature, the *Zhouli* became a veritable treasure-house for officials searching for imperial precedents; for antiquarians studying the history of early ritual practices and utensils; for linguists hoping to reconstitute the archaic Chinese language (the *Zhouli* being the only Rites classic to employ pre-Han script for a few characters); as well as for reformers intent upon recreating its structural perfection by a total reorganization of government and society.

The *Zhouli*'s bureaucracy was organized under six ministries: (1) The Office of Heaven had charge of both the political and domestic aspects of the royal household, so that its chief officer functioned as both the king's majordomo and his prime minister. This office supervised all general administration, including the appointment and supervision of officials in the five other ministries, and the running of the royal household. In the latter capacity, it was the employer of the palace chefs, guards, hunters, bailiffs for the royal lands, court physicians, vintners, valets, gatekeepers, accountants, furriers, a superintendent of the icehouse, several pickle makers, keepers of bedclothes and screens, female tutors and magicians, bronze casters, silk dyers, and a bevy of seamstresses. Such keen attention to the private provisioning of the imperial household may seem frivolous, but it points to an important feature of the ideal Chinese government in antiquity: a blurring of the lines between public and private, so that the ruler is thought to govern—forge community and confirm just hierarchy—just as effectively by setting his household administration in order as by appointing just and capable officials over his subjects. (2) The Office of Earth had charge of local administration for the territories outside the royal domain; its duty was to promote agriculture, education, and social welfare programs, offering outright grants to the poor. In times of shortage, government regulators from this ministry were to fix market prices for basic necessities, especially grain, so as to prevent rapid inflation and market speculation. (3) The Office of Spring was the ministry in charge of all rites and ceremonies, including divinations, musical performances, and astrological observations; this same ministry was responsible for compiling historical records and storing the state archives, procedures that had evolved from the recording of oracle bone divination results. It was responsible, as well, for the material production of ceremonial paraphernalia, such as clothing and carriages. State rituals, sacrifices, and record keeping, in other words, are not incidental to good government, but good government itself. (4) The Office of Summer, a kind of war department, was in charge of recruiting, training, quartering, and transporting the state's armies, as well as planning for fortifications and fire brigade units. This same ministry oversaw the horse breeders and trainers, and the mapmakers necessary to empire building. (5) The Office of Autumn had the direction of all matters judicial and diplomatic. It oversaw the enforcement of the penal code, the registration of population and contracts, and the administration of prisons, including executioners. In addition, it arranged the reception of foreign envoys from the various feudal states. (6) The Office of Winter was purportedly in charge of public works, economic production, and state monopolies. Unfortunately, accounts of this sixth ministry were lost in Western Han, and in their place is a section entitled the "Record of Inspecting Public Works" ("Kaogong ji" 考工記), which concerns the construction of cities, palaces, moats, chariots, weapons, musical instruments, jade instruments, and agricultural tools. In general, the *Zhouli* coordinates the responsibilities of every single office in this six-part bureaucracy of the ideal imperium so precisely that the whole fits together as neatly as "the overlapping scales of a fish."

To illustrate one of the *Zhouli* ministries, a list of positions within the Office of Heaven includes one prime minister and two vice-premiers; chief stewards and personnel officers for the palace; a palace garrison commander; kitchen functionaries, including tasters for the royal table, butchers, palace cooks, specialists in preparing food for sacrificial offerings and gifts, and sous-chefs; bailiffs for the royal hunting grounds; huntsmen; meat-driers; royal physicians; royal vintners; supervisors of the icehouse; eunuchs in charge of ritual vessels and preserved foods; valets in the royal living apartments; procurement officers for palace furniture; royal treasurers and accountants; chiefs of the harem, gatekeepers; the queen and various secondary wives and concubines, all of whom held bureaucratic rank; the harem prayer-masters, and so on. A complete job description is supplied for each post. For instance, the text explains the duties of the chief royal physician in the following manner:

In charge of government regulations concerning [the duties of] physicians. He collects the poisons [used in homeopathy] and medicines so as to supply the physicians in their work. Whenever those in the state [bureaucracy?] are afflicted with illnesses, with ulcers on the head or with wounds to the body, he visits them, and then sends to them physicians with an appropriate specialty to cure them. At year's end, he examines the work of his physicians, so as to adjust their stipends. Those with a survival rate of ten [patients out of ten] rank highest; those who lose one in ten are next; those who lose two in ten are next, and then those who lose three patients in ten. Those who lose four in ten rank lowest.

Even the duties of the humble "footwear master," ranked below the gatekeeper and seamstresses of the women's quarters, are described in meticulous detail; the master is said to be "In charge of [supplying and caring for] the ceremonial footwear used by the king and queen. He makes red and black double-soled shoes, red-bordered shoes and yellow bordered shoes, shoes with green on the double seam of the toe, plain single-soled shoes, hemp single-soled shoes [for summer], the ruddy brown formal footwear for outside and inside, the work-shoes, and the casual wear, so that for the sacrifices of the four seasons, they are suitably dressed." Apparently, the higher the position, the less specific the job description: The duties of the highest official, the prime minister, are so broad as to require rather more abstract categories, such as oversight of the Six Canons, the Eight Handles, and the Eight Precepts.

Amid this welter of detail, it is the summary of the Zhou king's powers and duties that appears most striking. This summary, repeated verbatim at the beginning of each of the six sections, describes the king as *minji* 民極 (the ultimate [standard] of morality for the common people): "It is the king who establishes the domain, who divides the regions and arranges the official ranks, who apportions the domain and demarcates the outlying areas, who establishes the bureaucratic offices and divides their responsibilities, so as to become the ultimate [standard] of morality for the common people."

Because good government rests chiefly on good men rather than good laws, as in all texts closely associated with Confucius, the *Zhouli* prescribed educational institutions for all levels of court and countryside. The better to realize a society of good men, the king's power over certain aspects of government was described as nearly absolute. For example, the king framed the laws for the empire; appointed and demoted members of his bureaucracy; decided upon punishments (although the petition to punish was to be composed by the prime minister); personally investigated all aspects of the bureaucracy; retained all governmental powers, even when away from court on a royal progress; had the sole right to pardon wrongdoers; offered all state sacrifices in person; acted as commander-in-chief of the army. Nevertheless, in many important matters of state, such as the appointment of an heir, the transfer of the capital, and declarations of war, the king might not act unilaterally but had instead to seek the approval of his officers and commoners. The king's power was also conditional in the sense that the king expected to be corrected by some few high-ranking appointees like the prime minister and the Lord Protector, though, curiously

enough, no special mention is made of remonstrance by his blood relatives.*
And since the *Zhouli*, unlike many early texts, holds law to be an important
instrument of government, its ideal ruler hardly qualifies as the Oriental despot
of popular imagination.

Still, the scope of prescribed government is enormous by modern Euro-
American standards, for the *Zhouli* depicts a state directly responsible for the
physical, mental, and moral well-being of even the least of its subjects, and consequently for supplying their most basic needs, including security, employment,
and education. For the very young, the aged, the infirm, and the incapacitated
there was to be full welfare relief. In return, the state's subjects must work hard
for the community good or risk exclusion from important ritual activities. Given
the protoscientific belief expressed in the *Zhouli* that different climates produce
different human temperaments, the good king saw to it that educational methods
and fiscal policies were adjusted to suit each locale. Such latitude followed from
one of the *Zhouli's* major assumptions: that good government policy, like personal morality, cannot be governed by a single universal set of standards (contra
the assumption behind the modern Euro-American rule by law), for it must
recognize and respond to wide variations in human characters, abilities, and
experiences. Unity as a viable goal requires coherence, continuity, and cooperation, but never absolute identity or uniformity. This view of government mandated frequent consultation by state representatives with local leaders prior to
the implementation of policy; also, the ruler's judicious application of statutes
in the penal code to account for individual circumstances. By doing all the
above, the ideal administration depicted in the *Zhouli* embodied the model of
the antique sage-kings, who knew that "[good] government takes accommodation to the people as its basis."

THE *LIJI*

The title of the *Liji*, whose modern edition is in forty-nine chapters, may be
translated as *Rites Records*, where the word *ji* 記 (records, notes) connotes secondary traditions on the rites, however old those traditions may be. (Compare
the *Shiji* 史記, *Archival Records*, cited above, which likewise dates to mid-Western
Han.) The *Liji* is full of exemplary tales, many of them astonishing or amusing,
about the deeds and sayings of Confucius and his disciples, with some of the
most memorable centering upon the ritual expressions of filial piety paid to
the living or the dead. Numerous chapters in the text contrast and compare

---

*The earliest chapters of the *Documents* portray the king working in concert with his
brothers and uncles, who are expected to counsel and remonstrate with him. The silence
of the *Zhouli* on this matter suggests a late date for composition of the text.

ceremonial practices ascribed to the Three Dynasties of antiquity, the Xia (now generally considered to be entirely legendary), Shang, and Zhou. One chapter depicts a perfect moral influence emanating from a central royal domain of one thousand *li* square to pervade progressively distant outlying zones occupying an additional nine thousand *li* square on a strict cartographic grid. The same chapter calls for the execution of anyone found guilty of "splitting words [manipulating language] in order to break the laws, confounding names in order to alter conventions; and holding to corrupt ways in order to throw government into disarray." Another elucidates the marvelous efficacy of good music in settling one's person and the state. And one essay, Records on Education (Xueji), reads like a modern training manual for teachers, full of useful tips about sparking and maintaining student interest, so that students soon "feel comfortable with their studies and close to the teacher": don't mumble in class; don't unduly pressure students with hard assignments or constant testing; promote study groups, so that students become less isolated and better informed; let students develop their own love of the subject; and so on.

But the *Liji* is best known for its treatises on the underlying significance of ritual training, several of which apparently preserve snippets from edited transcripts of Han scholastic court debates on set topics. Interspersed among such notes, the *Liji* supplies commonsensical rules about everyday etiquette: "When there are two pairs of shoes placed outside the door, one enters only if voices are heard" and "Do not roll the rice into a ball; do not bolt the various dishes down; do not slurp the soup." Included as well are prescriptions governing the polite arts and the characteristic occupations of the aristocrats, charioteering and archery, for example. Avenging a parent's murder, though technically illegal, was nonetheless considered a solemn filial duty, and the *Liji* stipulates the appropriate procedures. (Local officials usually chose not to prosecute avengers, lest they offend popular mores.) Strict rules mandate the segregation of male and female; even married couples were permitted no physical contact outside the bedroom, lest romantic love take precedence over the fundamentally communal loyalties to parents, clan, and ruler. Therefore, "male and female should not sit close together, nor have the same stand or rack for their clothes, nor use the same towel or comb, nor let their hands touch in giving and receiving. A sister-in-law and brother-in-law do not exchange inquiries about the other [lest a romance, let alone an unlawful liaison, develop]."* Husband and wife, father and mother, older and younger "had their parts [in ritual] to personally perform." And since all of the "myriad sorts of things" in the triadic realms of

---

*Modern readers tend to forget how pervasive sex segregation and spatial symbolism were in European society until the twentieth century.

Heaven-Earth-Human are bound in seamless community through their ritual roles, the *Liji* further mandates the conservation of natural resources: in spring, hunters are not to take young animals or eggs. Finally, the *Liji* offers instructions for the disposal of damaged or worn-out ceremonial paraphernalia, lest the sacred quality of the rite be diminished by careless disposal.

As a work compiled from many sources, the *Liji* is not without internal contradictions. One chapter emphasizes the incomparable dignity of the "noble man" while another stresses the noble man's refusal to "dignify his own projects" and his willingness to "abase himself and honor others." One passage in the *Liji* exalts the position of women, while another seems to denigrate it. (The *Liji* is much less concerned with gender relations than with generational hierarchy—the submission of all members of the younger generation, male and female, to those in the older generation, who have granted the young the most precious gifts of life, nourishment, and education.) Similarly, one chapter lauds the filial piety of sons who ruin their health in mourning their dead parents, while another curtly condemns those whose extravagant mourning for parents harms their bodies.

Contradictions notwithstanding, important themes thread through the *Liji*. Much stress is laid on love of parents, living and dead, and respect for one's teachers and superiors as the basis for proper social conduct. "Repaying good with good, and ill with ill" is affirmed as the basis of civil order;[*] those who "repay ill treatment with good" (as Jesus advised) may enhance their social standing by acts of leniency, but in the end such acts only reward evil and thereby confuse ordinary morality. Many rituals publicly honor those who have contributed selflessly to the fortunes of the community and the state. Thus, "when one is holding an article belonging to his lord, though it may be light, he should seem unable to sustain it. . . . When he meets his teacher on the road, he should hasten forward to meet him, then stand with hands joined across his breast." But the vast majority of social obligations are viewed as mutual. By advising parents that a child must "never be allowed to witness a single instance of deceit," the text implies that even parents, rulers, and teachers merit respect only by virtue of exemplary conduct.

Other important themes are the complementarity of the ritual and musical systems, and the relation between (inner) self-cultivation and its formalized expression in visible (outer) etiquette. Music is the chief means to harmonize society, bringing men and women to recognize their fundamental kinship with one another, whereas rites are the chief means to establish social hierarchy and

---

[*] Compare the standard Greek definition of justice, which Socrates questioned: "Do good to your friends and evil to your enemies."

make the distinctions upon which moral discrimination rests. Music functions to regulate the human emotions (thought to come from within), while the rites act to regulate human desires (thought to arise from objects external to the self). Both rites and music are needed, therefore, if the person is to find a harmonious balance between the desire to develop his or her innate singularity and the equally pressing need to uphold larger societal concerns. On the relation between self-cultivation and ritual, the *Liji* treatises are not in perfect agreement. They do agree, however, that, "the noble man would be ashamed to wear the proper clothes but lack the proper demeanor, or have the proper demeanor but lack the proper phrases, or have the proper phrases but lack the proper character."

Citations from the three *Rites* canons, taken out of context, are often used to prove the inegalitarian nature of early Chinese society, especially in the spheres of gender and politics. By some accounts, ritual managed to persuade a segment of the population to accept its inferior place in society unwittingly. It is equally possible, however, to employ the three texts to prove quite the opposite, that they promote a kind of egalitarianism in several senses: they assume that everyone can be perfected; they stipulate that a code of manners, aristocratic in origin, be learned by and applied to all humans; they advocate the assignment of social rank according to virtue and merit, defining both in terms of relative contributions to the larger society; and they aim to school each person, through theory and praxis, in the very social skills that facilitate effective interaction. Accordingly, it should come as no surprise that nonelites in early, medieval, and late imperial China were at times more eager than the social and political elites to embrace the precepts set forth in the *Rites* canons. The rites could empower commoners to join the elites just as easily as they empowered elites. (The subversive aspect of the rites is evident as soon as one considers the uses the apocrypha attached to the *Rites* canons were put to.) Once one accepts that, a long overdue reassessment of the *Rites* canons can begin.

ONE IMPORTANT ISSUE RELATED TO THE RITES

The *Zhouli's* detailed description of an ideal patrimonial state supported by highly structured institutions proved irresistible to such advocates of top-down reforms as Wang Mang and Wang Anshi. Down through the ages, the Cycle of the Rites (Liyun) chapter in the *Liji* also inspired rebels and reformers, including Kang Youwei. Why do committed Confucians look to the three *Rites* texts to justify social change, when the normalizing or normative function of the rites, meaning their ability to conserve the social order, is admittedly so strong?

Several preliminary observations are in order. First, from the beginning, governing by the rites, as opposed to the "two handles" of punishments and rewards, was identified as the distinctively Confucian Way to rule. In the *Analects*, for example, Confucius asserts the self-evident superiority of rule by ritual: "If it is really possible to govern countries by ritual and yielding, no more need be said," since "love for other humans" constitutes "the greatest part" of good government. For several reasons, Confucius and his early followers believed, ritual rule would not only assure subjects of a just and beneficial reign, but also prove a boon to the ruler, who would find it the most effective way to govern. Training in ritual, after all, habituated persons to strict order and hierarchy while providing the periodic indulgences and spectacles that gave people welcome release from their daily drudgery. At the same time, it served to preclude or regulate unhealthy or unrealizable desires, making the expression of human feelings both refined and satisfying. Finally, the aesthetic coherence of individual rites made them deeply pleasurable to participants and audience alike, which tended to reinforce the desire to behave well. By contrast, the penal code hardly guaranteed better conduct. Written laws, which did nothing to reform the person from within, would more likely spur men to look for legal loopholes or to turn litigious. Rites worked to instill morality, in other words, while penal law could only define the illegal, notify people that crimes are to be avoided, and punish crimes after the fact. For Confucius, then, rule by ritual is manifestly better than rule by law, not only because it is inherently more humane, but also because it is more effective. Whereas rule by law at best can only deter crime, rule by ritual can preempt the impulse to crime by fostering in humans, through symbolic systems, the desire to create and enhance community, and so teach humans to satisfy their most basic needs without hurting others.

Second, if ritual is a tool for perfecting the self and harmonizing society, the performance aspect of the rites rendered this tool particularly effective. Correct performance of the rites, after all, required the complex coordination of gesture, facial expression, and verbal formulae, an integration that in turn required thorough attunement to the ideas embodied in the rites. Therefore, alongside the metaphors emphasizing the restrictive and normative functions of the rites (for example, the rites as barriers and dikes), a counter set of metaphors expressed the rites as fluid movements akin to those found in symphonic music or choreographed dance. And insofar as the successful performance of the rites, unlike the reading of texts, demanded complete engagement of both body and mind, the messages embedded in artful ritual were apt to be internalized by sheer physical repetition of movements, until they permeated one's whole being, body as well as mind. Hence, the standard punning gloss: "Ritual (*li* 禮) means 'body' and 'embody' (*ti* 體)." As one Ru master wrote, "Once the rites affect the body, self-cultivation is carried out. . . . The body's daily advance in humaneness and the Right may then become unconscious," given the proper environment. But ritual accomplished more than the absolute integration of mental and physical activities designed to give visible form to the virtues. Always the assumption was that the sheer artistry of the ritual performance, displaying an imposing, yet graceful nobility of spirit that had become virtually second nature, made ritual a supremely powerful educator of all who witnessed it. Simple desire to recreate the beauty of the ritual led men to develop the far more elevated desire to attain the splendid charisma attached to the social virtues (fig. 14).

Third, the rites confront, address, and appear to explain many troubling aspects of human existence. It is hardly coincidental that the important rites

Figure 14. Sacrificial dances and music offered to Confucius, illustration 2. The liturgical text in succession stipulates every gesture to be made by hand, feather wand, and body, schooling the officiants in the proper ceremonies by which to best express their gratitude to the Sage for his teachings. From *K'ung tzu: On the 2540*[th] *Anniversary of Confucius' Birth*, 181.

mark crucial transitions—birth, puberty, marriage, and death—for rites are designed to help participants and onlookers embrace change rather than resist it. Rites do this in a number of ways. For instance, they remind participants and onlookers of the passage of time through changes in the colors of vestments, in the choice of rites, in the very selection of calendars to be employed at each ceremonial occasion. They also lend great dignity to occasions that have a component of fear and grief. But if new patterns are to emerge, the ritual obviously must begin by disordering the old. Breakdown, in other words, becomes the necessary prelude to breakthrough.

Preparation for the rites (fasting, purification, lustration, meditation) begins the process of breakdown by interrupting the normal, numbing routines of daily life, the better to induce in participants a deep receptivity to change. Such preparation can also signify, to oneself and others, the commitment necessary to focus one's energies on the solemn rites, being mindful of the benefits accruing from serene acceptance of the imminent, irresistible change. The ritual proper highlights the aura of change by its temporary inversions of the social order. In addition, rites theory reiterates the virtues of change, providing positive examples in the early sages' fashioning (*zuo* 作) of new artifacts of culture (for example, the well, the plough, the boat, writing, and the ritual institutions themselves) on the model of patterns in Heaven-and-Earth. The sages offer models of beneficial changes that are at once old (based on enduring patterns) and new.

Of course, the rites cannot induce widespread or profound social change—cannot function in any respect—except within a context of social cohesion, a context the rites themselves help to create and maintain. For this reason, rites theory unambiguously stipulates that the ritual system binds the entire empire "from the Son of Heaven on down to the common people" into a single community of practitioners, despite the obvious social segmentation. Successful ritual practice, by its very nature, aims at imagined communities and immersion into the Other. Ideally, sacrifice, to take but one example, entails "directing the self to [the object of sacrifice]"; mourners are to direct their thoughts to the dead, recreating the specific attributes of the departed until that person "lives again" in their minds, thereby constituting "a union [of the living] with the disembodied and the unseen."

Fourth, the *Rites* texts and ritual practices, because of this attempt at union, tend to evoke a coherent picture of ideal worlds in which hierarchy is always offset by reciprocity, so that the social order may become entirely equitable, if not entirely equal in the modern Euro-American sense. Equity, according to the ritual theorists, required that each receive from each his proper due, taking into account kinship ties, gender, age, and relative societal contributions. Each in return was to contribute according to his or her abilities. (This meant that the rites could at once foster strong community while accommodating a host of personal and situational differences.) And insofar as fulfillment of the rites essentially entailed periodic redistributions of wealth in each community, except in times of natural disaster when most rites were suspended, the rites could mitigate, rather than exacerbate, extremes of wealth and poverty, another effect making for social stability. One *Rites* chapter goes so far as to claim that the ideal underlying the rites is to have the elite "share advantages with the common people." (In some Chinese villages today, the rites still function this way. According to published reports, poor farmers in the southern provinces enforce local customs by which the rich foot the bill for monthly communal feasts.) Ritual power, then, does far more than merely continue existing social relations. The *Rites* canons, while accepting the inability of ordinary people to fully grasp or articulate the miracle of the rites, impel them all nonetheless toward higher ethical standards, thereby disrupting personal complacency and altering the social status quo. For all the foregoing reasons, both ritual practice and ritual theory work to provoke transformation.

It is understandable that the average person does not grasp the full power and scope of the rites, as the profoundly transformative aspect of rites (especially the major rites) cannot but remain, at base, a mystery. Indeed, the rites' very function is to recreate and convey the complexities of the Dao, leading participants and onlookers alike to glimpse the larger mysteries that daily life manages to obscure, allowing them an intimation of the "Secret [that] sits in the middle and knows." All major rites, then, like the cosmogonic Dao itself, evolve out of undifferentiated chaos, a heightening and mingling of emotions. Typically, then, as a necessary first step toward effecting social change, the rites mirror or even heighten the participants' already somewhat disordered emotions, in order to further their reorientation to a new situation or new relation. Hence the extravagant lamentations by the chief mourners at a standard funeral. Presumably in such extreme cases, the emotional darkness into which the rites plunge the person may be the only way to bring out invisible truths in the course of the day. Rites theory openly and repeatedly acknowledges its intention to play upon the mixed nature of the emotions, the better to move the person from one emotional state to another. For instance, in offering sacrifice the participant "cannot but rejoice in the opportunity to offer the sacrifice. Still, when it is over, he cannot but be saddened," presumably because the conclusion of the sacrifice signals a break in connection to the dead. Similarly, the traditional marriage ceremony makes explicit reference to the occasion's commingled joy and sorrow, joy at the union, with its implied promise of descendants, sorrow at the intimation that the older generation is edging toward death. Even today, a solemn memorial service in rural Taiwan is incomplete without its "teasers," hired actors done up as cheap whores whose lewd antics delight the crowd of humans and gods assembled to watch the procession. Such rituals of festive play and even harsh comedy, far from being humdrum repetitions that reinforce hackneyed thought, are "paradoxical and dangerous enterprises . . . capable of making improbable, impossible claims." Even rites theory, at least in the *Liji*, seems aimed at overturning expectations, as when it employs terms normally reserved for the highest conventional virtues to describe less-than-ideal behavior.

Like the cosmogonic Dao itself, then, the rites unfold from undifferentiated chaos to increasing differentiation and order.* Once the participants can direct their minds and bodies to the ineffable realities, two key components of solemn ritual may begin to come into play: physical construction of the ritual site and sumptuary regulations. Solemn rituals consistently require the construction of a special ritual site, one whose precise geographic location seldom matters. Basically, a new site is required if a new pattern is to emerge from present disorder. So a space is clearly marked off from the everyday world, in order that a temporary site of supersacredness (since All-under-Heaven is considered inherently sacred) be created there, whether a bamboo hut, an earthen altar, or a cell of space indicated by a vivid design drawn on the ground. It is within that marked-off space that the transformative process facilitated by the rites is said to occur. Even necessarily partial explanations of the mysterious processes at work there point to the very human need to be provided with a portion of neutral time and space within which to negotiate the usually incommensurate demands of *si* 私 (the self with its insistent needs and desires) and *guan* 官 (the world of conventions and laws with its stringent impositions). There, in this symbolic space that facilitates focused yet free-ranging exploration, the person may attain a sufficient insight into the workings of things, including the self, so as to arrive gradually at a solution that transcends the equally partial *si* and *guan*, going beyond dichotomous logic and system making. (Such transcendence is conceivable because maximum esteem for others is best expressed through maximum correctness of self-display.)

---

*According to Chinese cosmogonic theory, the Dao at its source is undifferentiated chaos, "without [coherent] form" (*wuxing* 無形), rather than nothing. As it unfolds in mysterious sequence, it proceeds by increasing differentiation until it engenders the myriad things. Death and dissolution only reverse this cosmogonic process, turning what has been highly differentiated (a human being, for example) back into the undifferentiated (the dust). Each act of creation mirrors this cosmogonic cycle. For example, a sculptor begins with an inchoate idea and refines it through several conceptual stages until she is ready to realize it in final form—a form then liable to disintegration. The rites would have us accept, even celebrate, the inevitable rightness of this cosmogonic cycle.

The goal is to epitomize impartial *gong* 公, that which is equitable when viewed in terms of Heaven or the Dao. For in the end the *gong* attitude or act is the only medium through which to reconcile the desires of the self with the demands of the world. Special sites facilitate this process of becoming *gong*, in part because they allow the person a temporary retreat from convention and conflict while offering an intuition into larger realities. Moreover, the accumulated quality and quantity of moral acts previously enacted at a particular site or type of site can work to enhance the person's "good understanding" (*liangzhi* 良知). Once the person has experienced that sense of *gong* within the self, the ritual site is always dismantled, for then the transformed person has not only seen how the sage ideally holds forth at center but also is imbued with the determination to maintain that type of balance in his own interactions with the world beyond the ritually demarcated space. In implicit reply to the Mohist argument that "spatial positions are names for what is already past," the early Confucians conceived of ritually demarcated space as a vital workplace in which the sacred commitment to *gong* was forged, as the first step toward a more just community.

If the participant failed to pursue this vision of centeredness with single-minded devotion, transformation became harder, especially when the person approached the ritual duties in a simplistic or opportunistic manner. Regrettably, the opportunist frequently substituted *guoli* 過禮 (overdoing the rites so as to advertise one's piety) for the altogether admirable *bianli* 變禮 (modifications of the rites designed to better communicate their proper spirit). In the process, he reduced the ineffable rites to a mere tool to wrest from the world the recognition or satisfaction of his own sizable ego. A person adopting an overly simplistic approach, on the other hand, could never hope to penetrate the true meaning of ritual, for a belief that the mere scrupulous observance of ceremony could generate right conduct forestalled the deeper realization that a true center in human relations is found only after the hard work of self-transformation.

Even for such dire failures, the ritual texts afforded an inducement and a path to the *gong* 公 state of mind via sumptuary regulations. Such regulations prescribed the maximum quantity and luxuriousness of consumer goods permitted to each rank in society; the higher one's rank, the more opulent one's clothing, housing, and vehicles might be. Sumptuary regulations, properly employed in a meritocratic society, served to identify for lesser mortals those exemplary persons who had achieved the transformative insights that made them able to contribute generously to the community. Moreover, the sumptuary regulations advertised to the not-yet-moral the palpable material advantages to be gained from *gong* behavior, for the regulations obviously worked to allow men of sufficient merit to gain great wealth and social prominence. Motivated by the prospect of such rewards, even the laziest among the state's subjects might be encouraged to begin the process of emulating those models of self-transformation. And once embarked upon that process, or so the theory holds, even the most obdurate might experience the profound pleasures to be had from extending their mutually empathic relationships; in freely contributing to society and promoting its transformation, such men created a kind of moral multiplier effect throughout society and state. Thus the rites were originally devised, as one influential theory holds, to satisfy desires rather than to curb them: to afford access to material goods while themselves providing less tangible goods, like spectacle, pattern, symbol, and perfect communion with a greater entity. Where well-constructed sumptuary regulations were in place, acts of goodness were crowned with conventional success, so even ordinary people came to desire change, rather than abhor it. This made ritual the least destructive (because most natural) way to promote both social reform and social unity. War and blood sacrifice, once identified as the key affairs of state, were no longer seen as the primary tools by which to generate order.

Consider, then, two of the most famous of the radical views embedded in the *Rites* classics: (1) the "well-field" system presented in the *Zhouli*, which mandates equal distribution of early China's major form of wealth, agricultural land, among the ruler's subjects; and (2) the utopian idea that "all men are brothers" presented in the Cycle of the Rites chapter of the *Liji*, which posits an ideal antiquity in which all goods were shared communally, with the result that selfish impulses were displaced by an orientation toward the common good. According to the well-field system of equal land tenure, which one modern scholar lampooned as "the most symmetrical story ever told," each well-field of one *li* square was partitioned along a grid resembling the Chinese character for "well" (*jing* 井), making nine square plots of equal size, like an American ticktacktoe board with added perimeter lines. Each of eight families would then be assigned a single plot, whose produce was theirs to keep. Together the eight families would share in farming the ninth and central square field, whose harvest they owed to the king as taxes. Irrigation and drainage ditches four feet wide and deep bounded each well-field. This pattern was then to be replicated with strict regularity throughout the king's land until it covered the entire domain. To the early Chinese, the well-field system epitomized the assumption that basic economic equity, ensured by the just state, can alone occasion the circumstances that allow humans "to befriend one another at home and abroad," while yet preserving the appropriate level of social hierarchy.

Even more unexpected is the insistence, in the Cycle of the Rites chapter in the *Liji*, that the rites system practiced in imperial China can induce in society at best only a "minor peace" because its premise has fundamental flaws that prevent the development of a true meritocracy, a true sense of integrity, and a true delight in good fellowship. As the chapter opens, Confucius has just attended a solemn sacrifice in thanksgiving for the harvest. Leaving the place, he heaves an audible sigh, prompting a disciple, Ziyou, to ask the source of his grief. Confucius replies,

> When the Great Way was practiced, All-under-Heaven was public-spirited. They chose men of worth and ability [for public office]; they practiced good faith and cultivated good will. Therefore, people did not single out only their parents to love, nor did they single out only their children for care. They saw to it that the aged were provided for until the end, that the able-bodied had employment, and that the young were brought up well. Compassion was shown to widows, orphans, the child-less, and those disabled by disease, so that all had sufficient support. Men had their portion [of land], and women, their homes after marriage. Wealth they hated to leave unused, yet they did not necessarily store it away for their own use. Strength they hated not to exert, yet they did not necessarily exert it only for their own benefit. Thus selfish scheming was thwarted before it could develop. Bandits and thieves, rebels and traitors did not show themselves. So the outer gates [of family compounds] were left open. This was known as the period of the Great Unity.
>
> Now the Great Way has fallen into obscurity, and so everyone in the empire is family-minded. Each loves only his own parents and cares only for his own children. Wealth and strength they consider to exist only for their own advantage. Hereditary succession among the great men [the lords of the land], they take to be a sufficient rite. Inner and outer walls, ditches, and moats, they take to be adequate defenses. As for the rites and duties, they think them the main structures by which to rectify relations between ruler and subject, to consolidate relations between father and son, to induce concord between elder and younger sibling, to induce loving harmony between husband and wife. By them, they set up institutions and measures; by them, they lay out fields and hamlets; by them, they judge men of courage and understanding to be worthy; by them, they consider merit to accrue to men's personal advantage. Thus selfish schemes are invented. Warfare derives also from this.

This passage from the Cycle of the Rites chapter is far more radical than the well-field system: It not only presumes that a just society will grant its members equal, or at least equitable, access to economic wealth, as the well-field system does; it argues further that even the ritual system institutionalized in Confucius's own day, when considered the supreme Good in itself, undermines the brotherhood of man and precludes the universal benevolence that would proceed from an awareness of this brotherhood. Presumably even those outside the Central States cultural sphere (the "barbarians") can understand that more important than the rites are the ideas embodied in the rites: specifically, caring for others, especially the needy, in a morally serious society. Often misconstrued as a Daoist or Mohist interpolation in a *Rites* classic, the Cycle of the Rites beautifully expands upon three of the most moving passages in the Confucian *Analects*, the first insisting that no person of true humaneness need ever feel alone since "all within the Four Seas are brothers"; the second enjoining the good man "to behave when dealing with those outside the home as though in the presence of important guests";* and the third encapsulating "the Master's dearest wish" in just three simple lines: "With the aged, to comfort them; with friends, to keep faith with them; with the young, to cherish them." The Cycle of the Rites chapter, then, in keeping with the spirit of all three *Rites* canons, would have us rethink and then reorder the proprieties that inform our social relations and customary habits.

ON THE ORIGIN OF THE RITES

The transformative potential of the rites makes sense as soon as we trace the origin of the rites to gift exchanges, first between the living and dead and later among the living. The first Chinese dictionary, Xu Shen's *Shuowen jiezi* (ca. AD 100), defines the character used for "rites" or "ritual" (*li* 禮) as "serving the spirits to bring about good fortune." No such character has yet been found in the earliest Chinese writing, the oracle bone script of late Shang, but the classical scholar Wang Guowei (1877–1927) proved conclusively that the early Zhou character *li* evolved from the character *feng* 豐 (abundant). The character *feng* shows two jades placed in a bronze *dou* vessel as an offering to the spirit-ancestors residing in Heaven. The connection between *feng* and *li* suggests that the earliest notions of ritual centered around spirit offerings made in hopes of securing the powerful ancestors' blessings on future endeavors. And certainly gift-conferrals defined the early Western Zhou nobility, whose presumed gentility became a chief source of inspiration to Confucius. Thus the linkage between gifts and ritual informs almost all early discussions of the *Rites* theory.

---

*The contrast between the Christian ideal and the Confucian is obvious here. Confucius does not enjoin the impossible (that we love our neighbors as ourselves), but the possible (that we treat our neighbors as people of consequence). Still, some Confucian teachings require adherents to realize the profound truth that "Heaven is my father, and Earth, my mother. . . . All men are my brothers and all things, my companions," as in Zhang Zai's famous "Western Inscription."

For instance, two key chapters of the *Liji*, the Meaning of Sacrifice (Si yi 祀義) and the Music Records (Yueji 樂記), both define the rites as requital or repayment (*bao* 報) for favors given, a gift for a gift. Other chapters, including On Self-Presentation (Biaoji 表記), insist that requital plays a crucial role in strengthening compassion so that it becomes consistent, civilized behavior. The opening chapter in the *Liji* states, "What ritual upholds is the give-and-take. If I give out but nothing comes in return, that is contrary to ritual. If something comes, but I give out nothing in return, that is equally contrary to ritual. Humans who observe the rituals are secure; those who do not are in danger." Clearly, early Chinese ritual masters consciously articulated a fundamental lesson more recently explicated by the modern anthropologist Marcel Mauss. Gifts of time, of gesture, and of food, as well as of more valuable material objects, are a powerful method by which to create irrevocable ties between human beings. The institution of a gift cycle was at once free and constrained, disinterested and self-interested. The social ties that it created (based on notions of honor and dignity, rather than coercion) produced a firmer foundation for a stable and just society than the charity or commercial exchanges known to relatively "advanced" societies, both of which tend to create ill-will between individuals precisely because they are exploitative, condescending, or inherently unbalanced. In premodern China, every gift had to be returned (though not all requitals needed to be of equal monetary value), so that within and between generations an ongoing cycle of exchanges established the basic obligation of every individual to both give and accept; as a charming lovesong from the *Odes* has it, "Throw me a quince / I'll requite it with beryl. / Not as an even swap, but to make love last forever." Numerous ritual regulations in ancient China governed the ways in which gifts (including gifts of foods, pets, carriages and horses, and even fiefs) were to be presented so as to lend honor to both recipient and giver, thus strengthening the long-term socio-cosmic bond between the human and divine orders. Long accustomed to thinking in terms of mutual ties, the early Chinese may well have found it easier than we do to presume mutual interest and to impart mutual satisfaction, for the gift exchange presupposes a fundamental kinship between donor and recipient, leaving some part of the giver's inalienable spirit in trust with the receiver. Could such a continual emphasis on circular exchanges wherein temporary loss turns to gain also have led to a greater acceptance of the adage, "Only change is constant"?

Loss is gain: the inherent power of the rites, both in theory and in practice, rests partly upon an appreciation that paradox rules human existence, paradox defined not as mere inconsistency but as a grave dilemma inherent in life that nonetheless mysteriously enhances rather than diminishes existence. Insofar as that sense of paradox embodied in the rites matches human experience, the rites can be trusted. "Surely the rites are ordered after men's feelings!" the *Hanshi waizhuan* proclaims. The special character of early Confucian theorizing about the rites, therefore, consists in this: its willingness to confess that all injunctions found in the *Rites* canons can be no more than guideposts to proper human behavior because the achievement of ritual order at each point relies upon an exquisite sensitivity to distinctions between people and situations, one inspired by a single-minded dedication to social needs. The result is a negotiated "art of holding all in one's hand."

Perhaps the same idea—that loss is also gain—prepared the early Chinese to accept other paradoxes at the heart of learning by Confucius's plan: (1) that the full development of each person's singular nature depends, at least initially, upon strict adherence to that seemingly most conformist of activities, ritual, which stresses relatedness rather than uniqueness; (2) that the realization of one's human potential through the distinctively human institution of ritual results in the acquisition of a second nature that is godlike (*shen* 神) in its transformative powers; (3) that the Confucian emphasis on the ritual expression of integrity (*cheng* 誠) pulls the person outward and inward, as the salutary union with Heaven-and-Earth corresponds to the signal ability to unify one's thoughts and deeds; and (4) that the true sage in ritual activity engages simultaneously in miraculous "creation" (*zuo* 作) and faithful "transmission" (*shu* 述) through ritual, the only tool or system capable of merging the aesthetic with the instrumental. Certain self-proclaimed disciples of Confucius among the classicists were "conscious, direct, and aware" that such paradoxes or peculiar incongruities lay at the very heart of ritual, requiring in life a series of discrete resolutions informed by experience and taste.

Ultimately, this frank acknowledgment of tensions in human existence allows the *Rites'* canons to frame the argument that perfect conformity with the rites demands a strong sense of balance, as the mourning chapters of the *Liji* make plain. If society is to work well, respect for hierarchy must be offset by a readiness to recognize important commonalities among members of the community; formal obligations incurred in society (for example, those owed by the son to his "official" mother, his father's primary wife, as opposed to his birth mother) must also be balanced against emotional debts (for example, those owed by the son to his wet nurse and birth mother). In essence, ritual celebrates "conduct by the Mean," defined by the Chinese as the balance point between emotional extremes, which lies nowhere near the lowest common denominator. Like the cosmic Dao itself, "Rites trim what is too long and extend what is too short, do away with surplus and repair deficiency."

Because of this capacity to induce balance within the ritual participants,* they

> extend the forms of love and reverence, and step by step bring to fulfill-
> ment the beauties of proper conduct. Beauty and ugliness, music and
> weeping, joy and sorrow are opposites, and yet rites make use of them all,
> bringing forth and employing each in its turn. Beauty, music, and joy
> serve to induce an attitude of tranquillity and are employed on auspicious
> occasions. Ugliness, weeping, and sorrow induce an attitude of inquietude
> and are employed on inauspicious occasions. But though beauty is used,
> it should never reach the point of sensuality or seductiveness, and though
> ugliness is used, it should never go as far as starvation or self-injury.
> Though music and joy are used, they should never become lascivious and
> abandoned, and though weeping and sorrow are used, they should never
> become frantic or injurious to health. If this is done, then rites have
> achieved the balance point. . . .
>
> The beginning of the two emotions [of joy and sorrow] are present in
> man from the first. If he can trim or stretch them, broaden or narrow
> them, add to or take from them, express them completely and properly,
> fully and beautifully, . . . then he has achieved true ritual.

To the extent that humans' love of paradox or search for balance informs their distinctive responses to human existence, the *Rites* canons have valuable lessons to teach, lessons that people may be more prepared to hear as post-modernist discourse bring them to place ever greater value on aesthetic orders. Among these lessons, are, first, that patterned behavior is necessary as a way of communicating respect for others. (Acknowledgment of this necessity may inspire the all-important question, "What kind of patterned behavior is most suitable to modern society?") Second, that emphasis on unifying symbolic prac-tice (orthopraxy) probably makes for a less divisive society than the doomed search for a correct unity in thought (orthodoxy). Third, that some prevailing Western notions of self as a fixed entity determined by genetics and early expe-rience may prove more destructive to social harmony and personal growth than traditional Chinese notions that stress the self-in-process as the sum total of meaningful human interactions. And fourth, that there is a valuable distinction, nearly lost today, between work, which by definition is absorbing, gratifying,

---

*These ideas are most fully addressed in the famous Doctrine of the Mean (*Zhongyong* 中庸) chapter of the *Liji*, a chapter that constitutes one of the Four Books in Zhu Xi's edu-cational schema. The comparison with Aristotle's *Nicomachean Ethics* is illuminating.

empowering, even transporting, and tasks done for survival. In ancient times, as one *Rites* canon tells us,

> When they entered the dance, the ruler, holding his shield and axe, went to the place for the dance. The ruler took his place at the head of those on the east. In a square-topped cap, wielding the shield, he led his many officers [in the dance], in order to give pleasure to the royal dead. Thus, the Son of Heaven in sacrificing joins All-under-Heaven to give them pleasure. And the lords in sacrificing join those within their borders to give them pleasure. . . . Sacrifice is the greatest of blessings. Now when those above have such blessings, then their favors will surely be granted to those below.

If modern life, increasingly bereft of community and suspicious of shared social responsibility, could gain some semblance of an akin order, playful yet solemn, civil yet discriminating, full of variety and industry, Confucius's injunction to "renew the old" spirit of the *Rites* would be fulfilled. A start made by merely "intoning the classics will have ended with reading the *Rites*." Already, some in Taiwan, in China, and in the Chinese diaspora—pop culture figures as well as leading academics—have begun to argue that the best response to the inhumanities, uniformity, and cultural subjection encouraged by the late stages of capitalism and Communism is "returning to *li*" in a "Confucian type of culture." Is this mere nostalgia or the tardy recognition, when all else has failed, that Confucius might well have been right after all? For "if it is really possible to govern with ritual and yielding, no more need be said."

Chapter Five

THE *CHANGES* (*YI* 易)

You should not resist fate
Nor need you escape it.
If you go to meet it
It will guide you pleasantly.
—Goethe

FROM AT LEAST THE HAN PERIOD, MOST
Chinese have traced the origin and transmission of the *Changes* divination manual, the *Yi*,* far back into the archaic past. In contrast to the other Classics more dependent upon the single figure of Confucius as author-editor, the *Changes* boasted no fewer than four culture-heroes contributing to its completion in four discrete stages. During the formative period of civilization, the Eight Trigrams were devised by the primeval ruler Fu Xi 伏羲 (also known as Bao Xi 包犧), who

---

*The *Yi* or *Yijing* (*Changes Classic*) is often transliterated by an older romanization system as *I ching*.

THE CHANGES

THE CORE TEXT consists of

the 64 Hexagrams or graphic symbols 卦

the 64 Hexagram titles 卦名

the 64 Hexagram Statements 卦辭

the 384 (64 × 6) Line Texts, one for each graphic line 爻 in each Hexagram

THE TEN WINGS APPENDICES consist of

the "Tuan" 彖 (On the Hexagram Statements), in two parts

the "Xiang" 象 (On the Images), in two parts

the "Xici" 繫辭 ("On the Appended Phrases"), also called the "Great Commentary" 大傳
  in two parts

the "Wenyan" 文言 (Sayings on Pattern), in one part

the "Shuogua" 説卦 (On the Trigrams), in one part

the "Zagua" 雜卦 (Interposed Hexagrams), in one part

and the "Xugua" 序卦 (Sequenced Hexagrams), in one part

The "Tuan" conveys a judgment on the Hexagram as a whole and on divinatory lines in particular, on the assumption that moral conduct directly parallels and reinforces the cosmic process. The "Xiang" offers a double focus on the graphic images, commenting both on the "great image" of each Hexagram (whose two component trigrams guide individual conduct in changing social and cosmic circumstances) and on the "small image" assigned to each individual line in each Hexagram. The "Xici" or "Great Commentary," which seeks to define the function of the *Changes* in the universe, will be reviewed in some detail in this chapter. The "Wenyan" sees the meaning of the sixty-four Hexagrams encapsulated in Hexagrams 1 and 2 of the *Changes* (with the former dubbed "The Key" in one recently excavated version). The "Shuogua" explains the cosmic significance of each of the Eight Trigrams, supplying the major correlations (e.g., characteristic direction, moral virtue, season, animal, body part, and so on) as it outlines the theoretical relation between the *Changes* and the Dao. The two final commentaries, the "Zagua" and the "Xugua," analyze the sixty-four Hexagrams in terms of pairs of contrasting or comparable Hexagrams.

THE EIGHT TRIGRAMS

Qian 乾 (also called "the key" 鍵) = dryness, firmness, initiating, the masculine

Kun 坤 = wetness, suppleness, gathering in, receptivity (but not passivity), the feminine

Zhen 震 = thunder

Kan 坎 = abysmal waters

Gen 艮 = mountains

Sun 巽 = wind

Li 離 = fire/sun;

Dui 兑 = lake

extracted the emblems from significant orders in the natural world of Heaven-and-Earth; the sixty-four Hexagrams, each with a separate Hexagram Statement, were generally ascribed to King Wen, predynastic founder of Zhou; the Line Texts were credited to the Duke of Zhou, son of King Wen and regent for the second Zhou king; and the Ten Wings, or Appendices, to Confucius. Thus the *Changes* in its successive phases of composition was thought to reflect the entire history of antique Chinese sagehood, from its first culture-hero down to Confucius himself. Given such massive authority, it was small wonder that the text was believed by Han to function as "an ancient thing that fixed fate."

To derive the *Changes* ultimately from Fu Xi's emblems was to believe that the oldest stratum of the *Changes* antedated by half a millennium any other written compilation of sacred materials, since traditions dated Fu Xi's reign to a period some five hundred years earlier than the time of the sage-emperor Yao, whose "Canon" begins the *Documents*, and more than a thousand years before Tang, one of the early culture-heroes mentioned in the *Odes*. Two items of accepted lore fostered the widespread perception that the *Changes* had been preserved faithfully from the archaic past: the highly structured sequence of its graphs was thought to preclude easy interpolations by would-be forgers, and the early *Changes* manuscripts, alone of all the Five Classics, had supposedly escaped destruction during the Qin Burning of the Books (213 BC) because technical manuals of divination and medicine were specifically exempt from that proscription. Consequently, most Chinese at one time, educated or not, embraced the notion that the authority of the *Changes* is so great as to be proof even against inept diviners; prognostications by the *Changes* were thought to be accurate so long as they were honestly performed. One famous thinker, Zhou Dunyi (1017–1073), spoke for many when he posed the rhetorical question, "How can it be that the *Changes* is simply the source of the Five Classics? It is the mysterious home of the gods of Heaven and Earth!" Ironically, then, a text not even considered a Ru classic until a century or so before the Han period rapidly came to be revered as the holiest of all the Five Classics—and thus the holiest of all things (fig. 15).*

This quality of mysterious holiness has engaged nearly every major thinker in imperial China. Perhaps no single work in China has elicited more interest from

---

*To date, the earliest extant text to list the *Changes* among the Classics is a "Collected Sayings" (*Yucong* 語叢) essay included in the Guodian finds (ca. 300 BC, reported in *Wenwu* 1977:7). One would like to know which sequence of the Classics the essay used, but the original order cannot now be ascertained because of the condition of the find. The modern editors have chosen to put the *Changes* at the head of the list of Classics in order to reflect the Eastern Han Archaic Script order. Note that traditions make the *Changes* both a man-made thing and a divine revelation.

Figure 15. (*top left*) Primitive people dressed in crude robes, worshiping the Eight Trigrams following the sage Fu Xi's invention of them (from Ming edition of *Kaipi yanshi futu*); (*lower right*) a picture of Confucius studying the *Changes* in his old age, in the company of his disciples (from Ming edition of *Kongsheng jia yu tu*, as reprinted in the frontispiece of the original edition of *Gushipian*, vol. 3).

scholars and laymen alike down through the ages. The table of contents to the *Jingyi kao*, a comprehensive survey of scholarly material from the Han dynasty through the seventeenth century, lists 2,050 works on the *Changes*, at least 500 of which are full commentaries. And some respected modern Chinese philosophers, including Xiong Shili (1885–1968), have continued to refer to the *Changes* as the foundation for their ideas. Outside China, the *Changes* is without a doubt the best-known Chinese book, in addition to being the most familiar of the Five Classics. Beginning with Gottfried Wilhelm von Leibniz (1646–1716) and continuing through Carl Jung (1875–1961) and Joseph Needham (1900–1995), the work has had considerable influence on leading intellectuals in Europe and America, who have mined it for alternate theories of structural change in the natural world. As a result, some twenty-eight versions of the *Changes* are currently available in the United States (though only four translations seem to be based on the original Chinese). To these positive measures of the *Changes'* impact in early modern and modern times, one may add the negative. Because a close reading of the *Changes* sharply challenged the dominant European worldview of their time, the first Jesuit missionaries to study and promote the *Changes* were all eventually declared insane or heretical. Centuries later, the People's Republic under Mao Zedong and Deng Xiaoping attacked the *Changes* on the ground that it reinforces customary predilections to "trust to fate"; the text has become a perennial target in the Party's periodic campaigns against "superstition."

To some degree, the pervasive and enduring impact of the *Changes* simply reflects the great concern that humans feel toward their own fates, for people consult books of divination to learn their futures and to improve their daily lives by discovering which objects, relations, and acts please or displease the spirits. The earliest written records in Chinese are the Shang oracle bones addressed to the gods by the ruling elite, which conveyed the elite's charges to heaven ("Fu Hao will bear a son") and sought the intercession of the ancestors in human affairs. Application to the gods through milfoil divination was later a component of many rituals regularly performed by bureaucrats and family heads on behalf of the state or patriline. At all levels of society, spirit communication through divination marked the beginning and end of the sacred rites celebrated in connection with momentous occurrences, including births, betrothals, travel, marriages, severe illnesses or prolonged infertility, appointments to office, the selection or accession of an heir, the appearance of strange portents, and deaths. So pervasive a role did divination play in the common religion of imperial times that the *Changes* is the only Classic to be included in both the Ru and Daoist canons, for use in and out of office. I focus here on the less overtly religious aspects of *Changes* theory, but readers should be wary of any view that portrays the Chinese as a people who have preferred to "keep spirits at a distance." Confucius's famous injunction was not intended to turn his adherents into secular humanists; it urged them to engage in a spectrum of ritual acts, including divination, lest wrathful spirits be provoked.

While divination in all forms has enjoyed enormous popularity in China for all recorded history, the *Changes* in particular has been revered or deplored because of the enigmatic character of its text. The text today reads as a jumbled compilation of omens, rhymed proverbs, riddles, and paradoxes, with snatches of song and story drawn from popular myth and archaic modes of divination. Tradition was right to portray the *Changes* as the product of multiple authors working in discrete eras, though it vastly overestimated the antiquity of the text. By the time the final additions to the *Changes* had been made and the received text included in the official canon, many of the early images had lost their original, direct meanings—some because of changes in the culture or in Chinese language, and some because the original divination text was radically reinterpreted through its Ten Wings, so that anachronistic philosophical and social concepts were read into the "core" Classic comprised of the six-line Hexagrams, Hexagram Statements, and their attached Line Texts. It is not surprising that early sinologists saw it as everything from a phallic cosmogony or textbook of logic to a Bactrian-Chinese dictionary. Neither is it astonishing that one Chinese authority insists that no Chinese scholar for the past two thousand years can honestly claim to have understood the text.

How, then, may we—more distant in time and possibly less open to the strange—usefully approach the *Changes*? Scholars know that the text originated as a diviner's manual and later acquired a reputation as a wisdom book useful to the nonspecialist. Some present-day interpreters celebrate this evolution, seeing it as a milestone in early thought, whereby the original divination manual embodying a belief in luck and chance (whose prediction and interpretation required the services of specialists at court) came to support the belief that changes are apprehensible and even controllable by persons of sufficient self-cultivation. Other interpreters, being more preoccupied with the powerful relations among words, images, and signs, prefer to stress the *Changes'* masterful employment of these multiple lenses, designed to instill in readers a simultaneous awareness both of the deep significance of ordinary human life and of the ultimately mysterious character of the cosmic processes.

The *Changes* encourages multiple readings while neatly balancing two contradictory propositions: that life is fated, and so outside our control, ruled by unseen forces, and that humans construct their own fates. In the *Analects*, Confucius suggests that the person "who fails to understand the fated [aspects of life] has no way of becoming a noble person," presumably because she ignores the distinctive boundaries within which the life of virtue must be lived. To inspire a clear-eyed commitment to humane behavior in the face of inescapable constraints, the received text of the *Changes* (representing, as we shall see, a revised and enlarged vision) successfully equates the achievement of the good life with the careful application of discernment and effort to the problems of self and society. As both the unseen forces and the visible world are ruled by divine patterns, both are natural, necessary, and fundamentally moral. And because the *Changes* represents a repository of all the key patterns needed for full human development, the moral person, with the guidance of the *Changes* and without the mediation of special religious experts, can achieve true control over many aspects of life, "riding" the positive cosmic energies that exist equally in the universe and in human beings' moral nature. Admittedly, the world at times may be vulnerable to destructive dislocations from within and without that make for temporary imbalances and injustices, but good acts create a congruence of patterns within Heaven-and-Earth and a consciously patterned self so powerful as to integrate self, society, and cosmos.

According to the *Changes*, application to the text could conceivably benefit even "petty persons" devoid of ethical concerns. The text itself promises to teach and enlighten ordinary persons, so that "stupid men grow unfoolish and sly men abandon their deceit." Of course, not all persons in every age have looked to the *Changes* to strengthen their will to embody and engender the patterns of the moral Way. Perhaps the vast majority of those casting the *Changes* have simply wished to better their luck. And while some scholastics devoted entire lifetimes to the invention of arcane "numbers-and-images" interpretive techniques (see below), ordinary users with mundane aspirations could, after receiving an answer from the spirit world, return promptly to everyday concerns, without expending precious time and energy in frustration and fear.

THE CORE TEXT

Origin and Dating

Tradition distinguishes four separate parts within the received text aside from the Eight Trigrams, those three-line graphic forms supposedly invented by Fu Xi to replicate the basic types of configured energy (for example, lake, fire, mountain):

- Layer I   The sixty-four Hexagrams, six-line graphs—broken or unbroken, supposedly signifiying yin and yang, respectively*—which tradition

---

*Yin literally refers to the dark side of the mountain slope, and yang, to the southern, sunny side of the slope. From this the terms come to mean "dark" and "bright," respectively. In the *Changes*, yang is allied with Heaven, so it is seen as catalyst and progenitor;

said were produced from all possible combinations (8 × 8) of the Eight Trigrams.

- Layer 2   A single Hexagram Statement assigned to each of the sixty-four Hexagrams.
- Layer 3   The 384 so-called Line Texts (6 × 64), each attached to a single one of the six graphic lines that make up each of the 64 Hexagrams. Typically, a Line Text consists of a single image coupled with its own prediction formula (for example, "of benefit to use to have an audience with the king").
- Layer 4   The so-called Ten Wings appended to the core text of the *Changes*, composed of seven commentaries (three of these in two parts). The most famous of the Ten Wings is the Xici 繫辭 (On the Appended Phrases), known to many simply as the "Great Tradition" or "Great Commentary" (Dazhuan 大傳). From Han on, most citations from the *Changes* are to the Ten Wings, especially the "Great Commentary."

If we must now reject many traditions about the archaic origins of the received text, including the Eight Trigrams as origin of the *Changes*, this division of the received text has at least the advantage of alerting us to the huge gap in chronology and conceptualization that separates the earlier Hexagrams, Hexagram Statements, and Line Texts (hereafter the "core *Changes*") from the later Ten Wings. As this basic distinction between the core *Changes* and the Ten Wings underlies any sophisticated understanding of the history of the received text, readers should familiarize themselves with the standard technical vocabulary used in connection with these two parts of the received *Changes* (summarized in the table found at the opening of this chapter) before moving on to consider complex questions surrounding the origin and dating of the *Changes*. To underscore the difference between these two halves of the extant text, this chapter treats the history and content of the core text separately from the Ten Wings.

Modern scholars in their reconstructions agree that the earlier stratum in the *Changes* consists of the sixty-four Hexagram titles, the single Hexagram Statement found under each title, the Hexagrams formed of six parallel lines that are

generative and often fearsome, it is never self-effacing. Yin, which is allied with Earth and equally sacred, is characterized as fecund (like fertile fields or life-giving water), full of latent potential, supportive, and self-effacing. According to Yin/yang theory, all change in phenomenal existence is produced by the operations of these two phases called yin and yang, which are relational modes rather than fixed entities. (For more on this and on the Five Phases, see Key Terms.)

either divided (broken) or undivided (straight), and the six Line Texts attached to each Hexagram.* A typical Hexagram Statement in the core text, like the following example taken from Hexagram 24 ("Return"), establishes one or more themes common to the whole Hexagram:

> *Return. An offering.*
> *In going out and coming in: no illness.*
> *Friends come: no blame.*
> *Turning round and going back, his path.*
> *Seven days to come and return:*
> *Benefits to those with somewhere to go.*

After each generalized Hexagram Statement, the *Changes* text puts six Line Texts, one for each graphic line of the Hexagrams, read from the bottom line up. The Line Texts typically consist of two main parts: a primary compelling image (for example, "three journey together," "a crane calling in the dark," or "floods of tears"), followed by one or more prediction formulae (for example, "unlucky for meeting a superior" or "favorable for going to war").

In one plausible theory, the Line Texts in the core *Changes* evolved when two quite different kinds of sources were combined, omen-verses (often in the form of brief jingles, on the model of "Red sky at night / Sailors' delight") and oracular prose statements loosely based on formulae found on the Shang-Yin oracle bones and bronzes (for example, "Benefits to those with somewhere to go"). As the two sources were combined, the punch lines of the omen-jingles (in this example, "Sailors' delight") were dropped, presumably because they were too well known to need restatement. The incomplete omen-verses were then coupled with the prose statements, so that one of the Line Texts might finally read something like, "Red sky at night. Benefits to those with somewhere to go." On occasion a brief mantic formula would be added, especially where its insertion produced an internal rhyme that made the prognostication more memorable. In such cases, the mantic formulae, usually only one or two characters

*The core *Changes*—as opposed to the Ten Wings—makes no reference to the Eight Trigrams. And commentators do not often relate the shape of the six-line Hexagram to the title, Hexagram Statement, or Line Texts. Hexagrams 27 ("Corners of the Mouth" ☲) and 50 ("The Tripod" ☲) are exceptions, however: Hexagram 27 is likened to an open mouth and Hexagram 50 to the form of that ritual vessel. Less plausibly, the Tuan appendix says that Hexagram 24, "Return," represents reversion graphically, as its single yang line on the bottom "returns" to five yin lines.

in length, then characterized the entire Line Text as *li* 利, *heng* 亨, *hui* 悔, *yuan* 元, or *zhen* 貞, or some combination thereof.*

Major sources of imagery in the Line Texts include (1) observations of the skies and weather; (2) observations of human behavior, especially involuntary movements (belching, sneezing, twitching, and the like); (3) aural and visual puns; and (4) historical anecdotes, with most referring to legendary events of Shang and early Zhou. Those images depending upon close observation of natural phenomena seem most familiar, not only because they resemble peasant lore the world over, but also because they reiterate the logic of divination, by which humans avidly search for signs in the world at large that may be portents from the gods:

> *A feeling in the big toe . . .*
> *A feeling in the calf . . .*
> *A feeling in the thigh . . .*
> *Fidget, fidget, back and forth:*
> *A friend follows your thoughts.*
> (Hexagram 31)

> *Go forth lame, come back praised . . .*
> *Great lameness: friends come.*
> (Hexagram 39)

> *The thunder comes crash, crash,*
> *Laughter and talk, ho, ho . . .*
> *Thunder comes sharply:*
> *Innumerable cowries lost.*
> (Hexagram 51)

---

*Originally, these mantic formulas referred directly to divination practice. *Li* meant "beneficial [to divine]"; *heng* 亨 probably meant *xiang* 享 (sacrifice offered to the gods), though it may have referred, as Waley suggests, to a rite that fixed or stabilized the prognostication or served as a loan character for *ji* 吉, meaning "auspicious," as Shaughnessy suggests; *hui* 悔 meant "determined [through divination] with regret"; *yuan* 元 referred to the great or primary sacrifice; and *zhen* 貞 signified that the divination had been "determined with assurance." From the Warring States period on, however, many commentators took these mantic formulas to describe moral virtues. *Li* meant "moral benefit" or "what accords with duty"; *heng* meant "morally penetrating," "steadfast," or "the confluence of auspicious things"; *hui* meant "morally regrettable"; *yuan* meant "the greatest good"; and *zhen* meant "morally upright" or "manageable." This process of moralization had already begun by the time of compilation of the "Wenyan" appendix in the Ten Wings. For further information, see Gao Heng, *Zhouyi dazhuan jinzhu* (1973), 5ff.

Fording the stream:
The fox wets its tail: Distress.
Dragging, the cartwheel: Determined.
  (Hexagram 64)

Line Texts that rely on a knowledge of historical anecdotes or early astrological observations require considerably more explication, at least for the modern reader. To take two examples: Line 5 of Hexagram 34, "Great Strength," says simply, "Lost sheep at Yi" in a terse allusion to the story of Wang Hai, leader of the predynastic Shang people. It was said that when Wang Hai, following the example of several earlier leaders, moved his capital north to a location closer to the "barbarians," he was killed by barbarians at Youyi. Many of the proto-Shang people were taken captive and their herds seized. The Line Text thereby warns against moving along old paths into dangerous territory. Nearly as laconic is Line 5 of Hexagram 54, "The Marrying Maid," which reads, "Emperor Yi gave his younger girl in marriage. The groom's sleeves: not as fine as the girl's. . . . A moon or more to see the auspicious." Emperor Yi, the second-to-last ruler of Shang (tradit. r. 1191–1155 BC), married his daughter to King Wen of Zhou in hopes of cementing his alliance with that powerful border vassal. The groom dutifully acknowledged his subordinate status by his less sumptuous outfit, but his ritual submission meant little once Emperor Yi's daughter had given birth to King Wu. For that event began the process by which the political Mandate would be transferred from Shang to Zhou within a generation, foiling the best-laid plans of Emperor Yi. And so the Line Text relays the rather obvious truth that what is good for the goose may be bad for the gander.

Fairly often the language of the Line Texts resists interpretation. It is only now, as excavated materials make for steady advances in the study of archaic Chinese language, that the archaic meaning begins to be discerned in some puzzling cases. For instance, the top line, Line 6, of Hexagram 54, "The Marrying Maid," opens with the statement, "The woman holds the basket, but no fruits are in it." On the surface, the Line Text describes a botched betrothal ceremony in which the proper presents have not been exchanged, an interpretation that fits a parallel image following it in the Line Text: the failure by a man, presumably the groom, to draw blood from the sacrificial sheep, as required by the ritual. But a woman holding a basket also conjures up notions of fertility, for "bloody basket" is the name given a woman's pelvic region. The phrase "no fruits" then predicts future infertility. The couple cannot pass the ancestors' charisma down through the generations, the ritual faults mentioned in the text being either the symptom or the root cause of the disorder.

Readers generally feel freer to discern patterns when each group of six Line Texts clusters around a single visual emblem, with additive imagery or incremental repetition throughout, as in Hexagram 52, in which all the Line Texts but one name human body parts from feet to head in their proper order, or Hexagram 53, with its wild goose:

> *Lines 5 and 6* = *When the wild goose skims the tumulus, . . .*
> *Line 4*   = *When the wild goose skims the tree, . . .*
> *Line 3*   = *When the wild goose skims the open land, . . .*
> *Line 2*   = *When the wild goose skims the rock-ledge, . . .*
> *Line 1*   = *When the wild goose skims the bank, . . .*

Hexagram 1 itself, usually considered the prototype for all the others,[*] displays this same sort of graduated change (also this rough correlation of number to height), for in Line 1, the dragon is submerged; in Line 2, it comes out in the fields; in Line 3, it works busily through the day; in Line 4, it leaps over the deep; in Line 5, it flies; and in Line 6, a flock of headless dragons soars overhead, an indisputable reference to the turning Green Dragon constellation. Those looking for special signs in the heavens had noted the Green Dragon's slow progress through the night sky, which begins in spring when it becomes visible in the eastern quadrant of the sky and ends in autumn when it sinks headfirst below the western horizon.

But in some Hexagrams, talk of incremental or sudden change permits an examination of a single theme from different angles. Hexagram 44, for example, appears to be a multifaceted discussion of fertility and infertility (apparently leading up to the birth of a godlike culture-hero), for after the Hexagram Statement, "The queen is strong. Do not marry [another] girl," the Line Texts supply a number of related images: an emaciated piglet nursing frantically (Line 1); two conventional images of fertility, seeds ready to burst (or, alternatively, ripe melons) and fish (Lines 2 and 4); a halting gait (Line 3), which suggests the pregnant woman's slowed movements; the traditional binding of the ripening womb, which holds within a brilliant sign, a child (?) come from heaven (Line 5); and, in the top line (Line 6), the queen swelling in late pregnancy or, in an alternative reading, being toasted with wine. "Distress but no blame" attends the welcome pregnancy.

So striking is the core *Changes'* concern with ideas of graduated change, timely behavior, and the necessity for multiple perspectives that when Line Texts

---

[*] In the Mawangdui silk manuscript of the *Changes*, Hexagram 1 is entitled "The Key" (Jian 鍵) instead of Qian 乾, as it is in the received versions.

in a single Hexagram lack any apparent connection with one another, scholars surmise that the original organizing principle (be it graphic, phonetic, semantic, or historical) has been lost to later readers. While such losses occurred in connection with every text in archaic Chinese, since that written language lacked the punctuation, inflection, and determinatives (also called radicals) that serve to pin down the precise meaning of particular characters, such losses affected more of the core *Changes*, whose short phrases were too brief to establish the kinds of patterns for scansion and parallelism that later readers tended to rely upon in interpreting difficult passages. The very malleability of the inherited stock-in-trade of the old court diviners, owing to linguistic ambiguity, made the core *Changes* the perfect vehicle for those who sought to read into the ancient *Changes* divination manual the existence of a wisdom book, replete with high-sounding talk about the most abstruse and abstract virtues.

To demonstrate just how divergently a single *Changes* Hexagram could be read, two standard translations of a hexagram are given below, the first reflecting early preoccupations with the mysterious turtle divination process, facilitated by the sacred ritual vessels with their *taotie* tiger designs, and the second reproducing the more moralized reading favored by later commentators: As can be seen, the earlier *Changes* is blunt and concrete by comparison with the abstracted elaborations of later commentators:

Hexagram 27 (#15 in the Mawangdui MS)
Line 1, the bottom line:

Dispensing with your numinous turtle	You let your magic tortoise go,
And viewing our shortened jaw.	And look at me with the corners of
Inauspicious.	the mouth drooping. Misfortune.

Line 2:

Say upside-down jaw;	Turning to the summit for
Threshing the warp at the	nourishment.
northern jaw	Deviating from the path to seek
To be upright is	nourishment from the hill.
inauspicious.	Continuing to do this
	brings misfortune.

Line 3:

Threshing the jaw;	Turning away from nourishment
Determination is inauspicious.	Perseverance brings misfortune.

For ten years do not use it.	Do not act thus for ten years.
There is no place beneficial.	Nothing serves to further.

Line 4:

Upside-down jaw:	Turning to the summit for
Auspicious.	nourishment brings good fortune.
The tiger looks with eyes	Spying about with sharp eyes
downcast.	like a tiger,
His appearance is so sad.	with insatiable craving.
There is no trouble.	No blame.

Line 5:

Threshing the warp	Turning away from the path
Determination about a dwelling	To remain persevering
is auspicious.	brings good fortune.
One may not ford the	One should not cross the
great river.	great river.

Line 6, the top line:

From the jaw:	The source of nourishment
Danger;	Awareness of danger
Auspicious;	brings good fortune.
Beneficial to ford the great river.	It furthers one to cross a great river.

Perhaps in response to such disparities in understanding that have left few traces on the historical record, the multiple authors of the Ten Wings, working during the late Warring States, Qin, and early Western Han periods, sought to reframe the context for the divination results in the core *Changes* in order to affirm the supreme utility of the *Changes* in wider, moralizing contexts.* Given the laconic and vague pronouncements found in the core *Changes*, later commentators could mold the mantic pronouncements of the core Classic more or less easily into a moral system of complex coherence in their search for the larger cosmological foundations for fate. The very indeterminacy of the *Changes* would facilitate "the resolution of doubts."

*Du Yu's (AD 222–84) postface (*houxu* 後序) to his commentary to the *Zuozhuan* states that a manuscript copy of the *Changes* excavated in AD 279 from the tomb of King Xiang of Wei (d. 296 BC) did not include the Ten Wings, though it did include a lost text of yin/yang explanations. Recent finds at Baoshan, Guodian, and elsewhere show that interpretive essays in the classicizing mode were probably associated with the *Changes* for about a century before unification of the empire in 221 BC.

While tracing the power of the text to its great age in the reign of the legendary Fu Xi, scholars before the mid–twentieth century commonly held also that divination by milfoil, as basis for the *Changes'* oracles, began only in late Shang or in Zhou. New archaeological evidence (some of it inscribed on Shang oracle bones) suggests a more complicated picture of early divination. Excavations show that the Shang-Yin and Zhou rulers, both before and after the Zhou conquest of Shang, practiced several kinds of divination, including one method that relied on counting bamboo stalks and another on manipulating milfoil. This mixture of methods continued, even as divination by milfoil came gradually to be used outside the court. The Great Plan chapter in the *Documents* has the ruler relying on both types of divination, after all, and the *Odes* sing, "Divine with a tortoise shell / Divine with the milfoil stalks." The *Zuozhuan* records twenty-four cases of turtle divination and twelve of milfoil, with at least one diviner favoring turtle over milfoil. An excavated tomb at Baoshan belonging to an official of the southern state of Chu who died in 316 BC outlines a procedure that relies on turtle and milfoil in turn, suggesting that divination by milfoil may have become full partner to fired oracle bones, even if it once functioned as mere supplement.

Archaeological and literary evidence alike attest to the increasing popularity of divination by milfoil in late Zhou, Qin, and Han, a popularity having both theoretical and practical bases. In theory, the milfoil plant (familiar to American gardeners as yarrow) was divinely suited to predicting the future because the graph for "milfoil" puts the graphic sign meaning "old" and "to test" under the graphic signifier meaning "plant." Milfoil by implication could lay claim to great age and a preordained function in testing. The visual pun, possibly strengthened by an aural pun linking "milfoil" (*shi* 蓍) to "time" (*shi* 時),[*] seemed to confirm the inherent capacity of milfoil stalks to transmit timely communications between the living and the dead, whose collective persons represented the sum total of wisdom and experience residing in Heaven-and-Earth. Two practical considerations probably also helped divination by milfoil eventually supersede divination by turtle in importance. Diviners

---

[*] In ancient times, in addition to this *shi* 蓍 mentioned in the main text, three other characters were regularly used for milfoil, all of which have graphic components indicating the vast age or magical properties of this particular kind of stalk: *qi* 耆 (Morohashi no. 28849), which can also mean "very aged," "to arrive at," or "ultimate"; *tao* 檮 (no. 15713), the right-hand of which signifies "longevity"; and *shi* 筮 (no. 26070), whose bottom half means "magician." Some traditions also mention the *tao* grasses as the favorite haunt of numinous turtles (no. 26070.1).

using milfoil avoided the trouble and expense of securing a steady supply of turtle carapaces. (For similar reasons, coins now serve as a convenient substitute for yarrow stalks, though their use in this context can be justified neither by long tradition nor by supreme utility.) And the number systems associated with milfoil divination meshed so well with those built into the correlative theories being promoted in some circles by the fourth century BC that both seemed to confirm not only one another, but the final perfection of the cosmos as well. In any case, diviners, professional and amateur, soon came to know the milfoil stalks so much better than the oracle bones that scholars by early imperial times retained only the haziest notions of the original techniques, interpretive methods, and underlying principles associated with animal pyromancy.

A discovery in 1976 of a cache of predynastic Zhou oracle bones (that is, bones used by the lords of Zhou before their conquest of Shang) therefore electrified scholars of early China, insofar as it promised to shed light on both the origins of divination by milfoil and its possible relation to pyromancy. A typical inscribed divination formula from that cache, recalling various oracular statements in the *Changes*, read, "The scribe-diviner You Fu made this precious instrument. Divined: 7-5-8." That some forty-odd inscriptions on these predynastic Zhou oracle bones, like those on a few Shang and Zhou bronzes, clearly referred to sets of numbers—some of six and some of three— inevitably brought to mind the six graphic lines of the Hexagram and the three graphic lines of the Trigram. Might these number sets constitute the direct precursors of the *Changes'* Trigrams and Hexagrams, with their attached Line Texts? Many were happy to conclude that they did. Before long the cache was hailed as constituting "the [original] *Changes* belonging to King Wen of Zhou."

But even true believers in these number sets as origin of the Trigrams and Hexagrams have had to confront several related puzzles. If divination by oracle bone and milfoil evolved truly in tandem, what impulse first pushed the milfoil diviners to go beyond the simple yes-or-no format employed in oracle bone divination? And if these number sets of three and six really served as precursors of the Trigrams and Hexagrams, respectively, why does the core text of the *Changes* make no explicit reference to the Trigrams? Admittedly, some imagery in the core *Changes*, especially in the enigmatic Hexagram Statements, lends itself to a reading of the Trigrams as eight significant "natural" paradigms in Heaven-and-Earth. As parents, Qian 乾, representing dryness, the masculine, and the impulse to initiate ☰, and Kun 坤, representing wetness, the feminine, and the impulse to complete ☷, together bear and beget:

☳ Zhen = thunder

☵ Kan = abysmal waters

☶ Gen = mountains

☴ Sun = wind

☲ Li = fire/sun

☱ Dui = lake

But knowing neither the exact historical relation of Hexagram to Trigram, nor the exact method devised to derive mantic number sets, one can only suppose that the mantic number sets evolved into the simpler system of broken and unbroken lines now in the core text of the *Changes** because of graphic similarities between those lines and the ancient forms of the characters for "six" and "eight" mentioned in the number sets.

When the graphic symbols for the Hexagrams, the Hexagram titles, Hexagram Statements, and Line Texts came together to form a core *Changes* remains a matter of intense speculation. Some modern scholars opt for a date as early as the tenth century BC, seeing the core *Changes* as a conscious composition of one or more editors, though the text was subject to modification until it was stabilized in the first or second century AD. Others posit a continual, nearly unconscious process of evolutionary accretion, with the hexagrams acquiring local meanings through oral transmission until such time as the core text coalesced and was written down, possibly as late as the fourth century BC. On the one hand, in its references to abductive marriages, slaves, cowries used for currency, and war captives sacrificed to the gods, the core *Changes* appears to

---

*In the two earliest editions of the core *Changes* now known, the Mawangdui silk manuscript and the Shanggudui (Fuyang) bamboo slips (both dating to early Western Han), the numeral one — signifies yang, while the numeral eight 八 (with its broken line) signifies yin. See Li Ling, *Zhongguo fangshu kao* (1993), 242, 260–71. Besides the Baoshan (Hubei) finds dated to ca. 316 BC, important finds at Tianxinguan (late fourth century BC) and at Wangjiatai, tomb 15 (mid-third century BC?), apparently use columns of numbers to indicate hexagrams instead of the graphic conventions using broken and unbroken lines).

preserve traces of Shang and early Zhou society. On the other hand, vestiges of such practices endured in some areas up to unification under Qin in 221 BC, and even in oral transmission the core text could have retained archaic grammatical and rhetorical features well into the Warring States period. Such obvious references to antiquity could also have been inserted into the text to make it appear more venerable. Most probably, given that the core *Changes* never once mentions an abstract philosophic concept, it predates the virtual explosion of theoretical inquiry ca. 500 BC. But the employment of terms not found on the oracle bones and the existence of numerous graphic variants in extant versions (mostly the sorts of phonetic loans and substitutions typical of different dialect areas) equally suggest a lengthy process of "tidying up" the text before the production of state-sanctioned versions. More precise dating is hard to establish.

How did the core *Changes* text finally come together? There are signs that the core *Changes*, like several other Chinese classics, may have first been written down when texts, being scarce, were typically memorized by disciples and explicated orally by masters. Many Chinese characters used for this first transcription of the core *Changes* would have been written without their determinatives (that is, radicals), for determinatives were not needed when the written text functioned mainly as an aid to memory or as sacred incantation or charm (the gods, ghosts, and ancestors needed no graphs to recognize meaning and presumably felt more comfortable with archaic forms of writing). But once written texts became available to wider reading audiences, as happened during the Warring States period, heretofore sacred readings kept originally within small circles would suddenly have presented themselves to readers quite unfamiliar with traditions of divination. Determinatives had to be added when the habit of phonetic borrowings in transcription gradually created so much ambiguity that it forced attempts at resolution. And with thinkers of various stripes openly competing for patronage, including the financial support of local elites, would-be masters of the predictive arts and purveyors of wisdom would have had not only to choose among several possible readings for most Chinese characters in the *Changes* text, but also to "correct" the text where it seemed defective, as it was bound to seem wherever it failed to support their own rhetorical stances.

Wisely enough, modern scholars, in their attempts to reconstruct the original core *Changes*, have focused on passages where the fit between the Chinese characters employed in the received version and their contexts seems less than perfect. For example, early imperial commentators read *fu* 孚 in its usual sense of "trust" in Hexagrams 9, 14, 17, 20, 49, 64, but why would Line Texts talk of "trust" filling an earthenware jar or of "the blood of trust" flowing out? Modern scholars surmise that it must be ants (*fu* 蜉, the sound component + the insect radical) filling the jar and the blood of war captives (*fu* 俘, the sound component + the human radical) spilling out on the ground. Everywhere peasants predict weather by watching the behavior of ants. And the blood of war captives, smeared on sacred vessels, was one of the most potent offerings made to the gods and ancestors whose advice was sought in divination. It is through such painstaking reconstructions that the restoration of one or more early *Changes* versions may yet be made.

The Core Changes *vs. the* Ten Wings

Clearly, the main problem in dating the entire received *Changes*, as the scholar-statesman Ouyang Xiu (1007–1072) realized a millennium ago, is that neither the core *Changes* nor the Ten Wings, let alone the two together, can possibly represent the work of a single diviner or compiler.* Substantial differences exist between the core *Changes* and the Ten Wings in grammatical usage, word meaning, type of material, and treatment of subject—differences due to the long centuries intervening between the composition of the core *Changes* and that of the Ten Wings, which must have been written in late Warring States, Qin, and early Western Han.

To list but a few of the most obvious discrepancies marking the two halves of the received *Changes* text: First, as mentioned above, the core *Changes* makes no mention of the Trigrams at all, though the Ten Wings consider the Trigrams' relation to one another and to the Hexagrams a vitally important subject, attesting to the mysterious symmetry pervading all the cosmic spheres. Second, the core *Changes*, unlike the Ten Wings, never seems to gloss itself. The core *Changes* never remarks upon the title, *Yi*, for instance, though the Ten Wings refer to it in no fewer than eighty-four passages. Neither do the Line Texts explain their own cryptic images or the relation of those images to either predictions or Hexa-

---

*The Ten Wings, though the product of a single impulse toward correlative thought, represents a collection of sedimented texts produced over several centuries, often in response to changing political dynamics. Each appendix in the Ten Wings shows signs of multiple authorship. The "Great Commentary," for example, gives two different stories regarding the discovery of the Trigrams: that they were a special revelation from Heaven, in the form of the River Map and Luo Writing and that Fu Xi found these patterns in the natural world. I treat the Ten Wings as a unit only because there is neither enough time nor enough knowledge to trace their separate histories. Scholars often do not know why a specific interpretive approach used before Song was important at a specific time or how it relates to conceptual tools used in the political arena.

gram graphs, a task that has been left mainly to the Tuan and Xiang commentaries included in the Ten Wings. Third, the core *Changes* employs no abstract philosophic terms at all, whereas several of the Ten Wings employ such terms in explicating the underlying cosmic and moral systems tying Lines, Hexagrams, and Trigrams together. Yin/yang Five Phases correlations also do not appear in the core *Changes*, though such correlations (at least in rudimentary form) underlie some of the Ten Wings, giving us a possible date of composition: The existence of such correlations makes it likely that the Ten Wings did not come together in a single corpus before those correlations were systematized, possibly as late as the first century BC, though some of the essays in the Ten Wings circulated as separate treatises in Warring States and early Han. The additional material included in the Ten Wings would have allowed early readers of these essays to read back into the core *Changes* the newest philosophical ideas and cosmological theories. With that accomplished, the antiquity of the *Changes* would work to bolster the prestige of new theories, just as the appearance of omniscience in the *Changes* shored up the text's claims to a divine origin.

In many cases it seems that the compilers of the Ten Wings worked to dispel some of the abstruseness of the *Changes* text. But apparently, in a number of cases, the compilers worked to maintain a degree of fruitful ambiguity in the text so that it could reveal truths on several levels simultaneously. By a simple recasting of the basic mantic images, to take one instance, the flying dragons of Hexagram 1 could easily become the supreme symbol for noble men, whose exemplary movements were always in complete conformity with the cosmic cycles, no matter whether they acted vigorously in the public sphere or remained in relative obscurity. From each such single conversion of meaning, numerous cosmic and ethical lessons spun out over time, the sacred lessons read into the text inevitably responding to the pressing issues of the day—so much so that several millennia later the modern philosopher Xiong Shili could see in the top line, where the dragons lack heads, canonical proof of the innate equal goodness of all men, above whom there should be placed no absolute ruler. Thus the *Changes*, in Xiong's mind, is the earliest known text to advocate political democracy. Such extensions from earlier readings, with their accreted layers of meaning, have served to keep the core *Changes* relevant to generations of readers.*

---

*Of course, upon occasion the compilers and their interpreters created additional interpretive problems in proposing elaborate and doctrinaire readings that relentlessly specified meanings, despite the notorious ambiguity of the document they intended to elucidate. In particular, conflicting numerological theories, as we shall see, derived from the mistaken belief that the text evolved from the mathematical regularities of Fu Xi's Trigrams.

Such semantic extensions have certainly contributed to the belief among those without technical training that even ordinary readers may find in the core *Changes* a repository of cosmic wisdom sufficient in kind and in quantity to prompt insights into all aspects of phenomenal existence and to guide human behavior in all spheres of life, even those that seem to modern minds quite unrelated to the religious sphere, such as career advancement. That the Ten

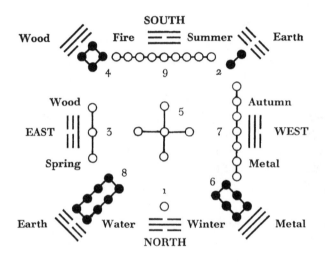

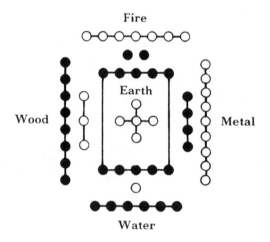

Wings do convince many readers of the absolutely sacred character of the core *Changes*—and so of its suitability as a medium of exchange between gods and men—is a measure of the rhetorical force it commands and the fascination that its systems of image and number exert. The text lends itself beautifully to discussions of time, the calendar, and fate, prompting reflection on the nature of timely action and opportunity. At the same time, its production of multiple perspectives seems to encourage discussions on the relation of reality to appear-

---

The River Map (top) and Luo Writing (bottom) are each mentioned once in the same passage in the "Xici." Conceived as magic squares produced by divine revelation, the River Map is often held to be the ultimate prototype for the Eight Trigrams. Various apocrypha identify both the River Map and Luo Writing as heaven-sent talismans whose appearance from the primeval waters of central China heralds the rise of a true king. Zhu Xi said of the River Map and Luo Writing, for example, "Heaven and Earth cannot speak, so they rely on the sage to write books for them. Were Heaven and Earth to possess the gift of speech, they would then express themselves better. The River Map and Luo Writing are examples of what Heaven and Earth themselves have designed." See ZZYL 65/9a.

According to legend, the round River Map (representing Heaven) consists of fifty-five spots arranged on the back of a dragon or horse that emerged from the Yellow River. The spots represent the Five Phases, which are thought to give birth to one another in a predetermined sequence: Wood produces Fire, Fire produces Earth (ashes), Earth (ores) produces Metal (when smelted), Metal (when molten) produces Water (for dew condenses on metal), and Water produces Wood (through irrigation). Each of the Five Phases are assigned two numbers, with even numbers representing the yin (or female) and odd the yang (or male). Even and odd are said to be united in harmonious union; hence the ability of this River Map to foster spontaneous production through the cycle of the Five Phases in a manner consistent with the constant laws of nature. In contrast, the square Luo Writing aligned with earth comes to symbolize impermanence and loss, for the Writing lacks the ten dots assigned in the River Map to Phase Earth.[*]

So far as we know, the writings of Shao Yong (1012–1077) and Cai Shen (1167–1230) are the first in which the Luo Writing was drawn with black and white dots in the manner of a Nine Palaces charm. Hu Wei (1633–1714), in his *Yitu mingpian* (Elucidation of the Changes' Maps) was one of the first scholars to systematically refute the traditional relation constructed between the River Map and Luo Writing, on the one hand, and the *Changes* and "Great Plan" chapter of the *Documents*, on the other.

---

[*] Though a Map and a Writing (possibly not these?) were certainly in existence by the time of Liu Xin (53-23 B.C.), scholars beginning with Ouyang Xiu (1007–1072) have questioned their divine origins and relation to the *Changes*. The writings of Huang Zongxi (1610–95) persuaded many to see the magic squares as extraneous to *Changes'* interpretation. Some in late imperial China even accused Shao Yong and Liu Mu of importing these magic squares from a Daoist reading devised by Chen Tuan (fl. ca. 950). For further information, see Larry Schulz (1982), p. 217ff.

ance or the relation of the part to the whole. The Ten Wings' glosses on the *Changes'* title and the "Great Commentary's" moralizing claims (examined below) shed light on just those issues. But before that, it may help to review available records on the increasingly complex understanding of the *Changes'* powers that evolved in the Chunqiu and Warring States periods, well before the compilation of the Ten Wings, for this understanding almost certainly facilitated the later incorporation of the Ten Wings into the *Changes*.

Evolving Uses of the Core Changes

Although more definitive answers about the history of the *Changes'* theory and practice will depend upon continued analysis and further archaeological finds, historians, in thinking about the process by which the core *Changes* came to have Ten Wings appended to it, have already noted an important evolution in perceptions of the core *Changes*. By this evolution, preceding but presaging the Ten Wings' theorizing, some literati came to view the text less as a divination manual and more as a repository of time-tested wisdom, though neither function was exclusive. Modern scholars, trusting to some two dozen semifictionalized accounts of divination chronicled in the *Zuozhuan*, which covers the years 722–464 BC, theorize that a shift occurred early in the seventh century BC because the *Zuo* entries prior to 604 BC show the *Changes* functioning exclusively as diviner's manual, in contrast to later entries, in which members of the elite cite the authority of the *Changes* without using any divination results as pretext for their observations. Two representative examples, supposedly spaced some fifty years apart, illustrate this difference. The first account focuses on an auspicious prediction process itself, but in the second men make predictions based on the *Changes* text without reference to any divination act. In the first entry, from 645 BC, the ruler of Qin is about to launch a punitive expedition against the ruler of Jin, who has failed to observe the diplomatic proprieties owed to Qin:

> Tufu, the court diviner in Qin, divined with the milfoil stalks and the outcome was: "Auspicious. Ford the Yellow River and the ruler's carriage will be wrecked." When the ruler of Qin demanded to know how such a prediction could ever be considered lucky, the diviner replied, "Ah, but this means great luck! After three defeats you are bound to capture the ruler of Jin, for the Hexagram encountered is *Gu* (Hexagram 18), meaning 'pest' ䷑. It says: 'A thousand chariots three times depart. After three departures, a capture of the male fox.' Now the fox is a *gu*, a pest, so this must refer to the ruler of Jin. The lower Trigram for the Hexa-

gram is wind, while the upper is mountain. The season right now is
autumn [when the harvest comes]. If we knock down their fruit and make
off with their timber [in the manner of a violent storm raging up the
mountainside], that means we will be victorious. And with Jin's fruit fallen
and its timber lost, what else could this mean but defeat for Jin?" [*Annals*,
15th year of Duke Xi of Lu]

The second example dates from 597 BC, when the leaders of the Jin army have
been debating how and when to attack the army of Chu. In utter defiance of
army regulations, which stipulate that all wings of the army must proceed in
unison, the arrogant Jin general Xian Gu in his capacity as assistant of the central
army leads that portion of the troops under his command to ford the river ahead
of the others, so that he can begin the attack:

> "This army is in great danger!" said [his commander] Xun Shou. "This is
> precisely the situation described by the *Changes'* Hexagram, 'Legions,'
> which says, 'An army proceeds by regulations. If they are not well kept,
> it is inauspicious.' In the conduct of state affairs, obedience brings good
> results. Disobedience does not. When the armies disperse, weakness
> results, as a marsh forms when the river is no longer held back.* Now,
> though regulations exist, each man does as he pleases. . . . [But once set
> loose,] the regulations go dry, as when water drains after a flood. . . . This
> leads to an inauspicious outcome! . . . This is what the *Changes* means!"
> [*Annals*, 12th year of Duke Xuan]

In this second example, a specific passage in the *Changes* is cited, but no divination has been performed. In contrast to the first example, in which the milfoil
divination predicts defeat for Jin regardless of any actions that may be taken by
those in the two enemy camps, in the second example the working presumption is that humans may improve their fates through strict observance of the
moral lessons embedded in the *Changes*.

For moralists who accepted the supreme authority of the *Changes*, it was
perhaps only a matter of time before the correctness of the prediction was

---

*Xun Shou here makes an explicit reference to Hexagram 7, "Legions," which is com-
posed of an upper trigram associated with rivers and a lower trigram associated with wet-
lands. He argues that while the river waters command great force, swampy waters have no
inherent power. Xun then continues to employ water metaphors to suggest the extent of
the impending disaster facing Jin as a result of Xian Gu's thoughtless act.

thought to depend upon the upright behavior of the parties involved in the divination procedure. This is made abundantly clear by two anecdotes included in the *Zuozhuan* and assigned to the sixth century BC, the first concerning Lady Mu Jiang, recorded for the ninth year of Duke Xiang (597 BC), and the second told of the rebel Nankuai, recorded for the twelfth year of Duke Zhao (530 BC), both of which concern success in interpreting the *Changes*. Lady Mu, a highly educated, capable woman, had been placed under house arrest in the Eastern Palace, charged with flagrant sexual misconduct and with outright treason against the government of her own son, Duke Cheng. Sometime during her confinement, a milfoil diviner appears in the narrative to predict Lady Mu's future. The diviner, anxious to please the well-connected Lady Mu or to comfort her, interprets the milfoil result (Hexagram 17, Sui) to mean that Lady Mu will soon be released from her incarceration. Lady Mu, who is far too intelligent to accept the diviner's interpretation, supplies an alternate and much more pessimistic milfoil reading that later proves correct:

> Of this Hexagram, the [Hexagram Statement of] the *Changes* says: "Sui: Great, successful, beneficent, firm. No blame." Now the word "great" describes those in charge of others; "successful," those who are the focus of admirable traits; "beneficent," those who induce that harmony that results from adherence to social duty; and "firm," those who manage human affairs. One who exemplifies humanity is qualified to be in charge of others. One happy in virtue is fit to conform with ritual. One who has benefited others is qualified to effect a harmony from duty. And one who is firm is qualified to manage all affairs. Such traits cannot be claimed falsely [as the oracle knows whether they exist or not].
>
> Only if I were to possess such traits would there be "no blame"—no matter what the prediction says. As I have been inhumane, I cannot be called great. Neither can I be called successful, since I have disturbed the state. As I have brought harm upon myself, I cannot be called beneficent. Neither can I be called firm, since I once abandoned my position for intrigue. Those who possess these four [good] traits are Sui. It is they who are described by the phrase "no blame." But I have none of these good traits, so how could I be Sui? I as a rule have chosen to do evil, so how could I bear no blame? I will most certainly die here. I will never gain my release.

In the second entry, the rebel Nankuai, in the course of plotting a rebellion, asks a friend, Zifu Huibo, to interpret blindly (that is, without sufficient knowledge of the specific situation) the divination results Nankuai has obtained: Line

Text 2 of Hexagram 5, which reads: "Yellow skirt. Supremely auspicious." Zifu Huibo, a student of the *Changes*, can say only what it ordinarily portends:

> "If it refers to a deed of loyalty and fidelity, then it is possible [that the lucky prediction will come true]. But if not, there will certainly be defeat. The outer figure indicates strength and inner warmth; such is loyalty. There is also harmony leading to fixedness, an apt description of fidelity. . . . Yellow is the color of the center but a skirt [unlike a blouse] is designed to adorn what is low. If the center be disloyal, it will not attain its proper color. If one below be disrespectful, he will not attain the proper ornament. And if the affair be no good, it will not attain ultimate success. . . . When the three virtues [of loyalty, harmony, and respect for superiors] are fostered, that makes for goodness. When these three virtues do not apply, the situation will not correspond with the [auspicious] phrasing of the milfoil divination."

There can be no clearer statement that personal virtue was by some point presumed to be the main prerequisite for obtaining an accurate and auspicious reading from the divine milfoil stalks. The great historian Sima Qian (ca. 100 BC) concurred: "The cracks respond to inner faith and sincerity. [When a divination is accurate,] may we not speak of a convergence between the two realms [of the pure inner spirit and the divine spirits]?"

Later *Changes* masters were wont to emphasize and elaborate this principle, advising amateurs to "first take up the words and ponder their meaning, so that the fixed rules [operating in the universe] will reveal themselves. But if you are not the right person [meaning a moral person], the meaning will not reveal itself to you," for the *Changes* only "takes on meaning in relation to the current situation." The text is not fixed or dead, in other words, because the same divination line is capable of yielding a great many constructions. As one person puts it, "The turtle shell is an image, the milfoil stalk, a number. Phenomena come into being and give rise to images, which are then multiplied. The images multiplied give rise in turn to numbers. But how can a . . . lapse in virtue ever be explained by [mere] numbers? . . . 'The ills of the people down below / Are not sent down from Heaven / . . . Contention is born of man.'"

One of the *Rites* classics explains divination as "bringing the matter to the attention of the August Ancestor." As divinations were meant to alert the gods to a particular person's wishes for the future, in the hope that the gods' blessings might be secured on behalf of a specific endeavor, it made sense that an auspicious divination would not work for a malefactor and that the *Changes* "could not be employed [successfully] to make reliable predictions about morally dangerous acts." For in the traditional way of thinking, even the gods and ancestors may not subvert the cosmic laws to favor evildoers, though the supplicants be their own relatives. By the same token, an overreliance on the oracles was said to be useless, if not downright harmful. Frequent application to the gods undermined the divinely ordained separation between gods and humans; as familiarity breeds contempt, to call upon the gods to intervene in every minor matter showed disdain for the spirit world. For obvious reasons also, a failure to heed the initial message sent from the gods turned good fortune into bad: "When the milfoil divination is auspicious the first time, but one draws the process out two or three more times, it will surely be inauspicious." Therefore the good person hoping for an accurate prediction—the only person who could reasonably expect such an outcome, according to the moralists—sought first, in the words of one commentator, "to make his actions proper before resorting to divination." Ideally a person would refuse to divine at all (a) if she found that she could not approach the act of divination with single-minded concentration; (b) if the issue was not in doubt; (c) if her plans were less than virtuous; and (d) if she did not intend to follow the instructions the gods issued through the result. So arduous was the ritual self-examination in preparation for divination that reports had Confucius himself feeling sure about only seven of each ten of his prognostications. And it is not surprising that Xunzi (d. 238 BC), one of the early Confucian masters, believed that "those who are really good at doing the *Changes* need not actually ever divine" for real expertise in the text presupposed remarkable insight into all the underlying patterns operating in oneself and the universe.

Injunctions placing some restrictions on divination practice reflected the ethical concerns of thinkers in Warring States and Han who believed that free will, rational choice, strategic action, and moral conduct should essentially determine the ultimate course of a person's fate. But even the most ardent adherents of Confucius in their daily round of activities often employed divination in their search for divine guidance (usually consulting the *Changes* but sometimes other well-known techniques, such as prognostication by the winds or physiognomy). To say, as some modern scholars are wont to do, that classicists as a group changed their conception of the core *Changes* from a divination manual predicting the future to a philosophical treatise outlining an ethical Way is to the ignore historical realities. (One only need recall the "evil-averting" [*bixie* 避邪] Eight Trigrams talismans placed above the lintels in literati homes to see this.) But it is no exaggeration to say that an emphasis on the cosmological and ethical power of the core *Changes* (which incidentally greatly expanded the possible interpretations the manual could produce) created the climate of thought later reflected in the Ten Wings.

THE TEN WINGS' SPECIFIC CONTRIBUTIONS

The Ten Wings on the Title

Given the new levels of ethical meaning ascribed to the *Changes* well before the inclusion of the Ten Wings in the received text, the Ten Wings' authors naturally sought to explain the significance of the title in order to demonstrate the full measure of the sacred text's depth and richness. Initially, the *Changes* was known as the *Zhou Yi*, or *Zhou Changes*, a title that laid implicit claim to the moral authority of the Zhou dynasty, whose early exemplary leaders (particularly good King Wen and the Duke of Zhou) were so much admired by Confucius. And because the Ten Wings claimed that King Wen, the Duke of Zhou, and Confucius each wrote parts of the *Changes*, the title *Zhou Changes* suggested the putative authorship and cultural context of the text's composition. But the character *zhou* 周 was not used only as a proper noun referring to Zhou times. In many passages it functioned instead as a verb, adverb, or adjective meaning "to go full circle," "full circle," or "comprehensive." For the early Chinese, as for the early Greeks, the circle embodied sublime perfection insofar as nothing could be added to it. Moreover, as all points on the circumference of a circle stand equidistant from the circle's center, the circle bespoke equitable treatment and equal access. Through such associations, the title *Zhou Changes* confirmed the "all-encompassing and all-inclusive" nature of the "Way of the *Changes*." The *Changes* faithfully represented all things in their entirety and in just proportion; it was also a text to which users could claim equal access. As one master remarked, "There is not a single thing that those who made the *Changes* did not bring together, from the obscure and bright of Heaven-and-Earth to the minute subtleties of the various insects, grasses, and trees." Only such a fully comprehensive text could be expected to mirror precisely the complex cycles of life and death, as a devout student of the *Changes* once observed: "For when the heavens and the sun turn in their circuits, hard and soft [= yang and yin, respectively] indeed make contact. Each returns to its place, so that it is a fixed rule that once ended, the cycle begins again. Now giving life, now giving death, human nature and fate are illuminated therein! . . . Even if he were to go against it [these cycles of fate], a person cannot, for it is the Mystery [of the changes] that silently by rule makes each attain its proper place."

The *yi* 易 in the title *Zhou Yi* (*Zhou Changes*) afforded the Ten Wings commentators equally rich opportunities for this type of imaginative glossing. Very early on, philologists in China decided that the archaic graph *yi* 易 had been devised as a subtle, if unmistakable, reference to two especially meaningful signs in the extrasocial world: that of the chameleon 蜴, symbolizing both the noble man's propensity to adapt to his surroundings and his willingness to conform to

Heaven's patterns, and that of the doubled light or enlightenment streaming from the conjunction of moon 月 and sun 日, indicating a perfect balance between yin and yang. Then, by a pun that worked equally well on the ear and the eye, *yi* 易 meant *xi* 錫 "to bestow" from "a superior to an inferior," for had not the *Changes* text been bestowed by the high gods upon the sage-kings for the express purpose of guiding lesser mortals in their decisions?

The "Great Commentary" appendix included in the Ten Wings, while alluding to all the foregoing explications, supplied three more of its own. According to the commentary, *yi* means (1) easy, (2) change, and (3) no change, terms that are paired with virtue, with *qi*, and with position, respectively. By definition, virtue is easy for the sage, who has so honed his sense of empathy and intuition that he anticipates change and accepts it effortlessly.* Despite the infinite variety of forms assumed by the changing *qi* in its operations, when a virtuous person steps outside her own limited perspective and looks beyond the confused diversities of perceptible reality to intuit the larger patterns informing the universe, this promotes the smooth transitions associated with incremental and appropriate change. (Hence the incremental alterations appearing in many emblematic images in the Line Texts.) Change, after all, is not the only constant, as fixed principles inform every interaction in the natural world of Heaven-and-Earth (for example, the natural distinction demarcating high from low) and then shape the noble person's activity. Thus when a truly noble person holds sway over the social realm, all change throughout the triadic realms of Heaven-Earth-Human can finally become suitably regular and predictable. In that sense, even this world of continual change can present a model of constancy or no change. The "Great Commentary" further promises that insofar as humans can reintroduce order into their interactions, they may come to understand, even embrace, change in ways that will grant them peace, stability, and security—and in some cases, considerable power—in their lives. As one influential tradition associated with the Ten Wings explained it,

The name *Yi* has three meanings: the easy, the changing, the constant. . . . The word "easy" is how we characterize its quality. No outer gate bars comprehension of true circumstances; no inner door blocks the spirit stored within. Its illumination penetrates the four quarters, so that distinctions are simply and easily established and Heaven and Earth made brilliantly clear. The sun, moon, stars, and planets are assigned their places; the Eight Trigrams are set in order. . . . Without trouble or bother, [the

---

*However, the term "easy" may have first meant simply that it was less trouble to divine with milfoil than with pyromancy.

myriad sorts of things] are quieted and freed of error. It is this which is its easy quality.

What changes is the *qi*. If Heaven and Earth did not change, they could not make their *qi* pervasive. The alternations of the Five Phases would then come to a standstill; the changing of the four seasons would then cease. . . . Should the ruler and ministers not change, they cannot bring the dynastic house to perfection. . . . Should husbands and wives not change, they cannot bring the family line to completion.

What does not change is position. That heaven is above while the earth is below, that the lord faces south while his vassal faces north, that the father sits while his child bows before him—these are [some of the principal] constants.

The Ten Wings, in their discussion of the *Changes'* title, begin to build a case for the benign character of change. As the one constant in the universe, change is shown to be necessary for social order and human insight. But this is not all. The Ten Wings testify at the same time, as we shall see, to the utter perfection of the *Changes* as guide to phenomenal change and to right practice.

The Ten Wings' Claims for the Core

Having forged tight connections between the *Changes* text, the natural patterns of Heaven-and-Earth, and a set of moralizing principles through their analysis of the *Changes'* title, the Ten Wings proceeded to prove their case for the uniquely sacred and supremely efficacious character of the *Changes* by seven linked propositions offered most clearly and compellingly in the "Great Commentary" to the *Changes*:

1. The ancient sages discovered the proper form of the Trigrams and Hexagrams after intense study of the divine archetypes of patterned change inscribed on the night sky, in the earth's configurations, and by the sacred divining tools. Therefore, the Trigrams and Hexagrams, which depict in mathematical combination all the possible alternations of *yin* and *yang*, yield a complete picture of all the possible dynamic processes.

2. Next, these same culture-heroes invented the basic components of human civilization (for example, weaving, music, markets, wells, ploughs, and the basic social institutions, including sociopolitical, age, and gender hierarchies), modeling each of these human constructs on the divinely inspired forms of the Trigrams and Hexagrams. In this way,

the sages saw to it that human tools and institutions, however artificial in one sense, were equally "natural" in another, for nothing unnatural could be adapted nicely to human uses and conduce to morality.

3. The myriad things emerge from an original state of undifferentiated *qi* called *wu* 無 (nothing), a shorthand expression for *wuxing* 無形, meaning that the *qi* in the primeval state is without form, inchoate chaos. Then in successive stages the *qi* takes on increasingly individuated forms, with *wu* producing yin/yang, which in turn produces the Four Virtues or Five Phases, which then in combination spawn the fully individuated myriad sorts of things of phenomenal existence. But at the high point of this development, the *qi* begins to revert again, moving ever closer to undifferentiation, until death spurs the final dissolution of form and individuality. All creative and productive human activity must follow this basic pattern set by *qi*.

4. So precise were the sages in modeling the *Changes*' text upon such set patterns that the condensed hyperreality of the *Changes* text parallels the supreme powers in the phenomenal world in all important aspects, not only replicating but reinforcing the fundamental relational processes at work in the triadic realms of Heaven-Earth-Human; as the *Changes* "has within itself" the complete range of natural patterns, it is one with the cosmos, an exact mirror and equal partner. (Were the *Changes* merely a representation of the cosmos, it would be both limited and lifeless, a sorry vestige of things.)

5. Therefore, those who seek to comprehend the full range of change and constancy in ourselves and in our world can do no better than to turn to the *Changes*' text.

6. The *Changes* can teach readers to distinguish significant from insignificant change, thereby enabling them to prioritize their concerns and pursuits. (Without the *Changes*, ordinary humans find it difficult to ignore the white noise generated by the ceaseless interaction of tendencies.) By focusing attention on the limited field of significant change, devotees of the *Changes* can achieve mastery over the changes that most affect their quality of life, since, by definition, such mastery is predicated on an exquisite sensitivity to the ethical implications of each evolving situation. They consistently act with circumspection in both senses of the word, the ability to see all around implying an akin ability to intuit the prudential course of action.

7. The inevitable result is human behavior that is easy (because it is natural) and efficacious (because it builds upon preexisting trends in perfect conformity with Dao). The operations of the master of the

Changes/changes become virtually indistinguishable from those of the cosmic Dao itself. In godlike fashion, the master exhibits an intuitive grasp of the sublime unity pervading all and wields knowledge and skill to shape the course of events appropriately. Thus, the sage reaches a state in which "the ideas contained in his mind and in external things are one, . . . so that no things lie beyond his nature and . . . his mind."

By these seven claims, the "Great Commentary" sought to persuade its readers that the only way to gain deeper insight into cosmic processes operating in ourselves no less than in the world at large is to approach change through the graphic symbols and literary images contained within the *Changes* Classic. Undoubtedly, the commentary's portrayal of active sages was designed to directly refute the portrait of sagehood offered in many early texts (including the *Laozi* and *Zhuangzi*) that present *wuwei* 無為 (not acting or intervening on behalf of any set goal) as the ideal. Arguing from common sense, classicists had advanced the observation that it is only the unfilial child who does not return with medicine for a dying father, only the disloyal subject who does not offer new policy measures for a declining state. But common sense would hardly prove to everyone's satisfaction the correctness of the commentary's claims attesting to the perfect utility of the core *Changes*. All such claims would seem compelling only to the degree that the Ten Wings' masters and their successors could show an infallible system embedded within the text. That explains the Ten Wings' frequent references to system and to symmetry, the subject taken up below.

The Ten Wings' Expansion of Divinatory Potential

As we have seen, the Ten Wings (chiefly in the "Xici," or "Great Commentary") present a complex argument by which the *Changes* classic, as its title suggests, functions not merely to represent the universe in words and images, but more importantly to inform and influence sociocosmic relations simultaneously inside and outside the text. In order to further demonstrate the perfection of the core *Changes*, the Ten Wing's authors predicated at least two additional sets of major symmetries, operating on separate conceptual levels. On one level, they drew attention to nine separate Line Texts (one each from Hexagrams 10, 15, 24, 32, 41, 42, 47, 48, and 57) said to encapsulate guidelines to moral behavior, constructing parallels between mantic images and social virtues. On a second, the Ten Wings' authors and their scholastic successors also outlined a series of mutually reinforcing interpretive methods based on symmetries, methods still in use today. The most important of these include (1) nuclear Trigrams, (2) inversion, (3) moving lines, (4) conversion everywhere, (5) correspondence, (6) coupling, (7) Hexagram Masters, and (8) waxing and waning calendrical correlations, each designed to turn the six graphic lines of the Hexagram into a potent set of relationships.

As we have seen, the idea of dividing the Hexagram vertically into two constituent Trigrams arose early on. From this idea, expounded principally in the "Images" appendix in the Ten Wings, there developed the dominant way of reading the Hexagrams in use today among adherents of the *Changes*. The "Images" commentary assigned to Hexagram 49, "Changeover" ☰, for instance, explains the six-line graph thus: "Fire in the lake: the image of changeover," an obvious reference to the graphic form of the Hexagram, where a Trigram-symbol for "lake" ☱ sits atop the Trigram-symbol for "fire" ☲; evidently, when two archetypal forces in opposition come together, it presages a tumultuous transfer of power from one ruling house to another. But in a desire to reveal the totality of the underlying cosmic order, thinkers pushed the Trigram concept one step further, proposing that the fundamental meaning of the Hexagram be seen as the product of two additional Trigrams, the so-called *nuclear Trigrams*, the bottom Trigram being composed of lines 2–4, and the top of lines 3–5.

Interpreters meanwhile drew upon a well-known pairing device, popular since the Warring States period and probably derived from the sequential ordering of the 64 Hexagrams found in the received text of the *Changes*, in which each Hexagram, except for eight in which inversion makes no difference, pairs with the inverted form of itself.* Pushing pairing to its next logical step, the *Changes* interpreters formed *inverse hexagrams* by the simple act of turning the original Hexagram upside down. With *moving lines*, the manipulation became a bit more complicated, for the traditional yin (broken) and yang (unbroken) values of each line had to be reversed, at least in stipulated cases. In the standard casting method for milfoil stalks, four divination results are possible: 6 (called old yin), 7 (young yang), 8 (young yin), and 9 (old yang). The extreme values (old yin and old yang) are said to be poised for a change, since Yin/yang theory has yin and yang *qi* reverting to their complements as soon as they reach the high point of their development. Old yin therefore moves to become young yang, and old yang moves to become young yin. Except in the very rare cases in which a divination procedure yields no sixes or nines, a single manipulation of the milfoil stalks quite naturally could be seen to produce two different Hexagrams (the first derived from the milfoil manipulation, the second resulting from changing all instances of old yin and old yang), the better to simulate the change

---

* In those eight cases, the Hexagrams are paired or moved by converting all solid lines to broken lines or vice-versa.

from present to future circumstances. Eventually there evolved a maximal conversion method called *conversion everywhere* [*pangtong* 旁通], in which all yin values in the original Hexagram are converted to yang, and all yang to yin.)

Alongside these interpretive methods, experimentation went on with notions of *correspondence*, already a preoccupation in the "Wenyan" appendix devoted to the explication of Hexagrams 1 and 2. Correspondence assumes that each line of the Hexagram has a single proper yin/yang value. Odd-numbered lines (lines 1, 3, 5, counting from the bottom up) should be yang and even-numbered lines (lines 2, 4, 6) yin; corresponding positions in the two Trigrams (lines 1–4, 2–5, 3–6) are then in harmonious resonance with one another. The degree to which a Hexagram matches this paradigm is then considered a good measure of its inherent auspiciousness or inauspiciousness (though the Line Texts sometimes contradict such assessments by position). In calculating degrees of correspondence, the two most important lines are the central lines of the bottom and top Trigrams (lines 2 and 5) predicting the subject/ruler, female/male, and child/parent relations. If these are properly yin (in line 2) and yang (in line 5), basic correspondence has been achieved. Of secondary importance is the relationship between the first and fourth line, where line 1 ideally should be yang and line 4 yin, a configuration symbolizing strong and capable commoners in low position who loyally serve the ministers occupying positions near to the king.

Contiguous lines in the Hexagram were, in parallel fashion, said to be in a *coupling* relation, with the higher line "resting on" the lower and the lower "receiving from" the higher. In Hexagram interpretation, the two most important coupled lines to watch have always been the fourth and fifth (read as official and ruler, respectively) and the fifth and sixth (read as ruler and sage, respectively). In the coupled fourth and fifth lines, the ideal relation has yin (the loyal subordinate) in line 4 and yang (the strong ruler) in line 5. But when it comes to the fifth and sixth lines, the ruler in line 5 ideally subordinates himself (symbolized by a yin or broken line) to the uncrowned sage in line 6 (symbolized by a yang line), whose more immediate understanding of the totality of the universe brings him closer to Heaven above. The implication that fixed sociopolitical hierarchies must retain their openness to the dynamic interplay of higher powers may also have informed the *Hexagram masters* concept explored in the "Tuan" appendix included in the Ten Wings. By this concept, each Hexagram has two masters: a governing master (usually line 5 in each Hexagram) and a constitutive master said to give the Hexagram its characteristic flavor, for example, the weak top line in Hexagram 43, "Breaking Through." When the governing and constitutive masters are both yang or both yin, the line is sure to be considered good and timely. (In such cases, the "Tuan" mentions only the one significant line of the Hexagram.)

Other theories at the same time focused attention instead on the correlation of each graphic line in the Hexagrams (6 lines × 64 Hexagrams = a total of 384) with the 365 days of the year, to facilitate exploration of the astronomical, mathematical, and musical symmetries expressing regular change in the universe.[*] For example, one scheme proposed by the *Changes* master Jing Fang (77–33 BC), the *waxing and waning* scheme, had four Standard Hexagrams marking the solstices and equinoxes, which left the sixty remaining Hexagrams each to stand in sequence for one-sixtieth of the solar year; that way the *Changes* could handily mirror the complex interactions of yin and yang *qi* over the course of the calendar year. Those who favored calendrical correlations, some of them famous diviners claiming to have rediscovered the lost mantic arts of the ancient courts, saw time as the single most important determining factor in the auspicious or inauspicious character of an event or relation. A few mantic experts of this persuasion went so far as to ignore the Hexagram Statements and Line Texts altogether because they were not necessary to express relations of time. The compiler of the popular tract *A Hundred Days to Mastering the Arts of Divination, Astrology, and Physiognomy* (*Buxing xiangshu bairi tong*, attributed to Li Dingzuo, ca. 750), to cite but one instance, had all the verbal texts that normally accompanied the graphic symbols excised from his manual, the better to illustrate his desire to have analysis proceed purely on the basis of each graphic line's association with the Ten Heavenly Stems and Twelve Earthly Branches of the calendrical system. With the stems and branches tied, in turn, to the Five Phases correlations slotting the myriad sorts of things into separate categories, the Five Phases correlations could sometimes supersede the original Hexagram images in importance.

Though none of the foregoing interpretive theories can now be situated in its precise historical context, one objective of this type of metainterpretation, or interpreting of interpretations, was to increase the number of avenues from which to observe and analyze divine change, either through the generation of secondary Trigram and Hexagram relations or in the radical expansion of ties between the core *Changes* and the established Five Phases categories of colors, directions, family relations, planets, body parts, domestic animals, and so on.

---

[*] An interest in astronomical, arithmetical, and musicological progressions by no means precluded ethical readings of the *Changes*, for extended ruminations on the harmonies prompted important ethical treatises, including Yang Xiong's *Taixuan jing* 太玄經 (comp. ca. AD 4) and Shao Yong's *Huangji jingshi shu* 皇極經世書 (ca. AD 1050).

(The sheer expansion of explanatory power must have delighted the *Changes* masters. The famous Zheng Xuan commentary to the *Changes* is an excellent example of this impulse to interpret the core *Changes* by multiple correlations beyond even those included in the texts of the Ten Wings.) As a result, many newcomers to the *Changes* have been able to see in it only a confused welter of numbers, graphic images, verbal emblems (the yellow skirt, the male fox, seed pods full to bursting), and extratextual connotations. In the face of such an overwhelming feeling it is best to consider why many early Chinese, like their counterparts in early Greece and medieval Europe, believed that emblems and numbers by themselves or in combination can encapsulate the universal regularities. Numbers in combination, after all, can beautifully express ideas of time, process, procedures, parity, symmetry, correlation, permutations, totality, incompleteness, probabilities, and clustering. And wisdom being largely equated with an ability to "cluster by categories" and "divide into groups" the myriad sorts of things and relations in the world, numbers served to express the basic functions and principles of the universe in precise formulae that erred in saying neither too much nor too little.

The "Great Commentary" itself offered three distinct explanations for the peculiar efficacy of numbers and emblems: first, that graphic images and numbers (especially numbers) capture aspects of reality, preserving them in a distilled form at once simpler and more transparently ordered than ordinary speech or writing; second, that only the clash of graphic images, numbers, and verbal emblems reflecting opposing perspectives can suggest the full complexity of the interplay of impulses informing the phenomenal world; and third, that the sheer incomprehensibility of such images and numbers, at once elusive and suggestive, contrives to catapult one ever more deeply into the Mystery, in contrast to conventional speech, which can hardly reflect even the current level of understanding.* Arriving at new insights requires such a marvelous medium with expandable capacities, a medium at once numerological, iconic, and metaphorical, for life's inexpressible richness overflows the petty particularities of mundane convention, as it would a narrow container. The Great Commentary puts it this way: "Just as the gods have no squareness [concrete, finite, perceptible forms], the changes/*Changes* have no [fixed] physical embodiment. Now yin, now yang, that is what we call Dao. . . . Things cannot be made entirely manifest through [mere] things!" In confronting whatever is

---

*As the "Great Commentary" puts it, "Writing cannot express speech completely and speech cannot express thoughts completely." That caused students of the *Changes* to value in their attempts to apprehend the absolute the other, conceivably less circumscribed tools at their disposal.

"above [perceptible] form," be it the gods or ghosts or Dao itself, numbers and verbal emblems play an intermediary role, being half in the substantial world "below form" (since they are perceptible to our senses) and half in the world "above" (since they correspond to no one tangible thing) (fig. 16).

But thinking that the existence of competing interpretive tools and theories on form and nonform threatened to obscure the very ensemble of processes captured within the *Changes'* text, some scholars particularly distrusted what they saw as the rather mechanical calculation of milfoil divination by the "[graphic] images-and-numbers" method, suspecting that it was far too rigid a formulation to grasp fluid reality. In response to such concerns, an alternate approach was promoted in Wang Bi's (226–249) Ethical Principle method. Wang Bi, believing not only that the Ten Wings perfectly capture the full meaning of the core text but also that each hexagram represented a single, unified concept, insisted that the *Changes'* reader should rely mainly on the Ten Wings in undertaking the two momentous tasks before him, determining correct interpretations and following through with right actions. Hexagram 1, or Qian 乾, for example, to Wang signified the organic totality of the vital order in all its latent power, which "stays ever on the right course," "comprehending the beginnings of things" and the dual nature of beings, as Qian itself is a composite of the responsive and the directive. To Wang's way of thinking, it was too time-consuming to learn the nature of every individual thing in the world. Rejecting the Han hermeneutics based primarily on the active manipulation and multiplication of Trigram correlations, Wang stated, "A multitude cannot control the multitudes, nor can motion ordain motion." Therefore, if ordinary persons are to manage change in the myriad forms it takes in the phenomenal world, they must recognize that, "in the final analysis, the myriad sorts of things, despite their myriad forms, are one." To learn about Hexagram 1, itself a perfect match for the ultimate unity and inherent order in the cosmos, is like "taking a post under the Pole Star . . . [from which vantage point of perfect centrality] the motions of heaven and earth are nothing particularly special."

Put another way, the *Changes'* adherent who would know the knowable course will find it enough to embrace the few eternal patterns of the high and the low, the one and the many—the social protocols, as it were, that are fated to hold in civilized communities—rather than getting entangled in the complex calculations and categorical correlations proposed by the mantic technicians. Wang Bi gave an example to prove that such basic protocols ruling human existence can certainly be mastered: "When the goal is to hurry things forward, making things appropriate is less important than making them be of immediate benefit [since that provides a greater incentive to act]. But when it's a

Figure 16. Detail of a silk manuscript of the *Changes*, showing the hexagrams at top. From *The Cultural Relics Unearthed from the Han Tombs at Mawangdui*, plate 18, p. 108.

question of ensuring that things will be preserved intact ad infinitum, immediate gain is less important than making things thoroughly appropriate." Alternate appeals to benefit and to appropriateness are like the alternation of yang and yin, insofar as one sometimes dominates and sometimes yields. By internalizing a few such natural patterns, which will help them adapt to present circumstances, perceptive men and women can "make their reason penetrate outward," testing the quality of their insights in the course of acting by observing the reactions in things, events, and relations outside the text. After all, both the Line Texts and the graphic symbols are only tools designed to help the reader comprehend underlying patterns. All too many readers, according to Wang Bi, were apt to take the constituent elements of the *Changes'* text too literally: "If the nuclear Trigrams are inadequate [expressions of the Dao], when applied to the changes in the Hexagrams, they become all the more inadequate. And if one then proceeds to take the Five Phases correlates into account, one immediately loses all the ground from under one's feet. Even if one is clever enough to puzzle out all sorts of things by means of such subtleties, one still has not got anything from which to derive the fundamental precepts [about Heaven-Earth-Human]."

Whereas many Han dynasty scholars had worked hard to preserve the images in interpretation, thinking them the principal key to unlocking the secrets of the cosmos, Wang Bi urged readers to discard the images as soon as they had outlived their usefulness. Of the three layers of meaning presented in the *Changes*, comprising words (*yan* 言), graphic symbols (*xiang* 象), and ideas (*yi* 意), the graphic symbols and their attached texts were only clumsy tools allowing a very preliminary level of understanding of the profound ideas inserted into the text by the antique sages: "It is like a trap used to catch a hare. Once you have the hare, the trap is forgotten. It is like the wicker basket used to catch fish. Once you have the fish, the basket is forgotten. In a sense, the words are traps for the images, and the images are baskets to hold the meaning. Therefore, whoever cherishes the words does not grasp the images, and whoever cherishes the images does not grasp the meaning." Humans were all too apt to forget that the ultimate goal of any human action, including divination, was simply to attain an understanding of the cosmic principles from which nature and fate derive. Determined as he was to discern and establish the general ethical ideas underlying the text, lest this ultimate goal be neglected, Wang Bi preferred to virtually ignore contemporary debates over the precise significance of the *Changes'* language in difficult passages.

With Wang in the mid–third century AD, readers of the *Changes* had available an entire range of the major interpretive approaches. Though the most fruitful approach to the *Changes* remained a matter of debate among classicists in late imperial China, with Zhu Xi (1130–1200) following Wang Bi and Lai

Zhide (1525–1604) promoting the Han Images-and-Numbers methods, the validity and usefulness of the *Changes* text, as divination tool or as ethical resource, were rarely doubted. Some few might insist, as Wang Can (177–217) did, that "the subtlety of inherent pattern (*li* 理) in the *Changes* eludes [mere] images of things. . . . Therefore whatever lies beyond the meaning, whatever the judgments show, remains firmly hidden, unable ever to issue forth [from the text]." But the *Changes*, employed with resourcefulness, flexibility, and practicality, has proved helpful on so many levels that it has handily survived all such challenges, deserving the popular assessment that the text is no less than "the absolute ultimate."

How is it that the received *Changes* had come so quickly to occupy such an important role in classicism? The historical Confucius, so far as we know, did not consult the *Changes*, which in his time was mainly reserved for professional court diviners. His early followers either ignored the *Changes* or disparaged it as a work emphasizing the operation of fate and luck, rather than virtue, in creating psychic and social security. Of Confucius's two greatest followers, Mencius and Xunzi, Mencius does not mention the *Changes* even once; Xunzi, who cites it in two of his thirty-two chapters, quite pointedly omits it from his list of Classics. Nonetheless, a mere two centuries after Xunzi, China's first major history, the *Shiji*, already portrays Confucius in later life as an ardent devotee of the *Changes*. And within a century or so after the *Shiji*, the *Changes* had moved to the heart of the classicist project, spawning ambitious forgeries and grand neoclassical imitations. Somehow, somewhat mysteriously the *Changes* was soon granted pride of place as the first among the Classics by Ru masters, long before the Eastern Han Archaic Script listing of the Five Classics acknowledged the fact. How had the *Changes* risen in the estimation of educated people, even those of Confucian persuasion?

Five possible answers spring immediately to mind. First, questions about the operation of luck, fate, and virtue in one's life, intriguing enough in any period, caught men's attention especially during the Warring States, Qin, and early Han periods, when frequent wars brought home the precariousness of human existence. Such questions then seemed all the more pressing when Han thinkers came to ponder the spectacular and totally unprecedented rise of Liu Bang, the Han founder, from the rank of ne'er-do-well commoner to Son of Heaven. Given that the content of the *Changes* (in the form of the Ten Wings) contributed vocabulary and systematic discourse reflecting upon discussions of the physical world and man's destined place in it—in a manner quite unlike the other Five Classics—the educated were bound to be drawn to it. Second, the precepts associated with the *Changes* via the Ten Wings and related traditions were seen to be consistent with the attitudes toward the divine expressed by

Confucius and his early disciples in Han and pre-Han accounts. One *Analects* passage insists that wise men know that one cannot "merely read the omens" because any prediction must be fixed by virtuous acts. Knowing that all life is made up of both the material and the spiritual, that below form and that above, the Chinese saw that the *Changes* could help them attend to one necessary side of life: "For the tangible, there are rites and music [through which to make contact]; and for the unknown, ghosts and gods" [to consult]." Moreover, all the interpretive approaches devised in and for the Ten Wings stressed the existence of structured and thus predictable change, emphasizing guided fate rather than random luck. In adapting the message of the *Changes* so that the text could also be read as a cosmic treatise on the patterns of fate and timely opportunity decreed by Heaven, Yin/yang, and the Five Phases, the mantic technicians and professional classicists in the Han and pre-Han periods had joined in crafting a significant accommodation that could satisfy all but the most skeptical followers of Confucius. For had not Xunzi defined gentlefolk by their ability to disregard mere coincidence while turning a single-minded focus on the constant principles, in order "not to mistake the nature of all things"?

Third, in the early days of classicism the absence of elaborate written traditions attached to the *Changes* might well have attracted innovative thinkers, and even the most scrupulous of scholars probably enjoyed having a relatively free interpretive hand to explore new ideas. (Regarding the less scrupulous, the Han histories do not hesitate to report that some highly influential readings of the *Changes* represented cynical forgeries foisted on an unwitting public.) Fourth, considerable fascination lay in the sheer wealth of significant patterns embedded in the graphic signs of the Hexagrams, in the mysteries revealed by Heaven in the form of numerological charts like the "River Map," in the verbal emblems presented in the Hexagram Statements and Line Texts, and in the extended explications and correlations of the Ten Wings. By the careful coordination of these multiple signs dedicated students of change might discern which meanings were most relevant among the connotations adhering to particular phrases and graphs. Fifth, and perhaps most important, was the state's interest in promoting the *Changes*. As we recall, from its inception in the pre-Qin period the Five Classics corpus was not merely "Confucian," and by about 300 BC, the corpus had become so authoritative to so many disparate groups that early centralizing states had a vested interest in adopting the *Changes'* principles and methods to affirm their legitimacy. Because the *Changes* backed its sound moral precepts by the divine authority of the gods, the *Changes'* oracular pronouncements could function as potent tools for social order among even the least civilized members of society. This, of course, may explain why it was cited so often in official spheres. One anecdote reported in a dynastic history, for instance, had the Ru master Yan Junping daily casting turtle and milfoil divinations in the marketplace, despite the low social status accorded fortune-tellers like himself. Yan consciously employed milfoil and turtle to dissuade his clients, all of whom were quite simple people, from dishonorable activities, on grounds that the gods had counseled them through divination to adopt filial piety, deference, and loyalty as the wisest courses of action.

THE TEN WINGS' SOLUTION TO FATE

Over the millennia, most Chinese have been wise enough to consider the role that external evils, as well as internalized ones, can play in altering the course, texture, and shape of human lives.* Thus a clear majority of the *Changes* Hexagrams make some reference to sacred rites of offering and divination, reflecting the general belief that regular offerings secure the ancestors' blessings and divert their wrath. At the same time, the observation and recording of natural phenomena in connection with divination have from the beginning of recorded history in China brought to mind the fundamental regularities in the cosmic processes: the unvarying sequence of seasons, of night and day. The stars circle the Pole Star eternally, prompting reflections upon time, timeliness, and time's critical junctures. If the *Changes* was "an ancient thing fixing fate," how were readers to play off time's eternal constants so as to determine their own fates and free themselves, as much as humanly possible, from the grip of external evils?

The types of guidance sought in the *Changes* ramified over time. Once the Ten Wings' interpretive modes had confirmed the moral and cosmic readings of the *Changes*, the chief business of the *Changes* no longer seemed limited to predicting one future event for one person at a time. Instead, people looked to the *Changes* to outline the main patterns prevailing in the cosmos and in human society, to suggest the sympathetic resonances operating in the universe, and to indicate the periodic signs of predictable trends, such as yin/yang and the Five Phases. Attempting to bridge the personal and cosmic levels, the main guidelines in the Ten Wings all described the sage in terms of a propensity for good timing (*shizhong* 時中) and precise positioning (*weizhong* 位中), on the theory that human activity proves efficacious only so long as it adjusts to the Dao's shifting

---

*Contrast the modern American tendency to dismiss the agency of the gods, chance, fate, hazard, and Mystery, which causes some to indulge in fits of hyperintrospection, blaming themselves for events entirely beyond their control, and others to be obsessed with the priority of the individual.

operations. The cyclical operations by which "now yin and now yang" wax and wane have been set from the dawn of time. Unfathomable and unavoidable, they and the visible changes spawned by them are fundamentally neutral in their embrace of all aspects of the world, though some of them may be (mis)perceived as inherently good by humans (for example, birth and maturation) and some as inherently bad (for example, death and decay). According to the Ten Wings, human behavior, to the degree that it anticipates and accedes to these patterned operations of yin and yang, will be timely, productive, and nondisruptive. Thus the true sage watches "the direction of events" and seizes the moment, while respecting the constraints of the unfolding situation. As one of the Ten Wings says, "The noble person, in consequence, labors to do everything at the proper time. . . . Vigorously, most vigorously, the noble person acts in accordance with the time, though most cautiously, wanting [always] to be blameless, despite the danger." The difficult task may be handily accomplished by acting upon a mere handful of insights, the easy Way of the *Changes* assures us:

> The sage carefully attends to the very first signs of change, knowing that he must take particular care at the beginning because the manner in which a project is begun affects all subsequent development.

> Having attended to the beginning, the noble man knows that it is advisable to be on the lookout for unintended consequences at every subsequent stage in a project: "If a person is always cautious [enough to anticipate problems] . . . , he or she will remain free of mistakes." It is especially important to be cautious in speech because loose talk quickly undermines good relations.

> Fortune is the product of long-term patterns, not short-term flukes: "The family that accumulates good deeds will always [over time] have more than enough felicity; and that which accumulates evil deeds, more than enough calamity. When an official kills his ruler or a son his father, this is not the result of a single day and night but a situation that has evolved gradually."

> Each act, however seemingly insignificant, has enormous potential to tip the balance in a person's character, since habit determines the strength of the will: "The petty man thinks to himself that a small good has no benefit and so he does not do it; he thinks that the small evil is harmless and so he does not eschew it. Thus wrongdoing accumulates . . . until it destroys a person."

> Problems are therefore best dealt with when first they arise, before they have grown to unmanageable proportions: "The noble man acts when

he sees the first beginnings of a trend; he does not wait for the final day of reckoning."

Moreover, the sage "never forgets danger when in a secure position, and never forgets death as long as he lives." In a low position he avoids cringing or flattering. In a high position, he is careful not to be arrogant and overbearing. Such a balanced response to any given situation (*he* 和) is possible only because the wise person sees all sides of a situation, "the obvious and the unobvious, the hard and the soft."

Though "what is called the Way of the *Changes*" consists of being "ever vigilant, from first to last, so one's principal acts may be blameless," the Ten Wings' authors made the Way easy to know and easy to follow for the weak-headed, the fainthearted, and the slack-willed. Aside from the passages setting out the text's claims to superiority, the Ten Wings eschew overt doctrine and explicit philosophizing, preferring simply to remind readers of the commonsense precepts they know already from proverbs and close observation of human behavior; these precepts will be enough to strengthen their resolve to act in appropriate ways. For once students of the *Changes* see that even the shortest speech or slightest gesture is no less portentous and consequential than a formal divination result, they will find countless opportunities for study and improvement; thus they may more quickly reach the ideal stage in which "the *Changes*/changes being known, there is a kin-feeling [with change itself]." And as soon as change is less feared, humans will make wiser decisions about how to cope with life's vagaries.

Still, the authors of the "Great Commentary," unlike many of their contemporaries, found practical wisdom and successful conduct to be insufficient goals in themselves. As thoughtful human beings, they sensed the special challenge presented by the persistence and pervasiveness of human immorality generated by ignorance or defiance of the cosmic laws. How to define the main external barriers to doing good (so as to argue for their removal) and explain why good people experience so much misery in their lives? Some of their contemporaries had already speculated that moral deformity and its ugly consequences are inevitable parts of human nature or the human condition. Absent a doctrine of original sin and assuming instead the inherent capacity of every human to "become a full social being" (*zuoren* 作人), how were moralists to convince quite ordinary men to undertake the single-minded striving for moral action that would be required if peace and justice were to be achieved? The difficulties of persuasion were only compounded by the authors' need to take into account three enigmatic, seemingly contradictory statements that all those working within the Confucian ethical tradition had inherited from their masters. The first had Confucius insisting that the "truly humane person has no concerns," other than the lifelong need to develop empathy. The second had Mencius proclaiming that "the noble man has cares (*you* 憂) to the very end of life," for unless those of virtue, intelligence, ability, and knowledge remain ever "afraid of losing their original virtue and of failing to incite others to virtue," they will never "attain true greatness." A third, the influential "Five Conducts" manuscript (*Wuxingpian* 五行篇) (ca. 300 BC), heaped on more confusion, for while it maintained that certain cares are preconditions to the development of empathy and wisdom, it also stressed the delight experienced by the truly humane person, whose "caring heart is incapable of grief."

In responding to such issues, the "Great Commentary" at first appears to offer equally contradictory pronouncements on the sage's concern or lack of concern, characterizing the sages as utterly "unconcerned" and yet "concerned." Clearly, readers are left to try to sort out the puzzle that the text presents. The Commentary mentions three aspects of goodness, by which it means "appropriate activity in a given situation." First, goodness for all the myriad things, among which humankind counts itself, is whatever Heaven decrees (*ming* 命), no matter whether Heaven is viewed as an anthropomorphic deity or as a convenient rubric for the sum total of impersonal, unconscious impulses (for example, yin and yang) giving shape to the universe. Heaven's decrees take a variety of forms themselves, from the gift of life itself (also *ming* 命) to time's constraints on the institution of the multiple hierarchies mandated in human society. Second, for humans (and to a lesser degree, other animals), goodness means acceding to Heaven's decrees, which are natural and so suitable, decrees that would have humans be social and sociable. Humans require associations if they are to fulfill the species' various aims, so a good society by definition (a) maximizes opportunities for social interaction; (b) relieves ordinary humans of the burdens (psychic and physical) they cannot carry; and thereby (c) avoids wreaking havoc with the possible development of unperfected humans. It is obvious that the natural human end must be to avoid loneliness and alienation, for "a person will always be content and happy if those without close ties come to join him, but he must be in constant danger and fear if those dearest to him leave him." As a result, a life is successful principally to the extent that a reliable network of social relations exists to sustain it. Third, ordinary humans mistakenly assume that the good lies in freedom from work and worry. Seeing that the myriad sorts of things in the extrasocial world of Heaven-and-Earth transpire without forethought and effort, they are apt to resent their peculiar lot as humans. By contrast, the sages, pinnacles of human achievement, have always freely chosen to sacrifice their ease and comfort to construct an ideal society that "makes the people easy" because "everything is in its proper place." In the words of Fan

Zhongyan (989–1052), they are "the very first to plunge into the torments of the world, and the very last to allow themselves to rejoice in its pleasures"—if only because they are all too aware of the difficulties of persuading themselves and others to act appropriately. Thus real culture-heroes live "in constant fear and trembling, as though facing a deep chasm or treading on thin ice, for they know that once their base impulses run away with them, they will not be able to advance [in the Way]."

The first and second points seemed so self-evident to thinkers in the early empires that they needed none but the most perfunctory of defenses. Life, which is indisputably better than the alternative, comes by some mystery as a gift from Heaven through one's parents. So great is that gift that no calamity can substantially lessen its value. The same goes for community. As anyone can see, only wounded animals or the sick among human beings withdraw from all contact with their kind, save when political ills demand temporary reclusion of the official. Point 3, however, is more complex and less self-evident, even counterintuitive. How can one call it good that the sages have worked and worried?* More specifically, how was it that not a single one of the three compilers of the *Changes* (King Wen of Zhou, the Duke of Zhou, and Confucius)—each considered a supreme moral exemplar who toiled unremittingly for years—received all the rewards Heaven has in its power to confer: long life, unsullied reputation, high rank, great wealth, and other forms of conventional success?

To readers of the "Great Commentary," the evident weakness of the charismatic forces for good must have presented a thorny problem. For oral and literary traditions left no doubt about the extreme humiliations suffered by these good men. King Wen, for example, had been jailed despite his faithful service to his overlord and his reputation for "accumulating good deeds and amassing charismatic virtue." The Duke of Zhou had been exiled from court, falsely accused of trying to usurp King Cheng's throne. Confucius, for his part, not only had failed to secure a high-ranking government post but also was beset in his various travels by troubles that reached almost ludicrous proportions. First under house arrest in Wei, Confucius was then detained in Kuang, with the threat of execution hanging over him. The men of Song had tried to kill him,

---

*Outside the group of dedicated Ru and Mohists, any statements linking sagehood as the highest form of humanity with burdensome worry seemed utterly laughable; most thinkers argued that the true sage, by definition, was one who could achieve greatness effortlessly, without expending his time, focusing his emotions, or exerting his will. In justifying such ideas of human excellence, thinkers pointed to the figure of the legendary Shun, who supposedly ruled the empire by simply folding his hands and letting his ritual robes hang loose. But *Analects* 15/11 offers the maxim, "One who gives no thought to distant matters will most certainly find cares close to hand."

and the men of Zheng had mocked him as a "stray cur." In Pu he was detained
a second time. In his home state of Lu he was slighted. Even when living in
exile "between Chen and Cai," he "got into trouble." Not to mention the sorrow
occasioned by the untimely deaths of several of his favorite disciples. When he
died "before his name was known," even the consolation of a good name had
been denied him, or so it seemed. Could it be that Heaven itself is unjust, as
several passages in the *Odes* and *Documents* allege, or were unthinking humans
responsible for such injustices?" Where was order, if supremely good men like
Confucius suffered such ills? Did this not prove that even the best men cannot
act to insulate themselves from pain and sorrow? If so, how are humans to keep
themselves from despairing?

According to the "Great Commentary," history demonstrates that great men
need to know injustice, for in such circumstances they are moved to devote their
full powers to helping lesser men bear personal misfortune. For had not King Wen
(then Earl of the West) set about composing the Hexagram Statements to the
Changes when he was imprisoned at Youli? Was it not when the Duke of Zhou
was under vile suspicion that he wrote the Line Texts of the *Changes*? And had
not Confucius compiled the Ten Wings and the *Chunqiu* chronicle to express the
depths of his distress? Judging from these examples, a painful alienation from the
prevailing power structures is a precondition for true compassion and insight,
whereby humans come "to bear no grudge against Heaven" since they "delight
in Heaven and understand fate." How is such an advanced state possible? And do
ordinary mortals, living in a time far distant from the golden age of the sages,
have it within their power to counteract or correct their unjust fates?

A close reading of the "Great Commentary" yields an answer to such questions. As people with ordinary emotions who have honed their powers of discernment, the sages are not particularly anxious about their own persons, their
allotted portion, or their own position in society. The sages recognize also that
in life some measure of sorrow and pain is decreed or fated by Heaven as the
end result of the complex interactions of interlocking cosmic cycles. For change,
however perfectly patterned, cannot ever "match," being the product of the
operation of two different polarities (yin and yang) combined in ever-varying
proportions; that the polarities will "rub against one another" is an immutable
law of the cosmos. And because "the patterns do not match, so fortune and misfortune are generated by it [the interaction of yin and yang]." Even the awareness of such disjunctions is the source of much misery in the world, in that
painful choices must be made. One thing in one stage of development cannot
possibly be another in another phase, and no single choice can claim absolute
value in all situations. Moreover, each separate phenomenal stage and thing
bound by time and place, insofar as it represents a cleavage from the Dao's orig-

inal wholeness, induces a sense of alienation and fragmentation. But wisdom consists of accepting the inevitable, so the sages do not add unduly to their burdens by taking responsibility for the difficulties engendered by predestined change; they do not then feel compelled to trace the origin of suffering to the nature of change. They recognize that a time out of joint is a situation of "no blame" in two senses: they themselves are not necessarily at fault nor is Heaven to be railed against.

The sages know, too, that the very processes that throw off occasional pain are those that make the world a source of unending wonder. Having glimpsed the splendor of the transcendent Way "above form," the sages are content not to manipulate external situations for their own narrow advantage; they "await Heaven's decrees," directing their own lives and those of others to a closer conformity with the organic structure of reality. That is what the "Great Commentary" means when it says the sages "take their ease," agreeing to "delight and play with" the manifold changes. Because the "principal concern for the sage is to walk in virtue," achieving the inner illumination that leads to beneficial change, the sages can shrug off a lack of wealth, rank, and fame as relatively minor annoyances. Thus they are spared the vast majority of anxieties that plague ordinary people, who loathe change and crave transitory gain, unaccustomed as they are to the larger view. After long years spent in ethical and cosmological investigation, the sages see that the course of change in the triadic realms of Heaven-Earth-Human never stands in the way of the fulfillment of their most pressing need as humans—that for the deeply satisfying companionship that overcomes alienation. Change is welcome, for it alone pushes them to set priorities and assess ultimate value. This realization, in turn, helps secure friendships and alliances with like-minded people, who will then provide the social network to see them through temporary travails. As a result, the Commentary promises that the noble of spirit will never be orphaned, friendless, and alone. Hearts and minds so conjoined, being "sharp enough to cut metal," can overcome any barrier while remaining "fragrant as an orchid."

Even others' misconduct the sages can accept, taking it as a warning to their own. Heaven's warnings deter people from hasty, ill-judged actions, so their conduct is "auspicious, with nothing that does not further." With such painful "chastisements" prompting them to renew their efforts in response to the mysteries of self, society, and cosmos, they merely stiffen their resolve "to develop to the full their own allotted lives and to abide by their commitments." At the same time, pain and sorrow offer necessary reminders of the travails that beset ordinary human existence. To some degree it is because the sages know adversity that they commit themselves to the care of lesser mortals, choosing compassion over detachment, in the knowledge that the choice entails a loss of freedom from anxiety. Thus are "great warnings" transformed into "great blessings" for the sages and all who come under their influence. Sweetest of all is the expectation that history will confer ultimate justice, though it may take some time. After all, though all three moral exemplars who wrote the *Changes* lacked the external requisites (the land base, rank, and factional support) to become Sons of Heaven, all three enjoyed immortal fame after death and sacrifices in perpetuity. Surely the ignominy they suffered once has been erased by subsequent recognition.

Like the bodhisattvas in later Mahayana Buddhism* (whose adherents may have been prepared for their devotions by the *Changes'* portrayals of heroic selflessness), the worthies and sages in the "Great Commentary" take for granted the necessity to work and worry on behalf of lesser mortals and harmony in the cosmic operations. Therefore, the noble person acts in such a way as to have the people "join with him, . . . [and] respond [to his proposals]," "gathering them" into useful societies where they can learn to value the good. The sage, seeing confusion all around, "stoops . . . to complete the myriad sorts of things, lest they be left behind" in their development. In its depiction of the sages, then, the Commentary lays out this general rule: the finer the human being, the more willing he or she becomes to "subordinate the self to others." This extraordinary self-abnegation on the part of the sage the Commentary aptly characterizes in a curious and so memorable phrase: "Those of insight, perception, and practical wisdom [who altered the course of civilization by their acts] had a godlike quality that was martial but did not kill."

Merely to contemplate the "confused diversities" of All-under-Heaven takes remarkable courage, a martial spirit. But the sages were determined to do far more: to arrange ordinary human beings in better orders and institutions that would prop up frail humanity in its efforts to achieve full humanity. One early characterization, therefore, has the sage "working that others might receive the fruit of his work. . . . He would have the people labor, but not to the point of exhausting themselves, and relax, but not the point of dissipation." Ever perceptive, the sages know that it will not do to drive others as they do themselves; anxious to support others in the manner of mother Earth, the sages tirelessly act to benefit others. Never do they let their own strengths overpower others in a "killing" compulsion. Hence the sages' determination, in bringing others

---

*Buddhist theory, however, portrays material phenomena as transitory, temporary, tentative, insubstantial, and so inherently false. The *Changes*, by contrast, asserts the absolute reality of patterned transformations. The term "changes" therefore connotes both the constant rules underlying the dynamic of phenomenal change and manifestations of those rules in the world of change. Accordingly, the Way is transcendent only in the sense that it is absolutely powerful and utterly mysterious. It is always part of existence.

out of darkness, to model their subtle interventions on the Dao's mysterious movement from inchoate mass to order and thereby obviate undue disruption. Drawing strength from the infinite vitality of Dao, the heroic sages receive a tremendous incidental benefit: on the whole they remain remarkably "unwearied" (*buyan* 不厭), notwithstanding the monumental effort they have invested in promoting the advance of civilization, so eagerly do they, despite "hesitation and hindrance," undertake the great enterprise (*daye* 大業) of bringing themselves and others to that blessed state of equilibrium in the Dao, by virtue of their charismatic power. In this respect they corroborate the promise of the *Odes* that "openhearted noble men are rewarded by the gods."

The authors of the "Great Commentary" of the Ten Wings, in laying out the problem and solution to wrongdoing, filled a gap, for the other Classics, as it happened, had failed to address this problem in any systematic way. Neither the chronicle format of the *Chunqiu* nor the brevity of the individual *Odes* songs lend themselves to extended treatments of complex issues. In set pieces the *Documents* presents dramatic models of good and bad rule, yet its scope rarely transcends court policy. And while the three *Rites* Classics illustrate both the theory and practice of exemplary social behavior, the *Rites* mandate the employment of the five emotions for communal harmony, rather than addressing those vague yet insistent feelings that the time is out of joint, that life is unfair, and that human nature is abhorrent. Only the *Changes*, through its appendices and traditions, faces the problem squarely, asking which of the host of misfortunes that beset humankind are attributable to forces outside the self (for example, to cosmic conjunctions of the sort that produce dynastic cycles). Insisting that "no blame" attaches to external evils, it does not hesitate to label the bad consequences of our own ill-judged actions as the very worst sort of calamity—that brought on by ourselves in willful ignorance.

Historically, such straightforward analysis made sense to conservatives and iconoclasts alike, buttressing the received wisdom about ethical relations with the latest theories about humankind's place in the larger world. And so while certainly the sheer wealth and variety of interpretive mechanisms (the images, the charts, the verbal emblems, and so on) provided by the *Changes* has helped convince readers that the text can lead them from a primitive state of "sluggish thinking" to an advanced perfection of the internal order, the striking simplicity and seeming inevitability of the Ten Wings' message has accomplished this also. In mirroring and confirming the celestial harmonies, the Ten Wings hold out the promise that, thanks to the sages' efforts (at once exalted and humble), students of the *Changes* can learn the key insight that the ineffable carries within itself a principle of radical intelligibility. In acting on that single insight, humans choose to adopt the divinely enigmatic but exquisitely transparent ways of the Dao. Then do "Heaven and Humans join and become one" (*Tianren heyi* 天人合一).

Conclusions drawn from the Ten Wings, especially the Xici or "Great Commentary," inevitably shape readings of the rest of the *Changes*, for that tradition brought to discussions of fate, faith, and works a well-defined and tenaciously held point of view. To silence the cynics who insisted that human beings showed little innate aptitude for the good, the "Great Commentary" offers a thoroughly optimistic view of humanity in which all persons desiring to do good can direct their own fates in all-important ways while improving those of others. By embodying the boundless generosity and compassion of Heaven itself, such humans conclusively demonstrate the inherent unity of the Heavenly and social orders. As Confucius said, to aid oneself and others, one needed to "work hard but not be aggressive, have merit but not consider oneself virtuous." At the same time, the Ten Wings' "easy" solution never underestimates the magnitude of the task facing the dedicated reformer. In acknowledging the complexities that arise when ceaseless change is interjected into the human equation, the *Changes* supplies one rationale for Confucius's seemingly contradictory pronouncements on *ren* ("full humanity"), which insisted that *ren* was both "easy to attain" and never finally attainable, so that the search for it was a "heavy burden" to be borne throughout one's life.

Confucius the historical figure was characterized in the *Analects* as one who was "determined to save the world, though he knew his efforts to be in vain." Legend tells us that in old age Confucius turned to study of the *Changes* and the task of composing the "Great Commentary." If the historical Confucius failed utterly in his repeated attempts to persuade the lords of the land to adopt the principles and practices of just rule, the legendary Confucius demonstrated to the satisfaction of most that the efforts of sages, painful and unrewarding though they may seem at the time, advance human development in absolutely crucial ways.

Chapter Six

THE *SPRING AND AUTUMN ANNALS* (*CHUNQIU* 春秋), AS READ THROUGH ITS THREE TRADITIONS

Its phrasing is subtle, but its points are wide-ranging.
—Sima Qian, on the *Chunqiu*

THE *SPRING AND AUTUMN ANNALS*
(*Chunqiu*) chronicles major political events affecting the small state of Lu, the home state of both the Duke of Zhou and Confucius, and its neighbors over the course of twelve ducal reigns extending some 250 years, from 722 to 481 BC. The term "Spring and Autumn" in the title is a standard synecdoche in which the two seasons stand for an entire calendar year; hence, the use of the term for a record of events arranged by year. Most scholars agree that the *Chunqiu* is based upon (perhaps is synonymous with) the *Annals of Lu* (*Lu Chunqiu*), one of many such works composed at the courts of the local rulers during the Eastern Zhou period (770–256 BC). It may seem surprising that the chronicle of Lu

253

survived when so many other archives were lost. Lu, after all, was a relatively powerless state whose very legitimacy depended largely upon that of Zhou, and the history of Eastern Zhou, which began with the flight of the king's court to a new capital site and ended with the murder of the last Zhou king, signaled nothing if not a precipitous decline in dynastic power. But by the late fourth century BC, the *Chunqiu* had already become far more than a state chronicle. As the only one of the Five Classics wholly attributed to Confucius, the *Chunqiu* had acquired the aura of an infallible guide to proper authority, its relation to power, and the conditions for timely transfers of power. As Cheng Yi would later write, "It is the *Chunqiu* [among the Classics] that shows the sage's application" of classical norms to these aspects of political life (see map in Introduction).

In the second century BC, when the Han house finally established the first stable empire in China, it recognized that authority, to be effective, must always be rooted in the past. The Han therefore claimed for its throne the special patronage of the Supreme Sage, Confucius, whose reputation rested on his unique mastery of precedents. Han legends insisted that Confucius had not only foreseen and approved the Han's receipt of the Mandate, but had also thoughtfully laid the groundwork for Han rule by providing in the *Chunqiu* chronicle instructive examples, good and bad, of historical figures and governmental institutions. Supposedly the *Chunqiu*, written "in anticipation of later sages [the Han rulers]," represented a store of knowledge for the Han comparable to that provided Zhou by the personal and institutional models laid down by Zhou's three virtual founders, King Wen, Zhou's predynastic ruler, and his two wise sons, the Duke of Zhou and the Duke of Shao. Confucius had decided that instead of presenting his ideas "in the form of abstract moral judgments, it would be better to illustrate them through the depth and clarity of actual events." It was therefore incumbent upon Han and succeeding dynasties to ponder the *Chunqiu*'s record of political successes and failures, for their possession of Heaven's Mandate ultimately depended upon their conformity with the ideals of good government revealed by Confucius in the text.

Unfortunately, the precise import of many *Chunqiu* entries was difficult to ascertain. Consider two typical *Chunqiu* entries, one for the twenty-eighth year of Duke Xi of Lu (632 BC) and one for the seventh year of Duke Wen of Lu (619 BC):

Duke Xi, the twenty-eighth year, winter: The duke met in Wen with the marquises of Jin and of Qi, the Duke of Song, the Marquis of Cai, the Earl of Zheng, the heir to Chen, the Viscount of Ju, and an officer of Qin.

Duke Wen, the seventh year, summer: Men of Song killed their counselors.

Even allowing for the "subtle phrasing" (*weiyan* 微言) attributed to Confucius, such terse entries seemed to offer little in the way of moral or political guidance. Fortunately for Han rulers and later readers three traditions traceable to the pre-Han period, the *Gongyang*, the *Guliang*, and the *Zuo*, expanded upon the laconic *Chunqiu* entries, providing enough background and interpretation to allow one to make sense of them. The *Zuo*, for example, explains that the winter meeting was called to conclude an alliance among the victors of the momentous battle of Chengpu in 632 BC, a coalition led by Jin against Chu, its strongest rival for hegemony. The *Zuo* entry reads,

In spring, the ruler of Jin, who was preparing to attack the state of Cao, sought permission to pass through Wei's territory. When the leading men of Wei refused, he went a roundabout way, . . . invading Cao and attacking Wei. In the first month, . . . he captured the Wei region of Wulu. In the second month, the Jin commander Xi Gu died. . . . The ruler of Jin concluded a pact with the ruler of Qi . . . in Wei. The ruler of Wei asked to join the pact, but the leading men of Jin refused to allow this. The ruler of Wei then thought of allying himself with the state of Chu, but even his own countrymen did not approve of this, so they drove him out from the capital to curry favor with Jin. The Wei ruler . . . took up residence in Xiangniu in Wei. Gongzi Mai, an official of Lu, was stationed in Wei to protect it from attack, and troops also came from Chu to Wei's rescue. But when the troops failed to win a victory, the Duke of Lu, afraid of Jin's anger, put Gongzi Mai to death, in order to curry favor with Jin. . . .

The Jin ruler then surrounded the Cao capital. Many of his soldiers, in storming the gates, died there. The men of Cao then took the bodies of the Jin dead and exposed them on the city walls, causing great distress to the ruler of Jin. Adopting a plan put forward by some of his subordinates, he announced that he would camp on the graves of the Cao ancestors. . . . The men of Cao, filled with panic and horror, put Jin's dead in coffins and had the bodies carried out of the city. The Jin forces, taking advantage of this panic to press their attack, entered the city on the *pingwu* day of the third month. . . .

Meanwhile, the men of Song, besieged by Chu, sent Men Yinban on a mission to the Jin army to report the crisis. The duke of Jin said, "The leading men of Song have come with a report of their distress. If I ignore them, they will break with our state. If I appeal to Chu to raise the siege, however, it will never consent. I would like to engage Chu in battle, but [our allies] Qi and Qin will never accede to that. What should I do?" [The counselor] Yuan Zhen replied, "If you intend to ignore Song's pleas, then at least allow it to bribe Qi and Qin and rely on them to appeal to Chu to lift the siege. In the interim, we can seize the ruler of Cao, divide up the fields of Cao and Wei, and present a part of them to the men of Song as a gift. Chu, because of its special ties with Cao and Wei, is sure to refuse the request from Qi and Qin that it lift the siege. Qi and Qin, pleased with Song's bribes and furious at Chu's stubbornness, will no doubt then be persuaded to join us in an attack on Chu." The duke of Jin, delighted with the plan, seized the ruler of Cao, divided up the fields of Cao and Wei, and handed a part of them over to the men of Song.

Now, here was something to sink your teeth into: a baroque tale of ruthless ambition, insidious guile, and complex stratagem, grist for the commentarial mills for centuries—all the more so because early classical thinkers sought to ascertain the moral course by "weighing" (*quan* 權) constant principles, judging them in light of the exact historical situation rather than applying the same ethical standard to all situations.

This concern for weighing the moral significance of political acts and agents, combined with the customary Confucian emphasis on the crucial importance of personal example (most especially of those in power), reinforced the time-honored value of keeping accurate records of court activities and celestial events. As he carried out one of the state's solemn religious duties, the state archivist (*shi* 史) was to serve as "the official maintaining impartiality."* "If the lord has any fault, it is the duty of the archivist to record it. . . . If he fails to record such faults, he deserves to die for the crime." Legend held that the unshakable integrity required of the state archivist was best exemplified in that unofficial historian Confucius, and the Sage's putative authorship greatly inflated the authority accorded the *Chunqiu* chronicle and its traditions. As a result, dedicated followers of Confucius, generation after generation, have looked to the text to faithfully reveal the workings of history.

CONTENT, DATING, AND AUTHORSHIP OF THE TEXTS

The *Chunqiu* text, unlike its commentaries, is authentic and early, being based on entries written down not long after the events they record. Archaeology con-

---

*Appended to the *Chunqiu* are stories of state archivists who chose to die rather than emend truthful, if highly unflattering, accounts of their rulers' deeds. In conflating canon and interpretive traditions, I follow Han thinkers, whose writings typically did not distinguish between the *Chunqiu* Classic and the three main interpretive traditions attached to it (though they were more likely to conflate the *Chunqiu* with the *Gongyang* than with other interpretive traditions).

firms that the *Chunqiu*'s portrayal of ritual observances, as well as the astronomical information preserved in the text's 122 reports on portents, is generally correct for the period. Such facts could hardly have been reconstructed or invented by a later forger, no matter how learned or clever. Moreover, the *Chunqiu* reveals a steadily evolving pattern of interstate relations that tallies with other evidence for the period. The earliest *Chunqiu* entries focus on Lu, the royal house of Zhou, and on six of Lu's immediate neighbors: Song, Cai, Chen, Cao, Zheng, and Wei. Gradually the chronicle includes states as distant from Lu as Qin (far to the west), Chu, and Wu (the latter two far to the south), reflecting the increased contacts brought by war and commerce between Lu and these outer states. Once again, no late forger could have devised such a faithful account of developing interstate contacts between Lu and its neighbors, producing this pattern of gradually expanding geographical coverage. All this suggests that the *Chunqiu* was probably completed by a single archivist (or group of archivists) in service to the small state of Lu, who in compiling the archival records of the past 240 years steadfastly refused to invent, expand, or edit entries when information was lacking. And nothing refutes the traditional belief in a single compiler, though not one shred of literary or archaeological evidence exists to verify that the faithful compiler was Confucius.

If one can imagine a single compiler putting together the *Chunqiu* sometime in the fifth century BC, the three main traditions associated with the *Chunqiu* remain something of a mystery.* Each is based on a slightly different edition of the Classic, and each uses slightly different language. The *Gongyang* reportedly contains Qi dialect words, and the *Guliang* words from Lu dialect, while the language of the *Zuo*, possibly from Jin, matches neither. Legends advanced on behalf of each tradition claim that all three date from about the time of Confucius. At least since Han times, the oral traditions of the *Gongyang* and *Guliang* have been traced back to Zixia, a direct disciple of Confucius, and that of the *Zuo* to a Zuo Qiuming or Zuoqiu Ming, usually, if erroneously, identified as an elder contemporary of Confucius. It now appears that both the

---

*The three traditions now taken as commentaries—*Gongyang*, *Guliang*, and *Zuo*—were not originally spliced with *Chunqiu* entries, as they are in most editions today. Some have speculated that it was probably He Xiu (129–182) who spliced the *Gongyang* with the *Chunqiu*; legend credits Du Yu (222–284) with doing the same for the *Zuo*, and Fan Ning (339–401) for the *Guliang*. The earliest extant edition that interspaces the three commentaries with the *Chunqiu* Classic, in the order *Zuozhuan*, *Gongyang*, and *Guliang* (with the extra *Zuo* entries marked as *fulu* 附錄), is the *Chunqiu sanzhuan* 春秋三傳 (recut in 1876). However, the imperially sponsored *Siku quanshu* (completed 1782) mentions Song, Yuan, Ming, and early Qing editions where the three commentaries were interspaced with the main *Chunqiu* texts.

Gongyang and the *Zuo* were transcribed in the late Warring States period, though the received version of the *Gongyang* may date as late as mid–Western Han. The *Guliang*, which except for its far greater preoccupation with the submission of women reads like a variant on the *Gongyang*, apparently was written down after the *Gongyang*, possibly as late as the first century BC. Because the *Guliang* was clearly not an ancient text, its claims to special consideration lay in its strong association with Lu, the home state of Confucius.

Through the ages many scholars have doubted that the *Zuo* was composed originally as a commentary on the *Chunqiu*. For one thing, the *Zuo* covers events for two decades after 481 BC, the date at which the *Chunqiu* canon stops, while omitting reference to scores of entries included in the chronicle. On some matters, the *Zuo* even contradicts the *Chunqiu*. To account for such anomalies, some scholars in imperial China assumed that the present *Zuo* reflects a not always smooth synthesis of various histories compiled by the separate states in the Chunqiu period. Following their lead, Henri Maspero considered the *Zuo* to be a pastiche, combining a commentary on the *Chunqiu*, similar to the *Gongyang* and *Guliang* in its format and its concern with ritual and ethics, with a much longer historical romance composed about the same time (late fourth century BC?) to cover events in the feudal state of Jin.* William Hung likewise saw the *Zuo* compilation as a response to what were in effect three separate versions of the same *Chunqiu* circulating in Western Han (one roughly comparable to the received text, which was presumably affiliated with a genuine pre-Qin edition; a second, incomplete *Chunqiu* text known to the *Zuo*'s author(s) after reunification under Han; and another *Chunqiu* text later known to Liu Xin), to which many additional passages, modifications, and loans had been interpolated from other commentaries and histories.

Though the *Zuo*, like the *Chunqiu* itself, is clearly a sedimented text of diverse sources, what appears probable is that it is the work of a single compiler or group of compilers who brought together disparate materials (only some of which were nearly contemporaneous with the events they report upon) and shaped them into a coherent whole with absolute assurance. It is equally certain that the *Zuo* existed for centuries before Liu Xin in late Western Han "put the *Zuo* in order, . . . quoting the words of the tradition in order to explain the text

---

*Because it supplies a wealth of background information, generally in extended vignettes that read like short stories, the *Zuo* is the longest of the three commentaries. It is, in fact, the longest of the Thirteen Chinese Classics, despite the fact that individual entries in the *Zuo* are noted for an incredible economy of narrative style that delivers a punch of unparalleled power. Over the years, the style and content of the *Zuo* have ensured its appeal to readers of classical Chinese, as numerous anecdotes attest.

of the *Chunqiu*." Assertions that Liu Xin forged the *Zuo* have been exposed as slanders. Modern scholars, in general agreement that the *Zuo* dates from the Warring States period (475–222 BC), continue to debate the precise century. Bernhard Karlgren concluded, largely on the basis of its grammar and lexicon, that the *Zuo* dates "between 468 BC and 300 BC." Recent scholarship seems to be converging on a date closer to 300 BC, a date made plausible by the numerous predictions in the *Zuo* that miraculously "come true" in the years 487–330.

In format, the *Gongyang* and *Guliang* texts are mainly question-and-answer catechisms (though short historical narratives have crept into forty some entries), but the *Zuo* reverses the ratio of catechism to historical accounts, creating narrative complexities and emotional resonances that are nearly unparalleled in pre-Han literature—as even its critics conceded. A comparison of early entries in the *Gongyang* with those from the *Zuo* illustrates the different impact the two commentaries have had upon readers. The *Chunqiu* opens in 722 BC, the year after the death of Duke Hui of Lu, with a succession crisis in Lu. Duke Hui's principal wife had died without issue, so his successor had to be chosen from among Hui's sons by his consorts. Among these, the two main contenders were the adult Xi (later Duke Yin) and the child Yun (later Duke Huan). Xi was the first to assume the dukedom, nominally as guardian for his younger stepbrother Yun. The first *Chunqiu* entry merely says, "First year, spring. The first month by the [Zhou] king's [calendar]," making no reference to Lu's newly installed ruler, Duke Yin. The *Gongyang*, however, intends to establish the moral claim of the younger brother to the dukedom by a series of glosses that together establish the exalted status of Duke Huan through his mother, while spinning a tale of treason and fratricide. The first gloss asks, "Why does the *Chunqiu* not say of the duke [Duke Yin] that 'he had assumed the throne'? Because it intends to get at the duke's intention. Why? The duke was going to pacify the state and then return it to Duke Huan. Why? Duke Huan was young, but of higher rank." A second *Gongyang* entry also implies Yun's right to succeed his father, though it ostensibly concerns the funeral gifts that the Zhou king sent to honor Lu's royal dead, Duke Hui and the deceased mother of Yun: "Duke Yin assumed Duke Hui's position for the sake of Duke Huan and so he announced the funeral of Huan's mother to all the lords of the realm. That being the case, then why does the text say it this way? To get at the duke's intention. And why does it talk of 'the envoy coming'? That means that the envoy was too late [to affect the succession in Lu]." Soon after, a third *Gongyang* entry notes the death of Duke Yin's mother and the duke's refusal to inter her in a royal tomb in a solemn state funeral. "Why is the word 'bury' omitted from the text? . . . Yin was not going to be duke permanently, so his mother could not be treated permanently as principal wife."

But however weak Duke Yin's claims to the dukedom, the *Gongyang* cannot countenance his assassination. Hence the *Gongyang*'s lengthy explication of a brief *Chunqiu* reference to an unnamed officer in Lu, dated to year four of Duke Yin's regency: "Why does the *Chunqiu* not call him ducal son? To denigrate him. Why? He [later] participated in the treasonous murder of the Duke Yin. . . . The ducal son said to [the future Duke] Huan, 'Allow me to create a disturbance during which to assassinate Duke Yin.' And then it was there, at the sacrifice to Zhongwu that they assassinated Duke Yin [seven years later, in his eleventh year]." After the assassination, the *Gongyang* concludes its moralizing by asking, "Why was the burial not recorded? It was suppressed because it was an assassination. Why in the case of an assassination is the burial not recorded? The *Chunqiu* does not record the burial if the duke's assassins have not yet been punished." The *Gongyang*, through such glosses, seeks to unpack the oblique literary style of the *Chunqiu* in order to verify the Classic's infallibility in laying down judgments.

Comparable entries from the *Zuo*, though in general agreement with the *Gongyang*'s view of Duke Yin's regency, supply the background needed to heighten the dramatic tension. About the succession crisis, the *Zuo* writes, for example,

> Duke Hui's first consort was Mengzi. When Mengzi died, a certain Shengzi succeeded to the role as principal wife and it was she who bore [the future] Duke Yin. Duke Wu of Song had fathered Zhongzi, who at birth had the characters "principal wife in Lu" inscribed on her hand. Therefore, Zhongzi was married into our royal house in Lu. It was she who gave birth to Duke Huan, and so when Duke Hui died, Duke Yin set her up in high rank and honored her.

Of the joint burial ceremonies for Duke Hui and Zhongzi, the *Zuo* then comments,

> The Son of Heaven is to be interred in the seventh month, when all the lords of the land have converged for the ceremony. The ruler of a state is to be interred in the fifth month, when all his allies have convened. A chief officer is to be buried after three months, in the presence of his fellow officers. A knight is to be buried within the month, in the presence of his relatives by marriage. Funeral gifts are presented before the burial. Visits of condolence are paid before the formal wailing. To anticipate such inauspicious events [by sending gifts ahead of schedule] is improper.

Omitting all mention of the ritual complexities presented by the interment ceremonies for Duke Yin's mother and the sacrificial hall built for Duke Huan's mother, the *Zuo* turns quickly to political events among Lu's chief allies, before taking up the tale of fratricide and treason. Of Duke Yin's assassination, the *Zuo* gives the following report:

> Yufu asked permission of Duke Yin to assassinate Duke Huan, as he himself intended to ask for the position of chief minister under Duke Yin. Duke Yin replied, 'It's because of his youth [that I did not hand the throne over immediately to him]. I am on the point of doing so now. I have had Tuqiu built for my retirement.' Yufu grew wide-eyed with fear [when he realized how he had misjudged the duke]. And so he turned around to slander Duke Yin to Duke Huan, requesting permission to kill him [Duke Yin, lest word of his own perfidy reach the reigning duke].
>
> [Sometime back], when Duke Yin was merely a ducal son, he had fought against Zheng at Hurang, at which point he was detained by the men of Zheng at the house of a Mr. Yin. . . . It was there that he [first] prayed to Zhongwu. . . . Upon his return to Lu, . . . Duke Yin set up an altar to Zhongwu, to which he made offerings in the eleventh month of each year. During such times, it was his custom to fast within a walled enclosure and lodge with a Mr. Wei. On the day *renzhen*, Yufu sent assassins to murder Duke Yin while he was at Mr. Wei's. He then raised Duke Huan to the throne and punished the Wei clan, some of whom were killed. The text does not record the burial [of Duke Yin], since his burial rites were not completed.

Not content to rely on the combined impact of elliptical rhetorical arguments, the *Zuo* tells the reader who did what and why and how. And while the *Gongyang* and *Zuo* in the foregoing example both condemn Duke Huan for sanctioning Duke Yin's murder, in many cases the three traditions diverge sharply, not only in matters of format, style, and approach to the material but also in moral judgment. On the important topic of revenge, for example, the *Zuo* asserts that the noble man's duty is to avenge deaths in his patrilineal line, even deaths many generations past, whereas the *Gongyang*, unless the case involves a ruler, would have the man first honor his obligations to more immediate family relations, paternal, maternal, and by marriage. In general, the *Gongyang* acquired a reputation for wisely "weighing moral priorities," the *Zuo* for upholding the absolute prerogatives of the state and family hierarchies.

Traditions so varying in approach appealed to different temperaments and different eras, and Chinese rulers often found it prudent to foster a spirit of competition among the interpretive schools. That explains why no single tradition managed to dominate *Chunqiu* interpretation over the centuries. The history of Han dynasty scholasticism is a neat demonstration of this point. During the first century and a half of Han rule, the *Gongyang*, as the older of the two interpretive traditions then in general circulation, was most influential; its proponents included such prominent scholar-officials as Dong Zhongshu. (In point of fact, in early Western Han the *Gongyang* tradition may have been the only tradition widely known.) A century later, the *Guliang* rose to prominence under Emperor Xuan's (r. 73–49 BC) patronage, in part because of the intransigence of *Gongyang* scholars on a theoretical point threatening the very legitimacy of the ruling house, in part because the *Guliang*'s interpretation of the Classic was more to Emperor Xuan's liking. A court conference in 51 BC granted the *Guliang* equal official recognition with the *Gongyang*. A few decades later, near the turn of the century, Liu Xin began to press for official recognition of the *Zuo*, on the grounds that its Archaic Script text best preserved pre-Qin traditions. Imperial recognition of the *Zuo* was hardly granted before it was withdrawn in retaliation for Liu Xin's association with the usurper Wang Mang. The *Gongyang* and *Guliang* came to the fore again, renewing rivalries between their respective adherents. Throughout Eastern Han (AD 25–220), the *Zuo* gained steadily in popularity within scholastic circles, no doubt because it was touted as promoting conservative values in this period of gradual reinfeudation. It was mainly adherents of the *Gongyang*, however, who were appointed court Academicians, a state of affairs that reflected and exacerbated the widening gap between official and unofficial learning.

Following Han, scholarship devoted to the *Chunqiu* interpretive traditions made monumental advances, with many *Chunqiu* masters borrowing freely from all three traditions. Nevertheless, memories of the competition among their respective adherents never quite vanished from scholastic discussions. Hence the intemperate language with which the scholar Zhong You (d. AD 230) lauded the *Zuo* as the work of a great official while excoriating the *Gongyang* as the work of a bun seller. The antagonisms surfaced once more, in somewhat distorted and distorting form, in the Modern Script–Archaic Script controversies of the late nineteenth century, which further politicized the age-old debates concerning the *Chunqiu* and its commentarial traditions.

THEORY AND PRACTICE IN THE *CHUNQIU* TRADITIONS

History as "Praise and Blame"

The approximately two and a half centuries covered by the *Chunqiu* witnessed the collapse of a political order that had evolved from the early Zhou state in the eleventh century BC. By the late eighth century, a multistate system of about 120 states and city-states operated under the nominal overlordship of the Zhou kings, who reigned ineffectually from their capital at Luoyang. The following 250 years were marked by incessant warfare of increasing scale and brutality, the powerful states swallowing up their weaker neighbors. Thirty-six rulers were assassinated and some fifty-two fiefdoms destroyed. By 481 BC, the date when the text of the *Chunqiu* ends, leaders of the forty-odd surviving states in China had virtually abandoned all pretense of fealty to the Zhou ruler as liege-lord. The dual religious and political authority of the Zhou kings had long been undermined by the desperate scramble for wealth and power among its feudatories, certain of whose rulers (precursors to the notorious fourth-century BC ruler of Zhao) had even taken to adopting barbarian dress and modes of warfare and, in a move equally upsetting to the cultural conservatives, had begun to arrogate royal powers to themselves.

Members of the Zhou elite, especially those in the old cultural centers, such as Lu, identified with early Zhou, must have feared losing what had once made their Central States or ZhuXia communities distinctive.* The *Chunqiu* itself relates this disorder, though its brief notices can hardly capture the tumult and misery attending the incessant warfare: "In the first month, our duke [of Lu] joined the Marquis of Jin, the Duke of Song, the Marquis of Wei, and the Earl of Cao in invading Zheng." "The subject population of Cai banished their minister Gongsun Qing to Wu." "In winter, the eleventh month, Wuzhi of Qi assassinated his ruler, Zhu'er." "In winter, we walled the town of Xiang." This is a catalogue of crises, plainly told. Yet the *Chunqiu* makes no apparent attempt to forge such notices into a coherent narrative or to pronounce judgment on the events.

Though no one knows who really compiled the *Chunqiu*, before unification in 221 BC pious legend had ascribed its compilation to Confucius, probably because the chronicle ends so abruptly—in the very middle of the reign of Duke Ai of Lu, three years before Confucius's death in 479 BC. The *Mencius*, compiled in the late fourth century BC, is the earliest extant text to offer any explanation as to how and why Confucius came to compose the Classic. In two separate passages, Mencius, the self-proclaimed disciple of Confucius, reports,

---

*The terms "Central States" (*Zhongguo* 中國) and "ZhuXia" (諸夏, literally, "all [descendants of] Xia") do not appear even once in the *Chunqiu* classic. Perhaps the text is too laconic to employ such terms or perhaps the text's compiler did not think of the states along the Yellow River as having a common heritage that differed significantly from that of the barbarians. Both terms are found in the three later traditions, however, with "Central States" appearing earlier and more often, and not a few *Chunqiu* commentators (but not this author) have seen the Zhongguo/barbarian distinction as the central theme of the whole *Chunqiu*.

When the world declined and the Way fell into obscurity, perverted sayings and violent deeds were on the rise again. There were even instances of regicides and parricides. In apprehension about this, Confucius wrote the *Chunqiu*. Strictly speaking, it was the Son of Heaven's prerogative and his alone [to authorize or write such a history]. For this reason, Confucius said, "Both those who would know me and those who would condemn me will do so because of the *Chunqiu*." . . . Confucius completed the *Chunqiu* and so struck terror into the hearts of rebellious subjects.

When [the Way of] the true kings had been extinguished, and the *Odes* lost, . . . the *Chunqiu* was written. It is the same sort of work as the *Sheng* of Jin, the *Tao Wu* of Chu and the *Annals of Lu*. . . . It models itself on the work of the state archivist. And its meaning, as Confucius himself said, has appropriated their didactic principles."

The *Mencius* saw in the *Chunqiu* an unofficial "official history" closely modeled on the annals sponsored by the courts of the major states like Jin and Chu and something far more: a text invested with secret meaning, designed both to reveal the Sage's reflections upon the imminent demise of the old order and to supply the key to a political morality capable of restoring the Golden Age.

Once Confucius's authorship of the text was accepted, two important questions remained: Confucius always taught respect for legitimate authority, so why had he taken it upon himself to award praise and blame when that was normally a royal prerogative? And why use such obscure language in the *Chunqiu* if he intended his judgments to be understood? The accepted answer went as follows: Confucius had deliberately adopted "subtle phrasing" (*weiyan* 微言, a phrase eventually read, by extension, as "esoteric teachings") because it would have been offensive, if not downright dangerous, for someone of his low rank to openly criticize the courts of his time. As Mencius had said, it was the sole prerogative of the Zhou king, not of his advisers, to make pointed moral pronouncements and to appoint court historians. If Confucius intended to vehemently protest the usurpation of royal prerogatives, he could not exercise such functions without appearing to be a usurper himself. At the same time, given his moral compulsion to adduce exemplary instances of rule and misrule, obedience and rebellion, he could hardly refrain from trenchantly criticizing the rulers of his day, whatever lengths he went to disguise certain of his judgments out of due respect for the hierarchical order.*

---

*Hence the *Gongyang*'s insistence that the *Chunqiu* disguises the crimes committed by the Zhou and Lu rulers and their blood relations, in deference both to their current high status and their descent from the culture heroes King Wen and the Duke of Zhou. See

That view, in turn, accounts for the honorary title accorded Confucius by tradition: Confucius is the *suwang* 素王 (the plain or uncrowned king, having no kingly regalia), who, in the absence of a true king ruling the real world from the Zhou throne, rules through a text, wherein he metes out rewards and punishments in the form of praise and blame. By virtue of his appointment from high Heaven, Confucius took on the great enterprise, once strictly reserved for the Zhou kings, of composing a "true history" as a way of restoring the realm to the rites and the Right. But as the times were so chaotic, Confucius could do nothing but refer to a just empire of Great Peace (*taiping* 太平) that had once prevailed, in order to make a series of implicit contrasts with current injustices. By this theory, the *Chunqiu* provides a compelling example of how texts can construct order, not only within their own confines, but also in the context of the larger historical world. At root, this is the main reason the figure of Confucius appears, with equal plausibility, to be a cultural conservator bemoaning the disintegration of a perfect society and as a radical reformer planning an improved world for the future.

Over the centuries, talk of the Sage's marvelous subtlety invited ever more subtle readings of his text, whose very brevity facilitated later exegetes in their attempts to read into it their own concepts of moral order. But the belief in Confucius's authorship, however emotionally satisfying, squared badly with relatively late legends (some recorded in the *Zuozhuan* itself) that had Confucius occupying high offices in Lu, positions from which he might have offered remonstrance more openly. Neither did it accord with the *Analects*, then regarded as the record of conversations within the Sage's inner circle, in which Confucius explicitly denied that he was anything but a plainspoken man. And why did the *Analects* make no mention of the Master working on or teaching a *Chunqiu*? Despite such puzzles, many ethical followers of Confucius accepted Mencius's attribution of the text, wanting to believe that the Master's vision informed every line and every word. Over time, the same assumptions about Confucius's subtle phrasing would be applied to all the Five Classics, since Confucius was said to have edited them all—but early Confucians looked to corroborate their theory first in relation to the *Chunqiu*. Thus they read into the rather bland statements recorded in the *Chunqiu* chronicle a masterwork by the

Chunqiu, entry for Duke Cheng, first year, *Gongyang* 6. Similarly, a *Gongyang* entry has Confucius recording verbatim in the *Chunqiu* a statement he knows to be erroneous, out of respect for the historical archives of Lu, whence the statement came. Oddly enough, the *Gongyang* hails that misstatement as "trustworthy history" because it exactly transmits the wording of the earlier archive. See *Chunqiu*, entry for Duke Zhao, twelfth year, *Gongyang* 1.

Sage that would reveal the deep moral structure of political acts not only for Eastern Zhou, but for all time.

To understand the interpretive difficulties these early Confucians faced, let us return to the typical *Chunqiu* entry cited above: "Duke Wen, the seventh year, summer: Men of Song killed their counselors." On first reading, the passage seems utterly devoid of subtle phrasing. Nonetheless, the *Gongyang*, *Guliang*, and *Zuo* all assume that it is fraught with deep significance. The *Gongyang*, for example, comments, "Why does it not name those who were killed? Song for three generations had had no [upright] 'counselors.' For three generations the ducal house had married within [the ranks of its own counselors, causing confusion in the ritual hierarchy]." By praise and blame theory, the failure of the *Gongyang* (and of the *Chunqiu*) to name the murderers should not lead one to conclude that their authors had no good information; the murders should be seen as somehow inevitable or merited. The *Gongyang* traces the motive for the murders to recent intermarriages between the ducal house and the families of its leading counselors. Such intermarriages often created a situation in which a counselor, the nominal subordinate of the duke, could be also his ritual superior, his father-in-law or uncle. Court ritual could thus easily become snarled in nettlesome questions over who should yield to whom under what circumstances and using what formulae. And because court ritual was then one of the two great affairs of the state, any counselors who had contributed to this dangerously destabilizing confusion in ritual hierarchy merited the death penalty, according to the commentators.

But where the *Gongyang* faults the Song counselors, the *Guliang* finds them innocent. (It is not unusual to find the three interpretive traditions associated with the *Chunqiu* disagreeing in their interpretations of key events.) According to the *Guliang*, the *Chunqiu* entry means to blame these enormous crimes squarely on the "men of Song": "The text calls them 'men' [that is, designates them generically as leading men in the state, rather than identifying them individually by name and rank] because it was a case of murder. Use of the term 'men' is designed to punish the guilty." In effect, the *Guliang* argues that the choice of the single word "men" to designate the murderers shows that the *Chunqiu*, and so Confucius himself, roundly condemns the killing of the counselors. The *Zuo* takes still a different tack. Arguing that the assassins were so numerous that the text had to indicate them by the general rubric "men," the *Zuo* infers that the counselors of Song must have offended large segments of the population. Hence, its final comment: "And so the *Chunqiu* says [by implication] that it was not their [the men of Song's] crime." Virtually every word in the *Chunqiu*, according to the commentators, was packed deliberately with moral significance, so that the seemingly straightforward record of a historical event inevitably acquired a moral subtext, a spin in today's parlance. In the case of the Song counselors, for example, a report that they had been murdered, executed, or assassinated would have carried a different emotional impact from the statement that they had been killed.

Some interpretive differences among the *Gongyang, Guliang,* and *Zuo* hinge less upon the specific import of the *Chunqiu*'s vocabulary in any one entry than upon the entry's general content. Two good examples may be given. The first concerns the famous battle of Hong, in 638 BC, which Duke Xiang of Song lost to Chu, mainly because the duke declined to strike when the enemy was at a disadvantage, crossing the river. In insisting upon an ancient code of chivalry, the duke forfeited his only chance to defeat a much stronger opponent. The *Gongyang* gives Duke Xiang its highest accolade, comparing him to good King Wen of Zhou, for "not forgetting important rites" in the aristocratic code of conduct. The *Guliang* criticizes Duke Xiang for ignoring the exigencies of the situation. And the *Zuo,* through the person of Gongzi Muyi, condemns the duke's disastrous miscalculation of his own troop strength. In a second example, dated to the year 619 BC, fifty-odd lords of the land have joined in building a wall around the tiny beleaguered state of Xing, thinking to save it from further depredations. The *Zuo* and the *Guliang* praise this rare instance of unselfish cooperation among the lords, but the *Gongyang,* ever wary of any encroachment on the Zhou king's age-old prerogatives, sharply condemns the act, seeing it as a sly attempt on the part of the allies to assert their authority over territory whose rightful overlord was the Zhou king.

Such disputes among the traditions did not preclude substantial agreement on one point, however. Proponents of all three traditions read the *Chunqiu* as a trustworthy history, one that colored its reporting without unduly distorting the nature of the events. The plain record of facts and the personal voice of moral discernment could meld so perfectly in such an ideal history as to convey concise moral judgments. In witness to this fact, the *Chunqiu,* "based on the events, modified its written account, the better to reveal the truth that it elicited." Students of all three *Chunqiu* traditions therefore studied the framing of a topic and the vocabulary, especially verbs and official titles, for clues to the author's moral verdict, believing that through subtleties of word choice the Classic conveys its grand meaning. Every literary device, even the precise phrasing indicating the day and month, was checked for its "subtle expression of the sage's judgment." Not infrequently, the commentators asked,

1. Why was this entry made?
2. What is meant or implied by the term X?
3. Why is the term Y not used in place of X?
4. Why does the *Chunqiu* text not record Z?

With all three traditions posing series of questions in dialogue form about nearly each and every line, the better to extract moral lessons from historical events, it is little wonder that the *Chunqiu* became the chief model for the "esoteric classics." The exegesis offered in the *Gongyang*, *Guliang*, and *Zuo* takes as its starting point three assumptions: that the *Chunqiu* is internally coherent, that it was composed to promote adherence to ritual and apportion praise and blame fairly, and that individual narratives were modified only when propriety required the sage-author to do so. All three traditions, in consequence, read the *Chunqiu* as the work of a single sage-author. (Apparently, the *Gongyang* and *Guliang*, but not the *Zuo*, assume that sage to have been Confucius.)

With sages for historians, the *Chunqiu* may have seemed far less important as history than as a guide to moral action. Modern-day readers, however, come to the *Chunqiu* commentaries with the opposite expectation, and so they are apt to find the praise and blame traditions contradictory, farfetched, and somehow antithetical to a historical project, even if they embrace postmodern theories proclaiming the impossibility of historical objectivity. In particular the *Gongyang* and *Guliang* traditions, and even more so the Han interpretations that elaborate them, make the *Chunqiu* history appear profoundly ahistorical in at least two senses: (1) they presuppose in the *Gongyang* an ideal political order called the Great Unifying Rule 大一統, which they consider to be at least as important as the events recorded in the text; and (2) they sometimes justify this ideal order on the basis of its supposed congruence with an originary principle of the cosmos existing before history, outside of history, and in the minds of the sage-kings, who by definition recognize important psychological, ethical, and political truths. To the Chinese, it was self-evident that cosmic principles, found equally in the natural universe of Heaven-and-Earth and in the best of humankind, pervaded all of history, needing only to be discerned and acted upon by those of true moral authority. In a just world, such as that imagined by the makers and masters of the *Chunqiu* traditions, the natural and the historical, the practical and the moral would invariably converge, allowing a true history to be not only accurate but edifying in its essentials.

On the Rectification of Names

As noted above, the *Gongyang* and *Guliang* largely employ a question-and-answer format designed to show how the *Chunqiu*'s wording reveals praise and blame. Like other catechisms, the *Gongyang* and *Guliang* typically present only a bare summary of their conclusions, seemingly justifying the philosopher Zhuangzi's complaint that the written word represents the mere dregs of the sages' original visions. Essentially, the two commentaries as we have them represent mere notes on what were undoubtedly extensive conversations, complete with memorable examples, in an age when most knowledge was transmitted orally from teacher to disciple. As a result, the *Gongyang* and *Guliang* notes often come across like oracular pronouncements, maddening in their obliqueness; their ambiguity and contradictions make them unlikely sources in which to delve for any elucidation, let alone resolution, of ethical problems. But by remembering how a single lecture note can serve to jog the memory and spark emotions, recalling lengthy explanations and forging complex connections, we can gain some insight into the ways in which these two commentaries were understood in Han and pre-Han times.

For modern readers, the most memorable entries in the *Gongyang* and *Guliang* may well be those that could spell life or death, entries on hereditary succession or the nature of kingship, for example, that were used as ammunition in court intrigues. Reading a memorial piously quoting the *Gongyang* precept "The mother takes her rank from her son" to justify raising an heir apparent's mother to the rank of empress over the current occupant, its momentous consequences are easy to imagine. History records, for example, that Emperor Jing of Han (r. 156–141 BC), incited to an intense dislike of his Lady Li by her palace rivals, took such offense at a memorial of this sort that he promptly ordered the memorialist executed and the hapless heir deposed. Well into the twentieth century, murders continued to occur with distressing frequency because of this same principle. Among Confucius's own descendants, for instance, was a Madame Dao, principal wife and therefore official mother to all the sons born to her husband, who ordered the murder of the biological mother of her husband's eldest son lest the birth mother come to surpass her in rank.

On the other hand, the concerns expressed in the vast majority of *Gongyang* and *Guliang* entries seem quite unconnected with present-day sociopolitical concerns, as modern states and customs tend to operate on principles different from those promoted in the *Chunqiu* interpretive traditions. Suffice it to say that modern readers are not the first to find the texts obscure and frustrating. Even Han readers, only a few centuries after the commentaries began to be compiled, found it hard to reconstruct the complex moral universe that presumably once prompted such pronouncements, so dramatic were the changes that preceded and accompanied unification under Qin and Han. Nonetheless, impelled by the sense of moral urgency that they brought to their reading of the canon, the Han masters of the *Gongyang* and *Guliang* traditions ignored other possible interpretive approaches to concentrate on establishing the *Chunqiu* as an encrypted statement of Confucius's political ideals. In doing so, the masters focused enormous attention on one short and rather enigmatic statement recorded in the Confucian *Analects*. In answer to the question how he would govern, if given the chance, Confucius supposedly replied, "I would definitely start with Rectifying

Names. . . . If names are not rectified, then words will not follow. If words do not follow, then affairs will not be completed. If affairs are not completed, then rites and music will not flourish. If rites and music do not flourish, then punishments and fines will be inappropriate. And if punishments and fines are inappropriate, then men will have nowhere to put a foot or hand. And so . . . the noble man with respect to speech leaves nothing to mere chance."

On a second occasion, in response to a similar inquiry, Confucius remarked, "Let the ruler be a ruler, and the subject a subject. Let the father be a father, and the son a son." From this it's clear that *zhengming* 正名 (rectifying names) in the *Analects* had nothing to do with calling a spade a spade;* it was an appeal to people to live up to the requirements of their societal roles, so that the names of their roles would correspond with the substance of their actions. Each man who called himself ruler should behave as a good ruler, fulfilling all the ritual and moral obligations invested in that role. Similarly, each man who called himself father should behave as a good father, and so on. Only when a person embodies, consistently and in the highest degree, the ideal qualities ascribed to his social roles can he live productively with others. His honor inheres not in externals (the social place to which he was assigned or born) but in his personal commitment to realize the true meaning of the roles he inhabits. Confucius insisted that if only the proper models for key social roles—ruler and subject, father and child—could be established, appropriate social reforms would follow naturally and easily.

Two logically distinct notions of rectified naming appear in such passages as the very foundation of good government: (1) acting in accordance with the connotations of the various names of one's social roles, so as to fulfill one's functions in society; and (2) making one's speech correspond with one's deeds, so that one becomes completely trustworthy. (Such notions ultimately contributed to a strong belief in the normative and regulative power of words as an arrangement of names of things, states, and events.)† Easy to dismiss as inane, if not

---

*A number of modern scholars have argued that the *Analects'* passage on the "Rectification of Names" does not fit the general tenor of remarks attributed to Confucius elsewhere. Arthur Waley in his translation, therefore, suggests that it was interpolated by logicians of the Warring States period; others have seen it as the work of Warring States professional "persuaders" (*shuike* 説客). Still, early classicists attributed this statement to the Master.

†Two centuries after Confucius, Xunzi's chapter on *zhengming* (chap. 18) expanded this second meaning embedded in the "Rectification of Names" theory. In Xunzi's time, when ideas of meritocracy were coming to the fore, rectification theory also seemed to require that commoners of good reputation be raised in office, given sufficient power to carry out their duties, and then held responsible for carrying out their duties in accordance with their

hopelessly anachronistic, this Confucian call to rectify names nonetheless constitutes a powerful vision of an ideal order in which names of performative force and regulative function help "to realize new worlds appropriate to emerging circumstances." Then does language fulfill its primary function to instill the correct moral values that should inform choice and action. By this theory, any well-ordered society runs basically on trust (*xin* 信). People must be able to trust that others will fulfill their ascribed (that is, named) roles, for few will bother to act like true sons if their fathers fall miserably short of being true fathers. As political and social superiors generally set the pattern of behavior for their inferiors, Rectification theory speaks of ruler and father before subject and son. But all members of the community must share, and know that they share, essential agreement on the specific meanings that underlie social labels and conventional language. It is not enough that members accede to conventions because they are lazy or coerced. They must themselves come to perceive the essential logic of each social role if they are to exemplify it in themselves and be instructed by it when it appears in others.

People who comprehend the essence of normative social roles see the wisdom of fulfilling their own roles, and so they exert a powerful suasive influence for good on the rest of the community. In a good community, a person can be expected to move effectively from one role to another, say, from son to father to adviser to the throne, as needed throughout the course of a lifetime, rather than having to improvise, often with disastrous results, as he goes along. In this way, correct naming ultimately becomes not only the main catalyst for proper social interaction through the rites but also a way of ensuring that hierarchy is balanced by reciprocity. Conversely, incorrect naming, however innocuous on the surface, becomes the chief factor in community collapse. So central was the Rectification of Names to the moral vision attributed to Confucius that even such critics of the Master as Zhuangzi assumed that his masterwork, the *Chunqiu*, was defined by its "talk of names and positions."

The *Gongyang* and *Guliang* commentaries preoccupy themselves with the question of whether specific historical figures fulfilled their assigned social roles, making basic sense of the *Chunqiu* by reading into it a Confucian narrative on the Rectification of Names. Wresting standards for present conduct from the text's obscure pronouncements, they aim to elicit the *Chunqiu*'s verdict on each

---

job descriptions, so that names and realities would perfectly correspond in both the bureaucracy and in the larger world. It is fitting, then, that many early texts attribute the *Zuozhuan* to the "school of Xunzi." Euro-American philosophy has only recently attributed a comparable measure of power to language in the aftermath of John Austin's (1911–1960) "performative utterance" theory, which notes that many utterances (e.g., "With this ring, I thee wed") constitute transformative acts themselves, as distinct from mere descriptions.

moral agent's relative success in exemplifying proper social roles in support of the Zhou order. Reading into the *Chunqiu* this notion of naming, the commentaries devised several additional corollaries regarding interpretation: (1) that Confucius meant his language to reestablish sharp distinctions between inner and outer, viewing the Zhou domain and the Lu state as inner in contrast to the other states of the realm and all the Central States as inner in contrast to the barbarians; (2) that Confucius by his word choice reminded readers of their solemn duty to "treat close kin as close kin" (*qinqin* 親親) by giving them preferential treatment; and (3) that Confucius intended his language to promote orthodox succession and unification, if not under Zhou (given Zhou's endemic weakness), then under some future regime. Every application of these interpretive principles was founded on the classicists' view of ritual, hierarchy, and humanity. For them, the scrupulous performance of assigned social roles constitutes the heart of the ritual system, which in turn is the basis for any humane political order predicated on an antique model. This is what the *Gongyang* compilers had in mind when they glossed the entry: "Autumn: A son of the Wu family came from the Zhou royal house to request monetary contributions from Lu":

> Why is he referred to as "the son of the Wu family"? In order to criticize. What was there to criticize? As the father had recently died, the son had not yet been invested with his rank. . . . Why is [the son of Wu] not identified as an envoy? It was a time of mourning [at the Zhou court], so there was no new ruler yet. [Consequently, no envoy could have yet been appointed.] Why does it record the phrase, "a son of the Wu family came to request monetary contributions"? In order to criticize. What was there to criticize? In matters pertaining to mourning, no requests should be made. Requests for monetary contributions do not conform with the rites.

To this, the *Guliang* adds,

> It was wrong to employ as an envoy a person who had not yet been invested with rank. . . . It is said: to present gifts is correct; to request gifts is wrong. Even if the Zhou royal house had not requested gifts, the Lu ducal house would still have had to present them [on such an occasion]. But even if Lu had not presented [the customary] gifts, it would still have been wrong for Zhou to request them. . . . The text criticizes both parties [for it also implies Lu's reluctance to send the customary gifts at mourning].

According to the *Gongyang* and *Guliang*, the Zhou royal house, and possibly the Lu ducal house as well, disgraced itself when it ignored the rules of etiquette prescribed for mourning ceremonies for leaders of state. Given the close blood ties between the courts of Lu and Zhou, Zhou's request for gifts and Lu's unwillingness to send them seem equally strange, a case of "kin not being treated as kin." Their specific ties were considered before the final verdict was rendered in the text: the actions "did not conform with the rites." Both of these glosses, typical of the *Gongyang* and *Guliang* in their analyses of *Chunqiu* entries, turn their focus on disparities between appearance and reality, names and circumstances, examining the text through the prism of Rectification of Names doctrine.

But the third major interpretive tradition attached to the *Chunqiu*, the *Zuo*, employs direct praise and blame considerably less often.* As a result, the Rectification of Names theory is less in evidence in its approach to the historical materials. In fact, consideration of the *Chunqiu*'s wording is less common in the *Zuo*, in which only some ninety passages out of thousands attempt to explain the presence or absence of a given term in the *Chunqiu*, a far smaller proportion than in the *Gongyang* or *Guliang*. This is not to say, however, that the *Zuo* lacks overt moralizing about the blessings of ritual rule. It contains some fifty *fanli* 凡列 entries added by Du Yu to explicate the proper customs and institutions ascribed to remote antiquity, plus about a hundred explicit moral judgments, some quite lengthy, attributed either to an unnamed gentleman (whom many have erroneously assumed to be Confucius) or to Confucius himself.

Still, the *Zuo* seems more concerned with supplying highly detailed and colored scenes of key events than it is with extracting from the *Chunqiu* a "hidden meaning" related to the Rectification of Names. Because the bulk of its text consists of such dramatic episodes, the *Zuo* appears less as commentary on the *Chunqiu* than a separate, at times even unorthodox, history of the period, with clear affinities to other accounts dating from the late Warring States, including the *Guoyu* and the *Zhan'guo ce*. A better rendering of the title in fact, would thus be *Zuo Traditions* rather than the usual *Zuo Commentary*. In relating its tales, the *Zuo* also appears to convey a mixed moral outlook, wavering, like so many of the patricians whom it portrays, between admiration for the politics of self-interest and nostalgia for an old aristocratic code predicated on honor and

---

*Perhaps it was the *Zuo* that influenced Zhu Xi to partly discount the prevailing interpretation of the *Chunqiu* as praise and blame history. Zhu said, "Confucius simply described things as they were, and right and wrong became apparent of themselves." Certainly Zhu distinguished the *Zuo* as historical learning from the *Gongyang* as classical learning.

loyalty. Neither virtue is unique to Confucian teachings, but rather is a pre-Confucian ethical holdover. How is it, then, that generation after generation of Han and later scholars concurred that the *Zuo* "fully discussed the phrasing" of the *Chunqiu,* so as to elucidate the teachings on *zhengming* most dear to the heart of Confucius? Given that the traditional conceptions of the *Zuo* nearly all assume a moral universe embedded in the text, is one to conclude that the Chinese, aside from a handful of skeptics, have deluded themselves for two thousand years about the true nature of the *Zuo,* and so, by implication, of the *Chunqiu* as well? Such a conclusion would do little to advance understanding of what these texts meant to their readers. The traditional search for coherence within the text, a topic worth serious consideration, raises an alternate possibility.

For though the *Zuo* differs in approach from the *Gongyang* and *Guliang* catechisms, there is one way in which it could be a considered a brilliant commentary on the language of the *Chunqiu.* The *Zuo* opens by immersing the reader in the complex rhetorical universe of the interstate system of the eighth century BC. The many political speeches inserted at the beginning of the *Zuo* appear to be careful, if edited, transcriptions of formulaic social discourse, presenting readers with traditional, appropriate (if highly idealized) ways of constructing persuasive arguments in early China. Then, as the chapters unfold, the *Zuo* proceeds to demonstrate the critical function of moral language as the basis for a livable society by that most provocative of rhetorical counterproofs: the *Zuo*'s historical entries simply portray the increasingly nightmarish quality of life as moral language gradually comes to lose all meaning.

Showing the awful social disintegration that follows when people's actions fail to match their titles and when people's words belie their actions, the *Zuo,* no less than the *Gongyang* and *Guliang,* underscores the pressing need for those in power to uphold Confucius's doctrine of the Rectification of Names. By this reading, naming in all its aspects—the roles, titles, claims, and modes of phrasing—certainly constitutes the central subject of the *Zuo* text. The praise and blame associated with right naming, however, is conveyed more subtly through the variety of social ills attending the incorrect use of language, rather than through a kind of catechism or, worse, a series of solemn pronouncements. Arguably, the *Zuo* presents the more compelling case for the proper use of language, as it also tallies with the pre-Han tradition (cited above) that had Confucius preferring to illustrate his points through actual events, rather than put forth abstract moral judgments. Thus, the *Zuo,* though it makes few explicit references to the Rectification of Names, may constitute the single best exemplification of that doctrine's wisdom, as its early promoters Liu Xin and Jia Kui (30–101) insisted. In effect, the entire history of the period, according to the

Zuo, warns of the chaos that ensues when there is no longer any congruence between social roles and conduct, words and actions.

A Reading of the Zuo

According to legend, the first century of Western Zhou (ca. 1050–722 BC) dynastic rule saw the establishment of a superior community in China called the ZhuXia (Xia descendants) or Zhongguo (Central States) order. Character-ized by peace, prosperity, and stability, the early Western Zhou, as the story goes, was overseen by exemplary rulers and manifested its perfect adherence to ritual by its scrupulous attention to rectified names. The rulers' vast authority rested not in military power but on an ethical civil administration and the broad support of their subjects. In those halcyon days, leaders placed enormous value on fulfilling the obligations of their social station and keeping their word, even at the risk of their lives. Integrity, sincerity, and loyalty were the bywords of the old regime, as legend had it:

> The former kings would display only their virtue, not their weaponry. Weapons were gathered in and used only at the proper time. Put to use at the proper moment, they were awesome to behold. But those who only make a show of weapons [without a show of virtue] will find that the people become accustomed to using them. . . . For this reason, the Hymn by the Duke of Zhou went,
>
> > *Now gather up the shields and pole-axes!*
> > *Now encase our bows and arrows!*
> > *We look to ourselves for fine virtue . . .*
> > *Confident that our king will preserve the Mandate.*
>
> Our former kings dealt with the people by enhancing and correcting their virtue; . . . they made them understand where benefit and harm lay; they used civil exemplars to teach them. . . . The reigns of Kings Wen and Wu highlighted the brilliance of the former kings, adding deep compassion to it. . . . The former kings did not devote themselves to arms; commiserat-ing with the people's pains, they sought to remove their woes. . . . If there were lords who did not pay the standard tributes, they looked to improve the system of titles. And if there were lords who did not pay homage to the kings, the Zhou kings sought to cultivate their own virtue.

By the *Zuo* account, for a short while in the early Chunqiu period this emphasis on "displaying virtue" was maintained, despite a steady weakening of the Zhou imperial powers. Then came a series of gross retreats from this orderly

ZhuXia civilization. In politics, first members of the royal family, then ministers and even counselors vied to usurp the names (that is, titles and assigned roles) and prerogatives of their superiors. The corruption of politics caused a gradual loss of faith in the normative and regulative functions of language, language being defined primarily as ritual language (that is, formulae instilling and affirming the proper social roles) and secondarily as formal rhetoric associated with public, political speech. Once language was no longer trusted, language forfeited its potential to reinforce accepted norms. That double decline occurred in logically separable stages, though they were frequently as messy in the *Zuo* drama as in real life. Yet through its careful selection of historical events and brilliant use of rhetorical devices, the *Zuo* makes the cumulative decline unforgettable.

As the *Zuo* opens, stage 1, corresponding roughly to the first thirty years of Eastern Zhou (722–692 BC), retains some sense of the old ZhuXia civilization, for it is common knowledge that "ritual . . . orders ruling houses, settles state altars, assigns men their respective ranks, and benefits future generations." Normative titles like ruler and father are apt to keep their agreed-upon meanings, and often virtue will be rewarded. Of course, certain persons fail spectacularly in their responsibilities, belying their roles out of woeful ignorance, selfish pride, or gross ambition. In contrast to later times, however, the consensus not only recognizes and condemns their ill-doing, but also contends that evildoers act badly at their peril. Especially with respect to this ability to make sound ethical judgments, then, the later stages witness a progressive devolution from the old Zhou.*

In stage 2, lasting roughly to 660, actors on the historical stage have begun to realize that virtue does not pay for either the individual or his family, given the various sociopolitical shifts. In response, the wise old advisers are forced to argue the practical advantages of virtue as it relates to specific current situations, with the result that the good seems less a function of virtue and more a function of temporary advantage. Meanwhile, the lords under increasingly nominal Zhou rule feel the need for an institution to reintroduce a measure of trust and stability into interstate relations. Eventually they devise the very imperfect institution of the hegemon (*ba* 霸), which at first seems to function well.

As Stage 2 gives way to 3, the first and second hegemons, dukes Huan of Qi (r. 685–643) and Wen of Jin (r. 636–628), but especially Duke Huan, miscon-

---

* Of course, by this reading, the *Zuo* must show that this decline in ethical judgment can be reversed under ideal rule, such as that by Zichan of Zheng (see below), which raises the level of political discourse. Thus the moralizing speeches of Zichan's contemporaries, including Shuxiang of Jin in 546 and 541 BC, dates which correspond to stage 4, would not have undercut a belief in the steady devolution of rites, music, and ethical language.

strue the nature of virtue and rectified names, seeing them either as mere tools of statecraft, tricks, or admirable pretenses. Their bad example leads to further unrectified behavior in the lesser lords, making usurpations more numerous and speeches increasingly bizarre. The statesmen most adroit in the use of righteous rhetoric often prove most perfidious when put to the test. All this dishonesty, stemming from an illusion of superhuman power and a disregard of human constraints, further weakens the fabric of civilization. Finally, language itself, as a result, becomes a kind of doublespeak.

In stage 4, corresponding to roughly the last century of the Spring and Autumn period, duplicity and usurpation are so much the norm that those in power, unless they are truly exceptional exemplary figures, are less wont to justify their actions by reference to conventional titles or to rhetorical speech. Names and naming, whether construed as social roles or as language itself, have lost all meaning for most. Self-interest becomes the typical accepted justification for all action, and naked force its instrument.

In outlining stage 1, the *Zuo* is not so stupid as to depict a world entirely without wrongdoing, where wrongdoing is defined as any action that breaks community by confusing or ignoring normative role definitions. It simply portrays the start of the Spring and Autumn period as a time when wrongdoing was easily recognized as such and so was swiftly punished by the gods or man. For that reason, the protagonists of the early *Zuo* entries live in a world in which benefit largely coincides with absolute conformity to ascribed roles. In this civilized society, in other words, loyalties to family and state need not conflict with self-interest. And self-promotion is less important than fulfilling one's hereditary role because failure to keep faith with others provokes violence against oneself and one's clan. A famous story dated to 722 BC, the very first year recorded in the *Zuo*, typifies stage 1:

> The Duke of Zheng had two sons by Lady Jiang: a firstborn son, Wusheng, and his younger brother, Duan. Because she had suffered more in giving birth to Wusheng, Lady Jiang favored Duan. She therefore tried to convince the Duke, against all precedent, to name Duan as heir. [This the duke refused to do.] After the duke died, Wusheng succeeded to the dukedom. Lady Jiang then begged Wusheng to give Duan power over an immense territory. Ignoring the advice of his counselors, Wusheng agreed to Lady Jiang's request. To his advisers, Wusheng said, "If Duan does too many things that are wrong, he is bound to bring ruin on himself." Eventually Duan rebelled. And after Duan's defeat, Wusheng in his anger vowed to keep Lady Jiang confined away from court in perpetuity: "Not before the Yellow Springs [the underground realm of the dead] shall we ever meet again!"

Wusheng in effect has told his mother that he will gladly see her in hell—and this in a society professing to honor age and filial devotion! As the tale continues, the reader learns that Wusheng soon came to regret his hasty vow:

> Ying Kaoshu, a border guard of Ying Valley, hearing of this, presented gifts to the [new] duke [Wusheng], who then had a meal served to Ying. Ying ate the meal but set the meat broth aside. When the duke asked him why, Ying replied, "Your servant's mother shares whatever food he eats, and she has never tasted your lordship's broth. I request permission to take her some." The duke replied, "You have a mother to take things to. I alone have none, alas!" "May I please ask you to explain the meaning of this remark?" asked Ying Kaoshu. The duke did, and confessed that he regretted his vow. "Why should your lordship worry? Dig into the earth until you reach a spring, and fashion a tunnel where the two of you can meet. Then who will say you have not kept your vow?" . . . The duke did as he suggested, . . . so in the end mother and son became as they had been before.

The moral lessons in this episode are clear: However much we might sympathize with the young duke, we must conclude that, compared with the filial Ying Kaoshu, he has failed miserably in his various roles. As ruler, Wusheng should have listened to his worthy advisers. As elder brother, he should have provided moral instruction to his younger brother, rather than tempting him to rebel by a gift of inappropriate powers. As son, Wusheng should not have blamed his mother for the events transpiring as a result of his own rash actions. Wusheng appears all the more culpable because he acted as he did at a time when the residual charismatic influence of the Zhou kings was still operative among Zhou subjects. But Wusheng retains some commitment to correct behavior. He is conscious, at least, that he must keep his vow at all costs. And once Wusheng shows himself ready to admit error, an astute adviser is there to deliver him from his dilemma, suggesting how Wusheng may at once keep the letter of his vow, as is noble, and abjure the dishonorable spirit behind it. Wusheng gains no obvious material advantage from restoring relations with his mother to what "they had been before," yet he is delighted to be able to return to the Way of the filial son, for he recognizes that this most basic of human connections is vitally implicated in his sense of his full humanity.

Given such a world, the reader, guided by the Ying Kaoshus of the early *Zuo* world, experiences no difficulty in assigning praise or blame to the agents in its early sections. Each person is judged according to a single criterion: to what extent does he recognize the social compact that lies at the heart of Zhou civilization? A mere thirty years later, as the *Zuo* reader learns, the current Duke of Zhou seeks to murder the reigning Zhou king. Though this dastardly plot is ultimately foiled, the reader has been alerted to the first signs of full-blown moral decline: in contrast to the first Duke of Zhou, who is credited with articulating the language of moral discourse for ZhuXia civilization, his successor consciously participates in its destruction! Stage 2 of decline sees less talk about the proper definitions of virtue, in part because the actors on the historical stage have begun to feel that virtue does not pay, either for the individual or for his family. Upright behavior expressed in ritual no longer yields conventional advantages because personal and family interests can coincide with the state's interests only when true rulers, determined to act like fathers and mothers to their subjects, are on the throne, encouraging the good. Once evil or merely incompetent rulers take charge, morality, personal and family interests, and the interests of society will usually diverge, if only because the throne no longer consistently recognizes and rewards good behavior.

One of the first stories to illustrate this undesirable state of affairs concerns events in 696 BC in the state of Wei: Duke Xuan of Wei committed incest with his father's concubine. From this notorious liaison was born a single son and heir, Jizi, whom Duke Xuan betrothed to a bride from Qi. But when Jizi's young bride arrived, she proved so beautiful that Duke Xuan promptly took her into his own bed. From their criminal union were born two sons, Shouzi and Shuo. Out of festering guilt and jealousy, Duke Xuan, his new consort, and Shuo, their son, conspired to have the innocent Jizi killed. But when Jizi's other half-brother, Shouzi, learned of the plot, he urged Jizi to escape. Jizi refused to flee: "Who would have any use for a son who disobeys his father's orders?" Both Jizi and Shouzi, who tried to defend his half-brother, were then brutally murdered by hired thugs. Though Jizi was faithful to the role of filial son and Shouzi to that of loving brother, both met violent, untimely deaths by the order of their parents. What could more clearly illustrate a ruler not acting like a ruler and parents not acting like parents? Notwithstanding their double failure as ruler and parents to preserve and protect, Duke Xuan and his queen flourished while their innocent victims died. It is only the *Zuo's* solemn act of commemoration that sets the record straight, thereby restoring justice to the world, and making the "studies of men here below . . . be felt on high."

A similar tale is told for the year 656 BC, three decades later. Duke Xian of Jin had a clandestine affair with his father's concubine. From this incestuous union were born two children, a daughter and a son, Shensheng, who became the designated heir. Duke Xian then had by other ladies of the palace four more sons: Chong'er, Yiwu, Xiqi, and Zhuozi. In his old age, Duke Xian became positively infatuated with the mother of Xiqi, a Lady Li, despite the unlucky omens attending her selection as consort. Lady Li, intent upon persuading the duke to replace Shensheng with her own son as heir and successor, availed herself of the pretext that Shensheng had made unwelcome and improper advances to her. Then, to preclude any possibility of Shensheng's return to favor, Lady Li falsely accused him of plotting to murder the duke. Shensheng's many supporters urged him to explain the matter to his father, but Shensheng refused, saying, "Without Lady Li, my father cannot take his rest or relish his food. If I try to explain, the blame will fall on Lady Li. My father is an old man. I could never be happy with such a course of action." Then Shensheng hanged himself.

What is the reader to make of two such grisly tales? Evidently, the initial wrongs, in this case incest and lust, so weaken the benighted person's constitution that gross incapacitation seems the only alternative to proceeding along the path to greater evils. Not even the unflagging virtue of their subordinates can restore the rulers to conscience. To the gaping contrast between their roles and their actions, between their own viciousness and their children's virtues, they are oblivious. It is two youths of misbegotten birth who, in seeing most lucidly the long-term consequences of their decisions, remain most mindful of their duties as sons and subjects. (Indeed, the moral courage exhibited by some youths and servants is a minor theme in the *Zuo*.) The *Zuo* account, of course, leaves readers in no doubt as to the source of much of the corruption: men and women in power have so habituated themselves to license that they refuse to "conquer themselves and return to ritual." But stage 2, in showing also how often just decisions by rulers and high officials to honor their obligations spell disaster to the state and death to their persons, draws attention to this growing perception of virtue's inutility, which the perceptive reader soon registers. To this perception, well-meaning wise men, typically court advisers, occasionally respond by giving short speeches extolling the practical advantages to be gained from "walking virtue's path."

Stage 2, then, having opened with the realization that disinterested social virtue no longer reliably conduces to personal as well as societal gain, continues with a few halfhearted attempts to salvage moral claims by showing that the employment of a particular virtue in a specific historical case may happen to be advantageous. A typical speech from this stage is that offered by Shi Wei to his ruler, the marquis of Jin. Shi Wei persuades the marquis that he would do best to cultivate the rites and music while displaying loving kindness to his subjects, not because such conduct would be right, but because the marquis' subjects can in that way be induced "later to be of [great] use" in attacks launched against Jin's neighbors. Because Confucius insisted that virtue could transform the state, the arguments posed by these men at court represent a major departure from the Confucian program to rectify names. The chief old-fashioned virtues are dubbed "small kindnesses, that do not reach to all, . . . minor acts of integrity that do not cover much," with the result that greater merit seems to lie in ana-lyzing legal and military procedures. In effect, virtue is no longer seen as the only rational choice, but as one of many possible rational choices in a world of proliferating and incommensurate choices, and once this happens, there is bound to come a time when it seems wiser, not just easier, to forsake long-term reliance on virtue for short-term gain. Notably absent from stage 2 are compelling argu-ments presuming any lasting benefits of cooperative community or any indica-tion that all orderly social interaction requires a fundamental reliance on principles of trust and just requital (*bao* 報).

As the very rhetoric of virtue changes, it first reflects then hastens the shift in the larger political realities. The current Zhou rulers, their authority eroded, are in no position to reward virtue reliably. Besides, the descendants of the royal house had abandoned virtue long ago. In response, the lords of the land devise a brand-new institution, that of hegemon, to ensure that virtue pays, at least in most interstate relations. In theory, the powerful hegemon is to deploy his troops in the service of the weak Zhou king, so that the hegemon's might serves the king's right(ful authority). Insofar as the hegemon combines in his person both martial strength and the moral authority (*weiyi* 威儀) invested in him by the grateful Zhou king, the institution of hegemon represents a plausible effort to restore a stable system that consistently rewards virtue.

Still, any alliance between king and hegemon can work only if the hegemon is entirely disinterested, for a hegemon acting in the name of the Zhou king must exemplify good faith toward the Zhou king and toward his peers, if his fellow lords are not to resent his anointment as primus inter pares. The hegemon must be especially careful to punish swiftly and impartially any leaders who fail to comply with compacts entered into by the community of states. And even under the best hegemons, there is the real danger that the hegemonic system, designed to bridge the gap between older notions of governance by the rites and the new realpolitik, will only reinforce prevailing notions that the virtuous deed seldom if ever achieves pragmatic goals. The world of the hegemons, after all, frankly accepts the need for an enforcer, a hired gun, to impose a marriage of the ideal and the real. Thus do state and society leave far behind the Confu-cian Rectification of Names, which calls for the natural conjunction of moral authority and political power. Despite the welcome measure of political stabil-ity reintroduced by the hegemonic system under the first two hegemons, dukes Huan of Qi and Wen of Jin, the question remains: Can an institution that relies upon a show of force rather than upon mutual trust and unforced good faith ever sustain, let alone build, a complex social order? In retrospect, it seems that the old adages were right: rule by force can have only very limited success; indeed, "those who use force will perish," like those "without rituals."

In relating the histories of the hegemons Huan and Wen, the *Zuo* concurs with those unhappy predictions. Though virtue, good faith, and mutual trust work to maintain good order through ritual, the hegemons sadly misconstrue virtue's fundamental centrality. Rather than keeping to virtue as the necessary and sufficient method by which to effect a Great Peace, they consider virtue merely one tool among many in a vast repertoire of statecraft. In many circumstances, treachery seems more useful than good faith, but just as soon as the hegemon wields power to further his private aims rather than the good of the community, his subordinates follow suit. Duke Huan himself dies an ignominious death. And the ruler of Chu, who breaks with his allies, finds his own subjects unwilling to risk their lives in his cause. Any equation of virtue and expediency fosters a situation in which no one can be trusted, thereby spurring a precipitous moral decline. The hegemonic system breaks down when the more powerful states fail to agree on the selection of a leader. Personal relations even within a small community become adversarial. Paralysis and disorder increase together.

The *Zuo* narrates a series of speeches that brilliantly mirror the onset of this malignant amorality. Early in stage 3, the key words of the old morality are newly defined. One speech, for instance, calls virtuous anything that persuades members of a military alliance to accept a particular overlord. Bloody battles become games, mere spectacles for viewing. War itself masquerades as a weird double for virtue, promising to yield all conceivable goods to all its participants, as one hegemon, Duke Zhuang of Chu, intones in an impressive, successful, and fundamentally corrupt speech: "Now the purpose of war is to prohibit violence, put weapons aside, preserve the great, . . . bring peace to the leading men and harmony to the masses, and enrich state resources." No Orwellian big brother is imposing this hideous oxymoron of peace through war on a compliant subject population. There is simply less and less belief in fundamental meaning or the ability of language to designate sociopolitical roles. Significant naming has become impossible. Whereas disputes once raged over the moral content of specific actions, stage 3 marks the steady subversion of moral language itself. Once virtue is conflated with victory, the standard definitions of key virtues, for example, good faith, courage, loyalty, good reputation and caring, are seriously distorted, when they are not rejected. As kinship cannot guarantee solidarity, generosity, or compassion, good faith is stunningly absent on the larger scale of interstate relations. Even at the moment of signing a treaty, while swearing their most solemn oaths, the signatories have no intention of upholding their pledges. Swearing by the gods or by one's family is either a cynical or a ludicrous move.

By stage 4, the same crisis deepens, as not only the assignment of moral priorities and the framing of moral judgments, but even the cold calculation of material benefit become dreadful exercises in futility. Hallowed precedents yield to "whatever the ruler wants." Ritual is employed to tart up debauchery and decay. "To plan" becomes a euphemism for "to murder." As the bewildering process continues, and normative language lies in total confusion, the constraints that it places on action falter. Duplicity becomes common. The jettisoning of the usual social bonds and the collapse of language into incoherence cause suffering on a scale that is hardly to be imagined. Children, women, and the old are especially vulnerable to the escalating brutality throughout stages 3 and 4 because the ritual system, thoroughly decimated, no longer keeps humans from their basest impulses. Entries devoted, for example, to the beautiful Lady Xia, who is part femme fatale and part victim, show her to have been abducted, traded, and forced to marry a dizzying succession of husbands and lovers. Her story begins with sexual license: "Duke Ling of Chen, Kong Ning, and Yi Xingfu all had sexual relations with Lady Xia. For a joke, they proceeded to wear her underwear to court. [The wise official] Xie Ye protested this, saying, 'When the duke and his ministers make displays of their debauchery, the people will find in them no good model to emulate.' " The three noble miscreants, miffed by Xie Ye's remonstrance, have him murdered. Some years later, King Zhuang of Chu also takes Lady Xia to his bed, but eventually he sends her home, blaming her for bringing bad luck to his household; too many men have fought and died over her. Next to lust after her is Minister Zifan of Chu, but he is warned off by Wu Chen, Minister of Chu, who eventually marries her himself and escapes with her to Jin. Years later, Zifan and Wu Chen then become deadly enemies over her. With the ruling councils of Chu at daggers drawn, the barbarian state of Wu seizes the opportunity to challenge its power. By the final centuries covered in the *Zuo*, the corrupt and corrupting political elites are hardly distinguishable in their attitudes from those who have never enjoyed the benefits of Central States civilization. Lacking all sense of "trustworthiness and a sense of social duty," the ruling class no longer continues even pro forma observances of the old rituals, and so the distinctive basis for cultural superiority in Zhou and Lu collapses. Scions of the nobility have sunk so low they can no longer plausibly assert their superiority over the ethnic "barbarians" living among them. In such a topsy-turvy world, the barbarian leaders, as Confucius once noted, often appear to be both more moral and more rites-conscious than the direct inheritors of Zhou:* with the Zhou system in utter disrepair, "it seems

---

*The Central States classicists, especially those from Lu and Qi, prided themselves on their superior knowledge of ancient texts and music. Yet many of the most splendid Eastern Zhou ritual bell sets and manuscripts have been excavated in areas once occupied by the "barbarian" states of Chu and Qin. See *Music in the Age of Confucius*, ed. Jenny F. So (Washington, D.C.: Freer Gallery of Art, 2000).

to be true that learning must be sought among the Four Barbarians." Two astute observers sum up the situation in an identical fashion, sensing that they are witnesses to "the final phase of an era."

Confused clamor and hubbub well up all around. In its early entries, the reader could count on the *Zuo* to offer clues to the proper moral judgment about any given scene. Typically, the protagonist would be introduced through an initial incident, whose symbolic implications, good or bad, would be borne out over time in successive lines or entries. But how to apportion blame when blame is nearly universal? Is it fair for cheaters to punish those who have cheated them? Is it permissible for untrustworthy persons to excoriate others for their lack of good faith? Is good faith owed to turncoats and traitors? In such a lawless state, can anyone claim with confidence that justice has been done or that the "evil one meets has been brought on [solely] by oneself"? The *Zuo*, one could argue, purposely refrains from sorting out this moral chaos. Instead it dramatizes it by juxtaposing claims and actions, words and deeds, in such a way as to highlight the bizarre discrepancy between them. Cognitive dissonance results. For example, what does "excellence" mean, when an "excellent" ruler of Chu is removed quickly from office? Whirled about in a historical milieu in which there is no chance to determine the best course of action in a given situation, the reader fully enters the unsavory and unsettling world portrayed in the middle sections of the *Zuo*.

To the end, the *Zuo* still seemed to indicate a possible way out of the morass by occasional interjections into its narrative of highly polished moralizing speeches by a few prominent figures. A classic example of such a speech occurs in an entry recounting attempts by an officer of Song, a state tied to the old Zhou order, to arrange an alliance between Jin and Chu:

On the *xinsi* day, they were about to make a pact outside the west gate of Song. The men of Chu wore armor under their clothing [intending to be ready for any skirmish] with Jin. [An officer of Chu,] Bo Zhouli objected, saying, "Surely we should not show our lack of good faith by wearing armor!" . . . [A fellow minister] Zimu replied, "For a long time there has been no trust between Jin and Chu. We simply wish to retain the advantage. So long as we achieve our aim, what's the use of keeping faith?"

Zhao Meng [a great officer of Jin and head of one of its ministerial clans] was concerned that the Chu contingent was wearing armor, . . . but Shuxiang [Jin's chief strategist] said, "What real harm can it do us? It does not do for even an ordinary man to be of bad faith, for bad faith ends, surely, in his own death. If they, having assembled the ministers of all the vassal lords, commit a breach of faith, they will surely gain no success by it. He who betrays his word is sure to suffer for it. . . . How can they injure us?"

Shuxiang concludes by advising Zhao Meng that "he has nothing to fear"; "they will be able to resist to the death" because they have a good cause. So impressive are men like Shuxiang, so noble in speech and so brave in heart, that readers may fail at first to realize that their speeches, in fact, mark a moral regression from earlier episodes. The very context for such acts of integrity has changed, virtue now being not the supreme Way of governing, but an instrument of some utility and no "real harm" when maneuvering in situations that are themselves inherently disordered. Thus the metaphors for virtue compare it with things that cool the heat and see it as one of many "implements of battle." Exceptional leaders, of course, prove exceptions to the general rule, as in the case of Zichan discussed below.

The reader approaching the fourth and final stage of moral decline, the last century or so of the Chunqiu period, will note a greater disinclination on the part of the historical figures treated by the *Zuo* to justify their actions by rhetorical speeches, as once was customary. The tendency to eschew rhetorical display is especially marked during the forty years under Dukes Ding and Ai. As before, the *Zuo*'s compiler/editor refrains from overt moralizing, but once naming (language, roles, and titles) is no longer a reliable guide to others' thoughts and actions, speech becomes redundant. The grand rhetorical speeches that once informed the reader's ethical understanding of earlier events in the *Zuo* are more conspicuous by their omission, though a few set pieces on ritual serve to underscore the debacles. Even the kind of public formulaic justifications once routinely offered before the undertaking of military ventures are often dispensed with. Shorter speeches, where included, generally enliven the narrative or introduce analyses of various historical processes. They seldom clarify moral issues. Most ironically, the virtue-talk about "service to one's lord" and "good governing" is mainly employed as a last resort by desperate men in desperate situations, as is evident from the following entry reporting a rebellion in Chu in 478 BC:

The men of Wu attacked the region of Shen in Chu. Sheng, the Lord of Bo, defeated them and requested permission to remain armed while presenting his spoils to the ruler. When permission was granted, he used the opportunity to initiate a revolt. In autumn, the seventh month, he killed Zixi and Ziqi at court and threatened the king. Ziqi [when faced with the rebel] said, "In the past I served my ruler with my brute strength.

I must end my life in the same manner." He tore a camphor tree up by its roots and used it to slay his attackers until he himself was killed.

[The rebel adviser] Shi Qi said, "Burn the storehouses and put the king to death. Otherwise, you will never succeed!" The Lord of Bo said, "That is impossible! Putting the king to death would be an ill-omened act and burning the storehouses would leave us with no supplies. How would we ever get along?" Shi Qi then suggested, "Take possession of Chu, govern its people well, and serve the spirits with reverence. Then you can elicit plenty of favorable omens and collect more supplies, as well." . . . But Sheng, the Lord of Bo, rejected this advice.

With virtue-talk reduced to ploys designed to fool others, entire *Zuo* entries are now devoted almost entirely to big-action narratives. Might equals right, and victory by any means is justified. Here is the entry describing the start of a revolt in Wei led by Kuai Kui, designated heir to the Wei throne, who is also younger brother to a Lady Bo married to the Kongs:

In the intercalary month of this year [480 BC], Hun Lianfu [who had had illicit relations with Lady Bo] and the heir apparent Kuai Kui entered the capital and took shelter at a garden estate of the Kong family. At dusk the two of them muffled themselves in women's clothing, mounted a carriage, and with the page Luo as their driver, proceeded to the Kong family mansion. When Luan Ning, senior retainer to the Kong family, asked the driver who they were, the driver reported that they were women relatives of the family. Eventually, they were able to make their way to Lady Bo.

Lady Bo, having finished her dinner, took a halberd and led the way for the group. The heir apparent and five other men, all armed, followed after her, carrying a pig [whose blood was used to seal their oath of alliance]. They cornered Lady Bo's son in the privy and forced him to swear an alliance with them. Then they threatened him until he agreed to ascend the terrace [to announce to all who were gathered there the heir apparent's seizure of state power].

Men claim to be women. Women lead men to violence. Not only is all turned upside down but, more's the pity, even the most intelligent of men are deluded into thinking, "That's just the way it [always] is." For example, the *Zuo*, describing the failure of the rebellion in Chu in 478 BC, comments,

The [rebel] Lord of Bo wanted to make Prince Zilü the new king, but Zilü refused. . . . In the end, the Lord of Bo put Zilü to death and forced tribes] joined forces to invade; when the very continuance of the Central States hung like a thread." The *Zuo Traditions* functions as commentary to the *Chunqiu* annals whenever it draws attention to the decay of ritual, the decline of community, the internal and external threats to civilization, and the strong connections among these evils. In revealing the dire consequences stemming from the collapse of an old rectified order, the *Zuo* joins the *Gongyang* and the *Guliang* in helping to usher in a revived, rectified order in a new imperial age.

Since no new order can be instituted if the naming crisis has not been solved, the *Zuo*, no less than the other two commentaries, reflects a four-step remedy for the follies of the Chunqiu era and its own time, with each step premised on an aspect of the Rectification of Names theory. First, one must find true rulers, who by definition practice ritual and promote frugality in order to ensure that the social compact is fair and workable. Again and again, the *Gongyang*, *Guliang*, and *Zuo* depict the degeneracy of the ruling families, including the Zhou, whose members have abandoned any semblance of benevolent rule. One duke of Jin, for example, amuses himself by shooting his slingshot at innocent subjects; no father and mother to the people is he. King Jing of Zhou misuses the power of music for his own pleasure, casting a bell whose sound is so intense that it causes him to sicken and die. A duke of Chu becomes so disproportionately angry over a minor ritual fault committed by a member of his court that he flops down onto a bench, which then tips into burning charcoal, so that he is burned to death. A duke of Zheng churlishly refuses to share a delicacy with one of his ministers, who takes offense at the public humiliation and plots to have him killed. And a later duke of Jin, at first terrified by apparitions from a ministerial family he had nearly exterminated on false charges, then grows arrogant enough to think that he can cheat his predestined death; in the end, he eats the grain he has been told to avoid, watches his stomach swell up, and hurries to the latrine, into which he pitches headlong, drowning in his own filth.

If better men are needed to lead the Central States, the good rulers must appoint true ministers, whose two main duties will be to help the ruler distinguish right from wrong and to spread the ruler's civilizing influence by suasive example. Through the help of these able officials, well-intentioned rulers can become strong rulers, capable of guiding All-under-Heaven. And once the governing elite is identical with a moral elite, its members can reformulate and forcefully restate moral priorities, to obviate any excuse for duplicity or conflicting loyalties. Rulers will join with officials in strictly enforcing sumptuary regulations, with the aim of increasing popular emulation of the reformed sociopolitical elite. By making visible the link between exemplary deeds and material privileges, sumptuary regulations give the general public great incentives to imitate their betters. When "tokens and titles" are not handed out lightly, they "create trust" and "are the embodiment of ritual." Finally, the entire polity, led by the ruler, must abstain from rhetorical deceit, speech that fails to correspond with either inner commitments or actions; as one character in the *Zuo* notes, the false words of petty men only attract enmity and blame. The Rectification of Names, well achieved, ends with conventional titles and daily speech both becoming true.

The foregoing reading, which envisions the *Zuo* as having been composed by a single committed moralist or group of moralists basing the work on disparate historical sources (some roughly contemporaneous with the events they purportedly describe), has the virtue of explaining why its accounts differ so markedly between one stage in the Chunqiu and the next. As we have seen, in the *Zuo*'s early sections, lengthy moralizing speeches abound, but as the book proceeds, such speeches, increasingly forced, tend to disappear, the exceptions being a few very long orations—larded in the text as ethical reminders?—on the efficacy of ritual rule. This would explain also why the *Zuo*, for all its obvious love of spectacle, never sinks to glamorizing battle, even as conflicts take center stage. Evidently, its author(s) kept more sober purposes in mind.

Whether the proffered reading corresponds with past reality or not, when lying and butchery proliferate, they lead inevitably to ruin and dishonor—that sequence of events the reader is apt to grant. But it is considerably harder to demonstrate to the reader's satisfaction that a pious return to ritual and correct naming can restore equity, hierarchy, and comity. However masterfully the *Zuo* seems to build its case, then, this four-step program for restoring community will strike some modern readers as absurdly unrealistic, unless they are wise enough to see that stable order and power depend more upon consensus than on force. Many early readers would have found it hopelessly naive as well. As if to quell such doubts, the *Zuo* gives two biographies, those of the exemplary Minister Zichan of Zheng (act. 554–496 BC) and of Confucius himself, that generate compelling new models of authority in the real world through the rhetorical voices generated in the text. The deeds of Zichan and Confucius, as counterweights to the pervasive moral decline, prove that turmoil and anarchy can indeed be brought back to communal order through the restitution of appropriate and dependable moral language. Zichan and Confucius, not the hegemons of military fame, are the true heroes of the *Zuo*.

EXEMPLARY LIVES: ZICHAN AND CONFUCIUS

Zichan, grandson of Duke Mu of Zheng, bursts onto the *Zuo* scene in 564 BC, when as a young man he suggests, contrary to the common wisdom, that Zheng may soon have reason to repent its recent victory over Cai, a victory achieved by Zichan's father, among others. Despite his youth, Zichan exhibits remarkable foresight and impartiality. By 557 BC, the records show Zichan actively engaged in politics; within four years, he rises to become one of six ministers in Zheng. Then, in 542, the prime minister Zipi, weary of trying to arbitrate the protracted struggles among the great families of Zheng, abruptly cedes his rank to Zichan. Until his death in 521 BC, Zichan continues to guide the affairs of Zheng from that elevated post.

To appreciate Zichan's great achievements, one must first realize the precariousness of Zheng's 鄭 domestic politics and interstate relations. Zheng, a small state near Kaifeng (Henan), was wedged uncomfortably between the two greatest military powers of his time, Jin and Chu. Long before Zichan became prime minister, internal strife among its aristocracy had seriously weakened it, affording Zheng's powerful neighbors ample pretext to intervene in its internal affairs. Knowing that even in a great state, internal dissension courts foreign invasion, Zichan steadfastly refused to take sides in any aristocratic quarrels, lest it hamper his ability to resolve them. Living by the maxim that "to seek to satisfy yourself at the expense of others is both improper and unworkable, but by sharing common goals, all can be secured," Zichan became a byword for probity and incorruptibility. At one point he even declined what many considered his fair share of the war spoils because such rewards were not in conformity with the ancient sumptuary regulations. By such means, Zichan intended to restore some sense of responsibility to the members of Zheng's noble houses that they might cooperate in securing the peace. Zichan meanwhile set about bolstering Zheng's external security, playing off one neighbor against the other whenever necessary. Zheng's neighbors, Jin and Chu, but especially Jin, had repeatedly pressured Zheng's rulers to accept their offers of protection. Delicately declining such disingenuous offers, which would have reduced Zheng to the status of a minor protectorate, Zichan managed to win the respect of both Jin and Chu. Without resorting even once to deceit—simply by seizing every opportunity to instruct the Jin and Chu rulers about the proprieties befitting the relations of great states to small—Zichan vastly improved the level of diplomatic exchange during the course of his many missions abroad.

In 547, for example, Zichan appeared in his military uniform at the court of Jin, where he had been sent to justify Zheng's recent invasion of Chen. An officer of Jin naturally challenged Zichan to explain both his attire and his state's recent incursion. Zichan then hastened to remind the Jin court of the pertinent facts: (1) that historical ties bound the rulers of Zheng and Chen, and that until quite recently Chen had relied upon Zheng for its protection; (2) that the present Chen ruler, defying past precedent, had not only allied himself with Zheng's enemy, but also, with the help of Chu, invaded Zheng territory; (3) that over a year ago, at the first intimation of worsening relations with Chen,

Zheng had applied to Jin for advice but received no answer; (4) that the former kings themselves had commanded that guilt be punished, and Chen was surely guilty; and (5) that Zichan's decision to wear armor, far from representing a taunting allusion to Zheng's recent military victory, was instead a reminder of the ties binding Zheng and Jin ever since the time of Duke Wen of Jin (hegemon 635–628). For was it not that gracious duke who had commanded the Zheng ruler, Zichan's forebear, to wear armor in token of his perpetual readiness to defend the great Zhou order? Zheng had no choice but to defend itself against invasion, Zichan insisted, and before deciding to punish Zheng for any slight enlargement of its territory, Jin would do well to remember that its own state had grown several times larger as a result of continual encroachments upon its neighbors. Zichan's meaning, however politely phrased, was eminently clear: Zheng's recent action was wholly justified, and Jin's record far from impeccable. An embarrassed Jin court, pronouncing Zichan's account reasonable, decided against punitive action. Thus did Zichan's masterful speech achieve a triple diplomatic coup: it averted a threatened invasion, it recalled Jin's special relationship with Zheng, and it reminded the Jin ruler of his sworn duty to loyally serve the Zhou king. Confucius reportedly exclaimed that if Zichan had fumbled his presentation, Zheng would surely have been lost: "How important it is to have a way with words!" "How indispensable is the gift of speech making," another official observed. "Zichan has that gift, so all the states are under an obligation to him. On no account may speeches be dispensed with."

But Zichan was not just a clever speechifier. His speeches as minister and prime minister were intended to show that state policy is best guided by ethical principles; his deeds, to reveal his determination to act always in good faith, in the belief that virtue was the one secure foundation for the state, propriety its bulwark, and ritual the single power capable of simultaneously reflecting and reinforcing the coherent orders of heaven, earth, and society. Thanks to the unusual clarity and consistency of his vision, Zichan, for the twenty-six years he served as prime minister, was able to promote the dignity of his state without cringing, boasting, manipulating, or contravening the proprieties. Ever alert to possible threats to his small state in interstate relations, Zichan at home proved an equally trustworthy if tough-minded public servant, totally dedicated to the welfare of his people. Confucius gave Zichan's administration his highest accolade, calling it humane (*ren* 仁), a term generally reserved for sagely conduct.

Of the many *Zuo* passages illustrating these admirable qualities, two incidents have been selected here, the first showing Zichan dealing with his social equals and superiors and the second with his social inferiors. A certain envoy from Jin, one Han Xuanzi, had a favorite jade ring whose match belonged to a merchant in Zheng. The envoy begged the ruler of Zheng to get the ring for him, and

> *It's Zichan who our children trains*
> *Our fields to Zichan owe their gains.*
> *Should Zichan die, who can take the reins?*

In a final touching scene supplied by the *Zuo*, Zichan lies on his deathbed talking to his successor, Zi Taishu. Reviewing his long career, Zichan tries to explain why he occasionally imposed harsh punishments (three mutilating punishments and two executions). He begins, as always, by modestly pointing out his inadequacies as a leader. Granting that the "most virtuous people" can govern with absolute leniency, leaders of lesser virtue like himself need to employ every tool at their command to keep the people on the straight and narrow: "When the fire is fierce, the people will keep their distance, and the victims will be few." Harsh punishments for a few recalcitrant criminals serve to deter the rest. Beyond this one speech, Zichan has little advice to give because his tenure in office had already taught that every bureaucratic appointment contributes to the relative health or weakness of the body politic; his successor should therefore always choose the best officials, without reference to aristocratic privilege or personal preferences.

Upon Zichan's death, the people of Zheng plunged into deepest mourning. Confucius himself shed tears because Zichan truly "exemplified the loving care transmitted from the ancients." No one doubts that Zichan's superb powers of leadership guided his small state of Zheng through perilous times. After all, when Zichan assumed power as chief minister, the state of Zheng was riven by warring factions. Under his guidance, peace was restored and the integrity of Zheng's borders maintained. But mere decades after Zheng's rulers began reversing his policies, Zheng confronted disaster again. Zichan's biography thus provides incontrovertible proof of Mencius's oft-derided assertions that the leader of even the smallest state can not only contribute to the ZhuXia civilization by unifying his people and harmonizing interstate relations, but also increase his reputation after death, as members of the elite come to honor his restoration of ritual.

For Confucius, the *Chunqiu* records only birth and death dates, but nine entries in the *Zuo* paint an unusually vivid portrait of the Sage.[*] The first of these, dated to 534 BC, shows Confucius as a young man of seventeen. Already the reader learns, thanks to the narration's flash-forward to the deathbed scene

---

[*]Two solar eclipses were said to be visible in the ninth and tenth months of 552 BC, presumably right before and after Confucius's conception or birth. The *Gongyang* and *Guliang*, but not the *Chunqiu*, record the eclipses. Note also that in early China, deathbed statements were assumed to carry the special ring of truth.

of Meng Xizi many years later, that Confucius will exhibit a profound, even miraculous understanding of ritual language. Meng, a learned official in Lu in charge of court ritual, says, "I have heard that there is one of perfect apprehension called Kong Qiu (the courtesy name of Confucius), a descendant of sages." After recounting the meritorious deeds performed by various ancestors of Confucius, Meng Xizi continues, "And I have heard also that if sages of brilliant virtue do not achieve their rightful place in the world, their descendants always include a person of perfect apprehension. Will this now come true in the person of Kong Qiu? Should I die, you must put [my sons] Yue and Heji under his supervision. So long as they serve him and study the rites with him, they will be assigned their rightful places."

Though this entry has whetted the reader's appetite to learn more about this paragon of wisdom and virtue, some fifteen years elapse in the *Zuo*'s account before Confucius appears again. The *Zuo* then laconically observes that "when Confucius was local magistrate," the Sage corrected a ritual fault having to do with the burials of the dukes of Lu. Yet another decade lapses before Confucius reappears, such long intervals serving to heighten the reader's curiosity about this man of perfect apprehension. What marvelous task will he undertake? Will he prove successful? If not, why not? Succeeding entries on the Sage answer these questions, beginning with an entry detailing political events in 500 BC:

In the 10th year, summer, Duke Ding of Lu, [Confucius's home state,] met with the Marquis of Qi at . . . Jiagu, with Confucius assisting his duke. [Prior to the meeting of the two rulers,] Limi of Qi had advised his marquis, "Confucius knows ritual, but he lacks martial courage. If you send armed men from Lai to coerce Lu's ruler, you will certainly get what you want." The Marquis of Qi agreed to this.

[Later,] because of this [the armed men], Confucius had his duke withdraw from the meeting. He said, "Our two lords have hitherto had good relations. But when armed captives from afar are used to throw a meeting into confusion—well, this is not the way for the lord of Qi to make good-faith compacts with another lord. Those from faraway should not enter into compacts with those in the ZhuXia [cultural sphere inherited from early Zhou], nor should barbarians make trouble among us. Captives should not meddle in alliances. Nor should arms compel friends. With respect to the gods, such conduct is inauspicious. With regard to virtue, it is an offense against duty. With regard to mankind, it is a ritual lapse. Milord must certainly not do thus." The Lord of Qi, hearing this, then abandoned his plan. [Fig. 17]

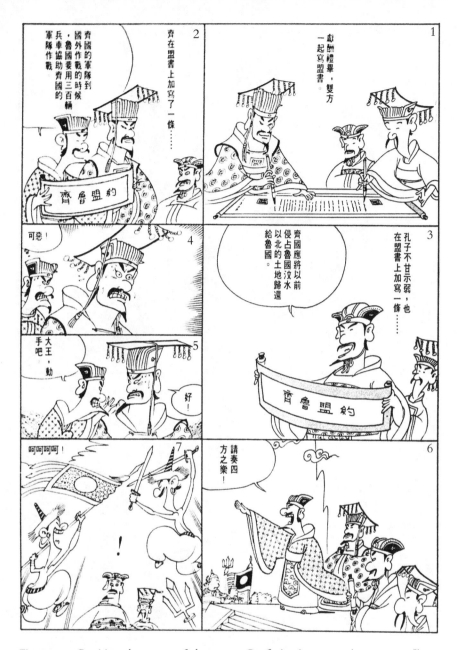

Figure 17a. Revising the terms of the treaty, Confucius intervenes in events at Jiagu, according to the cartoonist Cai Zhizhong, *Kongzi shuo: Ren zhe de dingling* (*Confucius Says: Exhortations by the Humane One*) (Taibei: Shibao wenhua, 1987). The duke of Lu and Confucius both wear plain robes, while the marquis of Qi and his adviser wear patterned silk. Both dukes wear the pearl-strung hat that shows them to be rulers of states, and both advisers wear the stiffly pleated caps reserved for high officials. Scene 1. Confucius looks on as the duke of Lu and the marquis of Qi sign the first text of the treaty. Scene 2. The Qi party adds a provision to the treaty saying that Lu must provide Qi with troops whenever Qi wants, or suffer a penalty. Scene 3. Confucius replies that Qi must then pay a similar penalty if it fails to return the land it has appropriated from Lu. Scenes 4–5: The marquis, furious that his plans have been thwarted, has his adviser order some men attached to his party to participate in a war dance (Scenes 6–7).

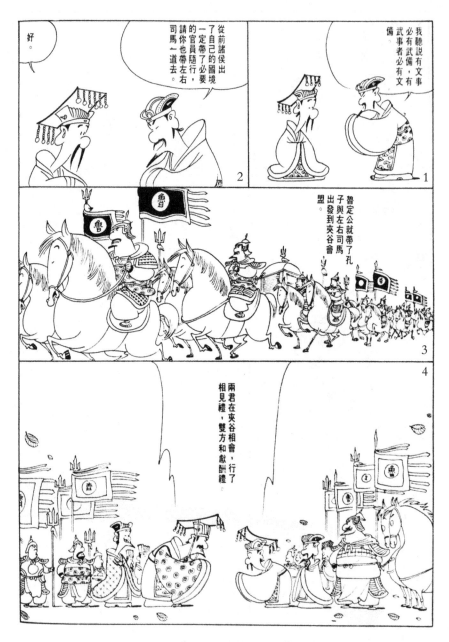

Figure 17b. (*Cont.*) Confucius as the moral power behind the throne of Lu. Prior to working out the precise terms of the treaty of Jiagu, Confucius sets up the preconditions for Lu's eventual success: Scene 1: Confucius advises the duke of Lu that even peace-making missions require military preparedness. Scene 2: Confucius therefore urges the duke, who will be leaving his own territory, to travel with a full complement of civil and military officers. Scene 3: The procession leaves Lu to go to Jiagu, where the two states will enter into a treaty of alliance. Scene 4: When the two rulers come face to face at Jiagu, they meet as equal parties, thanks to Confucius's foresight.

When the two states of Qi and Lu later were on the point of swearing an alliance, the men of Qi added a codicil saying, "Whenever our Qi troops leave their borders, if Lu does not follow us with three hundred armed chariots, let there be fearful consequences, as per the covenant between allies." Confucius sent Zi Wuhuan to bow and reply, "May there be similar consequences if you do not return our fields north of the Wen River, as we take part in the covenant."

Through his apt reminders about correct ritual, Confucius single-handedly shamed the Qi negotiating party into forgoing intimidation, restoring annexed territory, and dropping its plans to enlarge Qi at Lu's expense. The representatives from Qi, however reluctantly, had to agree to return to Lu its former fields, lest they lose face.

Once the formal alliance was concluded, the Marquis of Qi, who still harbored dishonest intentions, announced that he would hold a feast to celebrate the successful signing of the pact. As the *Zuo* tells it,

> The Marquis of Qi was on the point of feasting the Duke of Lu when Confucius said to Liang Qiuqu, "Why is it that you, sir, have heard nothing of the way the old relations were conducted between Qi and Lu? Once the business [of swearing the alliance] has been accomplished, to go on to further celebrate it by a feast is to belabor the affair. Moreover, the bronze ceremonial vessels belonging to the state cannot be taken outside our gates, and celebratory music is out of place in the wilds. To feast with a complete set of implements would be to forsake ritual, but if the implements were an incomplete set, it would be like using chaff and unripe grain. To use chaff and unripe grain is insulting to rulers. To forsake ritual is bad for one's reputation. Whatever were you thinking of when you planned this? Now a feast is a way to display virtue. If no virtue is displayed, it would be better to do without it."
>
> Only then did the parties, in fact, forgo the feast. [Sometime later] the men of Qi came to return the fields of Yun, Huan, and Guiyin [in response to Confucius's earlier speech].

This first major episode with Confucius as protagonist tells the reader quite a lot. Confucius is reputed to know all the ancient precedents. He tends to be underrated merely because he, unlike most men of his time, does not overvalue martial swagger; still, his willingness to speak out shows extraordinary courage. He is a stickler for proper observance of the rites. Not only the proper forms, but also the proper attitude must be maintained in human relations. Confucius moreover commands a singular ability to look well below the surface meaning of events to more fundamental realities. (By contrast, the Duke of Lu and the rest of his company seem diplomatic babes in the wood, utterly oblivious to the potential pitfalls of signing the codicil to the alliance or attending the feast.) That same sensitivity to the fit between language and reality helps Confucius make Qi a real ally, not just a nominal one. As master of the Rectification of Names, the Sage brings his native state of Lu considerable conventional success. Lu is not coerced by Qi; its power enhanced, Lu begins even to frame the alliance on its own terms by virtue of its greater moral authority.

Other entries reiterate these themes. According to tradition, "the sage makes his person tranquil and waits for a sign. And when it comes, he names it." In old age, Confucius has so honed his sage ability to see beyond present convention that he has gained quasi-magical predictive powers. When a fire breaks out near the palace precincts in Lu, Confucius knows immediately that it will engulf the ancestral temples of dukes Huan and Xi, whose construction violated propriety. Shortly before his death, Confucius also accurately predicts that his disciple Zilu will die in a rebellion and his disciple Zhai return safely home. Forestalling any possible suspicion that Confucius is simply a wizard with no practical abilities, a fourth entry shows Confucius in full battle mode, ably commanding those who will rescue Lu's duke from a would-be usurper of the ministerial clans.

The *Zuo* leaves the reader in no doubt that, given the chance, Confucius proposes to devote his remarkable abilities, as well as the resources of his home state of Lu, to rectifying names. From an entry recorded two years before Confucius's death, readers learn that a certain Chen Huan of Qi has assassinated his ruler. Because there can be no clearer case of an "official not acting like an official," Confucius deems the assassination morally reprehensible. In consequence,

Confucius fasted three days, then three times requested permission from the Duke of Lu to attack Qi. The duke said, "Lu has long been weakened by Qi. If you go to attack it, what is likely to happen?" Confucius replied, "Chen Huan has murdered his ruler. Half of the subjects are not on his side. If we take the masses of Lu and add one-half of Qi's population to them, Qi can be conquered." The duke said, "Tell Jisun [the head of the leading ministerial clan in Lu, then controlling policy]." Confucius declined to do so [since that would be to acknowledge, even to acquiesce in the Jisun clan's usurpation of powers]. When he had left the audience, he told others, "Since I come after the counselors in aristocratic rank, I dared not remain silent about this."

The passage has several implications. Both to fulfill his duty as a privileged subject of the ducal house and to foster general morality, Confucius must forcefully remind his rightful ruler of his sworn commitments to avenge the regicide. At the same time, Confucius cannot but refuse to talk with Jisun, since Jisun had no conceivable right, hereditary or moral, to determine policy for Lu. Confucius the official "acts like an official"—he conscientiously fulfills his social role—by distinguishing what is owed to the different parties in government.

As the *Zuo* closes, it bears witness to the final tragedy of Confucius. However often the ruling families in the states of Wei, Chen, or Lu consulted him, in the end they always ignored his advice. One Han text, put in the form of an imaginary dialogue, explains their failure to employ Confucius:

> Someone says, "Few men of Lu were virtuous. How was that, when they were so fond of questioning Confucius?" Reply: "It's because they in Lu never were able to question Confucius properly. Had they questioned him properly, then Lu would surely have become [a second] Zhou in the East [that is, it would have gained enough authority to found a new dynasty]. . . . When Confucius was employed by Lu, the men of Qi were sore afraid of him and so they returned the borderlands they had seized. . . . Lu did not really employ true classicists. Had it done so, Lu would have had no peer in the empire."

To employ Confucius properly, the decadent rulers of the Chunqiu period, including the dukes of Lu, would have had to accept the ethical constraints inherent in a Confucian "return to ritual" via the Rectification of Names. Instead, they resented Confucius's continual criticism of themselves as men refusing to accept the limits of their normative roles in society. And they also feared Confucius, knowing that he could institute a new order if ever he gained the ear of a receptive ruler. Thus they did everything in their power to hinder his advancement. Even in death, however, the model Confucius continues to instruct others about the importance of rectified language and to provide an example of the nobility of failure. The *Zuo* entry reports,

> Confucius died. The duke of Lu in eulogy said of this, "High Heaven gives us no comfort, for it has failed to leave us this one old man to support us on the throne. Ah, woe is me! Without you, Confucius, who has been like a father to me, there are none whom I can take for my own rule!"
> Zigong [Confucius's disciple] said, "In all probability, our ruler [Duke Ai of Lu] will not die a natural death in Lu. For the Master once said,

'Lapses in rites lead to stupidities. Lapses in naming lead to error.' The term 'stupidities' means failing in one's ambitions, while 'lapses' means failing in one's deeds. In life, the duke could not find it in himself to use Confucius. Now in death, adding insult to injury, he eulogizes him. That is contrary to the rites. That is not what is meant by correct naming. Our ruler has doubly erred in this."

Obviously, Confucius's disciple Zigong had learned his master's lessons well. Hollow words that do not correspond to deeds can never restore peace and glory to the state of Lu, nor the duke's belated praise of Confucius make up for his former neglect. Confucius has died, an apparent failure since no ruler ever adopted his ethical Way during his lifetime. But the *Zuo* subtly indicates that his Way is far too powerful to end, in part because the exceptional strength of character exhibited by the Sage has been inculcated in his loyal followers (fig. 18). Nearly without exception, the Sage's followers prove to be resourceful, loyal, and courageous. Zigong, in a manner very like that of his teacher Confucius, uses precedents and rhetoric to win back territory for Lu. Zilu, another disciple, is renowned throughout the empire for his absolute trustworthiness, so that even a desperate refugee puts more faith in a verbal promise from Zilu than in a written guarantee from anyone else. Most of Confucius's disciples rise to political prominence and high repute because they can be trusted to excel in the performance of their duties. Through them, the Way of Confucius will ultimately triumph.

Figure 18. Disciples mourning at the grave mound of Confucius. From *K'ung tzu: On the 2540th Anniversary of Confucius' Birth, 5.*

That after his death Confucius will go on to rule all of China is presaged by a single *Chunqiu* entry: "Duke Ai, fourteenth year, spring: Hunters capture a unicorn." The corresponding account in the *Zuozhuan* is brief: Confucius went to take a look at the marvelous animal, identified it immediately—another sign of his mastery of names—and had it carried back to the capital. That account is enough to remind readers of the popular legends circulating in Warring States and Han that embellished the *Zuo's* rather restrained remarks. In one such popular tale, Confucius, upon viewing the unicorn, asks, "Why has it come? Why has it come?" and then wipes away tears. Asked why he wept, Confucius replies, "The unicorn comes only when there reigns a king of extraordinary perception. This is no such time, yet it has shown itself." Notwithstanding his loyalty to the vassal state of Lu, Confucius is brought to the painful admission that Lu "has the name, but not the substance, of a great state." The Sage, as a subject loyal to Zhou, must also bewail the demise of the old Zhou order, for the unicorn heralds a new dispensation superseding Zhou. And if that new dispensation will come most happily under Confucius's own aegis, Confucius may still suspect that the unicorn's capture presages his own demise, for its perfect purity has not preserved the marvelous creature from brutal capture and death.

Even before Han, men credited Confucius with marvelous powers of insight, attributing to the Sage a perfect foreknowledge of political events in China. Fairly typical were the praises of one famous exegete, He Xiu (129–182), who wrote, "Infinite was his prescience. He knew that the Han dynasty would follow after a great chaos. He therefore created models to sweep away the chaos, transmitting [his moral order] to the Han."* It is easy to scoff at this vision of the omniscient Confucius. After all, Confucius appealed for the restoration of an ideal order that had never existed. And the Han dynasty, despite the supposed patronage of the Supreme Sage, collapsed after four centuries, occasioning a major crisis of confidence in the belief system associated with Confucius. Nonetheless, the figure of Confucius, failed visionary and embattled historian, has proven so compelling down through the ages that every era has had to rein-

---

*Classicists in Han and post-Han repeatedly struggled with the question of why Confucius did not succeed to the Mandate of Heaven in his lifetime, ushering in an era of Great Peace. (A similar question, of course, could be asked regarding Zichan.) Yang Xiong (53 BC–AD 18), the most subtle theoretician among the Han classicists, concluded that virtue was only one of a number of factors that must converge if the Great Peace is to be attained. As Confucius lacked a territorial base, he could only plan for the future dispensation, not institute the future now (*Fayan*, chap. 10). Zichan's virtue, perhaps, was simply not enough to implement the Great Peace. Granted, Zichan could order his state for a generation or two, but only Confucius could establish a higher order enabling future generations to realize a more perfect civilization.

vent the noble figure of the Sage to meet its own needs and expectations. Perhaps because he was both clear-sighted and generous in the pursuit of his ideals, the figure of Confucius has served as a lodestar, inspiring strong moral commitments in support of his cause:

> Here is one, unfortunate,
> Terror-stricken, driven afar, . . .
> With nowhere to go.
> But if my several brothers and relatives
> Will follow the laws of Heaven
> And give no aid to those crafty evildoers,
> Obeying the decrees of the former kings,
> And averting punishment from Heaven, . . .
> Then I will have my wish.

LATER INFLUENCE OF THE *CHUNQIU*

Modern readers, possessed of the most up-to-date archaeological evidence, know three facts about the Chunqiu period of which Han and pre-Han classicists were unaware. First, there had never been any sustained period of strong, centralized rule overseen by rites-minded early Zhou rulers; the three commentaries' shared nostalgia for an earlier imagined past reflects more their authors' moral aspirations for the present and future than their knowledge of Zhou conditions. Second, the three traditions nonetheless faithfully reveal certain major trends in Spring and Autumn and Warring States society, by which sacrificial-auguristic states led by hereditary elites gave way to bureaucratic, contractual, meritocratic states whose impulses toward centralization were predicated on unprecedented economic growth and increased cultural exchange, sometimes in the form of war. Third, the ensuing breakdown in social order during the period covered by the *Chunqiu*, however horrifying to those who witnessed it, spurred men to consider more carefully what kinds of institutions would best uphold a stable and just society.

So while the *Chunqiu*'s compiler(s) may have feared that the distinctive Central States way of life was giving way to barbarism, the historical record perused from the vantage of hindsight demonstrates quite a different scenario: the ZhuXia culture associated with the Central Plains region of China had begun to absorb and impress itself on neighboring cultures (being significantly changed in the process), so much so that such "barbaric" states as Qin, far to the west of the Central States, would be indelibly altered. In curious ways, then —ways mirrored, consciously or unconsciously, in the Three Ages theory discussed below—the breakdown of one old order, the elegiac Western Zhou of invented memory, paved the way for an entirely new stage of civilization in China: a unified, bureaucratic empire that would ultimately justify itself by claiming Confucius as its supreme prophet and model of successful statesmanship. This empire to some degree, of course, rested too upon invention. Responding to the intensity of the feudal states inhabitants' desire for unified, benevolent rule—desire that in the battle-torn centuries before 221 BC made men "crane their necks and stand on tiptoes" to look for any sign that peace would come—the authors of the *Chunqiu* and its commentaries (as interpreted by Han classicizers) projected onto the distant past a just empire that yet heralded the greater perfection of rule by classical principles.

Three hundred years after Confucius's death, the Han dynasty (206 BC–AD 220), the first stable centralized empire in China, claimed to rule by virtue of its adherence to the precepts of Confucius. But as we have seen, Han theory went further, claiming that Confucius, even as he was reporting on the chaos of his own time in his masterwork, foresaw and prescribed the path toward a future age in which All-under-Heaven would be unified under Han. As He Xiu, an important master in the *Gongyang* tradition, wrote, Confucius, "in chronicling the age which he knew through transmitted records, portrayed an order arising amidst decay and disorder." In Han classicism, then, the other four Classics reflected the old dispensation of Zhou, but the *Chunqiu*, ostensibly a tale of early Eastern Zhou, presented a plan for the future. Because Han thinkers, including the self-described skeptic Wang Chong (27–97), were united in their agreement that Confucius had composed the *Chunqiu* with perfect prescience as a guide for Han rulers, the intense scrutiny of the text that naturally followed led literati to read into the *Chunqiu* four notions that would come to preoccupy later thinkers throughout East Asia. The first was that membership in a political order was properly defined and delimited not by ethnicity but by complex cultural criteria; the second, that events, trends, and agents in history must be judged always from a single perspective, whether they prompted or impeded the achievement of *da yitong* 大一統 (grand unity) and *zhengtong* 正統 (ordaining the proper line of dynastic succession); the third, that a cycle of Three Ages of progressive acculturation would allow the final restoration of the legendary peace and prosperity of early Western Zhou; and the fourth, that naming, the fit between actions and normative social roles, must figure in every instance of administering justice.

According to the Three Ages doctrine, human cultures comprised three discrete stages of development: a present dog-eat-dog chaos could, if moral reforms were pursued by enlightened rulers, ameliorate and lead toward a future Age of Approaching Peace, finally attaining the ideal Age of Great Peace, defined as a time when "the Yi and Di barbarians advance and enter the aristocratic system [of the Central States], so that All-under-Heaven, far or near, small or great, is one." In such a time, all would "uphold humanity, attend to social duty, and condemn double naming [deceptive or confusing wording]." In the Age of Approaching Peace, the Chinese living within the geographic borders and ritual systems of the Central States would still feel a need to separate themselves culturally and politically from the barbarians without, but the Age of Great Peace would find all humans, regardless of ethnic origin, embracing the Central States ritual system as the single cultural standard most "in conformity with human feelings." The new utopia would formally recognize the inherent superiority of the Confucian Way, those teachings that claimed to be a refinement of the old Zhou model carefully preserved in Confucius's home state of Lu. Race and heredity would then be obviated as criteria of human values. It was for this reason that Confucius supposedly drew attention to acts of compassion and social duty in the *Chunqiu*, recording for all time even the smallest acts of goodness.

How were those currently in power to usher in the Great Peace heralded by Confucius? Given the legend that Confucius was once local magistrate in Lu, one important method was to judge court cases strictly on the basis of principles said to underlie the composition of the *Chunqiu*. Since the *Chunqiu* taught primarily through "piecing together statements and comparing events, so as to create precedents from them," we are fortunate to have some of the legal decisions handed down by the famous Han dynasty *Chunqiu* masters with reference to the Classic. One extant pronouncement on case law ascribed to Dong Zhongshu, probably the most famous jurist to explicate the *Chunqiu*, concerned a son condemned to death for injuring his father, a capital offense by statute under normal circumstances: "*A* had a son, *B*, whom he entrusted to *C*. *B* was raised and trained by *C*. [On one occasion], having drunk far too much, *A* revealed to *B* that he was *A*'s son. *B* was furious, [thinking that *A* was calling him a bastard], so he hit *A* with a staff twenty times. *A*, feeling that *B* was his son, was unable to contain his anger at this, so he reported *B* to the prefectural officials." No jurist in the lower courts had thought to question the verdict, but because Dong considered the Rectification of Names the single most important precondition to the longed-for Great Peace, he considered the case solely from that angle. As *C* had been *B*'s true father in every way but the biological, *A* could not reasonably claim the rights due a true father, according to the Rectification doctrine. As Dong wrote,

A was the biological parent of *B*. *A*, being unable to raise *B*, had entrusted him to *C*. In his intentions, then, he had long ago severed [the parent/child relationship]. Even if *B* beat *A*, *A* should not have had him brought to trial.

In other words, the privileges of fatherhood belong only to one who has acted as a father; one cannot be accused of unfilial behavior toward someone who has never behaved as one's father. Here the *Chunqiu* was held to corroborate the legal principle that in determining innocence or guilt, intentions and actions trumped other important considerations, including hereditary position, biological connections, and social rank. That may shock some modern readers, in that Dong's understanding of the *Chunqiu* by no means exalted the inflexible law-and-order mentality that the modern age tends to associate with Confucianism. What is more, when deciding upon the ruler's obligations to his subjects, the *Chunqiu* masters could be equally adamant in their opposition to oppressive state power. Whenever the throne tried to raise taxes unfairly, impose monopolies, or privatize public resources, the *Gongyang* masters were among its most vociferous critics. Admittedly, the *Chunqiu* traditions were occasionally employed to shore up imperial prerogatives, as when certain *Gongyang* masters advocated the utmost severity in dealing with aristocratic rebels. But more often they were employed to offset absolutist tendencies in that a close reading of the *Chunqiu* promoted the unshakable conviction that Heaven would gladly forsake any dynasty whose rulers ceased to act like true (that is, humane) rulers. Thanks in part to the *Chunqiu* and its commentaries, imperial policy as reflected in the legal code and in customary law proved sufficiently equitable to promote a stable and civilized polity.

Other, often overlooked, contributions of the *Chunqiu* to imperial culture should be mentioned, however briefly. Legends about Confucius compiling the *Chunqiu* may be partly responsible for the dramatic expansion under the imperial dynasties of earlier bureaucratic structures designed to edit and promulgate official histories for the literati's edification. Invoking the authority of Confucius, histories written on the model of the *Chunqiu* claimed a monumental power to illustrate the strength of personal character as it affected public life, to suggest the pathos of human commitments played out against the larger forces of history, and to exalt the virtues of courageous remonstrance. Early theorists were fond of saying that the *Chunqiu* "praises the very most minor of good deeds and criticizes the most minor of evil acts." By this simple phrase, they charged successors of Confucius with the solemn duty of carefully assigning praise and blame when compiling "veritable histories" (*shilu* 實錄) for the dynasties. Perhaps this goes some way to explain why even state-sponsored dynastic histories, despite their implicit commission to glorify the current powerholders of the state, included such a wide variety of divergent, even oppositional materials (for example, disparate omen interpretations and accounts of contentious court debates) that their compilers cannot be accused of merely working to advance the imperial project. Indeed, it is surprising how powerfully their works posed the implicit question, Why has no dynasty in recent memory ever attained a lasting Great Peace?

Confucius's legendary connection with the *Chunqiu* may also account for the tendency among many members of the Chinese elite to strive for historical fame in preference to religious salvation. An ardent longing for historical fame implies a keen awareness of the essentially transitory nature of human existence offset by a firm belief in the possibility of history continuously transmitted. Legend has it that Confucius, stung by his failure to persuade contemporary rulers to cultivate human kindness and conscious of his impending death, turned in his old age to compiling the *Chunqiu* so that later generations might benefit from his special understanding. Of himself, he reported, "I am someone who shares a path with the scribe and the shaman, but whose final destination is different." That the desire to secure a place in history in China would thenceforth be linked both to classical learning and singular virtue is attested as early as Han by an anecdote of the period: "When the Confucian master Yang Xiong was writing the *Model Sayings* [a text modeled on the Confucian *Analects* that includes brief moral pronouncements on historical events], a rich man of Shu offered a sum of ten million cash if Yang would only mention him in the book. Yang Xiong [though poor] would not hear of it. 'Now a rich merchant whose actions lack humanity and a sense of social duty is no better than a deer in a sty or an ox in a pen. How could he be mentioned for no reason at all'?"

Some may reasonably object that the real importance of the *Chunqiu* text lies in the ideas read into it, not in those of the canonical text itself. No matter. So long as statesmen looked to the *Chunqiu* Classic and its three main traditions for guidance, the miraculous rule by the uncrowned king Confucius operated to all intents and purposes as accepted fact, vindicating commentators who imagined Confucius writing the *Chunqiu* as a blueprint for future governments. So potent a source of inspiration did the *Chunqiu* remain well into the twentieth century that Japanese imperialists prior to World War II found themselves mining the text for quotations to prove that Confucius's final and most momentous dispensation was destined to take place under their "co-prosperity sphere." And even now the political appropriation of the figure of Confucius, drawing ultimate inspiration from the *Chunqiu* commentaries, continues among those determined to tout the superiority of a distinctive Chinese way.

Chapter Seven

CLAIMING THE CANON

The search for "true patriotism" and . . . true Confucianism, the true teaching
. . . all were symptomatic of a loss of a sense of givenness in the realm of
values following the collapse of the imperial Confucian civilization.
—Jon L. Saari

Modern China is the product of . . . modernist discourses originating in the West
and native institutions, . . . historical social conditions, . . . and native reaction-
formation. . . . Therefore, any diagnosis of power in contemporary China is a
critique neither simply of the West nor of China's tradition, but of their offspring:
China's modernity.
—Mayfair Mei-hui Yang

IN 1850, THE CASUAL OBSERVER MIGHT
well have concluded—wrongly—that certain values and institutions long associated with the figure of Confucius would continue to be widely honored. After
all, states employing the rhetoric of Confucian morality to organize and catalyze
their populations were to be found all over East Asia: the Manchu Qing dynasty
in China (1644–1911), the Tokugawa government in Japan (1600–1867), the
Chosŏn dynasty in Korea (1392–1910), and the Nguyen in Vietnam (1802–1884).
Heterogeneous as their official theories and practices were, never before had so
many classicizing bureaucracies in so many neighboring states launched such
intensive efforts to expand their school and examination systems while dissemi-
nating texts on classical learning and ethical teachings to the literate population.

By the early twentieth century, however, the marginalization of classical learning had begun all over East Asia. To account for the dilution of earlier traditions in China, one scholar, Lionel Jensen, has gone back to the Jesuit construction of the master Confucius (Kong fuzi) in the late Ming and early Qing (late sixteenth through seventeenth centuries), wherein Confucius appeared as a sort of patristic father or pagan precursor to Jesus Christ and classical learning as the moral complement to Christian religiosity. Jensen seems to presume accommodations between the Qing court under Kangxi (1699–1722) and the Jesuits, each promoting its separate agenda through selective interpretive frameworks of the Chinese past. Jesuit accounts of Chinese customs and teachings affected eighteenth-century European intellectual formulations in a number of fields, including biblical chronology, linguistics, and world geography. But the degree to which Jesuit activities influenced Qing thought is debatable, particularly when the Jesuit presence in China declined precipitously after 1706. More importantly for modernity in China, from the sixteenth century groups of scholars, for example, the early proponents of *kaozheng*, or evidential research, and the later adherents of Modern Script Learning, had been busily devising alternate forms of political discourse that reflected their criticisms of the state-sponsored understanding of the classical traditions.

With the Opium Wars of 1839–42, when China was forcibly opened to Western imperialism and Protestant proselytization, the stakes of the game changed: the once leisurely explorations of intellectual problems at the court of the early Manchu emperors yielded thereafter to more pressing matters of political and cultural survival. In the early decades after 1840, even Chinese converts to Christianity had at best only a hybrid notion of Western ideas, as is indicated by the case of Hong Xiuquan, leader of the Taiping rebels, whose visions of God and the utopian state bore the stamp of long-standing Chinese traditions. But in the aftermath of the Taiping war (1850–64), which devastated nearly two-thirds of the Qing empire, conservative statesmen within China, in cooperation with the Manchu ruling house, rededicated themselves to the task of restoring and reinvigorating the old orders. In the process, they embarked on a variety of self-strengthening movements justified by the slogan, "Chinese learning for substance; Western learning for application." At that point, influential thinkers in China undertook to define the nature of the Chinese essence, on the presumption that Chinese identity, Manchu sovereignty, modernization efforts, and defensive formations would all benefit from a clearer definition of China's distinctive contributions to world civilization—contributions that many loosely equated with the official and unofficial traditions said to derive from the Sage-Master Confucius. Confucius and the Ru were henceforth to serve as "banners for contemporary political mobilization."

Conceivably, such links might well have been forged had China not met ignominious defeat in the Sino-Japanese war of 1895. The shock convinced many Chinese patriots that decades of self-strengthening efforts, absent central planning and coordination, had accomplished nothing, and as a result the turn of the twentieth century saw a search for scapegoats and more radical solutions by which to keep the state from further humiliations. Anger spilled over in response to the corruption of the late Qing imperial court under the Empress Dowager Zixi, and some, adapting the language of nationalism and social Darwinism from the West, began to question whether the Manchus as a conquest dynasty were not themselves the root of the problem.

Among those who remained loyal to the ruling house was Kang Youwei (1858–1927). Ironically, it was Kang, that most ardent of reformers inspired by the model of Confucius, who led many intellectuals to openly question the authority of the state-sponsored classical learning by the publication of two controversial works. In the first (1891), Kang alleged that the Archaic Script versions of the Classics (including the *Rites of Zhou*, the *Zuo Traditions*, and half of the received text of the *Documents*) had been forged in Western Han by an unscrupulous classical master, Liu Xin (d. AD 23), to advance the political ambitions of the usurper Wang Mang. In the second (1897), Kang depicted Confucius as a bold religious prophet who, following Heaven's revelations, had planned, but failed as the result of political machinations, to effect the massive political reforms required to keep China from falling victim to its own intellectual sterility and cultural backwardness. These books, in presenting the Sage as messiah in a forward-looking, unilinear, evolutionary history, repudiated the direction that classical learning had taken for nearly two thousand years. Having alienated the conservatives, Kang also encouraged skepticism toward tradition among the reformers, for neither the superiority of ZhuXia civilization nor the manifest legitimacy of the old state institutions could be taken for granted if both were predicated on cynical forgeries. In essence, Kang asked Chinese to choose between their traditionally received historical identity and a personal allegiance to Confucius as devised by Kang. Kang himself had shown the way by his portrayal of Confucius and his rejection of most "Confucian" history. Within the space of a few years, Kang, like some elemental force, a "volcano or hurricane," had cut a ruinous swath through vast areas of tradition that had before this gone largely unchallenged.

Following the collapse in September 1898 of the Hundred Days movement, which had sought to quicken the pace of institutional reform under the Qing, Kang Youwei, in exile and with a price on his head, set out to articulate an audacious vision of a future Great Commonwealth (*datong* 大同), outlined in a manuscript (1902) whose contents were quietly shared with select members of his circle. Asserting that classical references to the Great Way and the Great Peace concealed a "hidden message" (*weiyan* 微言) predicting the establishment of an ideal state, Kang envisioned a future in which

> The world and the nation will be things which humans . . . will call their own, for they will not be things owned privately by a single individual or family. . . . All men will jointly share the means of production and the labor now required for the maintenance of their families, seeing to it that the old are taken care of, the young raised, the poor dealt with charitably, and the sick healed. . . . Although women are weaker, they will make their own completely autonomous decisions and their oppression will not be permitted. . . . Boundaries will no longer exist. Humans will form a community in peace; thus will they be able to attain a "Perfect Equality" through their common efforts.

Kang's *Great Commonwealth Writings* (*Datong shu* 大同書) foresaw a universal state under a federal elective body that would eliminate suffering and inequality gradually through the progressive inculcation in all humans of the three cardinal Confucian virtues of *ren* (full humanity), *gong* (fairness and public spirit), and *shu* 恕 (kindred feeling for others). Ostensibly rooted in the classical virtues, the radically egalitarian Great Commonwealth advocated the complete destruction of the basic traditional institutions of family and state.

As Kang did not attempt in his revolutionary blueprints, published or unpublished, to "reanimate the old" (*wen'gu* 溫古) by a seamless extrapolation from extant classical traditions, relying instead on new terminology and new arguments, he and his disciples epitomized for many a "new sort of Confucian interpretation, an effort to keep Confucius important." In effect, their activities alerted Chinese intellectuals to the grim possibility that Confucius himself might be doomed to oblivion unless his adherents could somehow adapt the teachings ascribed to him to prevailing Western theories. Literate Chinese suddenly confronted tensions that had long existed, almost unnoticed, beneath the surface of classical teachings. Even those steeped in the Classics could see that state-sponsored training had often favored certain conventions to the exclusion of others. Some of Kang's detractors, meanwhile, faulted him for retaining the Confucian axiom that ethical perfection should be the single goal of all humanity, since they saw human development as the amoral product of larger, autonomous forces in the biological, economic, and geopolitical arenas. No wonder Kang in his lifetime was considered the "most admired and the most hated member of the Chinese race."

Kang's insights, widely disseminated and wildly provocative, never dissuaded men less loyal than he from blaming the Qing for its failure to modernize. Opponents of the Manchus said that the Qing was ill-equipped, psychologically and materially, to respond to new realities in defense of China's interests. Attempting to defuse criticism, the Manchu government in 1905 decided to jettison the classical examination system altogether,* even though (a) the system was already in the process of being converted to support a modern civil service system; and (b) a shared commitment to the canonical texts had served to bind local elites tightly to the central court. In that the examination system in Qing China, even more than in earlier eras, was "almost the only point at which the central government cut deeply if briefly into lives normally little affected by events outside their locality," its abolition sounded the death knell for the moribund Qing. In abandoning the scriptures, the Manchus at one stroke forfeited the crucial support that most educated Chinese would have lent a dynasty intent upon revitalizing its classically based system. For once the state ceased to sponsor an examination system widely perceived as meritocratic and so, by definition, "in the public interest" (gong 公), the imperial system became correspondingly less identified in the minds of educated Chinese with the continuance of their way of life.

At the same time, the Manchus' virtual admission in 1905 that the key institutions of imperial China could not be adapted to modern needs (an admission that seems highly questionable in hindsight) accelerated the process already under way by which the name of "civilization" was transferred from China's indigenous social, intellectual, and political structures to almost any alternate model imported from Europe, America, or Japan. After 1905, when literate people no longer found the basic Confucian teachings "naturally" reinforced by aspirations connected with the political structure, classical learning would continue under markedly different auspices—for some, as a part of elementary education detailing a way of life increasingly more notional than real. Declaring Confucius's birthday a national holiday (1904) and establishing a School for the Preservation of Antiquity in the birthplace of Confucius (1906) were hollow gestures. With divisions over the meaning and import of Confucianism proliferating daily, dedicated classicists in the last years of the Qing and the early years

---

*In December of the same year, however, the Manchu court, while continuing to condemn Kang Youwei, announced that Kang's idea of Kongjiao ("Confucius-religion") would provide the basis for a revived Chinese culture; thus the newly organized Ministry of Education mandated schools to maintain the cult of Confucius under the guise of "national religion" 國教. In 1893, the Manchus had already agreed to send an official to the Chinese Legation in Washington, D.C., to represent Confucian tradition to the World's Parliament of Religions.

of the Republic could at best hope to persuade others that the current crisis called for something less than total rejection of China's supposed Confucian past.*

Many critics of Kang reckoned that China's plight was the direct result of the wicked barbarian regime of the Manchus, who had maliciously foisted a false understanding of politics and ethics upon the Chinese to weaken them. Thus, they argued, a return to the "national essence," including select classical teachings, still constituted the best bulwark in the Chinese struggle against repressive government, civil war, and imperialist aggression. Because the Classics were Chinese, they must be a repository of something of value, a rational humanist morality, perhaps, or a skeptical historical tradition, or even a universal value system based on duty, if not ritual. Many national essence proponents therefore dwelt upon Confucius's major contributions as educational leader and social thinker, making the Sage simply one among many pre-Qin advocates of *gong* 公 (public-spiritedness), the old virtue redefined as the key to modernity. In response to the swelling ranks of the "antiquity doubters" who insisted that few passages in the Classics had any factual basis, some like Zhang Binglin (1869–1935) portrayed the Classics as the chief authentic records of China's ancient history, even if the argument for the venerability of the Classics downgraded Confucius's status from Supreme Sage to premier historian of China. Always, the leaders of the national essence movement looked for "congenial stock [within Chinese tradition] with which to organically link the thought-systems of modern Europe and America, so as to build up . . . [Chinese] science and philosophy on a new foundation permitted by the internal assimilation of old and new." In truth, the badly shaken defenders of classicism were engaged in hastily conceived rearguard strategies of amalgamation with Western ideas, combing the Chinese Classics for passages that could be made to support the latest reforms, weighing Chinese institutions to ascertain which elements were compatible with the new nation-state, and rallying support by attacking the "worship of . . . other countries without reservation." Their conjunction of

---

*Many scholars assume that the traditional examination system could never have served the purposes of a modern civil service system. It is hard to imagine why, given that the modern British civil service system was long served adequately by qualifying exams for candidates that tested knowledge of the Greek and Latin classics in a formalistic, literary, and moralistic curriculum. Also, the basic educational and examination systems of the Qing functioned quite well, suggesting that the state would have done better in its modernizing efforts to have continued modifying those systems rather than abandoning them. Modifications were already under way by the 1890s, with students in China being tested not only on the Five Classics, but also on the *Best Methods of Military Defense* and *Conservation of Waterways*.

Figure 19. Classical scholars being turned into modern experts in the sciences as they pass through a gateway labelled "intensive courses." From Sally Borthwick, *Education and Social Change in China* (Stanford: Hoover Institute, 1983), 142.

sociocultural angst and ardent nationalism, ending in a curious compound of political radicalism and cultural conservatism, had its price, however. Even those who continued to read the Five Classics faithfully no longer necessarily exalted them as timeless sacred canons (fig. 19).

More shocking, even the fallback positions were difficult to maintain. Zhang Binglin, for instance, soon found himself joining Liu Shipei (1884–1919) in a reconception of the entire Chinese past, proposing that the most impressive features of archaic civilization in China be traced to an influx of Western groups from Central Asia, either ancient Chaldaeans or peoples from the Pamirs. By these scholars' rationale, if the ancient cultures of China and the West had once shared the same origin, the modern Chinese, as opposed to the outlander Manchus, would more likely attain the modernization that had hitherto eluded their state. In such desperate theories positing a biological entry into the narrative of modernity we can discern the pain of this generation of classically trained thinkers, living in a new Republic but intellectually and emotionally rooted in the imperial past. As one of them put it,

The larger problem is: How can we Chinese feel at ease in this new world which at first sight appears to be so much at variance with what we have long regarded as our own civilization? For it is perfectly natural and justifiable that a nation with a glorious past and with a distinctive civilization of its own making should never feel quite at home in a new civilization, if that new civilization is looked upon as . . . alien . . . and forced upon it by external necessities of national existence. And it would surely be a great loss . . . if the acceptance of this new civilization should take the form of abrupt displacement instead of organic assimilation.

In depicting Confucian learning as a component of national essence reducible to the "three ties" binding minister to ruler, son to father, wife to husband, the classically trained thinkers had exposed such traditions to still greater abuse, as "the conventionalism which paralyzed Chinese thought," the corrupt and corrupting ethical prop of peculiarly antiquated and inflexible systems in China, Korea, and Vietnam. But given the speed, scope, and intensity of change in the early part of the twentieth century, Chinese intellectuals of all political persuasions would assume the need to fix a definitive narrative about Confucian learning within the larger context of Chinese history.

That need generated four movements in the twentieth century: the May Fourth movement (1919–26); the New Life movement under Chiang Kai-shek (1934–37); the "antifeudal" movement led by Mao Zedong, culminating in the "criticize Lin Biao, criticize Confucius" campaigns of the early 1970s; and the New Confucian Revival movement of the eighties and nineties inspired by a group of philosophers in search of a Chinese philosopher-king. Each of the four movements emerged at a time when members of the elite sought to encourage massive changes in society, in the hope of restoring China to its rightful place in world politics. Each movement has sought to redefine tradition in an idiosyncratic manner, reinventing the past (radically essentialized) so that it might more successfully engage the awesome specter of modernity, lamentably confused with both Western civilization and industrialization. Participants in these movements typically expressed a mingled pride and hostility toward their own heritage and a corresponding defiance and admiration toward ideas imported from the West; they championed the unparalleled antiquity of the Chinese past in one breath, while denouncing in the next its sheer weight threatening to crush the fragile seeds of change. Such extraordinary ambivalence reflected, of course, the reformers' inability, in calculating the continued viability of Chinese classicism, to resolve two incongruent images: first, that classical learning in the past had helped to establish the superiority of Chinese civilization well beyond China's borders, and second, that throughout the East Asian cultural sphere, the ideology and institutions associated with Confucius had become a patchwork of beliefs and practices (few of them directly traceable to the Sage) used by the ruling classes to justify oppressive features of the local sociopolitical systems.

These disparate movements shared the presumption that culture, Chinese or imported, is an autonomous entity, alive and powerful, capable of transforming anyone who comes in contact with it. But they came to no firm conclusions whether the survival of their distinctive civilization depended primarily upon the transmission of the past preserved in literary and artistic masterworks or upon the physical race of Han Chinese imprinting its particular genius on the entire organic sweep of historical experience. If culture inheres in the records of high civilization, what must be done to preserve them? And if culture is the natural product of a superior race evolving through time, do the old systems represent anything more than outdated superstructures? Following hard upon just this sort of question, the urge to break away from conventional categories of thought in order to derive more dynamic notions of authority has catalyzed, at fairly regular intervals in modern Chinese history, radical reorientations toward Confucian learning.

THE MAY FOURTH MOVEMENT

Many China-watchers regarded the 1905 abolition of the examination system based on the "Confucian" Classics as the first clear sign of the mighty system's inevitable collapse. The downfall of the Qing dynasty in 1911 dealt another severe institutional blow to classical learning, for in 1912, the very first year of the new Chinese Republic, Cai Yuanpei (1868–1940), the Republic's first Minister of Education, ordered the formal study of the Classics removed from the nation's public school curriculum. Over the next few years, the Republic, plagued by mounting internal dissension and external assault, felt it could offer only haphazard support to the elaborate state cult dedicated to Confucius, whose worship centered at Qufu (Shandong), the hometown of Confucius still dominated by his Kong descendants; local bureaucrats and regional warlords meanwhile began to refuse the Kongs their traditional perquisites. The further loss of institutional backing undermined still more the authority of the old-style rites, teachings, and texts tied to Confucius, their symbolic capital collapsing in proportion to the shortage of funds. In consequence, the new Republic witnessed a dramatic devaluation of classical traditions. Whereas most late Qing intellectuals had confidently defended classical learning as the chief glory of Chinese civilization, adopting the slogan "No Confucianism, No China," more of the Republic's first generation took Confucianism as a code word for "outmoded imperial institutions." Naturally enough, when the radical May Fourth thinkers came to attack most of Chinese tradition, classical learning became their chief target. Steeped in the Western presumption of Oriental Despotism, an icono-clastic nationalism, and "an almost mystical faith in progress," the student leaders of May Fourth in their determination to take charge of China's destiny were primed to invoke the "natural principle" that the old must give way to the new. As the incredible wealth and power of the imperialist nations became apparent, Chinese modernizers charged that Confucianism, with its supposed aversion to change, had stifled the very ability of all East Asian peoples (with the exception of the presumably differently Confucianized Japanese, who were modernizing with relative ease)* to undertake the most natural of human functions: innova-tion and self-renewal. Confident that it was always "better to make mistakes because of distrusting antiquity than to make mistakes because of trusting antiq-uity," they urged their fellow intellectuals to smash what they called the old "Confucian Curiosity Shop" and all its contents, so that China might better entertain those brash newcomers, "Mr. Science and Mr. Democracy."

The majority of radical modernizers, we must remember, felt no special sym-pathy for classical learning, being quite unfamiliar with it. Believing that China could never survive under a Confucian aegis, even if Confucian values and insti-tutions were to be revised, the young reformers mercilessly attacked the vestiges of the past at every opportunity. The dearth of firearms and factories in China, Korea, and Vietnam could be remedied easily enough, but Confucian culture itself, in instilling "peace, repose, the family, and the emotions," stood no chance in the Darwinian struggle against a West that emphasized competition, war, indi-vidual initiative, rule by law, and rational calculation. Thus the main obstacles to successful modernization were the constituent elements of the Confucian system itself: familism, regionalism, age and gender hierarchies, the veneration of precedents, and the promotion of special interests. Thus the father of the new Chinese Republic, Sun Yat-sen (1866–1925), denounced Confucian dedication to the patrilineal family as the single greatest obstacle to a Chinese nationalism based on progressive Western models. Characterizing the Chinese people as a "sheet of loose sand," incapable of binding themselves to the larger collective entity of the nation-state under the rule of law, Sun wrote,

*In explaining Japan's obvious success, Chinese intellectuals tended both to misread the evidence for Japan's Confucian past and to ignore, like many modernization theorists half a century later, the crucial differences between China and Japan in the late nineteenth and early twentieth centuries. China was some five times larger than Japan, so change was bound to come more slowly to it. China's far greater racial, ethnic, and linguistic diversity posed greater obstacles to modernization. And perhaps most important, China's most progressive Confucian ideals, in strictly limiting the rate of taxation on farmland, forestalled any massive state expenditure on the kinds of new infrastructure required to modernize. Meiji Japan, by contrast, put Confucian ideologies to work for it in its first phase of nation building.

The unity of the Chinese people has stopped short at the clan and has not extended to the nation. . . . A Chinese [under the imperial dynasties] ignored the downfall of his country. He did not care who his emperor was. All he had to do was to pay his grain tax. But if anything was said about the possible extinction of his clan, he would be in terror lest the ancestral continuity of blood and food be broken, and he would sacrifice his life to resist that.

In the view of many ardent nationalists, Confucianism was particularly reprehensible, as it had served as willing handmaid to successive foreign regimes foisted upon an unwilling China. It was the Mongol Yuan dynasty, after all, that had first enshrined a conservative wing of Confucian thought, the Cheng-Zhu school of True Way Learning, as state ideology through its examination system. And it was the barbarian Manchu rule that had compromised the integrity of sacred Chinese traditions when it led classical masters to invoke a broadly culturalist worldview, by which even Manchu conquerors could be adjudged good so long as they conformed with the Chinese cultural conventions, including the Mandate of Heaven theory. All such compromises were anathema to the new conceptions of state sovereignty and ethnic pride. As Chen Duxiu and Hu Shi put it in *New Youth* magazine in 1918, "It is Oriental [that is, backward] to compromise and only go halfway . . . for fear of opposition."

Other, equally damaging charges were soon leveled at the evolving construct of Confucianism. Was it not, as dominant ideology, also responsible for China's perceived failure to develop the logical method required for both modern science and modern philosophical inquiry? Hu Shi, pronouncing Confucianism to be "long dead," tried to show how and why Chinese thinkers, once "indisputable leaders in world culture," had taken a wrong turn as early as two thousand years ago (shades of Kang Youwei), when a Confucian orthodoxy preoccupied with the past had stifled more pragmatic and progressive non-Confucian schools of thought, particularly the Mohists and Logicians of pre-Qin fame. For proponents of women's rights and the claims of youth against the aged, the constructed Confucianism provided an even easier target, for it seemed abundantly clear at the time that the late system had embedded in its codes of conduct the inferiority of women and the young. Footbinding and widow chastity, both imposed in the late empires, were but two of the egregious examples of the oppression of women prompting Fu Sinian, a leading classical scholar himself, to declare the Chinese/Confucian family structure the "source of all evil" in the land. But it was the imperial state's promotion of filial piety that most enraged the May Fourth reformers, who found the "blind obedience" and "slave mentality" it engendered to be the chief source of twentieth-century China's inherent domestic and international weakness: "The effect of filial piety has been to turn China into a big factory for the manufacture of obedient subjects, . . . the slaves of Confucius." One powerful poem described arrogant Authority sitting on a hilltop, from which vantage point it directed slaves bound in chains to dig for minerals to enrich its coffers. (Note in passing the reformers' unwitting adoption of the profoundly Confucian notion that the health of the body politic depends upon the morality of those in its service. Few of the May Fourth reformers adopted the customary Anglo-Ameican distrust of the strong state as constraint upon individual independence.)

Though the May Fourth reformers could never agree on the best way to save China, they were united in their opposition to Confucianism as they understood it. The most radical of them delighted to see its obscene influence finally exposed in a new play by Lin Yu-tang entitled *Confucius Meets Duchess Nanzi*. First performed in 1922 in Qufu, Confucius's hometown, the play derided Confucius as a vulgar hypocrite and social climber, an apt symbol for all the abuses perpetrated under autocratic regimes upholding antiquated ethical codes. In hindsight, it is evident that the impassioned May Fourth reformers, alerted to the fearful realities of the modern world by an especially impressive group of intellectual leaders endowed with remarkable polemical skills (Chen Duxiu, Hu Shi, Li Daizhao, and Lu Xun, among them), adopted and then passed on a seriously distorted picture of the workings of the Confucian Curiosity Shop. To lend rhetorical force to their arguments and greater significance to their rebellion, the reformers, sometimes inadvertently, exaggerated the inimical effects of the faltering Confucian system on China's past and on their own beloved Republic. For instance, Chen Duxiu accused Confucianism of enjoining a strict caste system, making its continuation in any form antithetical to the democratic principles of the Republic. Similarly, Lu Xun in his *Madman's Diary* saw "men eating men" as the single thread underlying all history in China, with the high-sounding Confucian ethical phrases mere masks for widespread community-sanctioned violence. In their eagerness to absorb scraps of Western culture, it did not occur to many that noncultural and nonideological causes, for example, the agricultural involution exacerbated by the recent population explosion in China, might have sapped the strength of the imperial system, even if the West had never come to their shores. It was easier to denounce an old system in which they had little psychological investment than to try to comprehend the complex sources of their present monumental crisis.

Admittedly, the embattled young reformers, who saw only turmoil around them, had little time to consider the most prominent features of the late imperial Confucian system in a more sympathetic light as the product of a series of complex compromises worked out on every level under specific historical circumstances, compromises successful enough to have secured the imperium the allegiance of its subjects for millennia. Probably only those of scholastic impulses, operating in a less politically charged atmosphere, would have cared to ask in what sense footbinding, to take one instance, could be termed Confucian, when it was first promoted some sixteen centuries after the time of Confucius and never adopted by Confucians outside China. The reformers could not know that the early followers of Confucius had been censured for urging not too low but too high a status for women in the household. Neither could they, in light of China's recent debacles, calmly discuss the possibility that premodern China had proven itself as fit for modernity as the West, having more social mobility, greater material wealth, and no more consistent a pattern of repression than premodern Europe.

Unfamiliar with world history, given the limited number of Western works translated into vernacular Chinese, the May Fourth reformers, in their determination to fend off imperialist aggression, believed only that the reified progressive West, with its uncompromising individualism defended by the rule of law, had an insuperable advantage over the Eastern Other debilitated by Confucian despotism. Did it really matter that industrialization was an anomaly in the West itself, having developed only in a few countries, namely, France, Germany, England, and America? Ill-equipped as they were to compare the effect of the Bible on Euro-American cultures with the state-sponsored canon's effect on thought, the May Fourth thinkers firmly believed that the canonization of the Classics associated with Confucius in 136 BC had prevented the kind of intellectual pluralism that led inevitably to Western science and logic. In this they ignored a simple truth that seems patently obvious in our own postmodern culture: sacred texts can be made to mean whatever their proponents wish. And neither the Euro-American specialists on China nor the Chinese experts on Euro-America, two groups to whom the May Fourth leaders looked for special guidance, offered appreciably more nuanced assessments of the current international situation. The reformers had been served fairly fantastic decoctions of skepticism, romanticism, liberalism, scientism, pragmatism, socialism, social Darwinism, and anarchism—which they naturally passed onto others. Besides, change of such magnitude would probably have rendered totalistic solutions more attractive than piecemeal adjustments in any age. Their propensity to treat what they thought of as Confucian tradition as a uniform, unchanging entity responsible for the entire range of ills in old China was simply an example of the general human need, in troubled times, to demonize someone or something.

Nonetheless, in their insistence that, if China's political leadership proved inadequate to the task, culture could change politics, the May Fourth leaders set the general pattern for all subsequent movements in this century. The exaggerated tenor of their responses, which careened from grand utopian solutions to utter dystopian expressions of self-abnegation, from "the extreme of servile imitations of the past to the extreme of iconoclasm," would be reproduced in later intellectual responses as well. The reformers exhibited a perverse pride in branding Confucian tradition as singularly evil and oppressive, as if some distinction lay in characterizing their civilization as the very worst in human history if one could no longer confidently claim it as the best. Their manifesto, after all, characterized Confucian institutions of the past as "useless and irrelevant, . . . hypocritical, conservative, negative, bounded, class-divided, conventional, ugly, vicious, warring, restless, idle, pessimistic elements promoting happiness for the few instead of happiness for the whole society." (As Mao noted in his satirical essay "It's terrible; it's wonderful," the embrace of radical solutions in theory hardly prepared Chinese intellectuals to implement them in practice, and their discomfort with this disjunction seemed to increase their self-doubt and harden their line.)

For better or (more probably) for worse, it was also May Fourth and the reactions against it that defined for the century the semantic range of "mainstream [Confucian] tradition" as (1) emphasis on highly particularistic social relationships, especially filial devotion and family loyalty, whose most visible symbol was the religious act of ancestor worship;* (2) acceptance of the strong state as a benign, paternalistic, and interventionist presence; (3) respect for status and hierarchy, on the assumption that asymmetrical relations inducing a sense of reciprocal obligation are mutually beneficial and satisfying; (4) preoccupation with maintaining social harmony and cohesiveness; (5) stress on the importance of education and self-cultivation; (6) emphasis on thrift, industry, and the willingness to sacrifice personal advantage for the greater good; and (7) more humanistic or secular orientations. No interpretive line associated with any of the Five Classics, it must be stressed, ever invented any of these values in an East Asian country. At most, Confucian masters gave some of these values a more richly constructed philosophical framework, ensuring them a wider and deeper diffusion throughout society. Sadly, few analysts who have succeeded the May Fourth reformers have bothered to reexamine these connotations, perhaps because in most cases inherited slogans have served their modern political purposes equally well or better.

THE NEW LIFE MOVEMENT UNDER CHIANG KAI-SHEK

The leaders of the May Fourth movement had four ambitious goals: national independence, modernization, emancipation of the individual, and a just society,

---

*Such relationships have been assumed to be inherently opposed to Western individualism and universalism, as exemplified in the notion of equality before the law.

none of which was achieved during the brief New Culture movement (1919–24) under their sponsorship. That the aborted May Fourth movement would color the course of the New Life movement organized under Chiang Kai-shek was only to be expected, considering the number of May Fourth sympathizers who from 1924 made their way into the radical or conservative wings of the Guomindang party (GMD or Nationalists, better known as the Kuomingtang [KMT]). As educated urban elites, the May Fourth reformers and the New Lifers agreed on the basic principle that a unified national identity rooted in a strong nation-state was the best protection against internal and external threats. In support of that identity, they intended to express their "great optimism about the imminent change for the better in world affairs." May Fourth reformers and New Lifers also shared an utter contempt for aspects of tradition they deplored as superstitious, passive, and family-centered, seeing these as serious obstacles to an invincible national identity. Leaders of both groups looked to "culture construction" as the "propellant force" to root out such debilitating tendencies wherever they found them. Chiang Kai-shek himself stated that only "an unsentimental attack on the old culture" might restore China to a position of international leadership. Chiang and his circle of advisers, however, in a major departure from May Fourth beliefs, reserved the adjective "old" for the dying days of the Manchu empire, when the empire had supposedly been irreparably weakened by a turn to mysticism and a consequent disdain for secular concerns. New Life leaders in fact applauded the "stern moral character and insight into the working of the Confucian social process" they found exemplified by Chinese civil servants, even in the Manchus' heyday, and so they called new whatever required daily self-renewal in loyal service to the Chinese state.

The twisted terminology should alert us to the fact that any similarities in the May Fourth and New Life leaders' analyses of China's problems were overshadowed by blatant disparities in their goals. The New Lifers exalted dictatorship and the total abnegation of the individual as the most efficient ways to restore the nation to political, social, and economic strength: they intended to "nationalize, militarize, productivize." For the New Lifers, a closer coordination of civil and military affairs would ideally bring on the very abject loyalty and filial piety that the May Fourth reformers had located and decried in state-sponsored learning. Had his means equaled his ambition, Chiang Kai-shek would then have installed himself as emperor. Far from denouncing the autocratic values and institutions of the imperium, the New Lifers longed to reinstitute most of them. And, in contrast to the May Fourth movement, which had made its name by protesting imperialist intervention in China's affairs, the New Life movement under Chiang Kai-shek willingly collaborated with any imperialists allied with Chiang's regime.

Much of the difference stemmed from Chiang's analysis of China's current plight, which was premised on the bizarre notion that the Chinese people in some sense deserved the unequal treaties imposed upon them by the imperialist powers of the West and Japan. Beginning where the national essence movement left off, Chiang made the case that in passively accepting the Manchu culturalist claims to hegemony, the Chinese had let their moral fiber so degenerate that they lacked the requisite virtue and knowledge to prevent civil war, opium addiction, and foreign incursions, military, intellectual, or spiritual. Adding insult to injury, the May Fourth reformers had then failed to give due respect to Chinese tradition, inducing a further crisis of self-confidence in the Chinese masses. In consequence, the masses had become ever more unfit to mobilize to defeat China's true enemies, the Communists and, quite secondarily, the Japanese. Responding to the May Fourth reformers, who in their "blind worship" of all things foreign had overestimated the need to adapt China's ways to foreign ideas, the Chinese people, according to Chiang, held the view that basic material security was prerequisite to training in virtue and also that economic deprivation gave them the right to rebel. They had gotten it backwards, Chiang insisted, with disastrous consequences for a national wealth and power. For only when the Chinese became truly self-disciplined on a rigorous classical model would they acquire sufficient moral stamina to obtain adequate food and clothing for themselves via the absolute sociopolitical stability that was the primary requirement for a healthy economy.

But by Chiang's account, there was still hope. "The glories and the scope of . . . ancient Chinese learning," he wrote, "cannot be equaled in the history of any of the strong Western nations of today." And China's indigenous philosophy developed by Confucius was "superior to any other philosophy in the world." Accordingly, the New Life movement promised to "reinvigorate Chinese society by adapting existing institutions or businesses to new needs." The best way to promote thorough modernization in China was to present the masses with a carefully syncretized ideology embodying the best elements of Western and Chinese cultures, even when Western elements were preponderant. Employing this revised form of Confucian doctrine, Chiang would forge a modern nation-state of "one will and one mind," going beyond mere national independence to full national integration.*

---

*Chiang Kai-shek and his inner circle aspired to have China emulate many aspects of the fascist regimes in Italy and Germany, excepting, of course, their assiduous courting of national trade unions and their emphasis on Aryan racial superiority. Nonetheless, Chiang's military dictatorship always lacked the means of control available to Mussolini and Hitler. Chiang's requirement for his first vanguard, the Blue Shirts, was typically minimalist. The

In articulating such dreams, the New Lifers understood, as many May Fourth reformers had not, that to vast numbers of ordinary people modernization meant unprecedented industrialization and forced entry into international markets, with the strong possibility of civil unrest, economic decline, and political fragmentation. To calm those widespread fears Chiang Kai-shek announced that a revival of traditional Confucian virtues could ameliorate the worst of the modern problems. Political pragmatism, at base, therefore inspired the New Life movement to harness certain strategic "traditional values" to the goal of rapid modernization, yet Chiang seemed to believe that only such values, extracted from their cultural context and totally refashioned, could provide the unity of purpose among the common people required to usher in a wholly new political, economic, and cultural system. Once they had been made aware of the glories of their past civilization, he reasoned, the Chinese people surely would be moved to recreate that glory through greater "material creativity." And if the instability of the early Republican era had made many Chinese subjects long for the stability they associated with the old imperial system, Chiang would trade on that nostalgia, hailing the policies of the Tongzhi Restoration (1860–70) as China's guide. After all, those of China's citizens living in the old treaty ports, including the very workers who suffered most under Chiang's policies, were not entirely immune to the blandishments of Chiang's confident assertions about the fundamental superiority of Chinese culture over that of other nation-states. However much they detested the implementation of some of his political programs, they could yet applaud his repudiation of the May Fourth reformers' "smearing and slandering" the history of Chinese culture."

As historians have observed, in deciding "to make a revolution the heir of an ancient tradition," Chiang had learned a great deal from the powerful resistance that sank the May Fourth movement. Accepting the chief May Fourth stereotypes of Confucianism (that it was anti-individualistic, hierarchical, and

Blue Shirts were to dedicate themselves to three goals only: dictatorship, exaltation of the nation, and the concurrent total submission of the individual to the will of the supreme leader. But over time, Chiang came to rely increasingly upon the theoretically inclined CC Clique, led by Chen Lifu, which espoused "Cultural Construction on a Chinese Basis." The Clique called for a "selective syncretism" of the best elements of Chinese and Western cultures in order to foster "the nation's self-confidence" and to offset the baleful effects of accommodation with the "spiritually bankrupt" West. For more information, see Lloyd Eastman, *The Abortive Revolution: China under Nationalist Rule, 1927–37* (Cambridge: Harvard University Press, 1974), 40, and id., "The Kuomingtang in the 1930s," in *The Limits of Change: Essays on Conservative Alternatives in Republican China*, ed. Charlotte Furth (Cambridge: Harvard University Press, 1976), 191–210.

undemocratic) Chiang and his New Lifers staked their claims to legitimacy on a celebration of this very constellation of qualities, seeing them as more adaptable for their purposes than anything available in a comparable Western model. Certain that the May Fourth leaders had failed at least in part because they had called for too many reforms on too many fronts, Chiang called upon his New Life adherents to devise a coherent agenda ("concrete content," he called it) for restoring China to itself:

> Does the New Culture movement mean the advocacy of vernacular literature? the piecemeal introduction of Western literature? the overthrow of the old ethics and the rejection of the national history? the demand for individual emancipation and the turn away from nation and society? the destruction of all discipline? . . . the blind worship of foreign countries and indiscriminate introduction and acceptance of foreign civilization? If it does, the new culture we seek is too simple, too cheap, and too dangerous!

Given a coherent rationale eschewing partial reforms, Chiang supposed that the Nationalist cadres would be able to induce the masses to subjugate their wills entirely to government policy. By a judicious mix of the May Fourth techniques for mass mobilization and the New Life message, the Nationalists would move the patriotic citizenry from alienation to activism by normative appeals with nativist overtones, employing one of the few resources the GMD had at their disposal, given the precipitous decline in state revenues and the simultaneous "hyper-growth in the size and scope of government organization."

So in mid-February 1934, Chiang Kai-shek delivered a series of five speeches explaining the methods and goals of his New Life movement: "What is this New Life movement that I now propose? Stated simply, it is to thoroughly militarize the lives of the citizens of the entire nation so that they can cultivate courage and swiftness, the endurance of suffering and a tolerance for hard work, and especially the habit and capacity for unified action, so that they will be ready to sacrifice for the nation at any time."

The very survival of the nation depended upon a complete reformation in social attitudes and behavior, starting with the most basic activities of daily life, eating and dressing. With the help of ninety-six short rules disseminated to the masses in their simplest form, Chiang proposed to instill in China's citizens at all levels of society the proper kind of military discipline. Among these rules were the following:

Don't smoke or eat when walking!
Look straight ahead!
Keep your buttons buttoned!
Sit up straight!
Be prompt!

There was to be no spitting or urinating in public and no displays of bad manners. By bringing public behavior into perfect conformity with his expectations for a modern civilized nation, Chiang Kai-shek proposed to instill a more "militarized, productive, and aesthetic" way of life. Better hygiene and more orderly social interaction were the substantive keys that would unlock a "national renaissance."

Within days of Chiang's initial outline of the New Life movement, the GMD party organs were working round the clock to establish the first New Life Promotion Association. By February 21, 1934, the association was coordinating the national efforts of allied groups (the army, the police, and the Boy Scouts) to orchestrate New Life activities, to disseminate New Life literature, and to organize mass New Life rallies. By March 11, the first official New Life demonstration, held in the Public Athletic Grounds at Nanchang, Jiangxi, attracted an estimated one hundred thousand people, despite drizzling rain. By month's end, the same Jiangxi New Life Promotion Association, in conjunction with Chiang's Army for the Suppression of Communist Bandits, issued a circular telegram addressed to all of China's citizens hailing the new movement as "the only path for national salvation." Then in August, the GMD sponsored a gigantic birthday celebration for Confucius in Confucius's hometown of Qufu. Coming as it did a mere six months after the inauguration of the New Life movement, the celebration, absolutely unrivaled in its splendor in the cash-strapped Republican China, underscored the notion that Chiang's legitimacy, like that of the emperors of old, rested upon lavish sponsorship of traditional values. Mass meetings "spontaneously" organized in Peiping, Canton, Nanking, and other major Chinese cities soon made New Life a nationwide campaign. By the end of 1935, the GMD boasted that 1,132 local district chapters of the New Life Promotion Association had been formed.

The official paper counts of late 1935 notwithstanding, the New Life movement in two years had gained little real support from Chinese anywhere outside of the overseas Chinese communities. Even Chiang had to admit that, "with few exceptions, most places have not really accomplished the two basic objectives of cleanliness and orderliness." Coming when it did, in the aftermath of the carnage of World War I, Chiang might have anticipated that his program would garner more support from literate elites sensitive to Western opinion, for it was at this very juncture that prominent Western thinkers led by Bertrand

Russell, Spengler, and Bergson looked to "Eastern spirituality" to temper the corrosive effects of technocratic innovations coming from the West. Their passionate advocacy of what they called the Eastern way of life might well have breathed life into the New Life movement had Chiang and his advisers, who were so quick to ridicule the May Fourth reformers' intellectual incoherence, offered a persuasive narrative of their own. How was one to explain a revolution that claimed inspiration from the Zhou dynasty two millennia earlier? What moral insight could the upper and middle classes hope to gain from rules mandating them to sit up straight? And without reference to class struggle or imperialist exploitation (strictly forbidden as Communist-inspired by Chiang's GMD), how was one to explain the manner in which the Chinese people, proud inheritors of such a glorious past, had slipped into a moral, mental, and material morass from which they could extricate themselves only by dint of hard work?

To anyone who undertook in good faith to explore the proposed GMD syncretism, it was readily apparent that Confucius was unlikely to further Chiang's project. Though Chiang and his propagandists had seen in Confucian teachings the most effective—or at least the cheapest—means to promote the social order and personal discipline required for national unity, the gap between New Life dictums and Confucian views, as expressed in the *Analects* or the writings of Mencius and Xunzi, was laughably wide. Chiang Kai-shek and his advisers might pepper New Life statements with Confucian maxims, but neither their methods (for example, "healthy violence" to quash opposition and the ruthless suppression of trade union activities, which exacerbated economic injustice) nor their goals (totalitarian rule and the destruction of all private morality) could be made congruent with even the most conservative strains within the imperial traditions. In stark contrast to Chiang's ninety-six rules, for example, was Confucius's proud refusal to reduce social duty to neat dicta and his condemnation of blind obedience to the state. And while Confucian teachings held that each moral act became its own reward, in that social beings take pleasure in building true sociality, New Life teachings had no implications apart from the enhancement of GMD power. If the movement's espousal of four Confucian virtues—*li* 禮 (courtesy), *yi* 義 (dutifulness), *lian* 廉 (incorruptibility), and *chi* 恥 (shame)—did not wrest victory from the jaws of Chinese defeat, Chiang would happily jettison them in favor of the abstract quality he called native morality, which in his view threaded through all schools of Chinese philosophy. The New Life movement remained little more than "a distorted echo of Confucianism," its nominally Confucian precepts actually a perversion of traditional morality that aimed to insert itself far more intrusively into people's lives than any previous state-sponsored ideology.

If members of the Chinese elite who honored the Classics had reason to doubt and dislike the New Life movement, the masses had even better reasons to disdain it. For in seeking to engender a more constructive type of soldier-citizen, the movement had vehemently attacked ordinary Chinese as uncivilized, even bestial. According to Chiang and his henchman Wang Jingwei, the masses of Chinese people ate like "cows, horses, pigs and sheep." "Unbearably filthy," they were given to gambling and other morally retrograde forms of self-indulgence. Overly individualistic and self-seeking, stubbornly resistant to outside interference in their lives, the Chinese masses were said to be unqualified to engage in serious nation building. The banal New Life rhetoric, which drew upon Christian Moral Rearmament campaigns far more than earlier Confucian revivals, insisted that the state would be morally equipped to resist its enemies and win respect only when new citizens had been forged, sound in body and disciplined in mind, politically conscious and socially committed, forward-looking yet grounded in the past.

What the masses did not find offensive in GMD rhetoric, they may well have found irrelevant. What use was it to preach good hygiene and frugality in the countryside, where dire poverty and cramped living quarters were the norm? And what enthusiasm could be mustered by forced participation at New Life rallies, whose harsh regimentation suppressed genuine mass expression? Within months of the launching of the movement, the fundamental illogic in New Life theory had become obvious to peasant, worker, and academic alike:

> There was an obvious contradiction in . . . identifying Chinese morality with the principles of [traditional] social life and yet regarding China as having failed on precisely this count. . . . [Moreover,] the New Life movement was a mass political movement that rejected popular political initiative and organized the people's conduct down to its minutest aspects; it aimed to politicize the people, but denied them any political roles what-soever; it . . . reduced individuals to mechanical units; and finally, it was a social revolution that aimed to suppress emerging social forces.

Chiang's proposed remedies for China's ills smacked of fascism in cynical window dressing. There might be a restoration of rites at Confucian temples (November 1928), along with daily study of the "Confucian" Classics (especially the Four Books) in the army and in schools; a celebration of Confucius's birthday as a national holiday (1931); and the official recanonization of Confucius and Confucian heroes (1934). But how could such measures contribute to a resolution of the grave structural problems besetting a country at war with itself and others?

To Chiang's inner circle, such a question would have been considered treasonous, as would any suggestion that Chiang piously intoned a Confucian morality while using decidedly Legalist methods to eliminate his political opponents.

Chiang's capitalist backers welcomed reductionist formulas equating national regeneration with thrift and workplace discipline, if that would insure a steady supply of cheap workers. Thus Chiang continued in the same vein in his public pronouncements long after 1935, when the failure of the New Life rhetoric was already evident. Indeed, his pronouncements were required reading in all Chinese schools from 1943 to 1949. Unfortunately, the New Lifers' constant endorsement of its stereotypes of Confucian values only strengthened the literate public's perception that the defining characteristic of Confucian classicism was hidebound repression.

THE GREAT PROLETARIAN CULTURAL REVOLUTION (1966–1976), WITH ITS ANTI-CONFUCIUS CAMPAIGN UNDER MAO (1973–1975)

Defying Chiang's clumsy yet brutal attempts at ideological control, a number of prominent Chinese intellectuals formulated counteranalyses of China's past with the help of Marxist categories. Long before the military victory of the Chinese Communist Party in 1949, for instance, Guo Moruo's influential *Studies on Ancient Chinese Society* (1931) had challenged the conservative faith in a developmental model predicated on China's unique national essence. The book concluded that the Western Zhou period, sacrosanct to devout Confucians as the golden age of Chinese ritual culture, had been in fact a despotic slave society much like other slave societies organized elsewhere in the ancient world. The most conspicuous change in intellectual life after the founding of the People's Republic in 1949, then, was the new ubiquity of Marxist analytical terms in the political writings and activities of the Party. Most intellectuals in the fifties were too busy learning the use of these tools of their profession to propose reassessments of either Chinese history or Confucius, even if they had any interest in doing so. Before the role of Confucius, the Confucian masters, or classicism could be decided, more basic theoretical issues needed to be settled, especially the proper application of Marxist periodization to the whole of Chinese history. Hence the relative freedom with which Chinese intellectuals in the first decade of Communist rule explored the significance of Confucius's class background, ethical contributions, and pedagogical methods.

For his part, the "great helmsman" Mao Zedong seemed willing to grant Confucius, if not Confucian institutions, the benefit of the doubt. Probably Confucius had extended the old Zhou ethical principles to create a new concept of humanity progressive for its time, and the generally egalitarian thrust of Confucius's commitment to teach those outside his own class went unquestioned.

Initially optimistic that economic modernization would sweep away outmoded values, Mao Zedong first sought consensus on the legacy of pre-Liberation China, lest angry theoretical debates slow the hard work of socialist reconstruction. To that end, Mao balanced speeches warning against "neglect of the Ancients' legacies" (even when "feudal or bourgeois") with denunciations equating "the uncritical . . . copying from the Ancients" with "the most sterile and harmful form of dogmatism." No clear official position emerged from the early post-Liberation discussions about Confucian learning. During the Hundred Flowers movement (1957), certainly, the Sage was in disrepute, and some of his defenders landed in considerable trouble, but by the early 1960s, party opinion seemed to reverse itself. Perhaps a dramatic increase in the focused study of China's indigenous past, orchestrated from the top, would serve to counter the widespread perception of political drift following China's break with the Soviet Union in 1959 and the Great Leap famines of 1958–60.

The historian Wu Han was one of those voicing the concern that a strong nationalism would never develop without a more sympathetic portrayal of China's imperial past: "I have asked children for their comments [on China's history] and they all say, 'With the imperial dynasties all so corrupt, it is difficult for us to love our country, though we try to!'" And so by 1961–1962, when Mao's radicalism was challenged by party pragmatists, numerous academic conferences set out to explore the real significance of Confucius's teachings. One of these was convened by Liu Shaoqi, then chairman of the People's Republic, whose influential manual *How to Be a Good Communist* (1962) borrowed the Confucian language of self-cultivation in an attempt, not atypical for the period, to integrate Confucian and Communist ethics. Eager to adopt the perceived Party line, the national press and academic circles with very few exceptions chorused praise for Confucius. Of the virtual torrent of articles about the Sage produced in these years, most praised him for formulating the progressive concept of *ren* (full humankindness) as an instrument of emancipation. Tourists flooded into Confucius' hometown in Qufu (on average, 30,000 people daily).

But then, without warning, in September 1962, Mao issued his famous call, "Never forget class struggle," thereby launching the Socialist Education movement (1962–65) in the countryside. By late 1963, those academics who had presumed the basic relevance of Confucian morality in modern times were feeling a distinct chill. A few were openly criticized for having suggested that "Confucius was a savior for all times." After all, "Confucius worship" could undermine "things such as Marxism-Leninism, the theory of class struggle and the method of class analysis." Still, some redeeming features were granted the Sage. Even in the worst attacks on him, muckraking essays devoted to the stark class divisions prevailing in Confucius's hometown, the Sage continued to be characterized as an innovative and demanding teacher who encouraged the sort of diligent study that could lead to real achievements.

Four years later, in 1966, Mao launched the Great Proletarian Cultural Revolution (1966–76), in which the great laboring masses, supported by students, were primed to rise in opposition to the revisionist approach of Liu Shaoqi and the members of his faction, chief among them Deng Xiaoping (1904–97). Because Confucianism was associated in the popular mind with the Middle Path and with gradualism, Liu Shaoqi and his supporters were recast as secret Confucianists, and the academic conferences on Confucius held under their auspices as "black sessions" serving the counterrevolutionary bourgeois Right. To translate: Liu and his supporters, under cover of China's Confucian heritage, had tried to revive capitalism and class hierarchy in order to destroy socialism. By 1967, Red Guards posed the very loaded question, "What Poisons were spread by the Monsters and Demons at the 1962 Shandong Forum on Confucius?" Their answer came in the form of a chilling series of equations: "Lauding and Glorifying Confucius's Thought" were equivalent to "Maliciously Attacking Mao Zedong Thought" and "Propagating Confucius's Notions of Benevolent Government" to "Maliciously Attacking Proletarian Dictatorship" (fig. 20).

If the first year of the Cultural Revolution laid the groundwork for the full-blown anti-Confucius campaign of 1973–75, many academics seemed oddly blind to the veering political winds, even after Liu Shaoqi's expulsion from the party in 1968 and his death in prison the following year. Their period of complacency would prove short. The Great Proletarian Cultural Revolution sweeping across China soon became a "bloody vendetta" waged against "any supposed remnants of Confucianism." Its campaigns broadened to accuse many intellectuals and state bureaucrats of acting as "covert agents of the ancient Sage." Political reds (committed followers of Mao Zedong) attacked the "four olds" (old culture, old ideology, old customs, and old habits) to clear the way for the "four news" of proletarian culture, ideology, customs, and habits. At the same time, the Mao cult was carefully crafted to convert to state use any religious impulses connected with the traditional Confucius cult. By late 1972, official directives called for an intensified assault on the pernicious influence of Confucius, citing Qin Shihuangdi's harsh suppression of classical scholars and texts (see the Introduction) as glorious precedent for Mao's suppression of the current counterrevolutionary forces. For the first time in Chinese history, Confucius was portrayed as a ruthless opponent of progressive historical forces, the "number one hooligan" in the state. In proof of this, the propaganda machines gave a new twist to the old story of Confucius's execution of a robber, alleging that Confucius had acted as class oppressor to Shaozheng Mao, a Robin Hood–type champion of the revolutionary masses and a clear precursor of Mao himself. As leaders pushed for a thorough weeding out

Figure 20. The Cultural Revolution anti-Confucius campaign. A big-character poster in the upper left-hand corner denounces "The Old Confucian Curiosity Shop." A guard takes a sledgehammer to the elaborately carved marble entrance pillar to the main Confucius shrine at Qufu. From Jonathan D. Spence and Annping Chin, *The Chinese Century: The Photographic History of the Last Hundred Years* (New York: Random House, 1996), 200.

of "unhealthy currents" of thought designed to leave the state purified and unified, each assault was presented as a necessary and measured response to extreme reactionary violence.

Why was the second rhetorical barrage against the Master in 1972–73 so much more virulent in tone than attacks five years earlier, which had connected

Confucius with Liu Shaoqi? In the interim, in 1971, Gen. Lin Biao, Mao's heir apparent, had died, reportedly while defecting to the Soviet Union. Because Lin had commanded the People's Liberation Army, party sources claimed that the counterrevolutionary forces in the highest ranks of the hierarchy had grown inexplicably stronger since 1967, requiring more strident countermeasures. In reality, Jiang Qing and others in the Party worked to deflect guilt by association with the leftist Lin by portraying him as an ultrarightist, ultratraditionalist, and ultra-Confucianist, intending in the process to undercut whatever moderating influence Zhou Enlai possessed. To substantiate Lin's utter treachery and depravity, Party organs made much of the decision by Lin and his wife in 1969 to hang scrolls in their bedroom that read, "Of all things, this is the most important: Conquer thyself and restore the Rites." This aphorism from the *Analects* was enough to show that Confucian precepts continued to inspire the evil rightists. The tenuous connection was brought out by Feng Youlan [= Fung Yulan], then China's foremost philosopher: "[Efforts by Liu Shaoqi and Lin Biao to undermine socialism] were made in imitation of Confucius. The times may be different, but they were the same 'revive the old' theories on retrogressive lines. Their spirits were one; their aims were the same." And so in 1972, journals suspended at the start of the Cultural Revolution (including the *Peking University Journal* and two journals of archaeology) were allowed to resume publication so that they could contribute to the conduct of the campaign. New journals such as *Study and Criticism* sprang up, their first issues largely dominated by articles critical of Confucius and Confucians. Even before the full Chinese Politburo could meet to discuss the proper official stance to be taken on the Confucius question, Jiang Qing had convened her own forum dedicated to criticizing Confucius as reactionary slave-owner (September 1973).

Up to this point, much of the "Criticize Lin Biao, Criticize Confucius" campaign had been an internal political event conducted within the ranks of the Communist Party to strengthen the hand of civilian radicals supporting Mao and Jiang Qing, with the anti-Confucian aspects mere window dressing. But given the radicals' insistence that "ethics serve politics," it was only a matter of time before they initiated and directed a public anti-Confucian mass movement against Lin Biao and Confucius as joint villains. To ordinary people participating in the campaign, Confucius appeared to be a real target of CCP ire, not just a convenient cover for political infighting. All of Chinese society was soon mobilized to condemn Confucius's allegedly subversive hidden message. Specifically Confucian rites, especially the all-important mourning and wedding ceremonies, were banned as remnants of China's old slave society. The usual big-character wall posters went up. Poems and songs of criticism were composed and circulated.

While many of the most frequently employed attacks on Confucius merely repeated the slanders found in May Fourth writings, they were now, significantly, published under the names of ordinary citizens, usually older peasants who had been illiterate prior to 1949. The anti-Confucius campaign, in fact, had the distinction of being the first major political campaign in post-Liberation China ostensibly sustained entirely through the revolutionary fervor of "representatives of the masses." In simple fact, many renowned intellectuals and Party members were now under suspicion, on house arrest, or in jail. But a trusted group of China's intelligentsia could be enlisted to provide so-called documentary evidence of Confucius's villainy, some manufactured for the occasion under the supervision of the Communist Party. Exhibitions and public lectures, many by China's most famous historians and archaeologists, determined the relevant source materials upon which directed study classes and small group sessions would focus. For with Lin Biao safely dead, the Anti-Lin, Anti-Confucius campaign could now address the larger ideological issues that had remained unsettled in the aftermath of May Fourth: Must every peasant revolt in Chinese history be regarded as an expression of anti-Confucianism? Was China's shameful weakness in the international sphere due ultimately to the Han Confucians, who rejected the expansionist policies favored by Qin Shihuangdi and his Legalist advisers? Did not all Confucian institutions oppress women and peasants, contrary to claims of "benevolent government"? Had not the worship of Confucius acted as the indigenous opiate of the Chinese people? Was not Confucius, who claimed to transmit rather than create, ultimately responsible for China's presumed inability to innovate in the fields of science and technology? By the mid-1970s the anti-Confucius campaigners added a more damaging accusation to these revived May Fourth charges: had not Confucius's very pedagogical approach been designed to "chain the minds of many people, hampering the in-depth development of the proletarian educational revolution"?

The anti-Confucius movement peaked in ferocity in mid-1974, despite Deng Xiaoping's return to power as vice-premier in 1973. So fierce was the infighting that year between Jiang Qing and her clique and Deng and his recently rehabilitated supporters that a Central Committee directive handed down on July 1 had to issue explicit injunctions against political activities detrimental to economic production (that is, "fighting civil wars"). Heeding the message, the radicals gradually abated their attacks, only to resume them in 1975–76 in the course of a new CCP campaign aimed at bourgeois rightists and "deviationist winds." It was really only in October 1976 that many of China's intellectuals, who correctly perceived themselves to be the real targets of Jiang's latest campaign, could relax, for that month brought the precipitous downfall of the so-called Gang of Four, Jiang Qing and three of her most prominent supporters. By that point, the intellectuals and bureaucrats who had emerged victorious with Deng Xiaoping from intraparty

strife were ready to reconsider the possible relevance of Confucius and Confucian institutions to China's modernization project. The very bellicosity of Jiang
Qing's anti-Confucian harangues had lent Confucianism a certain cachet to many
who had been tarred repeatedly with the label of Confucianist. Opponents of
Jiang, schooled in the terrifying instability of the Mao years, had come to accept
the faulty ideological equation that Jiang had made between revolution and anti-
Confucianism, on the one hand, and political stability and Confucianism, on the
other. Interest in Confucian learning grew apace in some circles, if only as a possible corrective to the extremism of the Gang of Four.

Deng's inner circle, looking to bolster "socialism with Chinese characteristics," meanwhile began to promote its own version of Confucianism, both as
China's indigenous alternative to the Protestant ethic and as antidote to the "spiritual pollution" imported from the West. The first characterization, in stressing
Confucian humanism, made for good foreign press and a strong China lobby
in America supported by several sectors within the sinological community. The
second, in laying the groundwork for a special regional identity in stark opposition to the West, played superbly to fellow autocrats in Asia and most everyone at home, regardless of political persuasion. Its anti-imperialist rhetoric and
claims of Chinese superiority threw a much-needed sop to Mao loyalists, while
implicitly assuring the older intellectuals who had suffered under Mao that they
could escape the perceived ills of postmodern life: irrationality, nihilism, self-
centerdness, hyperactive libidos, absurdity, and gross consumerism. With a more
united front at home and abroad, China could look forward to resuming its
rightful place in the world, inasmuch as its unique model of state-directed cor-
porativity theoretically contained an internal self-correcting mechanism for
Western developmental errors. It was such reformulated progressivist visions that
worked to generate a New Confucian Revival, a neo-neo-Confucian movement in China during the 1980s and 1990s.*

*The origin of New Confucianism is usually traced to early 1958, when four
articulate spokesmen for Chinese tradition, Carsun Chang, Xu Fuguan, Mou Zongsan,
and Tang Junyi, published a signed manifesto in the Hong Kong conservative journal
Minzhu pinglun (*Democratic Tribune*) stating that the religio-philosophical tenets of
Confucian tradition—by which they meant mostly post-Song orthodoxy—had an
intrinsic value transcending space and time. Since all four thinkers were disciples of the
late conservative thinker Xiong Shili [d. 1968], one might plausibly trace the origins of
the movement back to the 1920s. But a new Confucian revival did not interest most
Chinese intellectuals until (a) the West itself had expressed more interest in Chinese civilization; (b) sufficient numbers of Chinese experts on the West had proclaimed their dis-
satisfaction with Euro-American models of modernity; and (c) such a movement had
received a strong stamp of approval from top political leaders like Deng Xiaoping and Lee
Kuan Yew.

THE NEW CONFUCIAN REVIVAL

The May Fourth, New Life, and anti-Confucius campaigns posed the crucial question troubling Chinese intellectuals ever since the Taiping Rebellion (1850–64): can an effective modern state be grafted onto a Confucian society? In effect, the Confucian Revival of the 1980s reversed the question, asking if Confucian values and institutions could be successfully grafted back onto a semi-industrialized, modernizing state. Modernization experts in the early part of the twentieth century had been sure that the requirements for maintaining the Confucian social order and those for ensuring China's survival in the modern world were fundamentally opposed, but the proponents of a Confucian Revival in China (the New Confucians, or Xin Rujia 新儒家) have always rightly disputed such a pat assumption.

To the New Confucians, who style themselves the third wave of Confucianism (after Confucius and the True Way Learning masters of late imperial China), political revolutions and social movements are passing events that leave the basic patterns of the human condition essentially unchanged. "Antiquity is now" for the good reason that, in the end, people in all ages face similar problems in trying to construct reliable fiduciary communities that promote human flourishing. New Confucian spokesmen therefore argue, in slogans that seem to play off Wei Jingsheng's promotion of "democracy as the [necessary] fifth modernization," that Confucian elements can and must be restored to modernizing societies in Asia, since Confucian humanism is an absolute precondition for a more advanced modernization on a distinctive, homogeneous Chinese model.

According to New Confucian theories of the eighties, key elements of the constructed Confucianism—principally, a strong work ethic, customary deference to the twin authorities of family and paternalistic state, and an emphasis on education, self-sacrifice, and thrift—had been preserved intact in the People's Republic of China, in Taiwan, and in diaspora communities, despite the rapidly changing contexts for those elements. Supposedly, such transnational Confucian values and institutions constituted a force like the old Protestant ethic, which had propelled modernization in early industrializing Europe. Confucian ethics, unacknowledged, had already catalyzed East Asian states (including China under the vanguard CCP) to modernize quickly and well. Common wisdom in East Asia was willing to credit a Confucian work ethic for the educational attainments, high rates of saving, focus on family-run enterprises, and a host of unrelated phenomena that together spurred the East Asian "economic miracle" in a postmodern globalized world. The New Confucian theorists had only to orchestrate such accounts by issuing a series of spectacular reassessments of Confucian contributions to China and East Asia. One minor theoretical hurdle remained,

however: because general opinion held that the orthodox teachings of late imperial China, in stressing personal moral development, had overlooked the concomitant need for cognitive knowledge, Confucian ideals, if they were to foster
the ability of New Confucian states and societies to do battle with the preda-
tory West, would have to be retrofitted within the alien framework of scientific
and technical expertise.

Despite the exaggerated claims made for the East Asian states' distinctive Confucian heritage, claims based on the persistence in everyday life of practices and
beliefs associated with the old imperial state and society, this Confucian Revival
was largely an artificial rhetorical construct, and Confucianism a foreign product
to be marketed or copied for local consumption. Since the turn of the century,
China, Hong Kong, and Singapore had employed Western-style curricula
in their schools. And in the People's Republic in particular, after forty years of
strident political reeducation campaigns, only the elderly retained much familiarity with what was once mainstream Chinese culture. Only in Taiwan, where
the Guomindang legacy still prevailed, was more known about Confucian
learning. So "deculturalized" were most Chinese, in fact, by New Confucian
standards, that in the early eighties Singapore's political leaders had to call in
foreign experts (nearly all American-trained or American-based) to teach citizens what was now to be their own heritage.

In some sense, this Confucian tabula rasa perfectly suited party leaders in
China as well as Singapore's Lee Kuan Yew. A Confucianism nearly devoid of
prior content could serve conveniently as an empty receptacle into which to
pour hypernationalistic content unalloyed by Western individualistic notions. At
the same time, the dominant political parties could teach respect for centralized
political authority just as easily and effectively through New Confucian theory
as through open class struggle. The high-minded political correctness of the
slogans "Confucian exceptionalism" and "Asian values" could justify almost any
Party initiative. But the special beauty of a crafted Confucian Way with socialist characteristics was that it gave automatic cover to those in power while virtually requiring the ruling party to remain as final authority. Tradition was still
to be responsible for a host of social ills, including corruption, cronyism, gender
and racial bias, so the ruling elites could continue to evade blame for any current
economic and political troubles. But tradition appropriately revised under Party
leadership would supply the necessary continuity for successful nationalist construction in the future.*

---

*Hence the understandable suspicion expressed by the more perceptive social com-
mentators in East Asia toward any reinstitution of government support for Confucian learning. For example, Yingdai Lung (b. 1952), a popular columnist in Taiwan, in a recent essay

However high their expectations for a Confucian Revival, Party leaders knew they could not simply mandate it. If a revival was to succeed, it would need to draw support from large segments of the older academic and bureaucratic communities who might otherwise, given their histories, have been wary of joining forces with the top leaders. Luckily for the New Confucian Revival, in the PRC a strong convergence of interests in the eighties and early nineties among the CCP leadership, older intellectuals, and minor functionaries (not to mention other Asian autocrats and some sinologists abroad) meant that members of these quite disparate groups would occasionally cooperate in converting Confucius from degenerate apostle of China's exploitative feudal society to potent symbol of China's unparalleled readiness for modernity. Upon the effective death of Chinese Marxism after Mao, elites became keenly aware of an ideological vacuum threatening further political instability. A plausible unifying theory presented for foreign and domestic consumption might fill that vacuum and decrease the forces of regionalism, while forging the much-desired economic and political integration of "Greater China," especially Taiwan, Singapore, and the overseas Chinese communities in Southeast Asia and the Americas.* But no simple substitution of crass hypernationalism for Marxism would work with China's more cosmopolitan citizens. As the academics and party rank and file realized, unabashed sinocentrism alone would not be enough to preserve their authority at the nexus of change and tradition, enabling them to remain "the sole legitimate subject of Chinese history."

Fearing technocratic visions and rampant materialism equally, since both implied new power centers, many of the academic elites and politicos found a perfect solution in an updated version of state-sponsored Confucianism with a heavy emphasis on correctness. The secure grounding of New Confucian appeals in academic logic reassured those whose careers and status were tied to

entitled "In the Shadow of Confucius," suggests that the PRC and Taiwan each brandish pro-Confucian slogans about the sanctity of the "Chinese-Confucian" identity as a way of staking their claims to legitimacy. Compare the many recent attempts to reassert the figure of Sun Yat-sen as *Guofu* 國父 (father of the country) in both Taiwan and the People's Republic. Numerous academic conferences and public ceremonies, many held in Nanjing, the old capital of the Republic of China, promote this cult of Sun Yat-sen, presumably to gratify GMD leaders while attracting the interest of overseas communities. Naturally, in the hagiographic process Sun has been stripped of all complexities, the better to present him as revolutionary archetype.

*Note the concurrent official promotion of the myth that China is the oldest, continuous civilization on earth, stretching back some four to five thousand years, a myth intended to gloss over the differences among premodern cultures and minorities residing within the boundaries of what is now the Chinese nation-state.

their mastery of rational theory and practice. Then, too, the very complexity of the rarefied New Confucian metaphysics held a distinct advantage. (The CCP's onetime insistence on "going to the people" notwithstanding, many intellectuals and Party members, viewing the masses as stupid, inert, and unselfconscious, were intent upon retaining their place as indispensable engineers of the masses' emancipation and vanguards of the revolution.) Most gratifying of all was the prospect that a unique sociopolitical creation of Chinese intellectuals, Confucianism, might become a universally touted "good doctrine" for the postmodern world; this would allow Chinese intellectuals to claim superiority not only over the masses, but over their Western counterparts, who had up to then "occupied a leading position in world culture." Trusting the New Confucian third-wave Confucianism both to skirt basic conflicts between science and religion and to inoculate China against the personal alienation and social disruption associated with advanced free-market economies, intellectuals, functionaries, and CCP leaders joined in hailing the elective affinities they dubbed Confucianism as "a culture better suited to the future era, [one] that will replace . . . contemporary Western culture."

Typical statements from true believers imagined that "once the Chinese race recognizes the cultural value of modern science, and then incorporates this scientific spirit into its cultural quest for unity and harmony [code words for social cohesion], a new culture representing the future of humankind will undoubtedly dawn on the horizon." In the eighties and early nineties, such hackneyed appeals to yet another cultural revolution marked the "dubious spectacle of Chinese intellectuals going through the revolving door of history without ever making a new entry"—regardless of the unprecedented sophistication of the New Confucian rhetoric, which equally rejected the May Fourth reformers' wholesale embrace of Western values and institutions and Chiang Kai-shek's simplistic revival of select elements from an imagined past. Over one thousand articles on Confucianism were published in China in the eighties. Scarcely less impressive—or depressing, depending on one's view—was the scale of work accomplished by the Academy of Chinese Culture (*Zhongguo shuyuan*), whose distinguished members in the early eighties included Feng Youlan (1895–1990), Liang Shuming (1893–1988), and Ji Xianlin (b. 1911). Though the Academy never received large government subsidies, it gladly lent its considerable international prestige to the gratifying prospect of an alternative modernity, not Western but Chinese in origin, of universal applicability. Only one year after Deng's restoration to power, it sponsored the first academic conference devoted solely to Confucian studies, at which plans were made to establish the China Confucius Foundation, with a main office in Beijing and a branch office in the newly restored Confucian temple in Qufu,

Shandong.* These two think tanks quickly came to operate in conjunction with the Chinese Research Institute on Confucius in Beijing (estab. in 1985) and numerous local Centers for Chinese Classical Studies, including one in Shen-zhen, a Special Economic Zone. With the blessings of the Central Party Sec-retary, these research centers hosted several international conferences that drew scholars from countries as far away as Australia, France, and America. The main topic of discussion: the manifest advantages of Confucian values and institutions in a modernizing world.

With the Chinese faith in traditionalism dying hard, even in the so-called modernist camp, more seminars, on topics like "Modernization and Traditional Chinese Culture" inevitably followed, with the American professors Tu Wei-ming and Cheng Chung-ying usually in attendance. Undoubtedly, the high point of such activities was the international congress convened in the People's Republic of China in 1994 to commemorate the 2,545th anniversary of the birth of Confucius. Gracing the opening ceremonies were four prominent Chinese members of Deng's inner circle: Gu Mu, widely credited as the prime architect of Deng's economic modernization policies; Li Ruihuan, chairman of the Chinese Peoples' Political Consultative Congress; Li Xiannian, a senior Party and government official (now deceased); and Zhou Nan, then Beijing's chief representative in Hong Kong. Also in attendance were foreign dignitaries (including Lee Kuan Yew, the strongman of Singapore, and Goh Keng Swee, Lee's closest associate), the heads of several foreign academic institutes, and some three hundred scholars invited from twenty countries. In a trickle-down effect, study sessions were soon set up at all levels of state organizations to consider the event's implications.†

---

*With the aim of "enhancing academic culture," the state-subsidized foundation in its promotional literature promises contributors from overseas Chinese communities that their names will in perpetuity be "inscribed on tablets, on individual tablets" or in "small pavil-ions [built] in their names in the native place of Confucius, depending on the amount of contribution." Less elevated expressions of interest in Confucius can be found elsewhere: Beijing's New World Press, for example, churned out a combination potboiler and bodice-ripper entitled *In the Mansion of Confucius' Descendants*. Related by a seventy-seventh-generation descendant of Confucius in the best tradition of prime-time melodrama, this tale of intrigue, vice, corruption, and murder was soon translated into many languages.

†In promoting such sessions, the New Confucians have resorted to much the same sorts of propagandizing efforts as the Maoists used. Meanwhile, many of those schooled in the avowedly pro-Confucian atmosphere of Taiwan and Singapore learn a smattering of "Confucian" teachings through the required, but uninspiring, "national studies" classes. A pupil at the Singapore Chinese Girls' School remarked, "I'm not really into it; it's boring. The Con-ethics class is when we take catnaps or read romances under our desks."

The scene cannot help but bring to mind a poster of the late twenties that appeared at the Peasants' Association in a small town near Nanchang. One side of the poster depicts an old Confucian temple; the other, a "world park," featuring Marx, Lenin, and a vacant third position. In the center a man in Chinese Nationalist uniform carries the portrait of Sun Yat-sen toward the Confucian temple. The legend reads, "Sun ought to be in the world park," but the GMD "wants him in the Confucian temple." Ever since the New Life movement's attempt to co-opt Confucius in support of autocratic rule, the CCP had denounced Confucianism as the reactionary tool of myopic elites. And before the latest Confucian Revival, everyone agreed that material progress on a Euro-American model and Confucian tradition were diametrically opposed. Granted, some central concepts of Confucianism (chiefly *ren*, *gong*, and *shu*) by adaptation and extension could be brought into conformity with Western principles, but only one reified force, that of tradition or modernity, could prevail in the contest for the heart and soul of China. Interestingly enough, the New Confucians, with the support of new powers in East Asia, have essentially denied any need to choose between tradition and modernity. By their lights, the Confucian temple stands at the front gate to the world park.

It is to their credit, no doubt, that the Confucian Revivalists tend to scoff at stark either/or dichotomies. Unfortunately, they substitute the curious proposition that two key Confucian concepts, self-cultivation and *minben* (taking the common people as basis), can be successfully merged with the wealth-and-power discourse, producing the very "inner sageliness and outer kingliness" (that is, charismatic authority and political domination) lauded in imperial times. During the eighties and early nineties, the New Confucian leaders could credibly claim that Confucian institutions accounted for the phenomenal economic success attributed to the PRC, the Four Dragons (Taiwan, Singapore, Hong Kong, and South Korea), and Vietnam as "little China," so long as they engaged in selective amnesia about the past. Hence the dramatic "rebound" of Confucianism "in the stock market of explanatory paradigms." The economic dynamism displayed by these six states in the old Confucian cultural sphere—a dynamism all the more stunning when viewed against the economic recessions and rising crime rates of many countries in Euro-America—conceivably led the New Confucians to hope that both people and Party, once relieved of their most pressing economic burdens, might prove receptive to the New Confucian education to full humanity. But tying the value of Confucian ethics too closely to the appreciation in East Asian stock portfolios soon cost the New Confucians much moral and intellectual capital. The East Asian economic crisis spawned by the stockmarket crash of winter 1997 quickly tarnished much of the sheen of "Asian values," making it plain that government sponsorship of New Confu-

Figure 21. Confucius worship by representatives of the developing nations devoted to "Asian Values." From *Far Eastern Economic Review* (Feb. 9, 1989), 30.

cian discourse could neither guarantee rising GNP nor eliminate strains in the social fabric (fig. 21).

The failures of the New Confucian experiment, however, go well beyond ill-conceived tactics accepting the pace of economic modernization as the only accurate yardstick for contending public agendas. In general, the New Confucian theorists have tended to avoid specific talk of ritual, though ritual learning lay at the heart of the traditions associated with Confucius. No less worrisome is their general reluctance to dispute the need for "authoritarian arrangements" in East Asia (though they have gone on record protesting specific atrocities, especially the Tian'anmen massacre). Presumably the New Confucians have been loathe to jeopardize their partnership with the political powers-that-be, since they share a single theoretical goal: the creation of a unified, public-minded populace under the direction of far-sighted and selfless elites inspiring emulation. For this reason, perhaps, the New Confucians have failed to gauge the feasibility of their projects under authoritarian governments. For it is questionable, first, whether a genuine ethics of humanism can be constructed within the ideological parameters of Asia's current party politics, and, second, whether China's youth can be brought to accept this new version of state-approved Confucian orthodoxy. For as the historian Bruce Cumings has observed, "The one constant 'moral center' since 1949 is China's zealous and absolute concept of national sovereignty, about which it has been a good deal more sensitive than the Western powers who introduced the idea to China in the first place." Besides, under the old dynasties the specific moral calculus employed for society and state, no less than the role of elite cultural codes, varied so much that a revival of certain aspects of classical training could not reasonably be expected to foster a unifying impulse within a single modern nation-state, let alone across East Asia.*

Immersed in their abstractions, the New Confucians have too seldom paused to remind their patrons of such inconvenient facts. Open to charges of opportunism, the New Confucians appear to many China-watchers to be "vulgar" rather than "true Ru," though the Greek philosophers' examples show the temptations that well-meaning thinkers experience when they figure their anointment of quite ordinary rulers as philosopher-kings can win their theones a universalist significance transcending temporal, spatial, and ethnic boundaries. (Such temptations must be stronger still for modern Chinese, who have seldom enjoyed a secure place in an accepted narrative of their own, but instead have had to scramble to negotiate their place in history within the tales thrust on them by Euro-American intellectuals.) In the meantime, the New Confucians' willingness to collaborate with ossified "soft authoritarian" regimes in Singapore and China may well have had the opposite effect of that intended. New Confucian rhetoric to date, however inadvertently, has left only one indelible mark on East Asian politics: in lending credence to the Party's ill-judged plans to whip up peasant, worker, and student xenophobia (as seen in the *New Trimetrical Classic*

---

*It must be said that outside the PRC and Singapore (e.g., in contemporary Taiwan, Hong Kong, and South Korea), New Confucian thinking has contributed much to democratic politics. In Taiwan, for example, the prominent intellectual Xu Fuguan (1903–82), certainly the most antiauthoritarian and prodemocratic of the New Confucians, repeatedly stressed that the promotion of the "more open" aspects of Confucian tradition would spur development in Taiwan. Xu and his allies freely admitted, however, that "for the last few decades, those who have opposed democracy and freedom have often gotten help from Confucian culture, which they treated as protective cover for autocratic rule." In Hong Kong under British rule, such anti-Beijing campaigners as Martin Lee used to oppose the humane traditions of Confucius to the evils of Communism. Since the 1997 transfer, however, Lee has changed the object of his condemnation to the unholy alliance forged between an antidemocratic, corrupt Beijing and proponents of the Confucian tradition. The politician Kim Dae Jung of South Korea, sharply disputing the rhetoric of Singapore's Lee Kuan Yew, has argued that Confucian learning represents a heritage of ideas and practices compatible with civil-political human rights, despite Park Chung Hee's autocratic reinvention of Confucianism for political purposes in the "New Mind" campaign of the late 1970s in South Korea. Even in the PRC, certain antiauthoritarian forces have recently begun to cite Confucius in their struggle against conservative CCP factions.

Figure 22. A page from the *New Trimetrical Classic* (*Xin Sanzi jing*), published in 1994, which intersperses hypernationalistic content with paeans of praise for China's thinkers and statesmen, including Confucius. This particular page (78) extols Deng Xiaoping in verse for his suppression of "chaotic vagrants who rebelled against the correct [party line]" (a clear reference to the protesters at Tian'anmen square): "Bravely he opened the country, a flying dragon [like that of the *Changes*' Hexagram 1, which symbolizes perfect virility]. The people are secure and healthy." The old *Trimetrical Classic* (also called the *Three-Character Classic*), available in many versions in imperial China, told a beginning student in about twelve hundred characters the story of Chinese civilization, making frequent references to the basic goodness of human nature, to the necessity to study and work hard, and to the glorious contributions of sages like Confucius to society.

issued in 1994), the New Confucians have helped unleash hypernationalistic forces that will be hard to control. Quite unschooled in ways of "separating . . . the government from themselves," the Chinese masses may at this point be susceptible to any jingoistic propaganda that promises to reintroduce order (fig. 22).

The foregoing discussion, spanning the increasing mistrust of Confucius from the 1890s to more positive assessments a century later, has sketched two nominally pro-Confucian and two anti-Confucian movements in the twentieth century. These four movements, so dissimilar at first glance, share certain characteristics: Each arose in response to an acute national identity crisis occasioned by the perceived need for rapid modernization (a process itself that, being viewed as foreign, elicited calls for greater cultural homogenization). Each built on the conviction that China was so close to dismemberment, disintegration, or destruction as to preclude gradualist approaches. Each envisioned the need for a dynamic, radical transformation of traditional culture, the so-called national essence, whose core they tended to locate somewhere in the classical literary heritage. Each evaded easy classification by the standard American political categories of liberal, conservative, and radical for, in seeking to totally "reorganize the national heritage" (*zhengli guogu* 整理國古), all four movements intended both to preserve and to reject, to neutralize and to energize discrete slices of traditional culture. Each movement saw its immediate goal as the restoration of order and authority within China, and its eventual aim as China's reassertion of its age-old claims to regional, even world, dominance, implicitly asserting the centrality of China in any ongoing evolution of Confucian teachings. Each movement in turn revealed the need of modern Chinese for the "psychological compensation" of asserting China's past or future superiority to the West. Confident of the appeal of their nationalistic slogans to a frustrated public, the leaders of each movement saw little need to endow their positions with intellectual coherence, balance, or precision. Instead, each, in seeking to create a select group of new men who would rescue China by their superhuman heroics, demanded of its followers an impassioned, single-minded devotion to a voluntarist creed, investing what was an essentially political program with messianic overtones, so as to create "a religion which was not a religion." (Note, by contrast, the PRC's persistent wariness toward the adaptation of religious tenets drawn from Buddhism, much less Daoism, for nationalist ends.)

Whether the movements were nominally pro- or anti-Confucian, none ever really focused on the special quality of Confucius's idea of cultivation: steady delight in learning to make the human connections that enlarge one's capacity for joy. Instead, each of the movements used the discourse of Confucianism to frame a sober national identity and to formulate ambitious national goals. Clearly, the naturalized categories of nation, tradition, Confucianism, and modernity have served mainly as enabling alibis for dreams of dominance. But a sense of profound cognitive dissonance arises when the very same rhetoric once employed by the May Fourth reformers in their fight against the forces of "Pan-Asianism and aggression" now informs the Confucian Revivalists' vision of a "Greater China" powerful enough to intimidate its neighbors politically and economically.

How to critique but at the same time inherit tradition, how to innovate while transmitting the past are age-old questions, questions yet to be answered well. The modern PRC thinker Gan Yang insists that "to break away from tradition is the best way to inherit tradition." If I understand his paradox, Gan suggests a sequential effort: serious, prolonged cultural and personal introspection must precede any evaluation of modernity and tradition, civil versus official culture, China and the West, socialism and capitalism. Otherwise, the inability to disentangle the clumsy dichotomies that lend themselves well to polemic but not to clear analysis will deter humans from finding a more adequate form of inquiry. Far too many of those dichotomies rest on convenient fictions designed to preserve a sense of Western superiority (for example, that classical learning in China prevented the growth of science and democracy or that it supported a tyrannical system inherently less humane and enlightened than those of Europe and America).

The present value of either Chinese classicism or Confucian ethics lies not in select traditions selectively revised to conform with the modern wealth-and-power discourse, but in the questions such traditions may inspire about the presumed goals, methods, and implications of global capitalism, polymorphous modernity, and current debates over the good life. A review of some observations made by early classicists may offer one route, though not the only one, by which to distance oneself from the insistent ideological preoccupations of the dominant American progressivist project. Ru masters in imperial times called for some mediation between past ideas and present institutions. Few were foolish enough to want to duplicate in their own times the precise conditions of the normative past. Instead, they sought to build attitudes analogous to those of classical antiquity, informed by the same humane spirit but suitable for their more modern lives. (Some professedly pro-Confucian rhetoric of the twentieth century, in urging a direct restoration of the distant past, seems distinctly anti-Confucian.) Ru learning, then, with its emphasis on constructive accommodation, may help to subvert the "crude antithesis between change and value on the one side, and permanence and valuelessness on the other."

"CONFUCIAN" LEARNING IN THE PUBLIC EYE

The previous sections note the elusive yet charged character of the cluster of concepts identified with Confucianism in twentieth-century China. Contributing to this elusiveness is the fact that Chinese classical learning, even in its heyday, employed few complex religious institutions and distinctive iconic images, except at the level of the school and state cults dedicated to the Supreme Sage (whose importance nonetheless should not be underrated). Confucian rituals required no distinctive architecture or ritual paraphernalia; Confucianism's liturgical formulae were adapted from common ceremonies. In consequence, few activities and even fewer sites in China were associated with a specifically Confucian life, the exceptions being the ancestral home of Confucius at Qufu; the Confucian shrines in the capital; the scholastic academies and examination halls; and, until the curricular changes mandated in 1912, that place of honor in the local schoolroom occupied by a portrait of Confucius. Elementary school students in late imperial times might begin their academic day with a ritual bow toward the portrait of Confucius at the front of the classroom, and degree holders honor the Sage in biannual ceremonies. But veneration of Confucius was largely expressed in reverence for the classical literary heritage, whose preservation was credited to the Master, in cultural reproduction, and in fellowships at every level of society that promoted the complex tasks associated with self-cultivation.

As Confucius did not preach an exclusive belief system, his professed followers expected to see correspondences between the Master's teachings and the recognized tenets of other belief systems. At its inception, Confucian learning was a philosophy in support of informed moral action, rather than a creed enjoining a discrete set of beliefs. Its primary goal was to humanize each and every social relation so that society as a whole could become civilized. The provenance of any specific practice was of little concern outside academic circles.* Most practices later identified as Confucian, ancestor worship and the marriage rites, for example, had originated centuries before the time of Confucius in the customs of the Central States aristocrats, and they became virtually synonymous with Confucian culture only because they had been imprinted in the habits of body and mind of successive generations performing the rites and reading the Classics.

---

*After the introduction of Buddhism and the development of religious Daoism, many embraced aspects of all three teachings (*sanjiao* 三教). Ancestor worship conducted by the head of household was the rule in most families, and few professional religious experts chose to forbid family rituals. In most religious rituals, the Chinese expected to employ rites and vocabulary associated with one or more of the Three Teachings, as the occasion seemed to demand. Thus the vast majority of temples in Taiwan, Hong Kong, and Singapore, include altars dedicated to Confucius, Laozi, and the Buddha, rather than to any single teacher or god.

But once the seemingly natural process of cultural reproduction broke down at the end of the nineteenth century, the scriptural teachings seemed doomed to aridity and eventual desiccation. Educated Chinese today are apt to know no more about their past than their Western counterparts do of theirs. Aside from the pervasive indifference of the entire postmodern world to premodern history, which deprives the educated of conventional incentives to undertake the study of tradition, at least three other factors account for the lack of serious engagement by Chinese with the past: the unthinking conflation of Confucian and Chinese, which makes a specific study of their own classical heritage seem superfluous; the switch in printed texts from formal literary language (*wenyan* 文言) to vernacular, which renders earlier writings unintelligible to those without special training; and finally, the multiple distorting lenses through which most view their traditions, such as the "international educational standards" prescribed by select Euro-American institutions (which barely acknowledge the existence of Confucius or Chinese classicism), the rhetoric of recent political movements, and the more informal posturing of older generations in China and abroad claiming to be the sole authentic representatives of culture. Neither does it help that consumer cultures awash in things and information are increasingly oblivious to anything other than the dictates of fashion. Thus indifference, distrust, and outright hostility color many responses to Chinese traditions, not only in Euro-America but in China.

In imperial China, educated persons presumably shared a pride in their command of and reliance on the authoritative literary tradition found in the Five Classics and Four Books. However much they might disagree on interpretations and issues, they sensed a bond of common commitments to what they perceived as the Confucian Way. Lately, this sense of common traditions has devolved to little more than appreciation for Confucianism as an exotic consumer product marketed to historical amnesiacs. Hence the recent upsurge in East Asia of Confucian tourism, replete with theme parks, tableaux, and affordable Confucian key chains. To take one example, Ocean Park, the largest amusement park in Hong Kong, celebrates "five thousand years of Chinese history," which it seeks to convey to tourists through a careful selection of artifacts, (reproduced or real including oracle bones and bronze tripods, antique clothes with detachable queues, Chinese lanterns, upturned roofs, and "Confucian" collectibles, all at affordable prices). A history theme park in nearby Shenzhen claims that customers can experience "all of Chinese history" in less than two hours via staged tableaux depicting historical figures like the wicked First Emperor of Qin. The current rush to restore Confucian temple sites throughout China, Taiwan, and Korea, often in gaudy styles with supernatural motifs more typical of Buddhist and Daoist temples in the old days, is yet another sign of the increasingly popular theme-park approach to history.* Since most tourists equate East Asian history with Confucianism, visits to specifically Confucian sites (mostly mausolea, temples, and ancient academic institutions) are seen as edifying visits to times past. The conceit of such tourism, of course, is that the designated Confucian sites can convey transhistorical Truth through performance art, videos, and souvenirs: "Ultimately, it is not just the touristic image which is plastic, but also the 'traditional' concerns and constraints of the host culture."

Traditions can be tenacious, however, to the degree that they are diffuse and elastic. The very elusiveness of Ru beliefs and practices, whose influence Confucius likened to wind bending the grass, may improve their chances of survival, especially when they enjoy in some circles the peculiar advantage of being at once exotic yet familiar, old yet new, foreign yet indigenous. Confucius himself was fully confident that the old Zhou culture he faithfully renewed would never die, and part of the traditions' enduring appeal, especially in rapidly growing economies, may derive from the long-standing associations they forged between culture and connoisseurship, tying the search for self-cultivation to an appreciation of the polite arts of music, poetry, calligraphy, and (later) painting. Such benign associations may yet bring some aspects of classical tradition back from the brink of extinction—when they are bolstered by the elite's ever-present need to assume the role of cultural conservator, a growing nostalgia for the old ways in protest against the new, a natural curiosity about distant roots, and the nativist desire for a distinctively Chinese futurist way between capitalism (blamed for widening disparities in wealth, environmental degradation, and cultural destruction) and communism (seen as intellectually moribund and dangerously inclined to bureaucratic totalism).

Some signs in East Asia and in diasporic communities suggest that the delving into the Confucian past has begun to go beyond the grossly superficial or the politically expedient. In Japan, a thoughtful biography of Confucius by Inoue Yasushi has become a runaway best-seller (some seven hundred thousand copies within the first two years of publication) while garnering a host of prestigious literary awards. Kaji Nobuyuki's equally influential *What Is Confucianism?* (1990, in Japanese) offers impressive testimony to the strong hold that Confucian teachings still exert upon Japanese religious views of illness, death, and the afterlife.

---

*A far more inspired move to reintroduce the modern Chinese public to the ideas of Confucius and the other early philosophical masters has come in the form of *manga* by Cai Zhizhong 蔡志忠, whose cartoons, depict all the most important passages in the classical texts. Cai's books, originally published in Chinese, are now available in English from Asiapac in Hong Kong.

In Taiwan, Confucius has become a familiar presence in modern life, as much a hero in popular media as in government-sponsored articles, his image helped along by a joint-venture feature film produced in 1995 by Taiwan and the PRC placing the Sage's life and times within the context of fabulous treasures on loan from the Kong family mansion in Shandong. Vietnam, diverting capital badly needed for industrial projects, has decided to restore as a national museum the Hanoi campus of Van Mieu, a Mandarin university built in 1070 on the Chinese model. In far-off Indonesia, a Confucian "church" headquartered in Surabaya, one of the last traces of Kang Youwei's evangelizing in Java, conducts weekly prayer meetings venerating Confucius as savior of the Chinese race while producing films for locals on the fundamental message of religious and ritual Confucianism. Following the downfall of Suharto, the faithful in Indonesia have felt free enough to demonstrate in public for state recognition as one of five local religions. South Korea, the most self-consciously Confucian society in East Asia, boasts a private university with a distinctive Confucian Studies department, yearly birthday celebrations to the Master and his chief disciples in select Confucian temples, and a national organization, the Yu-rin 儒林, dedicated to preserving and promoting classical values and institutions. In South Korea, too, several farming villages have chosen to adopt traditional Choson period clothing and customs and to guide young and old by the rigorous discipline enjoined in classical manuals. Hanhak 漢學, the Village of Chinese Learning, located in the central midwestern region of South Korea, is one such "culture village," whose residents since the early eighties have sought to achieve an integrated way of life they associate with a preindustrial past.

Tributes to Confucius and to classical learning continue to pour in. In a world linked ever more tightly together, it is important to consider what this signifies about East Asia, its future, and its relation to ourselves. It is equally important to know whether the ancient teachings of Confucius can offer us, in our present circumstances, any guidance.

IS ANYTHING WORTH PRESERVING?

Even at the end of the nineteenth century, Confucius's darkest hour, the figure of Confucius symbolized to some the desire for communication and cooperation between diverse worlds. For instance, the author of *Nie hai hua*, Zeng Pu (1872–1935), wrote a short story in which the Sage himself translates precious books from 120 countries, then urges his disciples to master the remaining foreign languages. For Zeng's many readers, classical learning had repeatedly proven its worth as a springboard from which to launch significant change. Nonetheless, as Lu Xun, the foremost writer of modern China, once observed, "Confucius has had bad luck" ever since the turn of the twentieth century. Time and time again, he has been vilified by well-meaning reformers and lionized by dubious characters. It remains to be seen whether Chinese modernizers will come down on the side of extending their traditions through conscious borrowings, for what determines cultural survival is the utility of the past to the present.

Some have theorized that it is often on the peripheries of the Chinese cultural sphere, in this case, among Asian Americans and non-Asian academics, that dynamic cultural innovations occur, thanks to the persistent and sometimes more disinterested questioning of exiles, immigrants, and anthropologists. Many academics and technocrats envision a future with increasingly fluid cultural boundaries, where some Asian values may enter America's homes via TV, VCR, and DVD. Few, at any rate, would be prepared to argue that the fate of Confucius is now exclusively a Chinese concern. Indeed, some academics, mostly self-styled new Cold Warriors like Samuel P. Huntington, portray a bitterly divided world locked in titanic struggle in which the forces of East Asian "Confucian societies," in alliance with Islamic Fundamentalism, seek to defeat those of Western liberalism.* Faced with such a bewildering variety of scenarios invented in the culture wars, honest people may feel justifiably confused about the potential of Chinese classical learning to heal or harm. But uncritical relativism invites a far more troubling prospect. It is not only in China, to be sure, that popular idols like Cui Jian lament, "We have no ideals."

The poet Su Shi once likened the classics to a store of incredible wealth whose purchase price is ideas: "Let us make a comparison: In the markets, a large number of goods are displayed. I want them to be at my disposal. Now there is a thing that I can employ for that purpose which is called money. If I have money, all this merchandise will be mine. Well, in matters of culture, all

---

*The heated rhetoric of the American culture wars is evident everywhere, from John Updike's recent novel *Toward the End of Time*, which takes place in an imagined twenty-first century after a devastating war between China and America, to books like *Who Killed Homer? The Demise of Classical Education and the Recovery of Greek Wisdom*, by Victor Davis Hanson and John Heath (New York: Free Press, 1998), which argue that the values of classical Greece are "the sole paradigm which will either save or destroy the planet" (xviii). While discounting such apocalyptic visions, the sociologist Richard Madsen still suspects that there is good reason to fear the economic, legal, and psychological consequences for America of increased competition with a powerful Asia promoting "Asian exceptionalism." As Madsen observes, "In the name of keeping pace with 'international competition,' Western countries like the United States are breaking the power of labor unions, dismantling much of their welfare states, and 'getting tough on crime' by suppressing previously accepted liberties" (4). "After Liberalism: What if Confucianism Becomes the Hegemonic Ethic of the Twenty-first Century," JRRI Working Paper 14 (November 1995), 6 pages (Japanese Policy Research Institute: www.nmjc.org/jpri/public/wp14.html).

the classics and histories will be at my disposal if I first have ideas." Since the time of Confucius, the Way has been sought as remedy against cultural drift and foreign conquest, evils now inflicted less often by arms than by technology, consumer culture, and the global economy. Strong claims can be made for the Five Classics, the *Analects*, *Mencius*, *Xunzi*, and the writings of the Western Han masters: that they represent a rich storehouse of useful ideas open to those who choose to deliberate on their own characters and regimes and those of others; and that readers engaging the texts in active conversations relevant to their predicaments will find themselves better equipped to wend their ways through the old rubble and shiny new lures spun off by unstable traditions in conflict, if only because they are no longer content to think themselves the passive recipients of the wisdom of the ages. The greatest gains from the early Chinese canons are likely to be had, then, when the texts are approached with the same expectations that readers bring to any newly encountered Western classic. The Chinese text may be more difficult to understand, but the difference is one of degree, not of kind, since the thoughtful reception of any work requires a series of negotiations between the author's cultural epoch and the reader's own. Prior unfamiliarity with the Five Classics is, in theory, no barrier to this sort of exploratory exercise. The early followers of Confucius, after all, distinguished themselves from other groups more by the quality of their moral commitments than by their knowledge of old writings. In this respect, their teachings suit the postmodern age admirably, for in speaking of tradition, we "talk not so much of texts, lineages, and institutions, but rather of communities of persons who keep tradition alive."

The preliminary comments offered below concentrate on four recurrent themes in early classicism, stressing good social praxis over culturalist constructions and intellection. Those themes are self and society; the tension between ritual and law; the interdependence of hierarchy and reciprocity; and the insistence on economic justice as precondition to moral behavior. The goal is less to decode ancient China than to heighten our awareness of the choices we make daily, as often by a lack of thought as by conscious acts of will. Certain aspects of postmodern life call for a thorough reconsideration of human values. Some have charged, for instance, that most Americans are so enmeshed in the language of individualism that they have lost their capacity to articulate their equally strong human need for community. Like individualism, freedom from tradition is virtually an American fetish, but a person lacking traditions must be forever engaged in the exhausting process of marshaling elements shopped from different cultures into the coherent patterns of life and self needed for a meaningful existence. A more satisfying alternative, by which the otherwise consuming passions can be transmuted into passions that sustain, is a return to a simple notion promoted in many classical texts: that a person best mediates incommensurate moral claims by placing self and identity in the context of multiple social roles (each having its distinctive point and purpose), so that her conduct achieves the highest standard of excellence in as many social roles as possible.

In the old days, the classical traditions (note the plural) had been nonexclusive, the province of dedicated amateurs, if you will. It was not only that a person could be a Ru in office and a Daoist at home, as the proverb said. An ordinary adherent of the Way had by turns to act as a devoted family member, a competent judge of rival scholastic claims, an accomplished practitioner of the polite arts, an informed participant in complex rituals, a responsible contributor to local community welfare, and occasionally a pragmatic politician. For the early Ru texts, like those of Plato and Aristotle, envision the human firmly embedded in a nested series of human relations stretching from family and friends to local communities to the state to All-under-Heaven. In China, the pre-Confucian virtues of filial piety, commonality, and loyalty to just authority were grounded in the belief that humans are fundamentally interrelated. The teachings of Confucius and his followers went further, hailing this relatedness as the single most valuable feature of human existence and so defining virtue, not as inner rectitude or submission to a savior god, but as the building of constructive communities.

Notions of Self and Society

Early Confucian texts say very little about human nature. The *Analects*, in fact, specifies human nature as one of the subjects about which the Master "seldom spoke." All Confucian learning rests on one significant claim, however: though humans at birth are little more than squalling bundles of needs and desires, they nonetheless share a crucial basic moral endowment from Heaven, whether Heaven is defined as the distant ancestors, the gods, or the cosmic workings. That basic endowment, if developed, allows humans to attain moral perfection in their lifetimes. As humans are equal in having the capacity to be moral and as morality alone makes for true and lasting human happiness, humans have an equal potential for happiness, notwithstanding patent inequalities in intelligence, talent, wealth, social station, beauty, strength, and health.

Most humans, because of early training, social custom, or a developed weakness, remain unaware of their innate perfectibility. They do not seek to attain it nor do they prize this potential within themselves. They therefore focus their available energies on the pursuit of lesser goods that are harder to secure and harder still to retain: wealth, social standing, long life, and sexual prowess. But those who receive sufficient insight and support from family, friends, teachers, and other role models can come to a deep appreciation of the intricate ties connecting members of the community. They will then wish to affirm and sustain those bonds by empathetic acts expressed in the conventional (and so communicable) language of rites, courtesy, and ceremony. It is at that point that the biological human becomes a fully realized human being bent upon exemplifying humankindness and humankind-ness (*ren* 仁). Repeated, productive social interactions give identity to the self while ameliorating feelings of alienation. Since self-transformation into full humanity is possible only within society, self and society need not always be at war with one another. Thus is serene happiness brought within human reach.

Early Confucian texts imagine the self as a work-in-progress, rather than as a product finished at birth or set by infant experience. The work that makes for progress, according to early Confucians, consists of performative acts, words and deeds—not thoughts, except insofar as those thoughts enhance the quality of human interactions. The ultimate good is so clearly linked to productive social interaction that one cannot be good when alone. Early classicism is therefore quite uninterested in prescribing or proscribing any form of private activity or inclination, unless such activities or inclinations affect the social climate. And because self-improvement and the improvement of society are complex goals difficult to attain, sustained effort counts for more in the end than any initial personal aptitude for virtue. The best society, therefore, does everything it can to encourage steadiness of moral purpose through meritocratic systems of reward, especially in education and in government. Echoes of this inform the classrooms of East Asia, which tend to emphasize achievements won through diligent cooperation while downplaying the special circumstances—inequality of money or brains—that divide one classmate from another. Self-esteem in those classrooms derives from doing one's best consistently; it in no way depends on being protected from an awareness of one's failures.

Failure, repeated failure, is in fact presented as a necessary and accepted part of the process of striving for excellence. As one early Confucian master, Yang Xiong (53 BC–AD 18), put it, any insight into true greatness entails sorrow as well as joy, for it presupposes an appreciation of the gap lying between that greatness and one's lesser achievements, a gap that realistically speaking humans may never be able to close. Yet it is the willingness to strive for greatness against all odds that lends human life dignity and scope. Confucius offered a revealing self-portrait when he called himself "the sort of man who forgets to eat when he works himself up over some problem, who is so full of joy that he forgets his worries and fails to notice the onset of old age." Another characterized him as one "determined to save the world while knowing that his efforts were in vain." Seeing each human life as a precious jade to be polished and carved, the Confucian strives for perfectibility in the face of human frailty, rejecting the views that humans are inherently flawed by original sin, that they are noble savages horribly corrupted by convention, and that they are molded and motivated mainly by a profound need to belong to their indigenous culture, which operates in their lives somewhat like an autonomous agent.

According to the negative stereotypes, propounded as often by interested, self-Orientalizing Asian elites as by Euro-Americans, Confucian classicism is inherently antidemocratic, anti-individualistic, and patriarchal. Patriarchal it has been, but every known society (even the matrilineal) has been patriarchal. Hierarchical it has been also, since only anarchists propose a society without hierarchy. Still, hierarchy does not preclude democracy. What matters is the type of hierarchy stipulated and the type of democracy desired. Surely it is pertinent that Ru learning as early as the fourth century BC advocated meritocracy, denounced monopolies, and promoted state-sponsored welfare institutions and comprehensive education, seeing in such measures the fundamental guarantees to human dignity. Was it really more oppressive than its Euro-American counterparts? Its overall record probably deserves two cheers, not three, insofar as it helped engender a society that was not uniformly humane. But Ru learning can be considered anti-individualistic only in the sense that it warns against the untrammeled pursuit of what passes for individualism in the modern world—a striving for complete originality—lest that unproductive pursuit, in taking precedence over the development of personal moral autonomy, dramatically curtail the real choices open to oneself and others.

Tensions Between Ritual and Law

To see rule by ritual in opposition to rule by law is to accept a false dichotomy. From the Chunqiu period on, thinkers took for granted a highly evolved system of legislation and jurisdiction. Excavated legal documents from such sites as Shuihudi and Zhangjiashan bear witness to the procedural care law officials were enjoined to use when ascertaining guilt and adjudicating doubtful cases, lest punishments applied in an arbitrary fashion directly threaten the state's interests. The very comprehensiveness of the early legal provisions—not the absence of rational law—may well have made the law's inherent limitations that much more obvious. In any case, the Confucius of the *Analects* contended that communities cannot flourish by law alone. At best, the law deters some people from committing crimes; at worst, it merely punishes criminals after the fact. Because laws do not lead humans to humane behavior, no truly just and humane society can rely principally on penal law. In addition, insofar as laws mandate a single (minimum) fixed standard of behavior, they work against Confucius's belief that no fixed rules can determine what is best for all parties in every situation. The pursuit of human goodness ultimately requires the constant weighing and reweighing of incommensurate goods to determine in each situation the most just solution for all concerned. On what single principle—might as right, majority rule, cost-benefit analysis, the Kantian imperative, or some mixture of all the above—could one base a universally beneficial set of laws? Humans, as complex social beings, require many things, including food, sex, symbolic systems, fellowship, and spectacle. Many basic necessities of human life are in limited supply, such that no legal contract, implicit or explicit, can ever guarantee a sufficiency for all. Ritual can work well to dispense such necessities appropriately while enhancing fellowship, as we have seen in chapter 4. Good laws should then supplement ritual in its mediation among the private impulses and interests at work in society, establishing an arena in which the public good can operate. Of course, if society is to benefit from its primary reliance on ritual, its rituals will require continual renegotiation and revision, for the rites as the conventional language for social interchange must respond to the changing concerns and priorities of the community if they are not to degenerate into fatuous formalities. Confucius makes this supposed disadvantage an integral part of his notion of the rites. That is why, for Confucius, it is not the Way that enlarges people, but people who enlarge the Way.

The negative stereotypes persist, despite evidence to the contrary, in associating Confucian teachings with rote learning and the willful negation of human rights, with, in short, dictatorial rule, in the classroom as in the body politic. These harsh stereotypes that originated in eighteenth-century fantasies about Oriental despotisms now are fed not only by distaste for the unsavory support "Confucian" learning has acquired in this century but also by knowledge of the radically different premises of Confucian ethical theory and Euro-American equality before the law. Enlightenment notions of social justice require a rational agent operating by choice or by mandate from behind a "veil of ignorance," since the main condition for basic fairness is the elimination of all personal considerations, and only a rational agent can operate autonomously and without reference to his own perceived self-interest. Therefore the modern American philosopher John Rawls, operating within Enlightenment traditions, suggests that justice is served only when three basic conditions are met: first, each person has a right to the most extensive liberty compatible with a similar liberty for others; second, all primary goods, liberty and opportunity, income and wealth, and the bases of self-respect, must be distributed equally unless an unequal distribution favors the least advantaged members of society; and third, whatever social and economic inequalities are allowed to exist must prove ultimately to everyone's advantage. Where there is unequal access to advantage, he further states, the equal liberties stipulated in the first condition may not be overturned for the sake of any efficiency implied by the second. Once justice has been determined by the rational agent according to these three conditions, Rawls insists, justice is best guaranteed by laws that bind all members of society equally.

Confucius's followers would counter that Rawls's theory of justice is based on a practical impossibility: no such rational agent has ever existed in human history, for no person is truly autonomous by nature in the sense that he operates entirely without reference to himself and others. English and American justice is therefore built on a fiction that has evolved from the Enlightenment insistence on a rights-centered justice rather than a virtue-centered vision of morality. Worse, the fiction is a destructive fiction tending to work against community consensus. If human beings are social animals whose lives necessarily reflect various traditions, should they not be led to seek the ultimate good in human existence within the context of the community's goods? For the Confucians, then, justice requires that persons be given their due according to their societal contributions.

Hierarchy and Reciprocity

From the Confucian view of humans as social and sociable animal there follows the early concern with fostering workable social relations. Basically, early Confucian texts prescribe the complementary operation of hierarchy and reciprocity. No complex society without hierarchy has ever existed. More important, hierarchy does not preclude meritocracy; it provides a viable structure to support such a society, insofar as it rewards diligence and publicly honors those who contribute to society's health, thereby nourishing others in the practice of virtue. Furthermore, hierarchy as a bureaucratic tool lends itself to the efficient distribution of goods and services. But hierarchy without reciprocity, without an acknowledgment of mutual obligations, easily degenerates into tyranny. (Reciprocity without hierarchy may be ideal, as the Cycle of the Rites chapter in the *Rites Record* is quick to concede, but it is hard to realize on a scale larger than the family or village.) Deference to superiors must be matched by the superior's obligation of benevolence to subordinates and the subordinates' freedom to remonstrate with superiors.

Such a balance between hierarchy and reciprocity rests ultimately upon early constructions of the body and body politic, for Ru texts tended to make analogues of the two as soon as accounts of social interaction began to raise the inevitable questions about ownership, autonomy, boundaries, and the distribution of scarce resources. Physical boundaries were viewed as emphatically permeable and expandable because the health of the body and body politic was thought to depend always on flow and change, rather than on fixedness. In addition, neither the body nor the state was ever considered the "possession of one man," as both are entities held in trust, in effect, works-in-progress extending over space and time. To the Confucian, the fluid boundaries of the body and body politic foster order, for order in the Confucian tradition emanates from a stable—precisely because it is not rigid—center attuned to social and cosmic patterns. In the body, the center was defined as the heart/mind, locus of the proper motivations for humane social interaction; in the body politic, as the sage-ruler or, in his absence, the sage-teacher. Early Confucian learning placed far less emphasis than we might expect on a distinctly interior or spiritual life, in contrast both to its later interpretations in China and to Western stereotypes of the mysterious East. For specific ritual purposes, however, early Confucian writings insist on unambiguous territorial and social boundaries, which can be promptly deconstructed once the ritual's specific aims have been achieved.

It was the logic of moral situations operating in relational space, in other words, not the precise location of any thing, person, or event, that mattered most to true Confucians devoted to notions of ritual efficacy. This was so in part because the secure acquisition of true power depended upon the steady buildup of charismatic virtue, not upon the land, persons, or things at one's temporary disposal. After all, a strain of Chinese folk wisdom preserved in the Five Classics, especially the *Changes*, argued that no possession, even land, is intrinsically good or lucky given that the relative benefits accruing from possession depend upon timing and location as well as the owner's present rank and situation in life. Most important, supreme power, in the end, means the ability to confidently call upon the aid of a unified community. The person for whom "the people are prepared to die" is most powerful. And conversely, "One can never 'gain' [even] an empire without the heartfelt admiration of the people in it."

Because, as one early classicist put it, "the Way of [true] humanity lies in making contact," the Confucians labored to devise appropriate methods to optimize the flow of wealth and services. Ideally, wealth is redistributed regularly through ritual gift exchanges and through the enforcement, under social pressure or under political and legal sanctions, of the ruling elite's duty to distribute grain and other basic necessities to the poor. Moral learning would circulate from the king and his officials throughout the realm and then back to the court, "exactly as vital *qi* circulates through the human body." The state would also facilitate the appropriate movement of persons and information within the realm. Ideally, too, social mobility is encouraged through largely meritocratic educational and bureaucratic recruitment systems—a revolutionary idea attributed directly to Confucius—and persons engaged in ritual would assume a variety of shifting roles, each identified with specific physical sites. Basically, "goods and grains [in company with people and ideas] should be allowed to circulate freely, so that there is no hindrance or stagnation in distribution."

Such complex views challenge prevailing stereotypes that link the capacity of Confucianized cultures to reduce interpersonal conflict with the imposition of sharp restrictions on personal freedom. Confucius expressed a desire to see "harmony without conformity" (*he er butong*), knowing that harmony requires difference. He also, according to popular legend, specifically denounced oppressive governments, thinking them more fearsome than tigers. And so critical was Confucius of smug conventionalists in his own day that it is hard to conceive of him as an advocate of conformity in ours. He taught that blind adherence to convention often deters humans from their pursuit of perfection.

Economic Justice as Precondition to Learning

Confucius and Mencius are very clear on this subject: the physical, emotional, intellectual, and moral aspects of a human being are so interwoven that no distinction of lasting utility can be made among moral, physical, and intellectual activities. Lacking secure access to food, shelter, clothing, and education, only the noblest of human beings can be brought to devote time and energy to larger moral questions. The just state must therefore assure its people economic opportunities and a social safety net, before it punishes any for immoral [that is, antisocial] behavior.

The notion that economic justice is the prerequisite for human development immediately calls to mind the rhetorical barrages to which all are regularly subjected on the issue of China's human rights. Most scholarly treatments of human rights in China continue to cull short excerpts from the historical record to support or refute China's future potential to adopt American standards of political democracy; meanwhile the "Asian value" proponents have managed to convince vast numbers of the proposition that biology and culture in East Asia dictate a preference for strict order and rapid industrialization, while precluding any impulses toward civil society. Two crucial considerations have been omitted from the accounts put forward by influential opinion makers, however. First, timing plays a key role as domestic state structures evolve (or persist) in response to shifting (or consistent) patterns in transnational relations, so that what passes now for a unique governmental approach in the East Asian states may define an interim stage rather than a separate Way. Second, proponents of democracy everywhere ignore at their peril an important idea articulated by C. B. Macpherson: that democracy's chief goal is to procure "substantive justice" for men and women, so they then are emboldened to develop their innate capacities as makers, thereby becoming fully realized humans imbued with a sense of self-worth and social place. Significant obstacles to substantive justice will remain for the majority of the world's population unless theorists of all persuasions consider the equal damage to democratic institutions wrought by external sources of political and economic inequality. For the moment, far too few condemn as specious the arguments of powerful interest groups intent upon denying the fundamental interdependence of political and economic freedoms in the name of Asian or American exceptionalism.

No less off center, the negative stereotypes accuse Confucian classicism either of justifying wide disparities in wealth or of quite the opposite: requiring humans to abandon all economic interests in acts of extreme asceticism. The New Confucians themselves have promoted the latter stereotype by their fondness for quoting the Song master Cheng Yi, who said, "It is a small matter to die, but a great matter to contravene the Way." Cheng Yi and the True Way Learning of later imperial China notwithstanding, the early Confucian masters valued life too greatly to forsake it lightly. While admitting that in rare cases adherence to the Right may require the sacrifice of one's wealth, one's rank, and even one's life, they also insisted that the urge to attain wealth and power were so natural that the Sage himself was not immune from it. Moreover they believed that when a community countenances unacceptably wide disparities in wealth, its disadvantaged members will inevitably shirk their duties with respect to the communal good. Social drift or even outright rebellion will result. In their views, privileged persons who do not acknowledge their obligations to others by sharing their blessings with the community will find "their persons in danger and their territories reduced." It is curious, then, that none of the recent state-sponsored delving into questions of tradition and national essence mentions the forceful arguments for land reform and greater economic equity made by the most prominent Ru teachers, from Mencius (d. 289 BC), Jia Yi (200–168 BC), and Dong Zhongshu (176–104 BC) down to the leaders of the Practical Learning movements in China and Korea.

Judging from the earliest records in Chinese script, the literate elites of the Central States cultures have never held a detached view of their past, but have looked to discover in it an autochthonous origin, a hidden message, and a larger, in some cases, global and cosmic, significance. Even when their narration of their sacred history has not invoked supernatural agencies, it has found in historical patterns the manifestation of a distinctive spirit said to imbue their lives with a unique and uniquely meaningful direction. The Chinese people are hardly unusual in this. The notion that history might be, as the philosopher Bernard Bosanquet put it, nothing more than "just one damn thing after another" does not attract most human beings.

In premodern times, the essential narratives attesting to the sacred history of the Central States past were thought to be contained in the Five Classics associated with Confucius. By the twentieth century, a new ideological relation between Chinese history and the Chinese Classics began to emerge, whereby nearly the entire history of the national past—braced to confront the confusing demands of modernity—was said to result from the spirit of an orthodox Confucianism, acting for either uniquely positive or uniquely corrupt ends. In the twentieth century, the Chinese past and the presumption of Confucian orthodoxy became so conflated as to be virtually indistinguishable by most. The richness, variety, and innovation were thereby reduced, and the shifting importance of canonical teachings collapsed into one flat, ahistorical model. In the cartoons, the wise Confucian became an atemporal "rigid, strict schoolman" in a funny hat spouting fortune-cookie aphorisms. Reductionism is to be expected when the twin myths of sacred history and orthodox Confucianism have been forced to play important roles in modern China's political life. Whenever the Chinese state has had reason to assess itself in relation to other states, all such foundational myths serve as major weapons in the ideological stockpile dedicated to collective unity.*

In the end, deciding what constitutes the true character of authentically Confucian teachings may be next to impossible. Historians have a hard enough time determining what people did; ascertaining which beliefs prompted actions is a far more daunting task. Still, what harm would it do to act upon a Confucian proposition: that the achievement of a decent society, defined by the Israeli philosopher Avishai Margalit as one in which institutions do not humiliate, depends more upon careful practice than orthodox belief, that what counts are performative acts—how you treat others, not how you rationalize your treatment of them. As we have seen, Confucian classicism makes other key presuppositions: that (1) human beings are born with an adequate potential to develop the desire to act morally, but they must all diligently cultivate that fragile potential; (2) such self-cultivation ideally gains a person social recognition and possibly state support; (3) the state, for its part, has a responsibility to provide the material, educational, and psychic opportunities sufficient for each person's full development, since deprivation makes moral action of any sort nearly impossible for most; (4) human beings exist not as atomistic individuals but as parts of "knowable communities" inextricably bound by shared history, shared rites, and customs, no less than by the common need to develop; (5) law cannot func-

---

*Such reductionism colors nearly all discussions about early "Confucian" ideas about women, for example. Little or no context is provided in the writings of the early Confucian masters for the rare comments and anecdotes that explicitly speak of women. Such comments and anecdotes as do exist are liable to quite different constructions. Scholars have many more records pertaining to the gender constructions employed by the state-sponsored classicism of late imperial China, and there revisionist scholarship is remaking our understanding of Confucian life for women.

tion as an adequate foundation for a workable society, since law only defines unacceptably antisocial behavior without encouraging better; (6) the performance of certain social rites, articulated by the community and reinterpreted as society changes, can help to habituate individuals to socially productive behavior, while relieving them from alienation; (7) only when humans are encouraged to see and take pleasure in their social lives will an ethic of shared responsibility finally emerge, leading to a truly secure society. In Confucian theory, "fairness" (*gong* 公) can be ensured only by the "public spirit" (also *gong* 公) of each community member, expressed in a willingness to share community resources in proportion to each contribution to the community.

The American philosopher Richard Rorty is probably right when he says that the current global situation cries out less for spiritual renewal than for practical ingenuity: how to put the brakes on growing economic inequalities? how to deal with military and ecological threats? how to contain population growth? A classical interest in human history and in local customs begins with four practical assumptions: that society needs to preserve some continuity with the past if it is to maintain its stability, because the past is relevant to the present and changing world; that the current situation is not necessarily the best of all possible worlds; that good institutions direct people's attention to their very human need for frequent ethical interaction; and that civilization results from an accumulation of conscious, ethical acts, and the acquisition of objective knowledge or material wealth is secondary to the process. Questions of what specific teachings, if any, to transmit from the past, and how, must be answered anew for each age, perhaps for each person. To reconstruct the genuine insights attributed to the Ancients in a modern form that facilitates the deliberative process, larger intellectual and emotional concerns must be integrated more closely with our daily activities and experiences. The conceivable reward for the hard work of integration: the possibility that a familiarity with the Chinese Classics may prompt new insights—some merely forgotten in our own cultures—into the all-too-familiar problems that plague humanity.

The great scholar-iconoclast Gu Jiegang (1893–1980) used to argue for "one Confucius at a time." By returning to one fundamental idea reportedly propounded by Confucius—that true humanity consists in a willingness to participate in collective living and to search for cooperative solutions—we may construct a Confucius more benign than many an earlier version. Though perfect justice will elude us, such conduct affords the same potential rewards in our own days as in those of Confucius: the remarkable pleasures to be found in imaginatively immersing ourselves in communities past and present, which can only increase our delight in Heaven's most precious gift of life.

Appendix I

KEY TERMS

Readers should note the problematic nature of key terms used in discussions of classical learning in China, including Confucius, Confucian, neo-Confucian, Confucianism, China, and "the West." The first five of these six terms are all foreign neologisms, having no exact equivalent in premodern Chinese, though they have been used so long in Western languages that they appear entirely natural. Of course, the primary criterion in determining good cross-cultural language— the language of interpretation—must be its explanatory power, not whether a term has native equivalents or enjoys chronological simultaneity. Therefore, certain eminent scholars in the field of Chinese studies continue to use these terms, believing that clear writing becomes absolutely impossible once these rubrics have been jettisoned. My own belief is that these grossly inexact terms generally do more to obscure than to enlighten. Therefore, I discuss each of the terms briefly below, before turning to two other important topics: *qi* 氣 (vital configured energy); and Yin/yang Five Phases 陰陽五行 theory (also known as correlative thought).

Confucius The Supreme Sage in imperial China was traditionally known as Kongzi (Master Kong) or simply Zi (The Master). His proper name was Kong Qiu, and his courtesy name was Kong Zhongni. The expression Kongfuzi, meaning Great Master Kong, first appeared, it seems, on inscribed spirit tablets dedicated to the Sage during the Yuan period, but it was the Jesuit missionaries of the late sixteenth century who popularized the term, in their determination to further elevate the status of the Master "in an almost patristic sense as the ancient prophet of Chinese monotheism." (From Kongfuzi comes the Latinized form, Confucius.)

The main problem in thinking about Confucius is this: While no one seriously doubts that Confucius (551–479 BC) was a historical figure, in the earliest extant records about the Sage, he already enjoys mythic status. This mythicizing process was well under way centuries before the Han imperial patronage was reserved for the Five Classics in 136 BC, so that the figure of Confucius often appears, even in early texts, simply to lend drama and authority. The source now commonly regarded as most reliable for the life and thought of Confucius is the *Analects* (*Lunyu* 論語), a work that purports to record conversations between Confucius and his disciples. But even the earliest passages in the *Analects* probably date to the fourth century BC, about a century or so after Confucius's death, and the *Analects* contains later traditions and outright interpolations. (The Shanghai Museum apparently has in its possession an as-yet-unpublished text that purports to transcribe conversations between Confucius and his disciples, many parts of which do not correspond with the *Analects*. And since that excavated text dates to ca. 300 BC, it too may reflect pious traditions not based on fact.) Scholars cannot reasonably hope to discern precisely what the historical Master really thought or said. Often, trying to ascertain the true personality and message of Confucius is like looking at a very darkened portrait done in oils: "At first you see nothing, then you begin to recognize features, and then you realize that they are your own."

Throughout this book, therefore, I have tried to follow the formula whereby "Confucius" refers to the semifictional creation of the *Analects'* compilers, supplemented—where this is possible without doing real violence to the *Analects'* account of Confucius—by portraits of Confucius preserved in related canonical works of early date, including the *Liji*. I follow this formula in the full knowledge that Confucius over time came to be "more than a man or a thinker, more even than a school of thought," a veritable "cultural phenomenon intertwined with the destiny of all of Chinese civilization." That this construction of Confucius began some two thousand years ago and continues today, having undergone a number of remarkable transformations and vicissitudes, is a substantial source of confusion in speaking about Confucius.

Confucian vs. classicist In China, the term "Ru" 儒 was used to describe the classicist who made the study of antiquity his chief pursuit. But the same term, quite confusingly, was also used in ancient texts more narrowly to describe committed followers of Confucius, who adhere in their conduct to the specific ethical Way of antiquity supposedly prescribed by the Master. Often these texts do not make clear whether their use of "Ru" refers to the larger group or the much smaller subset of moralists. Many Warring States and Han texts, however, sharply distinguish between the followers of Confucius and those among the classicists who are most career-minded, calling the latter "vulgar Ru." Texts in the post-Han period are apt to use the term "Ru" indiscriminately "to refer to a master of state ceremonial, a recognized teacher of Confucian doctrines, a philosopher who contributed to the elaboration of these doctrines, anyone who attempted to live by Confucius's teachings, any member of the civil service regardless of whether he lived in accordance with Confucius's teachings, any educated person regardless of official ambitions, or any conventional person (since it was conventional to quote Confucian doctrines in support of conventional behavior)." In recent centuries, the term has been used to connote "deference, urbanity, wisdom, moral probity, reasoned . . . classicism, and a learned, paternal authoritarianism, [all] the desiderata of Europeans doubtful of the institution of monarchy and despairing of religious war." The semantic boundary of the term has always been blurry. For clarity's sake, I try in this book to reserve the term "Confucian" for self-identified ethical followers of Confucius.

neo-Confucian As many scholars have noted, the term "neo-Confucian" and "neo-Confucianism" are Western inventions with no direct counterpart in Chinese. The learned Jesuit Jean-Joseph-Marie Amiot (1718–93) was possibly the first to use the term "neo-Confucians" to refer to Song thinkers. Apparently, the term "neo-Confucianism" came later still, in nineteenth-century Europe; Japanese writers adopted it as early as 1904. The term was meant to denote post-Buddhist developments in Confucian thought, dating from the Song onward. In theory, therefore, the term "neo-Confucian" carries three discrete meanings: (1) the thought of Zhu Xi; (2) the Cheng-Zhu school or True Way Learning movement (Daoxue), first adopted in 1241 as the basis for the state-sponsored examination system; and (3) the broader neo-Confucian movement that derived from many teachers besides Zhu Xi and evolved in many countries over many centuries, so that it was called by a variety of names in East Asia. Because of the tendency to confuse or conflate these three discrete meanings, Anne Birdwhistell, Benjamin Elman, Conrad Schirokauer, and Hoyt Tillman, among many fine scholars, have cast doubt on the usefulness of the category neo-Confucian. Tillman, for example, has objected that a fixation on the neo-Confucian rubric inevitably privileges the learning of Zhu Xi while obscuring the legacy of other important thinkers, thereby distorting scholarly perceptions of the larger picture of classicism in later imperial China. Elman bemoans the term's general lack of historical specificity. Although this book focuses on early Five Classics learning, readers should be aware of important tensions within later Confucian classicism, for instance, that between the desire to seek societal improvement through major institutional reforms and the desire to rest content with bureaucratic meliorism because of a sharper focus on personal self-cultivation.

Confucianism "Confucianism" is a term that I have reserved in this book for two fictive constructs implying a single orthodox synthesis. The first construct was devised by several groups in the nineteenth century, including Protestant missionaries and nativist conservative Chinese; it purported to encompass the entire semantic field registered by a complex of Chinese terms referring to sorts of people and ideas, including Ru (classicists): Rujia (classicist affiliation), Rujiao (classical teachings), Ruxue (classical learning). The successor construct, no less fictive and probably even more reductionist, was employed in four successive political movements of the twentieth century: the May Fourth movement, the New Life movement, the anti-Confucius campaign, and the New Confucian Revival, all of which have praised or excoriated Confucius as symbol of an Asia-specific religious ethos. These movements are the focus of discussion in the last chapter of this book.

"Orthodoxy" is a term I have generally avoided because historians of China do not agree that it ever existed, nor can they reach consensus on what it would have meant with respect to the imperial period in China. In the few cases where I do use it, I do so simply in connection with two facts: first, that in the Han and post-Han periods, some texts and interpretive traditions received state sponsorship while others did not; and second, that a narrow selection of Zhu Xi's teachings gradually became the basis of the state examination system over the course of the thirteenth through early fifteenth centuries. Nothing conceivably like a hegemonic orthodoxy ever prevailed before then. And even after 1414, when a *Great Compendium of the Five Classics* in 121 *juan* and a *Great Compendium of the Four Books* in 30 *juan* became the standard prep books of approved interpretations to be used in the state-sponsored examination system, challenges to the unprecedented authority of Zhu Xi's formulations continued.

China The term "China" derives from the Qin dynasty (221–208 BC), which was the first to unify nearly all of the territory now thought of as China proper. But until modern times, when the introduction of nationalism dramatically altered conceptual categories, those who lived within China's geographical boundaries did not think of themselves as Chinese. Apart from their strong clan and regional affiliations, people tended instead to identify themselves in one of three ways: (a) as inheritors of the Central States (*Zhongguo* 中國, usually mistranslated as "Middle Kingdom") civilization once presumed to center on the Yellow River plain; (b) as subjects of the reigning dynasty; or (c) as spiritual descendants of the Han or Tang dynasties, the two great empires of the premodern period when the culturally confident state felt assured of "the loyalty of a scholarly community eager for official service."

In the period prior to unification under Qin in 221 BC, the Central States civilization was centered in what is today north China, with a fluid boundary marked in the west by the Ordos desert, in the north by mountains north of the Yellow River, in the east by the sea, and in the south by the Yangzi River. Thanks to archaeology, we now know that important cultural contributions often came from well beyond these limits. Also, in many areas within China, so-called barbarians lived cheek-by-jowl with ethnic Chinese (the "Han"). In consequence, the scholar William Boltz has proposed for the premodern period to distinguish carefully between "China" and "the Chinese," using "China" to refer only to the geographic area of the present-day People's Republic, minus the Autonomous Regions.

Throughout this book I have tried to restrict the qualifier "Chinese" to three main uses: (1) as adjective for the language, written or oral, that has evolved from the premodern grammar and script forms of the oracle bones (ca. 1300 BC) into modern Chinese; (2) as qualifying adjective for an evolving ethnic group (Han Chinese as opposed to barbarian); and (3) as adjective pertaining to the modern Chinese nation-state, either in the People's Republic of China or in Taiwan.

There are, of course, related problems attached to the Chinese notions of dynasty and empire: Though Chinese scholarship, based on premodern traditions, continues to speak of dynasties extending back to the Xia, or pre-Shang period, I think it unlikely that there were true empires before the Qin and Han in the late third century BC.

"the West" This, too, of course, is a fictive construct designed to focus attention on a particular narrative, whereby a unitary civilization has unfolded from the time of the Greek thinkers—though it somehow, curiously enough, embraced in Judaeo-Christianity the religion of the non-Greek-speaking (that is, "barbarian") Jews—down to the present, culminating in that triumph of progress that began with the Enlightenment thinkers. Implicit in talk of "the West" is the fallacious though popular notion that the countries so situated (in the main) through a unilinear course of evolutionary development are on their way to the ultimate goal of progress through democracy and capitalism. In modern America, discourse about the West often nourishes the belief that modern America represents the final apogee of all of Western civilization. Equally absurd, of course, is the notion of a unitary East and Asian exceptionalism, ideas promoted first by the Japanese in the late nineteenth and early twentieth centuries.

What we tend to regard as modern Western civilization refers to only some few aspects associated with the post–Industrial Revolution world in England, France, Germany, and America. Much of European culture is casually ignored whenever texts speak of "the West" or of "Judaeo-Christian tradition." Nonetheless, the dramatic narrative of "the West" has been taken up by Chinese reformers and conservatives as well as by many non-Chinese—quite uncritically —who employ it as the antithesis or "mirror image in reverse" of everything that is unique in the history of China. For example, Nietzsche pitted "European-American indefatigability" against the "hundredfold-inherited contemplativeness of the Asians."

As a historian interested in the distinctive patterns produced by different cultures in different eras, I have often chosen in this book to employ the terms "Euro-America" and "Euro-American" coined by Arif Dirlik, in the hopes that the reader may thereby be alerted to the multiple discontinuities and non-simultaneities in the history of Europe and America, as well as the progressivist assumptions that color the naturalized term "the West."

qi 氣 The origin of the term is unknown. No Shang or early Zhou graphs can be conclusively identified with the concept. The character now used for *qi* shows clouds of steam rising over cooked rice. The graphic form suggests bubbling or boiling over; it may also imply some kind of nourishment. In fact, the root meaning of *qi* appears to be "vapor" or "breath." Like early Greek, Indian, Latin, and Hebrew philosophy, early Chinese belief presumes a "life breath" that vitalizes as it circulates through bodies or the air. Undifferentiated *qi* is the dynamic universal stuff out of which all the disparate things of the cosmos condense (at birth) and into which they dissolve (at death). As a form of breath, *qi* typically operates in rhythmic, floodlike pulses, alternating between inhalation (expansion) and exhalation (contraction) in regular cycles. Only bad *qi* is blocked or stagnant.

Perhaps the closest English equivalent to *qi* is "vitality." As latent energy stored in the Dao, *qi* is undifferentiated, but as vital energy operating in the universe, *qi* is definable in quality and characteristic in its configurations. By some mysterious process, the originally undifferentiated *qi* makes for distinctive entities. *Qi* can be congealed or compacted in liquid and solid forms. *Qi* comes in different grades. The lowest grade of *qi* (called turbid) is subject to various malfunctions, including physical deformity, muddled thinking, and excessive desire. The purest refined *qi* (the "quintessential" *jing* associated with procreative fluids) is reserved for two kinds of light-giving entities: the luminous heavenly bodies and the enlightened minds of the sages. As the basic stuff that informs the entire cosmos and binds all humans to the rest of phenomenal existence in Heaven-and-Earth, *qi* precludes an absolute dividing line between humans, other species, and things. Understandably, the notion of *qi* has also worked against the development of the transcendent/immanent dichotomy presumed by many European and American thinkers. At the same time, *qi* functions as the physical medium that allows sympathetic "mutual response" to take place between categorically related entities. Therefore, *qi* theory from the earliest times has been preoccupied with the nature and significance of macrocosmic influences on microcosmic processes.

By the first century BC, the single term *qi* signified both the "material stuff" in continual process in Heaven-and-Earth and the underlying dynamism predisposing that stuff to assume specific form. For the early Chinese, human *qi*, despite its obvious physicality, had a definite moral dimension as well. In the properly functioning heart/mind, for example, *qi* is said to gather at "the spirit abode." What is more, the will to do good is said to be "commander over the *qi*." A millennium later, Song thinkers were to draw a neater conceptual line between *li* 理 (internal principle) and *qi* (material stuff).

In the case of humans, a finite store of *qi* endowed at birth is somehow passed down from parents to child. The birth of a human being, in effect, represents an accumulation of *qi*. Over the course of an individual lifespan, the *qi* tends to become less active. Physical overexertion may cause it to "block." Tension and stress equally frustrate it. Immoral acts also are said to "abuse the *qi*" to the degree that they engender shame, anxiety, and restlessness, for these emotional states produce certain physical symptoms, such as constricted breathing and palpitations of the heart. Human beings, then, have some measure of control over the rate at which their original *qi* stagnates or is depleted. Balance in the mental and emotional spheres can be induced by the process dubbed self-cultivation. Various techniques designed to retain (and ideally augment) the *qi*'s activity include both moral and physical arts: moderation in daily habits, adjustment of posture, meditation as "inward training," habituation to goodness, and a calm acceptance of fate. The philosopher Mencius (?371–?289), for example, tells his disciples simply that "the way to make *qi*" is to "nourish it with integrity."

Master Han Fei (d. 234 BC) is one of many thinkers to link the conservation of *qi*'s vitality with the acquisition of political power and material wealth. Extending his imagery, it may help to think of *qi* as operating like money in the bank: An individual can deposit or withdraw *qi* from his fund. What's more, he can inherit a sum or bequeath it to his descendants. Like great reserves of wealth, a great reserve of vital *qi* represents the potential to influence others. *Qi* thus provides the basis for the charismatic power of the virtuous man. All Confucians insist that each newborn is credited with sufficient *qi* to realize the full human potential for sagehood, even though few are wise enough to develop their innate capacities.

In summation, early Chinese thinkers view all cosmic change in terms of the dynamic process inherent in vital *qi*. *Qi* is substance, activity, and vitality.

yin/yang Five Phases correlative theory The Chinese cosmological system, which assumed definite shape no later than the third century BC, envisioned the world in terms of two interlocking systems: yin/yang and the Five Phases (often translated, less accurately, as the Five Agents or Five Elements). This is sometimes known as correlative thought, or categorical thinking.

According to the theory, there evolved out of primordial chaos one cosmic pattern with dual aspects known as yin and yang. All of phenomenal existence reflects this pattern. The myriad things can be categorized as either male or female, light or dark, day or night, hot or cold, superior or inferior, and so on, with the first term of each pair representing yang and the second yin. This duality is one of the constant norms of the universe, as illustrated by the regular alternation of day and night, of summer and winter. Yin and yang, though opposing, are also complementary; the waxing of one invariably entails the waning of the other. To take an example from nature, the summer solstice is the longest day of the year, but, in another sense, it also marks the onset of winter; subsequently, the days grow ever shorter and colder until the winter solstice. The familiar figural representation of yin/yang emphasizes this fluid symbiotic relation. The curvilinear areas of dark and light enfold each other within a perfect circle that knows no beginning or end; the tiny seeds of each are discovered in the swelling contours of its opposite. At the culmination of one, its opposite is born, and on and on, in a constant process of advance and retreat, making and unmaking. In this way, "movement back" becomes "the Way of the Dao." Men of virtue in studying the cosmic patterns infer from this that in victory lies defeat and in humility, greatness.

Yin/yang may not seem so alien, since our language predisposes us to think in terms of positive/negative. But it is far more difficult for us to conceptualize cosmic process in terms of the Five Phases. The Five Phases invariably comprise Water, Fire, Wood, Metal, and Earth, though different orders of enumeration are preferred by various classical authorities. The phases are essentially five different types of process. According to one early authority, "Water goes down, fire goes up, wood is pliable," and so on. Each phase is said to rule (that is, to predominate in) a certain period of time (a dynasty, a season, a set of hours) before it gives way to the next phase. This connection with time resulted in conceptual overlays between systems of yin/yang and the Five Phases, as in the following chart:

Rising yang		Yields to	Rising yin	
Wood	Fire	Earth	Metal	Water
Spring	Summer	transition	Autumn	Winter
East	South	Center	West	North
Green	Red	Yellow	White	Black

The Chinese soon set about classifying all known entities into groups of fives, constructing exhaustive lists which they hoped would elicit order from the seeming chaos of the world. By laws of sympathy and repulsion, things accounted as categorically alike (that is, correlated with the same phase) were said to be drawn to one another whereas categorically different things repelled each other. According to the same theory, careful "inference by analogy from objects of the same kind" (*tui lei* 推類) could facilitate the intuitive apprehension of all parts of the ineffable Dao by some form of indirect communication that is simply not possible through logical argument.

Traditional scholars used to assume the existence of coherent Yin/yang Five Phases theory in deep antiquity. All available evidence now suggests that Yin/yang theory predates Five Phases theory, but that neither makes its appearance much before the Warring States period (475–222 BC). It seems, for example, that Yin/yang dualism, which tradition assumed to have originated with milfoil divination by the *Changes*, had not been widely adopted by divination experts as late as the third century BC, for a number of excavated texts (for example, those from Baoshan and Wangjiatai) employ number sequences rather than the now familiar yin/yang graphic symbols of broken and unbroken lines. If that is so, the *Zuozhuan* accounts of milfoil divination (see chapter 6) have been reworked to accord with later practice, and the "Xici" essay included in the received text of the *Changes* may be the oldest text associated with the Five Classics to imply a cosmic dualism. Michael Loewe has suggested in numerous articles a date of first century BC for the full elaboration and widespread adoption of Yin/yang Five Phases theory, as seen, for example, in the works of Yang Xiong 揚雄 and his contemporary Jiao Gan 焦贛. That date of first century BC may mean one of two things: either a coherent Yin/yang Five Phases theory was not widely adopted by the literati and court until the first century BC or correlative theory itself had not been completely systematized before then.

Appendix II

A NOTE ON CHINESE HISTORY

The Xia dynasty is entirely legendary (see Chronology). The Shang, some part of whose history is corroborated by written records, was centered in the Yellow River valley region.

The Zhou, as the first dynasty whose existence is fully attested, is often regarded as the first empire in China. In Euro-American accounts, it is usually treated as a feudal state because its overlordship was largely maintained, when it was maintained, by vassal lords related to the Zhou ruling house. By the Chunqiu period (722–476 BC), however, there was no doubt that the power and prestige of the Zhou ruling house had dramatically declined; in visible sign of that decline, the Zhou rulers were forced to abandon their traditional seat of power (near present-day Xi'an) and move to a new, eastern capital at Luoyang. (Chapter 6 of this book portrays that decline in some detail.) By the Warring States period (475–222 BC), in consequence, the charisma of the Zhou throne had so waned that six states (Qi, Chu, Yan, Zhao, Han, and Wei) "east of the passes" and Qin "west of the passes" (around Xi'an) struggled for mastery. It was Qin, the least "uncivilized" of the states in contemporary estimation, that finally unified the country in 221 BC.

Qin, though short-lived (221–209 BC), instituted the basic form of government that prevailed, except for periods of disunion, until 1911: central control and bureaucratic administration (over the centuries increasingly staffed by candidates chosen by civil service examinations from the literate population of males throughout the empire) replaced a loose confederation of local ruling elites exercising patrimonial sway. Marxist historical schemas label this entire period feudalistic, meaning, precapitalistic. No term could be more misleading, given the role of the central government administration in the imperial period, though the unsettled periods between dynasties saw attempts to "restore" feudal institutions ascribed to the Zhou dynasty of antiquity.

By the mid–nineteenth century, it was evident that the old imperial system, with its limited tax base and minimal local control, could no longer cope with problems internal and external. The Euro-American imperialists, by demanding that China accept a series of unequal treaties that negated its sovereignty, certainly advertised the weakness of the last dynasty, the Qing, or Manchus. But the Manchus faced perhaps even a worse internal problem: thanks in part to long centuries of peace and prosperity and in part to the introduction of new crops from America (peanuts, potatos, and sweet potatos, for example), China had experienced exponential population growth, and the strain this placed on the state's financial, educational, and human resources required a thorough reorganization of those resources.

As the Manchus were a conquest dynasty, some reformers within China attributed all contemporary troubles to foreign rule. After attempts to nudge the imperial bureaucratic regime closer to a constitutional monarchy failed in the summer of 1898, public opinion increasingly supported the overthrow of

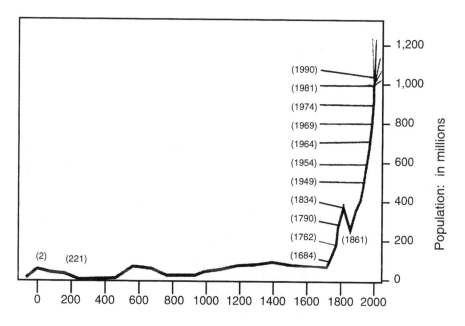

the Manchu dynasty. In 1911, under the nominal leadership of Sun Yat-sen (1866–1925), the Republic of China was founded.

Sun's GMD party never fully controlled the immense territory to which it laid claim. The party's main power base was in the most Westernized coastal cities, among literate elites trained directly by Euro-American missionaries or indirectly by Euro-American pedagogical methods. Having such a small power base, the GMD could not defeat the local warlords contending for power, expel or neutralize the imperialist presence in China (which the GMD denounced under Sun Yat-sen, then accommodated under Chiang Kai-shek), or, after 1919, effectively rival the Chinese Communist Party (CCP) and its growing number of sympathizers. By the 1940s, when China's territorial integrity was most threatened by Japanese aggression, it was clear that a showdown between Mao Zedong (Mao Tse-tung) and Chiang Kai-shek would come as soon as World War II was over. The civil war from 1945 to 1949 between the GMD forces under Chiang and the forces under the direction of Mao's CCP ended in ignominious defeat for Chiang Kai-shek, who fled with many of his inner circle to Taiwan, shortly before Mao announced the founding of the People's Republic of China in October 1949. The CCP still directs events on the China mainland, though the GMD has gradually relaxed its control over Taiwan.

SUGGESTED READINGS

CHAPTER 1. INTRODUCTION

Students of the Five Classics continue to be deeply indebted to two major translation projects: the first by James Legge resulted in *The Chinese Classics, I–IV* (Oxford: Oxford University Press, 1893–4) and the *Li Ki* (Oxford: Oxford University Press, 1879–91), and a second undertaken by Bernhard Karlgren in his study of the *Odes* and *Documents* is detailed in *Bulletin of the Museum of Far Eastern Antiquities* 16–27 (1944–45) and 20–22 (1948–50).

Readers will wish to familiarize themselves also with the works most closely associated with Confucius and two disciples, Mencius and Xunzi. Of the many good translations of the *Analects*, I still prefer that by Arthur Waley: *The Analects of Confucius* (London: George Allen & Unwin; rpt., New York: Vintage, 1932); for Confucius's disciples, see the *Mencius*, trans. D. C. Lau (London, Penguin, 1970), and *Hsün tzu: Basic Writings*, trans. Burton Watson (New York: Columbia University Press, 1963). The three-volume *Xunzi: A Translation and Study of the Complete Works* (Stanford: Stanford University Press, 1988–94) provides very useful sketches of the intellectual context of the Warring States period. To better understand the pre-Qin milieu in which Confucius and later followers operated, readers should consult A. C. Graham's masterful *Disputers of the Tao: Philosophical Argument in Ancient China* (La Salle, Illa: Open Court, 1989). Yu Weichao's four-volume *A Journey into China's Antiquity* (Beijing: Morning Glory Press, 1997) is an excellent introduction to the material civilization of early China, as it sheds particular light upon issues of textuality, rites, and music.

For the Qin attitude toward the Classics, the best analysis is Martin Kern, *The Stele Inscriptions of Ch'in Shih-huang: Text and Ritual in Early Chinese Imperial Representation* (New Haven: American Oriental Society, 2000). For events in Han, the most convenient overviews may be found in *The Cambridge History of China*, vol. 1, ed. Michael Loewe and Denis Twitchett (Cambridge: Cambridge University Press, 1986); and Mark Edward Lewis, *Writing and Authority in Early China* (Albany: SUNY Press, 1999). For the "grand play" of Chinese thought, Anne Cheng's *Histoire de la pensée chinoise* (Paris: Éditions du Seuil, 1997) is particularly valuable.

For late imperial classicism, see Benjamin Elman, *From Philosophy to Philology: Intellectual and Social Aspects of Change in Late Imperial China* (Cambridge, Harvard Council on East Asian Studies), or his later *Classicism, Politics, and Kinship: The Ch'ang-chou School of New Text Confucianism in Late Imperial China* (Berkeley: University of California Press, 1990); Thomas A. Wilson, *Genealogy of the Way: The Construction and Uses of the Confucian Tradition in Late Imperial China* (Stanford: Stanford University Press, 1995); and the satirical novel by Wu Jingzi (1701–54), *The Scholars* [= *Rulin waishi*], trans. Yang Hsien-yi and Gladys Yang (New York: Columbia University Press, 1992).

CHAPTER 2. THE ODES

More good studies of the *Odes* exist than for any other of the Five Classics. The most readable translation remains Arthur Waley's (1937), *The Book of Songs: The Ancient Chinese Classic of Poetry* (available now from New York, Grove Press, 1996, in a revised edition, with additional translations and a highly valuable Postface by Joseph R. Allen). Ezra Pound's translation, *The Confucian Odes: The Classic Anthology Defined by Confucius* (New York: J. Laughlin, 1954), often captures the spirit of the *Odes*, especially that of the State Airs, though the translations can be unreliable. James Legge's translation in vol. 4 of *The Chinese Classics* (Oxford: Oxford University Press, 1893–4), which reflects the scholarship of late imperial China and England, is also well worth consulting.

Beginning students of the *Odes* will find several general studies to be of great use. They should begin with Kenneth DeWoskin, *A Song for One or Two: Music and the Concept of Art in Early China* (Ann Arbor: Center for Chinese Studies, University of Michigan, 1982), Steven van Zoeren, *Poetry and Personality: Reading, Exegesis, and Hermeneutics in Traditional China* (Stanford: Stanford University Press, 1991), and Stephen Owen, *Readings in Chinese Literary Thought* (Cambridge: Council of East Asian Studies, Harvard University, 1992), chap. 1. (Most of Owen's entire body of work bears upon the *Odes* in interesting ways.) The full implications of DeWoskin's material become apparent when read in conjunction with comparative material from other cultures, for example,

Rosalind Thomas, *Literacy and Orality in Ancient Greece* (Cambridge: Cambridge University Press, 1992). Many will also want to read Marcel Granet's classic study of the odes as communal songs associated with fertility festivals: *Festivals and Songs of Ancient China*, trans. E. D. Edwards (London: Routledge & Sons, 1932), and that by Pierre Diény, *Origines—aux origines de la poésie classique en Chine* (Leiden: Brill, 1968). And for one of the best guides to the later use of the *Odes*, see *Han Shih Wai Chuan: Han Ying's Illustrations of the Didactic Application of the Classic of Songs*, trans. James Robert Hightower (Cambridge: Harvard University Press, 1952).

Shorter essays for the nonspecialist include Chen Shih-hsiang, "The *Shih ching*: Its Generic Significance in Chinese Literary History and Poetics," in *Studies in Chinese Literary Genres*, ed. Cyril Birch (Berkeley: University of California Press, 1974), 8–41; Chow Tse-tung, "The Early History of the Chinese Word *Shih* (Poetry)," in *Wenlin: Studies in the Chinese Humanities* (Madison: University of Wisconsin Press, 1968); David Schaberg, "Song and the Historical Imagination in Early China," *Harvard Journal of Asiatic Studies* 59.2 (December): 305–61; C. H. Wang, "Shih ching," in *Indiana Companion to Traditional Chinese Literature*, ed. William H. Nienhauser (Bloomington: Indiana University Press, 1986), 692–94; Pauline Yu, "The *Book of Songs*," in *Masterworks of Asian Literature in Comparative Perspective*, ed. Barbara Stoler Miller (Armonk: M. E. Sharpe, 1994), 211–21.

CHAPTER 3. THE *DOCUMENTS*

Two translations of the *Documents* are currently available: *The Chinese Classics*, trans. James Legge (Oxford: Oxford University Press, 1893–4), vol. 2, *The Shoo king*; and *The Book of Documents* (Stockholm: Bulletin of the Museum of Far Eastern Antiquities, 1952), which has been designed with the specialist in mind. Surprisingly little else of use exists on this important text, aside from specialized studies in Chinese and Japanese. Early legend-sets concerning the chief heroes of the *Documents* are the subject of Sarah Allan, *The Heir and the Sage: Dynastic Legend in Early China* (Taibei: Chinese Materials Center, 1981). Readers who wish to gain a sense of the major shifts possible in interpretive commentaries to the *Documents* may consult Michael Nylan, *The Shifting Center: The Original "Great Plan" and Later Readings* (Nettetal, Germany: Steyler Verlag, 1992), *Monumenta Serica Monograph Series* 24. Those who would know more about the fourth major commentary to the *Chunqiu*, that by Hu An'guo, will profit from Conrad Schirokauer, "Neo-Confucians under Attack: The Condemnation of Wei-hsüeh," in *Crisis and Prosperity in Sung China*, ed. J. W. Haeger (Phoenix: University of Arizona Press, 1975), 164–65. Readers interested in the sixteen-character transmission from the "Counsels of Great Yu," which was often seen as the basis of the Cheng-Zhu teachings, may consult Benjamin Elman, "Philosophy (*I-Li*) Versus Philology (*K'ao-cheng*): The *Jen-hsin Tao-hsin* Debate," *T'oung Pao* 69:4–5 (1983): 175–222.

CHAPTER 4. THE RITES

For a translation of the *Liji*, see *Li Ki, Book of Rites: An Encyclopedia of Ancient Ceremonial Usages, Religious Creeds, and Social Institutions*, trans. James Legge, ed. Ch'u Chai and Winberg Chai (1885; rpt., New York: University Books, 1967), 2 vols.; and of the *Yili*, *The I-li: Book of Etiquette and Ceremonial*, trans. John Steele (London: Probsthain & Co., 1917), 2 vols.

A number of good books on Chinese ritual are available. For early China, these include Herbert Fingarette, *Confucius: The Secular as Sacred* (New York: Harper & Row, 1972); Poo Mu-chou, *In Search of Personal Welfare* (Albany: SUNY Press, 1998); and Derk Bodde, *Festivals in Classical China: New Year and Other Annual Observances During the Han Dynasty, 206 B.C.–A.D. 220* (Pinceton: Princeton University Press, 1975). For late imperial and modern China, these include Chu Hsi, *Chu Hsi's Family Rituals*, trans. Patricia Buckley Ebrey (Princeton: Princeton University Press, 1991); and also by Ebrey, *Confucianism and Family Rituals in Imperial China* (Princeton: Princeton University Press, 1991); *Death Ritual in Late Imperial and Modern China*, ed. James L. Watson and Evelyn S. Rawski (Berkeley: University of California Press, 1988); Emily M. Ahern, *Chinese Ritual and Politics* (Cambridge: University of Cambridge, 1981); and Martin King Whyte, *Small Groups and Political Rituals in China* (Berkeley: University of California Press, 1974). For music, see *Harmony and Counterpoint: Ritual Music in Chinese Context*, ed. Bell Yung, Evelyn S. Rawski, and Rubie S. Watson (Stanford: Stanford University Press, 1966); and DeWoskin's *A Song for One or Two* (see suggested readings for the *Odes*). Various works by Miriam Levering introduce the concept of scriptural reading as rite. A very good short essay is Helen Siu, "Recycling Rituals: Politics and Popular Culture in Contemporary Rural China," in *Unofficial China: Popular Culture and Thought in the People's Republic*, ed. Perry Link, Richard Madsen, and Paul Pickowicz (Boulder: Westview, 1989), 37–53.

For general theory, the most useful texts include Catherine Bell, *Ritual: Perspectives and Dimensions* (Oxford: Oxford University Press, 1997); Ronald L. Grimes, *Beginnings in Ritual Studies* (Washington, D.C.: University Press of America, 1982); and Marcel Mauss, *The Gift*, trans. W. D. Halls, foreword by Mary Douglas (Paris, n.p.; rpt., New York, Norton, 1950).

CHAPTER 5. THE *CHANGES*

The correct procedure for casting the *Changes* can be found on pages 721–25 of the standard translation, Richard Wilhelm, *The I Ching or Book of Changes*

(Princeton: Princeton University Press, 1967). In contrast to the Wilhelm translation, which is largely based on the commentaries of late imperial China, a more recent translation of the *Changes*, that by Richard John Lynn, *The Classic of Changes: A New Translation of the I Ching as Interpreted by Wang Bi* (New York: Columbia University Press, 1994), reflects the commentaries of Wang Bi. A translation of the Mawangdui excavated version of the *Changes*, along with a number of appended essays, has been made by Edward L. Shaughnessy, *I ching, the Classic of Changes* (New York: Ballantine, 1996).

In this chapter, I have highlighted a neglected theme in the "Great Commentary," in contrast to most other studies of the "Great Commentary," which focus on the Sage's foreknowledge of events. See Willard J. Peterson, "Making Connections: 'Commentary on the Attached Verbalizations' of the *Book of Changes*," *Harvard Journal of Asiatic Studies* 42:1 (June 1982): 67–116. For an early master's understanding of the *Changes*' traditions, see Yang Hsiung [=Xiong], *The Canon of Supreme Mystery by Yang Hsiung: A Translation with Commentary of the T'ai hsüan ching*, trans. Michael Nylan (Albany: SUNY Press, 1993). Kidder Smith, Jr., "*Zhouyi* Interpretation from Accounts in the *Zuozhuan*," *Harvard Journal of Asiatic Studies* 49 (1989): 421–63, is quite insightful, as it builds upon Hellmut Wilhelm, "*I-ching* Oracles in the *Tso-chuan* and the *Kuo-yü*," *Journal of the American Oriental Society* 79:4 (1959): 275–80. Another article by Smith is also noteworthy, as it attempts to situate the *Changes* in the context of the other Classics: "The Difficulty of the *Yijing*," *Chinese Literature: Essays, Articles, Reviews (CLEAR)* (Dec. 1993): 1–15.

CHAPTER 6. THE SPRING AND AUTUMN ANNALS

The only complete translation of the *Chunqiu* (with a nearly complete translation of the *Zuo*) can be found in *The Chinese Classics*, trans. James Legge (Oxford: Oxford University Press, 1892), vol. 3, *The Ch'un Ts'ew*. A partial (and quite readable) translation of the *Zuo* may be found in *The Tso chuan: Selections from China's Oldest Narrative History*, trans. Burton Watson (New York: Columbia University Press, 1989). Much of the *Gongyang* and *Guliang* can be found translated in *Studies on the Gongyang and Guuliang Commentaries*, trans. and annot. by Göran Malmqvist, *Bulletin of the Museum of Far Eastern Antiquities* 43 (1971): 67–222; *Part II, Bulletin of the Museum of Far Eastern Antiquities* 47 (1975): 19–69.

Five classic articles on *Chunqiu* and its associated traditions are recommended: Bernhard Karlgren, "On the Authenticity and Nature of the *Tso-chuan*," *Götesborgs högskolas arsskrift* 32:3 (1926), rpt. as a monograph by Chengwen Press, Taibei, 1968; George Kennedy, "Interpretation of the *Ch'un Ch'iu*," *Journal of the American Oriental Society* 62 (1942): 40–48; Moss Roberts, "Double Judgements in the *Spring and Autumn, Kung-yang*: The Reign of Duke Yin," in *Nothing*

Concealed, ed. Frederick Wakeman, Jr. (Taibei: Chinese Materials and Research Aids Service Center, 1970), 21–34; Ronald C. Egan, "Narratives in the *Tso chuan*," *Harvard Journal of Asiatic Studies* 37:2 (1977): 323–52; and Eric Henry, "'Junzi Yue' versus 'Zhongni Yue' in *Zuozhuan*," *Harvard Journal of Asiatic Studies* 59:1 (June 1999): 125–61.

CHAPTER 7. CLAIMING THE CANON

A number of new works address gender relations in imperial China. For the early period, see Alison Harley Black, "Gender and Cosmology in Chinese Correlative Thinking," in *Gender and Religion: On the Complexity of Symbols*, ed. Caroline W. Bynum, Steven Harrell, and Paula Richman (Boston: Beacon Press, 1986), 165–95; Lisa Raphals, *Sharing the Light: Representations of Women and Virtue in Early China* (Albany: SUNY Press, 1998); and *The Sage and the Second Sex: Confucianism, Ethics, and Gender*, ed. Li Chenyang (Chicago: Open Court, 2000). For gender constructions for and by women of the late imperial period, see Susan Mann, *Precious Records: Women in China's Long Eighteenth Century* (Stanford: Stanford University Press, 1997); and Francesca Bray, *Technology and Gender: Fabrics of Power in Late Imperial China* (Berkeley: University of California Press, 1997). It is in light of these books that one should read such earlier accounts as those by Nancy Lee Swann, *Pan Chao: Foremost Woman Scholar of China* (New York: Century Company, 1932); and Tseng Chi-fen, *The Testimony of a Confucian Woman: The Autobiography of Mrs. Nien Zeng Jifeng, 1852–1942*, trans. Thomas L. Kennedy (Athens: University of Georgia Press, 1993).

For Euro-America's take on China, consult David E. Mungello, *Curious Land: Jesuit Accommodation and the Origins of Sinology* (Stuttgart: Franz Steiner Verlag, 1985); Andrew L. March, *The Idea of China: Myth and Theory in Geographic Thought* (New York: Praeger, 1974); and Harold Isaacs, *Scratches on our Minds: American Images of China and India* (Westport: Greenwood Press, 1958).

For the May Fourth movement, the classic work remains Chow Tse-tung, *The May Fourth Movement: Intellectual Revolution in Modern China* (Cambridge: Harvard University Press, 1960). Translations of the writings of Lu Xun are helpful, as are Chang Hao, *Chinese Intellectuals in Crisis: Search for Order and Meaning, 1890–1911* (Berkeley: University of California Press, 1987); Gu Jiegang, *Autobiography of a Chinese Historian, being the Preface to a Symposium on Ancient Chinese History (Ku shih pien)*, trans. Arthur W. Hummel (Leyden: E. J. Brill, 1931); and Leo Ou-fan Lee, "Modernity and Its Discontents: The Cultural Agenda of the May Fourth Movement," in *Perspectives on Modern China: Four Anniversaries*, ed. Kenneth Lieberthal et al. (Armonk: M. E. Sharpe, 1991), 158–77. For the late imperial and Republican civil services, see Benjamin A. Elman, *A Cultural History of Civil Examinations in Late Imperial China* (Berkeley,

University of California Press, 2000); and Wolfgang Franke, *The Reform and Abolition of the Traditional Chinese Examination System* (Cambridge: Harvard Monographs, 1960). For a recent revisionist history of Republican China, see *Reappraising Republican China*, ed. Frederic Wakeman, Jr., and Richard Louis Edmonds (Oxford: Oxford University Press, 2000). For the anti-Confucius campaign, see Kam Louie, *Critiques of Confucius in Contemporary China* (New York: St. Martin's Press, 1980). For more recent developments, see Jing Wang, *High Culture Fever: Politics, Aesthetics, and Ideology in Deng's China* (Berkeley: University of California Press, 1996). Perhaps the sanest discussions of Asian values can be found in Arif Dirlik, *What Is in a Rim? Critical Perspectives on the Pacific Region Idea* (Boulder: Westview, 1993); and Bruce Cumings, *Parallax Visions: Making Sense of American-East Asian Relations at the End of the Century* (Durham: Duke University Press, 1999).

APPENDIX II. CHINESE HISTORY

For more specific discussions of Chinese history, readers may wish to consult one of the following texts: Patricia Buckley Ebrey, *The Cambridge Illustrated History of China* (Cambridge: Cambridge University Press, 1996); Jacques Gernet, *A History of Chinese Civilization* (Cambridge: Cambridge University Press, 1982); Conrad Schirokauer, *A Brief History of Chinese Civilization* (New York: Harcourt, Brace, Jovanovich, 1991); and for the twentieth century, Jonathan Spence, *The Search for Modern China* (New Haven: Yale University Press, 1990). Readers with a particular interest in the development of classical learning may wish to consult John Berthrong, *Transformations of the Confucian Way* (Boulder: Westview, 1998).

INDEX